FROM
WASHINGTON
TO
MOSCOW

FROM
WASHINGTON
TO
MOSCOW

US-Soviet Relations and the Collapse of the USSR

LOUIS SELL

DUKE UNIVERSITY PRESS

DURHAM AND LONDON   2016

Printed in the United States of America on acid-free paper ∞
Typeset in Arno Pro by Westchester Publishing Services

Library of Congress Cataloging-in-Publication Data
Names: Sell, Louis, [date]–
Title: From Washington to Moscow : U.S.-Soviet relations and
the collapse of the USSR / Louis Sell.
Description: Durham : Duke University Press, 2016. |
Includes bibliographical references and index.
Identifiers: LCCN 2016006457
ISBN 978-0-8223-6179-4 (hardcover : alk. paper)
ISBN 978-0-8223-6195-4 (pbk. : alk. paper)
ISBN 978-0-8223-7400-8 (e-book)
Subjects: LCSH: United States—Foreign relations—Soviet
Union. | Soviet Union—Foreign relations—United States. |
Soviet Union—History—1985–1991. | Soviet Union—
History—1953–1985. Classification: LCC E183.8.S65.S35 2016 |
DDC 327.73047084—dc23
LC record available at http://lccn.loc.gov/2016006457.

Cover art: US president Ronald Reagan with Soviet general
secretary Mikhail Gorbachev in Red Square during the
Moscow Summit, May 31, 1988. © White House Photo /
Alamy Stock Photo.

THIS BOOK IS DEDICATED TO

men and women of goodwill who

served their country on both sides

of the Cold War divide.

CONTENTS

On a frigid Moscow morning in January 1993, George H. W. Bush and Boris Yeltsin signed the START II nuclear arms reduction treaty in the Kremlin's Vladimir Hall. As I stood with the US and Russian delegations behind the two presidents, I got that Yogi Berra feeling—"It's déjà vu all over again." After a few minutes, I realized why. In May 1972, Richard Nixon and Leonid Brezhnev had signed the SALT I strategic arms accords on this spot and a famous photograph showed the US and Soviet delegations standing behind their respective chiefs on the same Kremlin staircase.

As a newly minted Foreign Service Officer, I had worked in a minor capacity on the 1972 summit and as chief of the political section at the US Embassy in Moscow I helped in the negotiations of START II. Only twenty-one years separated the two events, but what changes had occurred. SALT I was considered by many to be a sign that the Soviet Union had attained strategic parity with the United States. But by 1993, the Soviet Union had disintegrated and its Communist system had vanished. Inside Yeltsin's Kremlin, Russian authorities tried hard to maintain the atmosphere of earlier summits but the signing was a muted affair.

Outside the Kremlin, destitution stalked the streets of the Russian capital. In one of the glittering but empty food stores along the city's New Arbat Street, I had seen Russians scuffling as shopkeepers wheeled in a cart carrying a few bony scraps of meat. The euphoria which had greeted the end of the Communist regime had long since disappeared. Yeltsin and hard-line opponents in the Russian legislature were mired in battles, which only ten months later would bring tanks into the streets to shell the parliament building. Economic reform had brought a sleazy "kiosk economy" to the streets of Moscow. On almost every corner, impromptu stands, often nothing more than metal shipping containers, sold a wide range of imported—or more accurately, smuggled—consumer items not available in Soviet times but now affordable to only a few.

My purpose in writing this book is to describe how the changes symbolized by these two events occurred. How did the Soviet Union—seemingly so confident and powerful in 1972—disappear less than twenty years later? Across history, empires have often vanished and in most cases the causes are relatively clear: foreign invasion, internal revolution, economic problems, natural catastrophe, or the like. Yet none of these obvious causes apply to the collapse of the USSR, an event which no Sovietologist, myself included, predicted.

Conflict with the external world was built into the Soviet genome, implanted via the Marxist-Leninist philosophy of competition between capitalism and socialism and the Russian historical experience of foreign invasion and external conquest. In this book, I will focus on US-Soviet relations across the final quarter-century of the Cold War and the role that superpower relationship played in the collapse of the USSR itself.

I also seek to give a flavor of what the US-Soviet relationship, which lay at the heart of the Cold War confrontation, was actually like for key players. I have drawn heavily on the accounts of participants on both sides and on the archival record that I had access to. Where relevant, I also draw on my own experiences.

This book appears a quarter century after the Soviet collapse, in a time when tensions in the US-Russian relationship following Putin's seizure of Crimea, invasion of eastern Ukraine, and military intervention in Syria have led some to warn of a renewed Cold War. The Russia of the second decade of the twenty-first century is not capable of mounting a Soviet-style challenge to Western interests across the globe. Nevertheless, the corrupt, xenophobic, and authoritarian Putin regime is a far cry from the Russia that most hoped to see emerge from the ruins of the failed Soviet experiment.

Understanding how the Cold War ended and why the USSR collapsed is critical for comprehending how Russia got where it is today. When it is relevant in the narrative, I discuss how developments in the waning years of the Cold War influenced what came later, but the story of Russia in the years of Yeltsin and Putin is beyond the scope of this book which ends in 1991, when it was still possible to be optimistic about the future.

Over the years many people helped me in the research and writing of this book. I would like to especially single out Dan Caldwell, Distinguished

Professor of Political Science at Pepperdine University, who read the entire text and provided encouragement and sound advice throughout this long project. Many friends and former colleagues discussed with me their participation in the events treated in the book or read parts of the manuscript as it was being written. These include Ambassador Mort Abramowitz, Shaun Byrnes, Ambassador Jim Collins, Ambassador Bill Courtney, Burton Gerber, Ambassador Arthur Hartman, A. Ross Johnson, Ambassador Jack Matlock, Judyt Mandel, Wayne Merry, Ambassador Joe Presel, Bob Pringle, Jonathan Sanders, Ambassador Thomas Simons, Ambassador Peter Tomsen, and Roman Wasilewski.

An indispensable resource for anyone writing on the Cold War is the trove of US and Soviet documents at the National Security Archive, especially the collection originating with my late friend in Moscow, General Dmitri Volkogonov. Svetlana Savranskaya and all of the staff were consistently helpful in assistance with materials. Professor Timothy J. Colton, while serving as director of the Harvard Davis Center, allowed me to become an associate and use its Russian-language library and archival sources. Mark Kramer, of the Davis Center, allowed me to participate in the Cold War seminar he has led there for many years, provided advice on access to archival material, and also provided inspiration through his own writings drawn from his unparalleled knowledge of Soviet-era archives. Professor James M. Goldgeier and the late James Millar, of the George Washington University Institute of European, Russian, and Eurasian studies, allowed me access to the Gelman Library and its collection of materials covering the Cold War era. I would also like to thank the staff at Duke University Press for their dedicated care and attention in helping bring this project to a conclusion.

As an independent scholar with limited resources and living in rural Maine, I was particularly dependent on "the kindness of librarians," especially the University of Maine at Farmington, Bowdoin College, and the Maine State Library, for access through interlibrary loan to books by participants on both sides of the Cold War divide.

I would also like to thank Waleck Dalpour, the chairman of the Department of Social Sciences at the University of Maine at Farmington, for the opportunity to teach as an adjunct for a decade. Angela Carter, of the Social Sciences department, provided countless hours of assistance with research material. Finally, I wish to thank my undergraduate professors at Franklin and Marshall College, who taught me the value of a liberal education in developing critical thinking, writing, and analytical skills—especially Sam Allen, who first showed me the richness of Russian history and literature, Sol Wank, who opened my eyes to the enduring power of nationalism, and Stanley Michalak, who initiated me into the complexities of Cold War politics.

And I must conclude by expressing devotion and gratitude to my wife, Cathey, for the patience she exhibited over the years it took to bring this project to conclusion.

First Visit to the USSR
Things Are Not as They Seem

"Vnimanije!" None of the American college students in the crowded train stopped at the Finnish border actually understood the Soviet guard's command to attention, but his burly presence demanded instant silence.

His next words sent a chill down my spine. Together with one of the female students in our group on its way to visit Moscow during spring break from a study-abroad program in Denmark, I was ordered off the train. As we climbed down from the green Soviet railroad car, I looked back toward the Finnish border. Only a couple of hundred yards away, it might as well have been the moon, which in that year of 1967 our two countries were still racing to reach.

Before we left Copenhagen, some of our Danish student friends had told us of a marvelous way to stretch our travel budget in the USSR. The Soviets, who basically viewed Western visitors as walking sources of hard currency, enforced an artificial exchange rate, making one ruble worth about one dollar. Outside the USSR, it was possible to buy rubles at a more realistic rate of four rubles for every dollar.

There was one problem with this scheme. Travelers were forbidden from bringing rubles into the USSR. I had cleverly conspired to fool the Soviet authorities by hiding the rubles in my sock, while my female friend had—so she told me—slipped them into her bra.

Walking to the station with the guard behind us, I wondered whether it was just a coincidence that two of us with illicit rubles had been summoned. Could I ask to go to the toilet and flush the rubles away? (This I learned later was presuming too much on Soviet bathroom technology.)

In the station an officer told us that we had improperly filled out our entry declarations. He slapped the forms onto the counter and pointed to where we had written our birthdates in the American fashion, with the month first, instead of in the European fashion with the day first, as the form clearly required, he sternly informed us. After we had filled out new forms, the officer said we were free to go.[1]

When I awoke the next morning the train was moving slowly through a dense evergreen forest, the branches of the trees drooping under a heavy load of fresh snow. Occasional clearings revealed "Peter and the Wolf" villages with tumbledown wooden huts clustered around a hand-cranked well. In later years, I enjoyed cross-country skiing through the lovely woods that surround Moscow and I learned to treasure the ramshackle charm of Russian villages. But few cities show their best side to arriving rail lines and Moscow is no exception. In the late winter dawn, the villages seemed more squalid than picturesque.

As the train entered the Moscow outskirts, strings of identical high-rise apartment buildings reinforced the gloomy impression. Even at a distance, these unpainted concrete towers seemed shabby and unappealing, surrounded by mounds of debris and acres of mud and dirty snow. Our train rumbled slowly past long platforms packed with masses of people on their way to work. Dressed in shapeless, dark overcoats and jammed tightly one against the other, there was something unsettling about these crowds. Not many people appear at their best on the morning commute, but an aura of unhappiness and resignation, together with a dollop of menace, hung over these sallow-faced and unsmiling throngs.

The Hotel Tourist, flagship of Sputnik, the Soviet youth travel agency, provided our first exposure to the contrast between the image of the USSR as a nuclear-armed superpower and the grim reality of daily life. A dingy multistory building far from the center of town, the Hotel Tourist was barracks-living at its finest. Each room slept six students and every floor had one toilet. Bathing was also provided, of course—in the basement was a large, collective shower. Cleaning and luxuries such as toilet paper were apparently waiting for the next five-year plan.

Sputnik had allocated three guides to our group. Olga, the leader, was a heavy-set woman in her thirties, who moved us efficiently through Moscow's crowded tourist sites. She was pleasant enough but could be counted on to deliver the official line on any subject, with a smiling air of "I've heard all this before," if critical questions were asked. Olga's two younger female assistants supported her on any issue that might come up. One evening, talk turned to the well-publicized trial the previous year of two dissident Soviet authors, Andrei Sinyavskiy and Yuli Daniel. The discussion continued for some time along predictable lines until eventually Olga excused herself, saying she had to go home to her family.

As soon as the door closed behind Olga, the behavior of the two younger guides changed. One of them jumped to her feet and cried out in an animated voice, "Now, show us the latest dances." Discussion of politics was abandoned in favor of pop music, film, and life "over there." Our guides had a deep hunger for information about how young people lived in the West and did not bother to conceal their longing for some of the cultural and consumer advantages of the capitalist system whose flaws they had only recently joined Olga in expos-ing. It was my first—but far from last—exposure to one of the eternal aspects of Soviet life—the contrast between "official" and private behavior.

Visits to Moscow State University (MGU) provided another example. Sput-nik had thoughtfully arranged for us to meet a carefully selected group for a discussion of everything the United States was doing wrong in the world, especially, of course, the war in Vietnam. More revealing insights came after we joined a group who invited us to their dorm rooms for a party.

I was struck by the difference between the Soviet and the American version of the late-night student "bull session," at least in its 1960s variety. For Ameri-can students of that era, politics was the most important issue. We had discov-ered that the world, including our own country—perhaps especially our own country—was full of injustice, and we were the generation that was going to change that. Soviet students gave the impression of being bored with politics. The Soviet system was a reality. They didn't seem to expect or desire any seri-ous changes, so why bother talking about it? The MGU students shared our guides' intense interest in ordinary life in the West. "What job does your father have, how much money does he make, how many rooms does your family have to live in, where do you go for vacation?" These were constant questions. For them, politics was simply part of the landscape.

Eventually one of the Soviet students took me to his dorm room. On the wall were three posters: Lenin, US president John Kennedy, assassinated four years previously, and the Beatles. Lenin, he said, was "not a bad guy," but he was essentially on the wall for "cover." JFK was there because he had been a world leader genuinely striving for peace. But it was the Beatles, he said, who were his true politics, and he showed me a collection of pirated Beatle recordings.

After a while we were left to our own devices, which turned out to be a big mistake from the point of view of our official handlers. We found our way into Moscow's youth subculture, aided by our Western appearance, the cachet of being American in Cold War Moscow, and, no doubt, the presence in our group of several attractive young women.

For me this experience centers around memories of Svetlana. Darkly beautiful and free-spirited, Sveta was an adventurer and a snob. She was determined to live her life independently and to the hilt, in the manner of her favorite poet Lermontov. Her father was a midlevel official in Moscow and, although she loved her parents and took advantage of his connections in such things as the purchase of Western clothes, she was indifferent to politics of any sort. The Soviet system she took as a given. She simply wanted to find her own personal space within its cracks.

For almost a week we were together every minute, falling deeply, passionately—and hopelessly—in love. On the night before my departure from Moscow, we considered various schemes of adolescent rebellion. I would not get on the train leaving Moscow and stay behind with her. We would go to the American embassy and declare that we wanted to remain together forever. But in the end we simply said good-bye, divided, as so often happened, by the immense differences of circumstances and systems.

Sveta and I wrote for a couple of years but eventually the correspondence trailed to an end. Every letter took months to arrive—no doubt delayed by detours through security authorities on both sides of the Iron Curtain—and we had our own lives to lead. At the time, I had no expectation of ever returning to the Soviet Union, and I do not believe she wanted to leave her home in Russia. I never saw Sveta again and I only hope that she ended up as happy in her choice of a spouse as I have in my own.

What stands out in my mind about that first youthful trip to Moscow was the way the underlying reality of Soviet life kept breaking through the highly embellished official version in which the Soviet authorities sought to enfold us. Things were not always the way they seemed—a lesson that was repeated on many occasions over the coming decades.[2]

CHAPTER 2

Leonid Brezhnev
Power and Stagnation

We remember Brezhnev as a doddering old man, clinging to power past his time. The shuffling gait, slurred speech, and gaffes such as reading the same page of a speech twice became the stuff of jokes and a source of embarrassment for many Soviets. Brezhnev's time became known as the "era of stagnation" and in historical perspective the term is well deserved.

But in his early years Brezhnev played the rough-and-tumble game of Kremlin politics with sufficient skill to defeat several challenges to his rule. Not an intellectual or an innovator, all his instincts were cautious and conservative. Nevertheless, he presided over an era of increasing professionalism and competence in the ruling elite and throughout Soviet society.

The first years of Brezhnev's rule saw relatively high rates of economic growth. The Soviet people experienced the beginnings of a modest consumer society. Individual apartments became more widely available and basic consumer appliances could be found to furnish them. Brezhnev brought a sense of stability to Soviet life, a feeling that things were improving and the expectation that they would continue to do so.

Brezhnev's international posture was active and aggressive. Under Brezhnev, the USSR invaded two countries, fought a border conflict with China, threatened the invasion of Poland, and together with its Cuban client used military might to install pro-Soviet Marxist-Leninist regimes in several African countries. In Southeast Asia, the Soviets provided Hanoi with massive quantities of weapons used to humiliate the United States. Brezhnev's military buildup turned Moscow for the first time in history into a truly global power. On the diplomatic front, a series of summit meetings in the 1970s symbolized the achievement of strategic parity with the United States.

This combination of domestic stability and international power is likely one reason why in the years after the Soviet collapse polls in Russia showed rising nostalgia for the Brezhnev era—memories which Vladimir Putin, who came of age under Brezhnev, skillfully exploited to buttress his own climb to power.[1]

Brezhnev Consolidates Power

Brezhnev's appearance at the top of the Kremlin ladder came as a surprise to many, perhaps even him. On the evening in October 1964 when Khrushchev was ousted, P. K. Ponomarenko, a senior figure under Stalin, met Brezhnev by chance outside the elite apartment building where both lived. In retirement and having spent all day at his dacha outside Moscow, Ponomarenko had not heard the news about Khrushchev's overthrow. Brezhnev looked downcast and when Ponomarenko asked what was wrong, Brezhnev replied, "We removed Khrushchev today." A surprised Ponomarenko asked, "So who is the new 'First'?" Brezhnev answered, "Just imagine, it's me."[2]

Brezhnev was widely expected to be a transitional figure. Many members of the new team had more impressive résumés and left no doubt about their own ambition for a higher role. Nevertheless, over the next several years Brezhnev moved skillfully to sideline potential challengers and cement his own place at the top of the Kremlin hierarchy.

Aleksandr Shelepin, former head of the KGB, presented the most serious challenge. Within the closed world of the Soviet elite, "Iron Shura" hardly bothered to conceal his ambition to achieve supreme power and his determination to return the USSR to a neo-Stalinist domestic course and a more confrontational posture with the West. Shelepin was the leading figure within the powerful Secretariat, in effect second secretary after Brezhnev. He also retained his position as head of the Party-State Control Commission and by virtue of this fact was deputy chairman of the Council of Ministers. Shelepin's client Vladimir Semichastny headed the KGB, which had provided the security muscle for Khrushchev's ouster.[3]

In the summer of 1965, rumors circulated within Central Committee circles that Shelepin would take over as party leader and Brezhnev would be relegated to his previous position as chairman of the Supreme Soviet, the powerless Soviet parliament. By the end of the year, it was clear that Shelepin had overplayed his hand. At the December 1965 party plenum, Shelepin lost control of the Party-State Control Commission. Mikhail Suslov, an acetic ideologue and former aide to Stalin, took control of the Secretariat and assumed the lead role in preparing for the upcoming 23rd Party Congress.

Shelepin further weakened his position in the run-up to the Congress when he proposed a radical party program that managed to offend almost everyone in the leadership. Shelepin called for a struggle against bureaucratism in the party apparat and the elimination of the system of "packets," by which members of the elite received special rations of food and other goods. Before the Congress, Minister of Defense Malinovsky pointedly stated that the army strongly supported the current leaders of the party and government and said rumors about dissatisfaction in the military were baseless, showing that the military stood solidly behind Brezhnev. Next year, while Shelepin was in the hospital having his appendix removed, Brezhnev used the defection of Stalin's daughter, Svetlana Alliluyeva, as an excuse to remove Semichastny as KGB chief. Shortly thereafter, a Central Committee plenum installed Shelepin in the powerless job of trade union chief.[4]

Kosygin and Economic Reform

Aleksei Kosygin played little role in the plot to oust Khrushchev but after its success he was the natural choice to be chairman of the Council of Ministers or prime minister. Personal relations between Brezhnev and Kosygin were strained from the beginning. Kosygin regarded Brezhnev as an intellectual lightweight and resented Brezhnev's interference with Kosygin's government turf. Brezhnev, for his part, was jealous of Kosygin's authority among the top elite and was angered by Kosygin's persistence in speaking his mind at Politburo sessions.[5]

At a Central Committee plenum in September 1965, Kosygin announced a series of measures that amounted to the most sweeping change in the Soviet economy since the establishment of the Stalinist central-planning system in the 1930s. Kosygin reversed Khrushchev's despised structure of territorial economic management, which had sent bureaucrats out of their comfortable Moscow billets into remote regional postings. Kosygin reinstated the powerful industrial ministries but he also sought a new approach that would couple more efficient central planning with somewhat greater independence for individual enterprises. The number of plan indicators each enterprise was required to meet was reduced from thirty to nine and a modest move toward the notion of "profit" was made by allowing enterprises to keep a greater share of what they earned.

Kosygin intended for the 1965 program to be the first phase of a more sweeping reform to be introduced in the next Five Year Plan. According to Dzherman Gvishiani, Kosygin's son-in-law and senior official at the State Committee for Science and Technology, Kosygin sought "the gradual evolution of the system of 'state management' of the economy into state *regulation* of the activities of the enterprise."[6] It turned out, however, that Kosygin's reforms collided with entrenched opposition at both the upper and lower levels of the Soviet system. Party leaders were unwilling to surrender supervision of the economy, which they feared could erode control over other areas of the system. Enterprise managers feared the limited autonomy the plan tried to give them. The Soviet central-planning system was so complex and basically so dysfunctional in practice that individual enterprise managers could not operate without the ability to turn to party officials for extrasystemic intervention—often quasicorrupt—to break through bottlenecks. Brezhnev, moreover, had no desire to see a potentially dangerous competitor gain credit for anything as important as rescuing the Soviet economy. The party apparat gradually whittled away at the reforms and by the time of the 24th Party Congress, in 1971, they had been quietly shelved.[7]

In 1966 Kosygin threatened to resign after Brezhnev successfully blocked Kosygin's efforts to cut the number of Central Committee departments dealing with the economy. Rumors spread that Kosygin would be replaced by Dmitri Ustinov, then the party secretary responsible for the defense industry. In the end, the Politburo rejected Kosygin's resignation as it did two subsequent efforts by him to quit, but the prime minister never lost his anger at Brezhnev's interference in the economy. In later years, Kosygin often returned from Politburo sessions "literally shaking with indignation at how thoughtlessly and hurriedly one or another important question had been decided."[8]

Brezhnev and Agricultural Reform

Brezhnev's first major domestic move was in agriculture, not surprising since farming was a perennial weak spot in the Soviet economy and agricultural failures had been one of the charges leveled against Khrushchev. In a speech to the March 1965 Central Committee plenum Brezhnev proposed a number of major initiatives. To stimulate output, prices that producers were paid for agricultural goods were raised and farmers were promised a bonus for grain delivered over the planned amount. Brezhnev also lifted legal and financial restrictions that Stalin had imposed on collective farmers, who were now allowed to have Soviet internal passports and given the same social benefits as urban workers. He also announced a major increase in capital investment in agriculture and launched a huge program of irrigation and soil improvement: major waterworks in Central Asia, land projects in the "non-black earth" regions of Russia, and planning for the diversion of Siberian rivers into water-starved southern regions.[9]

Brezhnev's agricultural policies, which continued more or less unchanged throughout the remainder of his tenure, left intact the rigidly centralized system of collectivized agriculture. In one respect, however, his approach marked a major departure. Soviet leaders had traditionally seen agriculture as a national milch cow, from which resources could be extracted to subsidize the development of more favored parts of the economy. Under Brezhnev, investment in agriculture tripled, rising to 30 percent of all state investment by some measures. Nevertheless, agriculture remained a major burden on the Soviet economy and its stubborn resistance to reform constituted one of the underlying factors in the crash of the entire system.

Anyone who visited a Soviet collective farm in the Brezhnev era, with its dirty and dilapidated buildings, surrounded by piles of rusting equipment and staffed by an aging, poorly educated, and often inebriated workforce, could see that much of this massive investment was wasted. Over the period 1970 to 1990, productivity in Soviet agriculture declined at an average figure of 4 percent per annum. By 1979 subsidies to offset artificially low food prices consumed at least twenty-seven billion rubles—more than one-quarter of total agricultural production.[10]

The results of this massive spending were meager. Although the USSR became the world's largest wheat producer in the 1970s, it still needed to import massive quantities of livestock feed. By the end of the 1970s, shortages were widespread. During my first tour at Embassy Moscow, over the period 1977–80, lines for milk would form as early as 6:00 AM and by 8:00 AM they had often completely disappeared. Soviet friends told me that outside of Moscow, the best-supplied city in the country, there were areas where milk was provided to nursing mothers on a prescription basis.

As diplomats, our family was sheltered from most of the hardships experienced by ordinary Soviets. We could purchase milk for our children from the Helsinki department store Stockmanns, which sent a weekly truck full of frozen milk and other items to a small commissary the embassy maintained in a basement corridor. We also had access to the so-called *dipgaz* (diplomatic gastronome), where small quantities of fresh and canned goods from various parts of the then-expanding Soviet empire could be purchased at rip-off prices for hard-currency coupons. Despite its grandiose title, the dipgaz was roughly comparable to a seedy mom-and-pop grocery store in the United States in the 1950s. It was, nevertheless, far beyond what was available to most consumers, who were barred by burly militia guards at the door.

My wife and I observed what this could mean to ordinary Soviets as we were leaving the dipgaz one midwinter Moscow morning, with small children in tow and carrying that week's purchases, including Bulgarian tomatoes, on top of our market basket. Seeing the tomatoes, which in that era were seldom available in Moscow even in the height of summer, an elderly Soviet approached us and asked eagerly, "Where did you get those tomatoes?" I showed the old man the dipgaz but added, probably somewhat guiltily, that I didn't think he would be able to enter. The old man straightened up and said, not angrily but with a kind of quiet determination, "What do you mean I can't enter? This is my country, isn't it!" I watched him cross the small parking lot and approach the guard. An argument ensued and the old man raised his voice. The guard pushed him away but the old man returned. Eventually, the guard pushed him aside so roughly that the old man fell helplessly into a snowbank.

Stability of Cadres

Brezhnev, who once said, "You can go a long way in politics with charm," was chosen as party leader in large part because no one expected him to rock the boat. Throughout their lives, Brezhnev's leadership generation had been buffeted by turmoil. They began their careers during the upheavals of the 1930s, often rising to responsible positions at an early age as older colleagues disappeared amid Stalin's purges. Next came four years of war, the hardships of reconstruction, Stalin's death, and finally waves of change under the impetuous Khrushchev. By the 1960s, the Soviet leadership wanted nothing more than a little peace and quiet and for almost two decades that is what Brezhnev gave them.

The new leadership reversed many of Khrushchev's unpopular personnel policies. The October plenum, which ousted Khrushchev, decreed that the positions of party chief and prime minister could not be held by the same person, as had been done by Stalin from 1940 to 1953 and Khrushchev from 1958 to 1964. A second decision, which at the time must have seemed reasonable to the fifty-eight-year-old Brezhnev and his mostly fifty-something colleagues, was that senior party and state positions should not be held by persons over seventy.

The new approach was popular among top party and state officials. At the 23rd Party Congress, spontaneous applause greeted Brezhnev's remarks proposing the removal from party statutes of provisions Khrushchev had inserted requiring a regular turnover of party officials.[11] The effect of these new policies was immediately evident. Under Brezhnev, retention rates for the Central Committee were always more than 70 percent, a striking contrast to the practice under Khrushchev, where typically 50 percent of the Central Committee was replaced at each congress.

Over time Brezhnev's policies inevitably led to an aging of the party-state leadership. By the late 1970s, no Central Committee member was under forty and the average age of the Central Committee elected at the 26th Party Congress in 1981, the last under Brezhnev, was sixty-two. But the Central Committee was a relatively spry body compared to the Politburo. In 1966 the average age of Politburo members was fifty-eight, but by 1981 it had risen to seventy, even taking into account the election of the fifty-year-old Gorbachev, more than a decade younger than his nearest Politburo colleague.[12]

Under Brezhnev the struggle for power did not cease but its rules became clearer and the consequences of defeat less dangerous. Whereas Stalin had his opponents shot or imprisoned and Khrushchev sent them to remote power stations, Brezhnev tended simply to ignore those he sidelined in the struggle for the Kremlin brass ring. Shelepin remained a member of the Politburo until 1975, long after he had lost out in his bid to replace Brezhnev. Kosygin hung on as head of the Soviet government until shortly before his death in 1980, despite the long-standing antipathy between the two men.

As time passed, however, the negative consequences of "stability of cadres" became increasingly evident. As the Soviet leadership aged, its capacity for work and its ability to engage seriously on the issues declined catastrophically. By the late 1970s, Politburo meetings were pro forma sessions. Brezhnev would read a short paper prepared by his staff that he probably had never seen before. Afterward there might be a perfunctory discussion followed by the obligatory unanimous approval. Perhaps the most egregious example was the 1979 invasion of Afghanistan, a disastrous decision taken in secret by a handful of Politburo members with no debate and over the objections of the military.

Stalin and Khrushchev had been careful to keep the leaderships of the national republics on a tight leash through regular rotation and by retaining many important positions, especially those related to security, in Slavic hands. Under Brezhnev, however, republic leaders gained virtual lifetime tenure. In Uzbekistan, Sharaf Rashidov created a vast system of patronage and corruption, which included foreign bank accounts, mansions, and reportedly even more unsavory practices such as a personal harem. When "the Uzbek scandal" began to emerge under Gorbachev, albeit only partially, it shook the national leadership and undermined the legitimacy of party rule.

The aging of the political leadership was also reflected in other Soviet institutions. Under Brezhnev the Academy of Sciences was possibly the only institution with a greater respect for geriatrics than the Politburo. Sessions of the academy, where aged members slowly helped one another to their chairs and then dozed peacefully through the proceedings, looked more like an old-folks home than a gathering of the top brains of an enormous and talented country.

Brezhnev and the Military

Brezhnev had an instinctive sympathy for the Soviet military, stemming from his experience as a political commissar during World War II and his postwar career in several key positions within the Soviet political-military complex. On occasion, however, Brezhnev was willing to take on the military. During the 1974 Vladivostok meeting with President Ford, he overruled military objections to a nuclear arms deal during a long-distance shouting match with Minister of Defense Grechko. But such instances were rare. Brezhnev's basic approach to politics, avoiding potential threats to his position by accommodating the desires of the major players of the Soviet establishment, meant that the generals enjoyed a virtual blank check during his eighteen years in office.

Never Again

In the fall of 1962, during meetings devoted to clearing up the aftermath of the Cuban Missile Crisis, then-Soviet first deputy foreign minister Vasily Kuznetsov told US official John J. McCloy, "We will never let you do that to us again." It was not a remark meant to be taken lightly. Grigory Korniyenko, a senior official at the Soviet embassy in Washington at the time and later the Ministry of Foreign Affairs' (MFA) chief "Americanist," recalled grimly that the "twenty-fold superiority which the United States had in the area of strategic weapons at the time of the Caribbean crisis had made them masters of the situation." The lesson that Moscow drew from the incident, according to Korniyenko, was to "strengthen the (Soviet) leadership in its efforts to achieve nuclear parity with the United States by means of the accelerated growth in strategic weapons."[13]

Determination never to suffer a repeat of the Cuban humiliation reinforced powerful memories stemming from the 1941 Nazi surprise attack. Until the very end of the USSR, the Soviet military was led by men whose formative experience in life had been their participation in what the Soviets—with good reason—described as the Great Patriotic War and they were determined never to allow a repetition of the disastrous setbacks the USSR had suffered in the early stages of that conflict.

In November 1987, Chief of the General Staff, Marshal Sergei Akromeyev, recounted his wartime experiences for Colin Powell, then serving as Reagan's national security adviser. Akromeyev described how after enlisting as a seventeen-year-old in 1941 he had been sent to the front during the siege of Leningrad, where "for 18 months I never set foot inside a building even when the temperature dropped to 50 below. We were always fighting and always hungry. . . . Of my high school class of 32 only I and one other survived."[14]

The experiences Akromeyev described were seared into the consciousness of him and others who shared them. Akromeyev told Soviet ambassador Dobrynin that his motto was, "National security along all azimuths. We proceed from the worst possible scenario of having to fight the United States, its West European allies, and probably Japan. We must be prepared for any kind of war with any kind of weapon. Soviet military doctrine can be summed up as follows, 1941 shall never be repeated."[15]

Military Spending Takes Off

The first year of the post-Khrushchev leadership saw a battle over military spending. In a May 1965 speech, Nikolai Podgorny, who with Brezhnev had led the "Ukrainian faction" in the plot to oust Khrushchev, asserted that the Soviet people need no longer "suffer . . . material restrictions . . . to strengthen our defense ability."[16] With his chief rival, Shelepin, calling for stepped-up competition with the United States, there was little incentive for the new general secretary to side with Podgorny. In a July 4 speech, Brezhnev asserted that it was time for "long, intensive, tenacious and disciplined work on a mass scale" to strengthen Soviet military power.[17] Prime Minister Kosygin initially seemed to line up with Podgorny, but only two weeks after Brezhnev's speech he backed off, saying that "in the current situation . . . it would be against Soviet national interest to economize on defense" despite certain advantages that would result if "very large sums" could be diverted.[18]

After Podgorny was sidelined at the end of 1965 by being moved to the largely ceremonial position of Supreme Soviet chief, the way was clear for a major increase in military spending, which continued until almost the end of the Gorbachev era. According to data published after the Soviet collapse by Yuri Maslyukov, who was for many years a senior official in the Soviet defense industry and ended his career under Gorbachev as deputy prime minister and chair of the Military-Industrial Commission (MIC), in 1960 real budgetary expenditure on defense amounted to 15.3 billion rubles. By 1970 it had almost doubled to 29.2 billion, accounting for over 29 percent of total Soviet budgetary expenses, or 7.3 percent of Soviet net national product. Maslyukov asserts that Soviet military spending grew steadily from 1965 to 1989 and that at its maximum it was 77.3 billion rubles, accounting for 16.1 percent of all budgetary expenses and 8.4 percent of total GNP.[19]

Throughout the Cold War, the true level of Soviet military spending was a highly contentious topic of debate among Western analysts. The CIA developed sophisticated methodologies for estimating Soviet military spending, a task complicated not just by the secrecy in which the subject was shrouded but also by the very different nature of the two economic systems. For years, the CIA estimated that military spending amounted to 6–8 percent of the Soviet gross national product. In the mid-1970s, a Soviet émigré undergoing a routine interview at a US army facility near Munich unexpectedly announced that by accident he had been allowed to see the real—and highly classified—figures for spending on new weapons procurement. After this windfall, the agency went back to the drawing board and calculated that the real burden of Soviet military expenditures amounted to 11–13 percent of gross national product.

In 1992 I separately asked former Soviet foreign minister Eduard Shevardnadze and Russian parliamentary speaker Ruslan Khasbulatov, an economist by profession, how much the USSR had really spent on defense. Without any hesitation, both told me the military had consumed 40 percent of all state spending. At the time I thought this was too high, but in retrospect it may not have been far off. In 1990 a former General Staff officer told a US military interviewer that 40 percent of the Soviet GDP went to the military while a senior Central Committee economics official reported after the Soviet fall that by 1987 military spending had reached 34–36 percent of Soviet net material product.[20]

Achieving Nuclear Parity

By the second half of the 1960s, Brezhnev's increase in Soviet military spending had led to the deployment of new strategic weapons that, in the words of probably the most well informed student of Soviet nuclear weapons now in the West, "finally allowed the Soviet Union to achieve strategic parity with the United States." In 1964 the USSR had 200 ICBMs, all vulnerable and technologically deficient SS-7s. By the end of the decade, the Soviets had deployed 860 new and capable SS-11 ICBMs and 170 huge SS-9s, the first of the "heavy" ICBMs that in the coming years gave the USSR a massive advantage in the "throw weight" or destructive capability of its missile force. The Soviets also began an ambitious construction program of strategic nuclear missile submarines. By the end of 1969, the Soviets had launched twelve Yankee-class boats, which were patrolling regularly off the US coast.[21]

The creation of this second-generation missile force in the second half of the 1960s was "the largest single weapons effort in Soviet history." In the eight years between Khrushchev's ouster and the signing of the SALT I arms accords in 1972, "senior Kremlin leaders engineered what can only be described as a spectacular turnabout in Moscow's military fortunes."[22] At the time of the Cuban Missile Crisis the United States enjoyed an approximate four-to-one advantage in deployed strategic systems; measured in terms of nuclear weapons actually capable of reaching their targets, the US edge was probably several times greater. By 1972, when the SALT I accords were signed, the Soviets had put in place a reliable capacity to retaliate with devastating effectiveness against any American strike and were laying the groundwork for a strategic nuclear force capable of threatening a first strike itself.[23]

Toward the end of the 1960s, the Soviets began to develop a successor to the SS-9, known in the West as the SS-18, whose massive eight-ton payload allowed it to be deployed with ten or more of what were called in the jargon multiple independently targeted reentry vehicles, or MIRVs. By the time the SS-18 deployments were completed, the over three thousand highly accurate warheads capable of being deployed on this component of Soviet forces alone could be seen as giving Moscow the theoretical capability of destroying all fixed US nuclear forces in a single blow.[24]

As the accretion of Soviet weapons continued, and with the United States mired in Vietnam, prospects for a fundamental shift in the nuclear balance in Moscow's favor seemed to increase. The Soviet economy was still growing and its future prospects seemed rosy, buoyed by the output of massive new Western Siberian oil fields. "Strategic superiority seemed far more attainable to the Kremlin in the early 1970s than at any time since the beginning of the Cold War." In the early 1970s, Soviet military leaders expanded their definition of the goal of strategic equivalence to include the concept of "deep parity," which meant that not only would the USSR seek to match US strategic nuclear capabilities, it would also seek to block US ability to project power around Soviet borders.[25]

The military buildup proved to be a double-edged sword. It dramatically increased Soviet power but by the end of his time in office Brezhnev seemed to have recognized that spending had gotten out of control. Several weeks before his death, at a gathering of the USSR's top commanders, Brezhnev urged the military to make more efficient use of the resources it received.[26] In candid conversations with US presidents Nixon and Ford, Brezhnev sometimes lamented in a seemingly sincere fashion how US-Soviet nuclear agreements had actually accomplished little in reducing the burden of nuclear weapons for both countries.

A Missile Civil War

Closed to the outside world and supplied by an ever-expanding budget, the Soviet defense establishment seldom faced the guns-versus-butter dilemma common in open societies. Disputes there were, but they tended to be about how to allocate expanding slices among various consumers. Generally such conflicts ended in providing something for everyone. A case in point is a clash within the Soviet military establishment in the late 1960s that was so intense its participants called it the "missile civil war," a conflict completely unknown to the outside world until after the collapse of the Soviet system but which shaped the structure of Soviet strategic nuclear forces over the second half of the Cold War.

On one side was academician Vladimir Chelomei, a distinguished missile designer, who had enjoyed considerable success through shrewd moves in the game of Kremlin patronage politics, such as hiring Khrushchev's son Sergei to work in his institution. But by the late 1960s, Khrushchev was cultivating his garden and Chelomei's opponent in the missile civil war, academician Mikhail Yangel, headed the Yuzhnoe Design Bureau, which happened to be located in the Ukrainian city of Dnepropetrovsk, where Brezhnev began his political career.

Chelomei and Yangel squared off over two competing designs, which each argued should become the centerpiece of the next-generation Soviet ICBM force. Yangel, whose institute was responsible for designing the formidable Soviet heavy ICBMs, favored a four-warhead missile designated by NATO as the SS-17, while Chelomei backed the six-warhead missile designated by NATO the SS-19. Yangel's missile was considered more reliable and more survivable but Minister of Defense Grechko, who cared little about survivability since he believed that in a crisis the USSR should launch its missiles preemptively, favored Chelomei's design because it carried more warheads.

Behind the argument over the missiles was a dispute about the strategy of nuclear conflict. One side of the debate believed the USSR should rely on large numbers of relatively cheap missiles that would not need to be based in expensive hardened silos, as the United States had done with its Minuteman ICBMs, and which could be dispersed widely throughout the vast extent of Soviet territory. Yangel and his supporters, by contrast, argued that the USSR should base its ICBMs in superhardened underground silos capable of surviving an initial nuclear attack and being fired in a retaliatory mode.

Yangel's approach would require a major change in Soviet practice because the USSR planned to launch its strategic nuclear forces preemptively, in part because early Soviet missiles required hours to prepare for launch and were thus not suitable for a retaliatory strike, and in part because the Soviet military was determined never again to be taken by surprise. As Minister of Defense Grechko said at one point in the course of the debates, "We will not repeat the mistakes of 1941 and will not sit and wait until we are hit over the head."

On an even deeper level, the debate was also about the very nature of nuclear conflict. Many old-line officers clung to the notion that if nuclear war occurred it was the business of the Soviet military to win it. But by the late 1960s, with both sides already possessing thousands of nuclear weapons, some recognized that the concept of victory was meaningless in nuclear war and that the only realistic use for nuclear weapons was deterrence. As Yuri Mozzhorin, chief for thirty years of one of the USSR's leading missile-design institutes, told Grechko, "We have thoroughly worked out and modeled the results. . . . The war cannot be won."

To settle the dispute, Brezhnev convened a secret meeting of top Soviet military, industrial, and scientific leaders at Stalin's former dacha in the Crimea. After a long day of fruitless argument inside a tent set up for protection against the hot Crimean sun, which participants later wrote had begun with the General Secretary personally piloting the lead vehicle of the VIP motorcade in a hair-raising drive through the Crimean mountains, Brezhnev stood up to leave. As participants began to gather their papers and Brezhnev, who hated to be put in a position where he had to decide among competing views of powerful institutional players, was berating Grechko and other members of the Defense Council, Mozzhorin tapped the Soviet leader on the shoulder. "Leonid Ilich, everything that the military has said here is incorrect. It's all really the other way around. I must speak." Brezhnev gave Mozzhorin ten minutes, which he used to "describe the doctrine of deterrence and how strategic missile forces should be built and developed in contemporary conditions."[27]

Brezhnev appointed Academy of Sciences chief Mstislav Keldysh to come up with a solution. Working late into the night on a veranda overlooking the Black Sea Keldysh, Ustinov, and a small team of experts came up with a compromise that was essentially "all of the above." The USSR would build both competing missiles and base them in silos hardened to withstand a nuclear strike. The move brought peace to the warring tribes of Soviet missile designers but it was the most costly of all possible decisions, especially in view of the fact that at the same time the missile civil war was unfolding the Soviets were deploying over three hundred new SS-18s. The compromise decision also stated expressly that the USSR would employ the risky "launch-on-warning" policy for its nuclear arsenal—a stance it maintained until the early 1980s.[28]

CHAPTER 3 · Repression and Resistance

In 1964 a young Yugoslav scholar, Mihajlo Mihajlov, spent the summer in Moscow. Mihajlov's description of the Soviet intellectual scene on the eve of Khrushchev's ouster is infused with optimism. He characterized the Soviet Union as "attaching itself to Europe and moving toward democracy." Students at Moscow University were busily exploring the works of banned foreign and Soviet writers such as Franz Kafka, Vladimir Nabokov, and the poet Nikolai Gumilev, shot in the 1920s for being a member of the opposition to the Communists. Mihajlov concluded that "the basic character of the Soviet literary mood in the summer of 1964 was the expectation of a final liberation of literature and the arts from all possible restrictions of dogmatic Marxism."[1]

Five years later, another perceptive young observer of Russia, the American writer George Feifer, found that "the morale of Russian intellectuals is as low as it has ever been." Hopes for the future generated by Khrushchev's Thaw had vanished. Among intellectuals, "pessimism about Russia's political future is their dominant political mood and it is far-reaching, almost to the point of despair."[2]

Feifer was describing the outcome of a struggle in the early years of the Brezhnev era between the authorities and a segment of the liberal intelligentsia centered in Moscow, Leningrad, and a few other cities. The outcome of this engagement was never in doubt. The authorities were determined to suppress the modest flowering of intellectual independence Khrushchev had allowed. But the battle left seeds that survived the Brezhnev years and sprouted with renewed vigor in the era of Gorbachev's glasnost.

Initial moves by the new Brezhnev administration on the ideological front seemed hopeful. One of Brezhnev's earliest acts was to remove the hated

Tromfin Lysenko, who had exercised baleful control over Soviet genetics for years. The most visible excesses of Khrushchev's antireligious campaign, which had led to many churches being destroyed, were cut back. In 1965 historian Aleksandr Nekirch published *June 22, 1941*, which for the first time in the USSR revealed the full story around Soviet entry into the war and pointed to Stalin's responsibility for the disastrous Soviet defeats in its early stages.[3]

But these positive signs were not long in being reversed. Shortly after Khrushchev's ouster, Brezhnev installed the reactionary S. P. Trapeznikov as the chief of the Central Committee Department of Science and Learning, where he had responsibility for the Soviet scientific and educational establishment. It soon became clear that the new Brezhnev administration was beginning "a gradual conservative turn in ideology that in its turn influenced all aspects of the external and internal policies of our country and party."[4]

The Battle over Stalin's Legacy

The first ideological battle was over how to handle Stalin's historical legacy, in many ways the touchstone of Soviet politics since 1953 and even in the twenty-first century a defining aspect of the Russian political landscape. Before the 23rd Party Congress, in 1966, rumors about a rehabilitation of Stalin provoked counteraction among the liberal Soviet intelligentsia. A protest letter was signed by twenty-five well-known figures in the Soviet scientific, literary, and artistic community. Protest meetings were held in Moscow scientific institutes and lecture halls, sometimes addressed by victims of Stalin's repression. These gestures may have had some effect, because at the congress there was no mention of Stalin.

In December 1969, shortly before the ninetieth anniversary of Stalin's birth, the Politburo approved an article that presented a positive picture of the dictator as a military leader and civilian statesman. When word reached foreign Communist parties, Polish leader Gomulka and Hungarian leader Kadar flew to Moscow to urge reconsideration. During a break in the proceedings of the Supreme Soviet, Brezhnev assembled the Politburo for an impromptu debate. Always eager to duck controversy, Brezhnev began by asking whether it was necessary to publish the article at all. Suslov, under whose direction the article had undoubtedly been prepared, said the country was waiting for it, especially in Stalin's native Georgia. Podgorny, who at the 22nd Party Congress under Khrushchev had first proposed that Stalin's body be removed from its resting place beside Lenin, said that if the article were published, it should include "who was killed and how many were killed" by Stalin's hand. The conservative Ukrainian party chief Pyotr Shelest argued passionately for publication. For him, "what was important was Stalin's achievements . . . the war. The building of Socialism."[5] Straddling the debate, Brezhnev concluded that an article would be published but it would have a "calm tone" and there would be no mention of those killed by Stalin.[6]

On December 21, Pravda published an article that highlighted the "mistakes and distortions" connected with Stalin's cult of personality and formally upheld the line of the 20th and the 22nd congresses. A small bust of Stalin was installed beside the Kremlin wall but plans for a major monument were shelved. Brezhnev had established an approach to dealing with Stalin's legacy that amounted to pretending that the man who led the USSR for almost thirty years and who established the essential elements of the Soviet system had never existed. His name almost never appeared in the Soviet media and the purges that claimed millions of victims were ignored or glossed over in vague references to an era of "mass repression."

The neo-Stalinists were turned back—for good, at the leadership level, as it happened. But Stalin's memory continued to enjoy support among parts of the Soviet population. When I lived in Moscow in the late 1970s, small photos of Stalin adorned the windows in many trucks and taxis, a kind of spontaneous "hard-hat" protest against the treatment of Stalin as a nonperson. Taxi drivers whom I asked about the practice emphasized Stalin as war commander. For them, Stalin was the "Great Leader," and they often said the USSR needed someone like him to return. They did not deny the existence of the purges but tended to see them as necessary or even in some cases as positive, the iron hand that Russia needed to keep on the correct path.

In December 1979, the hundredth anniversary of Stalin's birth, rumors were widespread about possible steps to glorify Stalin's memory. On December 21, I went to Red Square, almost deserted on a frigid, snowy morning. A police cordon kept people well away from the Lenin Mausoleum and the wall behind it, where Stalin and other former Soviet leaders who had managed to die in political good graces are buried. While I watched, a small group of men and women dressed in what looked like expensive foreign coats, apparently members of the Stalin family, emerged from a small door in the Kremlin wall and walked slowly to the end of the row of markers where Stalin's tomb is located. They laid a wreath, stood for a few minutes with bowed heads and then returned to the Kremlin. That was the only visible commemoration. By 1979 Brezhnev was a doddering old man and neither he nor any of the other old men around him had any desire to rekindle the sharp debates of a decade earlier.

A few days later a trip to Stalin's Georgian homeland produced a different impression. On the ride in from the airport we asked our taxi driver what Georgians thought about their illustrious countryman. "That's a difficult question to answer," he replied ambiguously but added that he would take us to a place that would show us what we wanted to know. We soon found ourselves in front of a charming, old-style Tbilisi home, knocked on the door and were met by a beautiful young woman. She ushered us inside and we saw that her family had transformed their home into a museum to Stalin. Every wall was covered with pictures and mementos glorifying Stalin's life. The lovely walled backyard had been turned into a sculpture garden where visitors could sit on benches and contemplate statues or other mementos of the dictator, including one with him as a Christlike figure summoning small children to his side. The girl's parents were not home. When we asked her what she thought of Stalin, she replied simply, "He was a wonderful man." I left marveling at the incongruity of this beautiful young woman seemingly entranced by the memory of one of history's greatest mass murderers.

A more complex picture emerged at a party we attended that evening thanks to an invitation from an unofficial artist. Amid the usual impressive Georgian consumption of alcohol, an intellectual explained that Georgians had an ambiguous attitude toward Stalin. He was genuinely revered as a local boy who made good in Moscow, a magnet for ambitious Georgians for centuries. Stalin had also taken on something of the traditional Georgian reverence for larger-than-life heroes outside the law, in part for his role in organizing a series of spectacular bank robberies in Tbilisi in the early years of the twentieth century, with proceeds going to finance Lenin's Bolshevik party. But Georgians also understood that Stalin had been responsible for killing more of his own people than any other figure since Genghis Khan. Another person had a simpler take. "Yes, Stalin killed many Georgians but we still love him because he killed so many more Russians."

Tanks in Prague Crush Hope in Moscow

The decisive turning point in the Brezhnev administration's battle to reverse the intellectual flowering of Khrushchev's Thaw was the 1968 invasion of Czechoslovakia. Liberal Soviet intellectuals were captivated by the daring of the Czechoslovak reformers. People tuned in avidly to BBC and VOA to follow developments in Prague. Heated discussions in workplace corridors and around kitchen tables reflected hopes that the success of reform in Prague could dispel gathering conservative clouds in the USSR.

Andrei Sakharov wrote that "even from afar, we were caught up in all the excitement and hopes and enthusiasms of the catchwords, Prague Spring." Vladimir Lukin, who worked in Prague at the journal *Problems of Peace and Socialism* and who became Russian ambassador to the United States in the

1990s, returned to Moscow in the summer of 1968 and immediately found himself in demand for seminars on the Czechoslovak reforms. Inevitably, rumors ricocheted through the Soviet capital. According to activist Lyudmila Alekseyeva, in the summer of 1968 Brezhnev was reported to have swept aside his prepared speech at a meeting of Moscow party leaders and cried out, "Don't you see everything is falling apart!" The incident itself seems improbable but—as was often the case in the information-starved Moscow environment—the rumor probably reflected something of the hopes of the intellectuals and the anxieties of the authorities.[7]

The clank of tank treads in the squares of Prague was recognized as the death knell of change in the USSR. "For Soviet public opinion the invasion in Czechoslovakia was the end of illusions about revolutionary humanism and the communist idea."[8] Nevertheless, the invasion had a lingering impact that was largely unnoticed at the time but that proved significant later. Memories of the Prague Spring endured among influential segments of the Soviet elite and help explain the rapid support among the Soviet intelligentsia for Gorbachev's glasnost.

Karen Brutents, a senior official in the Central Committee International Department, said that he and other liberal-minded colleagues greeted the news of the invasion as a signal that the Soviet leadership had turned away from all reform. Learning about the move on the eve of the arrival of Soviet troops, Brutents and Anatoliy Chernyayev, later Gorbachev's closest adviser on foreign affairs, went home and drowned their sorrows in a bottle. The morning after, as they listened to BBC reports from Prague, Brutents hoped for the failure of the Soviet invasion and the leadership that had launched it. Brutents reported that for him and like-minded colleagues the invasion began an era of political "double-think," when there could be almost no agreement with anything in the official ideology or in the behavior of the current leadership except for some international actions.[9]

The Beginnings of the Dissident Movement

In the late 1970s, when I lived in Moscow, Mayakovsky Square was usually deserted. A statue of the poet looked heroically into the distance, as if seeking an escape from the clouds of noxious fumes that seeped up from the sixteen-lane ring road thundering underneath the square and from the ugly mass of the neo-Stalinist Hotel Peking that loomed over it. In July 1958, however, when the statue was erected, Mayakovsky Square became the setting for the first stirrings of what later became known as the dissident or human rights movement. After the dreary official ceremony, many in the crowd began spontaneously to recite poetry. People continued to gather at the square throughout the summer for what amounted to a cultural "happening." Eventually, this display of spontaneous creativity proved too much for the authorities and the gatherings were banned.

In September 1960, young students led by Vladimir Bukovsky began to gather again at Mayakovsky Square. Youthful participants read poetry and sang songs. The atmosphere of this second round was more youthful, more critical, and no doubt also more rowdy than the earlier literary gatherings. In 1961, as part of a campaign to ensure order in the Soviet capital prior to the 22nd Party Congress, the leading organizers received prison sentences. "We were fighting for the concrete freedom to create and it was no accident that many of us . . . later emerged with the movement for human rights. We all got to know one another in Mayakovsky Square."[10]

On December 5, 1965, Soviet Constitution Day, Aleksandr Yesenin-Volpin, son of the poet Sergei Yesenin, organized a demonstration at Moscow's Pushkin Square, which he called a Glasnost Meeting. "The idea," Yesenin-Volpin said, "was to get the state to live by its own laws."[11] Soviet citizens had been conditioned to live as if they had no rights. But what would happen if people acted on the assumption that they did, in fact, have the rights the state itself said they did?[12] On this simple proposition, initially dangerous for its adherents but ultimately fatal for the Soviet system itself, was founded the Soviet human rights movement.

At that first demonstration about two hundred participants carried banners and handed out leaflets that demanded glasnost and "Respect the Soviet Constitution." Many years later, Volpin's wife remembered the event: "The wind of liberty was whistling in her ears." About twenty people were briefly detained and forty students were expelled from university. Bukovsky and two others were confined in a psychiatric prison, one of the earliest known uses of this brutal tactic against the regime's internal opponents.[13]

Fourteen years later I attended one of the last of these Constitution Day demonstrations. On a dark and cold Moscow evening a few score people gathered, determined to keep alive the tradition. Some hastily unfolded placards, which few succeeded in reading before the bearers were bundled off by plain clothes police swarming thickly around the square. One of the participants was Andrei Sakharov, who less than a month later would be forcibly exiled to the closed city of Gorky. If anyone standing in the square that evening had been told that a decade later Sakharov would be a member of an elected Soviet legislature and that two years after that the entire Communist edifice would come crashing down, he would have been considered eligible for an insanity verdict. Yet it did happen and it was the courage of the people in the square and of their predecessors, by then many of whom were in jail or exiled, that played an important role in that subsequent train of astonishing events.

The Trials Begin

One of the themes of the 1965 demonstration at Pushkin Square was to protest the arrest of two Soviet writers, Andrei Sinyavskiy and Yuli Daniel, for publishing their works abroad. In February 1966, they were brought to trial in a courtroom packed with government stooges. The event was accompanied by a media campaign that featured orchestrated letters condemning the young writers by some of the leading figures in the Soviet cultural establishment, harkening back to the Stalinist show trials of the 1930s. But 1966 was not 1936 and neither the accused writers nor their supporters outside the courtroom were willing to play by the old rules. Sinyavskiy and Daniel conducted such a vigorous defense, including pointing out the awkward fact that there was nothing in the Soviet criminal code prohibiting the actions of which they were accused, that they managed to turn the trial into an indictment of the authorities who had staged the event.

Outside the courtroom in the frigid Moscow winter, something equally important was happening. Not intimidated by the media campaign or by the gangs of plain clothes police who thronged around the courtroom in a remote Moscow suburb, friends and supporters gathered to show their solidarity. Also in the crowd were Western correspondents drawn by the novelty of the USSR's first show trial in a number of years. Eventually the two camps joined up in a nearby snack bar and established a link that quickly became an important element in the inability of the Soviet authorities to crush the nascent human rights movement.

Stories filed by the Western correspondents were promptly broadcast back into the USSR by foreign radio stations. The dissidents had obtained access to a powerful source for spreading information that was outside the control of the Soviet authorities. The KGB could still, of course, arrest whomever it wished. But it was no longer possible for the Soviet authorities to simply flick away internal critics without anyone noticing. And as knowledge about the activities of the human rights activists spread, the cost of the repression to the Soviet authorities in terms of blackened international reputation and eventually to their diplomatic relations with the Western democracies grew.

Despite the flimsiness of the charges and the eloquence of the defendants, the result was never in doubt. Sinyavskiy was sentenced to seven years confinement and Daniel five. Nevertheless, participants in the process felt that in some respect they had won. The defendants admitted they had sent materials abroad but they did not acknowledge that this was illegal and they did not ask for mercy. "The government attacked; we fought back. It was the beginning of the twenty-year war waged by the Brezhnev government against the intelligentsia."[14]

In 1968 the Soviet authorities staged another dissident show trial. Aleksandr Ginzburg, Yuli Galanskov, and two others were accused of compiling a collection of documents on the Sinyavskiy-Daniel trial. Learning from the earlier fiasco, the Soviet authorities carefully prepared the "trial of the four." They introduced two new offenses in the criminal code, Articles 190/1 and 190/3, that made it a crime to disseminate false or slanderous information about the Soviet system, which the Soviet authorities in practice defined as any information that might be embarrassing. In the time-honored tradition of Stalinist show trials, the authorities also managed to break two of the accused during pretrial interrogation. Hoping to intimidate the movement through the severe sentences and the spectacle of some of the accused testifying against each other, the Soviet media gave broad publicity to the trial.

Ginzburg received five and Galanskov seven years in a strict regime labor camp, a sentence that proved fatal for the sickly Galanskov. One again, however, the result was not what the authorities had expected. The trial triggered a new round of protests from well-placed members of the Soviet intellectual elite and an outpouring of support from ordinary citizens across the country. An appeal signed by a young scientist named Pavel Litvinov, the grandson of Maksim Litvinov, foreign minister under Stalin, and by Daniel's wife Larisa Bogoraz attracted considerable attention for the vigor of its protest and because the signatories boldly added their names and addresses. Widely circulated by hand and also heard throughout the USSR on foreign radios, the Litvinov-Bogoraz appeal stimulated a number of supporting letters from other Soviet citizens. Approximately fifteen letters of protest signed by about seven hundred people reached Western journalists in Moscow; the number that never got beyond the KGB must surely have been much greater.[15]

Jewish Emigration

The more conservative climate that accompanied the new Brezhnev administration brought with it a heightened level of officially inspired anti-Semitism. Informal quotas began to be imposed more rigorously on the entry of Jews into prestigious educational institutions and career fields. In 1949, 14 percent of the scholars in the prestigious Academy of Sciences were Jews, but by 1980 the proportion was half that.[16] Criticism of Israel in the media often seemed to cross the line into attacks on Jews as a people. Articles with more than a hint of ugly, old-style Russian anti-Semitism sometimes made their way into the press and such attitudes were understood to be quietly flourishing under high-level patronage in conservative party, security, and intellectual circles.

Anatoly Shcharanskiy, the informal spokesman of the Soviet Jewish community in the 1970s, reflects the typical background of the postwar urban Soviet Jewish population. Shcharanskiy's nineteenth-century grandfather was a religious Zionist who dreamed of moving to Israel, and one of Shcharanskiy's uncles actually did so. Shcharanskiy's father, born in Odessa before the revolution, believed that communism would solve the problems of Jews as it solved the issues of poverty and oppression in Russia. Like most urban Jews of his generation, Shcharanskiy grew up "completely unaware of the religion, language, culture, and history of my people."[17] In the Ukrainian industrial center of Donetsk, where Shcharanskiy was born, there were neither synagogues nor Jewish schools. In youth "the beginning and end" of his Jewish awareness was a consciousness of the anti-Semitism of the street. Nevertheless, Shcharanskiy grew up loving Russian culture from which he believed he initially derived all his "dissident passion."[18]

The 1967 Six Day War set off a wave of enthusiasm among the Soviet Jewish community. Inspired by the achievements of Israel, Soviet Jews began to rediscover their identity and make a conscious effort to reacquaint themselves with the religious and cultural traditions of their ancestors. Worried about prospects for the future, a small but growing number of Soviet Jews began to apply for permission to emigrate. At the end of the 1950s, a grand total of three Jews had been allowed to leave the USSR but in 1966 that number rose to 2,047.

The Soviet authorities responded to the new and unsettling phenomenon of increased Jewish activism with the old standby of repression. After the Six Day War official propaganda against Israel increased in volume and viciousness, diplomatic relations with Israel were broken off, and emigration was essentially ended. In 1968 only 229 Soviet Jews were allowed to depart. Numbers only began to rise again a few years later as prospects for US-Soviet relations improved. For the next two decades, until the Gorbachev era, Jewish emigration followed this pattern depending on what advantage the Kremlin believed it could extract from either opening or closing the spigot.[19]

Samizdat

The intellectual ferment of the Khrushchev era sparked the appearance of what became a new branch of Russian literature, created outside official channels and generally circulated by hand in typescript copies secretly pecked out on manual typewriters with as many carbon copies as could be made. Called *samizdat*, from the Russian for "self-published," it included poems, short stories, novels, camp memoirs, economic and sociological analysis, works of any genre and of every artistic and political flavor. Some samizdat was crackpot, the type of work that could not have been published under any system, but much was of the highest quality.

Reading samizdat was virtually a universal experience for Soviet intellectuals. The best samizdat was highly prized and circulated rapidly. Sometimes a person receiving a sought-after work, say the latest Solzhenitsyn novel, might stay up all night reading the treasured text before it had to be passed on to the next reader. As with almost every aspect of Soviet life there is a joke to cover this situation. A grandmother is having difficulty getting her granddaughter to read *War and Peace*, which looks too boring and official. So the grandmother, in a heroic feat worthy of Tolstoy's characters themselves, stays up at night typing the entire text of the novel—which her granddaughter eagerly devours once she believes it is samizdat. According to a study conducted in 1970 by one of samizdat's most avid readers, the KGB, more than four hundred works on economic, political, and philosophical questions had appeared in samizdat in the preceding five years.[20]

In our apartment in Moscow in the late 1970s, I always kept a supply of banned Russian-language books that had been published abroad, known as *tamizdat*, from the Russian for published "over there." Dissident or refusenik visitors would freely help themselves to the material while the rarer official guests might sneak a glance at the forbidden fruit but usually left it on the shelf. On one occasion, after a small dinner party at our apartment for Soviet environmental officials, one of the younger guests pulled me aside as the others were leaving and asked if he could borrow my Russian-language copy of Vladimir Voinovich's *The Life and Unusual Adventures of Private Ivan Chonkin*, which describes the hilarious misadventures of a Soviet counterpart to the Austrian "Good Soldier Schweik." Since Chonkin's exploits include desertion, followed by his capture of a KGB detachment sent to arrest him and its rehabilitation through honest labor, Voinovich's novel could most definitely not be published in the USSR.

I told the young official that he was welcome to keep the book but he insisted that he would return it. A few weeks later, at a meeting in the young official's office he handed the book back to me. He said he had enjoyed reading it and then, rolling his eyes at the ceiling, asked rhetorically when it could be published at home. A small incident in itself, it is nevertheless worth pondering what the effect was on the young official, a capable civil servant and a sincere patriot, of being reduced to covertly borrowing one of his own country's outstanding works of literature from a representative of its leading adversary. It is also interesting to speculate how many additional people, trusted friends of the young official, read the book before he returned it to me. This kind of intellectual subversion, like water melting away limestone, helped gradually undermine the legitimacy of the system even in the eyes of its own officials.

The Chronicle of Current Events

After the "trial of the four," Litvinov and other members of the burgeoning human rights movement decided to create a regular record of acts of resistance throughout the country. On April 30, 1968, the first edition appeared of the *Chronicle of Current Events*, one of the most remarkable samizdat publications in the history of the USSR and perhaps in the history of resistance to modern totalitarianism anywhere.

Over the next fifteen years, despite intensive Soviet efforts to suppress it, the *Chronicle* appeared every two months, with an eighteen-month break from 1972 to 1974, a total of sixty-four issues. The *Chronicle* avoided debates about how to reform the Soviet system. As British sociologist Peter Reddaway, one of the *Chronicle*'s earliest foreign supporters, wrote in 1972, long before anyone outside of Stavropol had ever heard of someone named Mikhail Gorbachev, the *Chronicle* sought to promote the "openness, non-secretiveness, freedom of information and expression subsumed in the ancient Russian word *glasnost*."[21]

The *Chronicle* circulated widely in Moscow and Leningrad and made its way to other Soviet cities by clandestine couriers. It quickly developed a network of underground contributors who provided information on developments in Ukraine, the Baltics, and the Caucasus as well as Orthodox and Protestant religious dissent.

Soviet authorities devoted considerable efforts to stamping out the *Chronicle*. Anyone found with a copy was subject to interrogation and arrest. It was a cat-and-mouse game played for high stakes, with successes and failures on both sides. Luck and quick thinking sometimes played a role. On one occasion, the KGB showed up to search the apartment of Galya Gabai, who was then helping the *Chronicle*'s first editor, Natalya Gorbanevskaya. Gabai threw *Chronicle* documents into a pot of borscht cooking on the stove. An acquaintance who happened to be in the apartment at the time stirred the "hot" borscht throughout the search until the KGB left empty-handed, and presumably also unfed.

The anonymous editors of the *Chronicle* typically made an effort to stay out of the mainstream of dissident activities but KGB pressure was relentless and the eventual outcome certain. What was astonishing, and no doubt infuriating to the authorities, was the willingness of new people to step forward to take over responsibility for producing the *Chronicle* as their predecessors disappeared into the hands of the KGB. Gorbanevskaya supervised the *Chronicle's* preparation until her arrest in December 1969. She was followed by Anatoly Yakobsen until his arrest in 1972. This sequence of editorship, arrest, and the appearance of a new editor continued at regular intervals until the *Chronicle's* final disappearance in 1983.[22]

At the end of the 1970s, I became involved with the *Chronicle* in its twilight era. By then the Moscow dissident community was a dwindling band under intense pressure. The *Chronicle* was still appearing, but its publication and dissemination was increasingly difficult. Shortly after a new edition of the *Chronicle* would hit the street, I would be approached by someone in the movement. Often in a packed snack bar, where the crowd and the steam from damp clothes would hopefully obscure surveillance, I would be handed an envelope with an original copy. Through this and other channels the *Chronicle* made its way abroad where it was printed in Russian and English translation.

Andrei Sakharov

No account of the human rights movement would be complete without mention of Andrei Sakharov, its most well known figure and without a doubt the most impressive human being I ever met. As a young man, Sakharov developed the first Soviet hydrogen bomb, a feat the USSR accomplished years before American intelligence thought possible. That success made Sakharov at an early age a full member of the prestigious Soviet Academy of Sciences and a member of the Soviet military technical elite, with access to the country's top civilian and military leadership.

Like many Western scientists involved in nuclear weapons research, Sakharov gradually developed doubts about nuclear weapons and some of the nuclear policies his country pursued. Sakharov first voiced these doubts to the Soviet leadership in the summer of 1961 as Moscow was secretly preparing to test the largest thermonuclear device ever exploded. In a closed meeting with top Soviet nuclear scientists, Khrushchev announced that the USSR would resume nuclear testing that fall, despite an informal moratorium that the USSR, the United States, and Great Britain had been observing since 1958. Sakharov volunteered that the USSR had little to gain from the move and as the meeting continued he scribbled a more pointed note to Khrushchev warning that resumption would jeopardize the "test ban negotiations, the cause of disarmament, and world peace."

Later, as the officials and scientists assembled in a Kremlin banquet hall, Khrushchev called for silence, raised his glass as if for a toast, and launched into a blistering attack on Sakharov. Holding up Sakharov's note and getting red in the face, Khrushchev accused Sakharov of "poking his nose where it doesn't belong." Khrushchev ordered Sakharov, and implicitly any other scientist who might be inclined to follow his example, to "leave politics to us,—we're the specialists."[23]

Khrushchev's outburst demonstrated in a particularly vivid way an important failing of the Soviet system: its difficulty in dealing with internal criticism. Sakharov writes that during Khrushchev's tirade everyone sat frozen, averting their gaze and afterward only one person spoke to him. Sakharov at this stage was hardly a "peacenik." The core of his argument was that resumption of testing would benefit the United States more than the Soviet Union yet Khrushchev was unwilling to even consider Sakharov's views. His harsh personal assault on someone who had done so much to enhance Soviet military power would obviously have a chilling effect on the willingness of other specialists to put forward criticisms, even well-founded ones. Khrushchev was notorious for his outbursts and afterward he would sometimes cool off and even try to make amends to the victims of his tongue lashings, as he did to Sakharov. But the impermeability of the Soviet establishment to internal criticism, let alone public scrutiny, eventually had serious consequences for the survival of the system itself, consequences that were especially marked in the secretive military field.

During the mid- and late-1960s, Sakharov gradually moved from the position of skeptical insider to public critic. Beginning in 1966, Sakharov began to participate regularly in the annual December 5 Constitution Day demonstration on Pushkin Square, joining the activists who would assemble around the poet's statue and silently doff their hats as a sign of protest against Soviet violations of its own constitution.[24]

In 1968 Sakharov produced an essay entitled "Progress, Coexistence, and Intellectual Freedom," in which he highlighted the notion of "convergence," the idea that the Soviet and American systems would eventually evolve toward each other, shedding hard-edged capitalism and totalitarian socialism and in the process ending the Cold War. Sakharov proposed a host of fundamental changes to Soviet society, including the abolition of censorship, repeal of laws violating human rights, release of political prisoners, and economic reform. He concluded on a note of high optimism, outlining a four-stage plan of cooperation in which the first was the creation of a multiparty system in the socialist countries, after which the Soviet Union and the United States would cooperate to eliminate world poverty and the reduction in national differences would lead to world government. "Progress" marked Sakharov's break with the system and led to his exclusion from the top circles of the party-state leadership, although some of the privileges associated with his status as Academician remained intact until the end, including access to a chauffeur-driven limousine in which he sometimes pulled up to the front of the American embassy.

By 1975, when his essay "My Country and the World" appeared, Sakharov had developed a familiarity with the dark underside of Soviet society that was very different from the privileged cocoon of the Soviet elite where he had formerly dwelled. He received a large volume of correspondence and a steady stream of visitors trudged up to his fifth-floor apartment on Moscow's ring road, seeking personal intervention by someone whom many treated with the reverence that Russian peasants had formerly ascribed to saintly intercessors.

With something approaching a novelist's eye, Sakharov began by describing the grim streets behind the glittering skyscrapers of Moscow's New Arbat: "A sea of human misery, difficulties, animosities, cruelty, profound fatigue, and indifference."[25] Sakharov attributed his more pessimistic view of Soviet prospects to his own new awareness of the "unusually large number of unfortunate people" in Soviet society, the solitary pensioners, the chronically ill who cannot gain entrance to a hospital, the drunkards, the prisoners, the victims of corrupt local officials and the local mafia, and the desperate people who besiege the waiting rooms of important officials.[26]

In 1968, with his leadership connections still largely intact, Sakharov had hoped that "Progress" might actually influence Soviet behavior. In 1975 Sakharov addressed his arguments primarily to Western readers. Sakharov welcomed the détente in US-Soviet relations, but he also warned against the "miscalculations and defeats" of Western policy because of its failure to understand the dangers of totalitarianism hidden behind the Soviet façade.

In 1973 Sakharov was first warned that he might be prosecuted for his "anti-Soviet statements." Sakharov responded in characteristic fashion. He invited Western correspondents to his apartment and informed them about the threats. The incident set off a major campaign against Sakharov in the Soviet media, beginning with a critical letter signed by forty-two Academicians, including many of his former colleagues. In response to fears that Sakharov might be arrested, the president of the US National Academy of Sciences, Phillip Handler, wrote the president of the Soviet Academy, Mystyslav Keldysh, to warn that Sakharov's arrest could end US scientific cooperation with the USSR, an intervention that Sakharov believed played a decisive role in ending the campaign against him.[27]

At the end of the 1970s, I was embassy contact with Sakharov for a brief period, one of the most memorable experiences of my government career. A quiet-spoken man, Sakharov also carried with him an unforgettable aura of penetrating intelligence, inner peace, and deep moral rectitude. In retrospect it is somewhat ironic that this man who created such a terrible engine of destruction was also perhaps the most saintly individual I ever met. Most of my conversations with Sakharov concerned developments within the Soviet human rights community. At no time did I ever attempt to discuss anything related to Sakharov's previous defense-related career, and I am confident that had I or any other US official attempted to do so Sakharov would have indignantly broken off the conversation.

Two meetings toward the end of our relationship stand out. In the first, Sakharov said he knew the Soviet authorities were closing in on him. The long immunity he had enjoyed because of his past services to the Soviet state was ending and he expected to be arrested at any moment. The KGB was entering his apartment in his absence and not even bothering to conceal the evidence of their intrusions. Taking from his ever-present battered leather briefcase a packet wrapped in brown paper, Sakharov said he had been writing his memoirs. He was concerned that the KGB might seize them and asked for help in getting them out of the USSR. He showed me several notebooks where every inch of paper on both sides was tightly covered with Sakharov's tiny but neat handwriting.

In a later conversation, Sakharov pulled out another brown paper packet from his briefcase. This proved to contain Sakharov's Nobel Peace Prize medallion, a disk of solid gold about five inches in diameter. Holding it in my hands I was filled with surprise at its weight and its value both monetary and otherwise. My other thought was one of sadness both for Sakharov and for his country. This great man, one of the twentieth century's outstanding figures, was forced to rely on the aid of a foreign diplomat to help protect his personal legacy. And his country, to which he always remained loyal, was abusing his contributions and wasting his talents in such an egregious fashion.

In January 1980, I learned about Sakharov's exile to Gorky from a BBC broadcast while I was visiting Baku with another embassy officer. I never saw him again. But the privilege of meeting him will remain with me as long as I live.

Aleksandr Solzhenitsyn

Sakharov and the Nobel Prize–winning novelist Aleksandr Solzhenitsyn were the most prominent critical voices of the 1960s and 1970s, but they could hardly have been more different. Sakharov was the quintessential "Westernizer," rigorously rational and convinced that the solution to Soviet ills lay in adopting the essential elements of liberal democracy without surrendering the positive features of socialism.

Solzhenitsyn, by contrast, was the classic "Slavophile." Solzhenitsyn was more sweepingly and passionately critical of the Soviet system than was Sakharov. Yet Solzhenitsyn also championed the notion that there was a special "Russian way" to national freedom, strongly infused with Orthodox religion, the collectivist tradition, and the Dostoyevskian concept of suffering as a path to redemption. Solzhenitsyn's austere religiosity made secular intellectuals uncomfortable, in the West and the USSR, and his sharp criticism of détente ran counter to the then prevailing notion that the rougher edges of the Soviet system could be smoothed through cooperation and contact with the West. Solzhenitsyn was a prophet and a loner. His pointed criticisms of those who deviated from his own strict standards often alienated even his supporters. Yet no writer did more to reveal how the apparatus of oppression formed the essential underpinning of the system that Lenin and his followers imposed on Russia and its neighbors.

In *The First Circle*, Solzhenitsyn wrote, "A great writer is, so to speak, a second government in his country and for that reason no regime has ever loved great writers." The Politburo seemed to agree. It discussed what to do about Solzhenitsyn on at least three occasions but remained divided for several years about how to respond. In 1969 Solzhenitsyn was expelled from the Writers Union but allowed to remain at liberty. The breathing space allowed him time to have *The First Circle* and *Cancer Ward* smuggled abroad, where they were published to critical acclaim. In 1970 Solzhenitsyn declined to travel to Stockholm to receive his Nobel Prize, fearing—with good reason—that he would not be allowed to reenter the USSR.

After Yuri Andropov became KGB chief in 1967, the Soviet spy agency stepped up its campaign against Solzhenitsyn. In August 1971, while Solzhenitsyn was standing in line at a food store in Novocherkassk, he was apparently injected with a toxic substance, possibly ricin, which the KGB and its Bulgarian ally used a decade later to assassinate a Bulgarian dissident in London. Solzhenitsyn survived but remained bedridden for two months. In late 1973, the KGB arrested one of the typists engaged in preparing Solzhenitsyn's monumental study of the Soviet labor camp system, *The Gulag Archipelago*. Fearing that his own arrest might follow, Solzhenitsyn authorized the publication in the West of *Gulag*, whose text had already been smuggled abroad by sympathizers.[28]

Based on Solzhenitsyn's experiences and on comprehensively researched recollections by other survivors, Solzhenitsyn's vivid three-volume account of the Stalinist labor-camp system can plausibly be said to have changed history. *Gulag*, Soviet shorthand for "Main Administration of Corrective Labor Camps," circulated widely in samizdat. The interest was so intense that many people devoured the tattered typescript copy in one sitting, before passing it on to the next reader. *Gulag's* meticulous compiling of fact after fact had a shocking impact on the Soviet intelligentsia. Unofficial historian Roy Medvedev said, "I think that few could stand up from the table having finished this book the same as when they opened its first page."

Gulag dealt the Soviet system a blow whose historical consequences perhaps even surpassed those of Khrushchev's 1956 secret speech. By the time I served at Embassy Moscow in the late 1970s, it was rare to meet an educated Soviet, even officials, who would pretend not to have read Solzhenitsyn's work. *Gulag* helped spread an emerging consensus within the liberal intelligentsia that the entire Soviet political system was flawed from birth.

Gulag's impact in the West was equally great. Entering the English language as a synonym for *concentration camp* and selling around the world in tens of millions of copies, the book completed the process of destroying the reputation of the USSR, even among its remaining left-wing supporters. After its publication the USSR lost all shred of pretense to stand on the side of progress and humanity. By shifting the political and moral climate against the USSR, the book also played an important role in the resurgence of belief in liberal democracy and thereby helped lay the groundwork for the political and ideological offensive of Western leaders such as Ronald Reagan and Margaret Thatcher in the 1980s.[29]

The Soviet leadership responded quickly. In February 1974, Andropov sent a private letter to Brezhnev implying that failure to move against Solzhenitsyn because of concern about the reaction abroad could lead to serious discontent among senior party and military figures. A few days later Solzhenitsyn was on a plane to Germany.[30]

The Empire Strikes Back

When Yuri Andropov was appointed to head the KGB in 1967, some were hopeful that he would be a moderate figure. Andropov was known within the extended village that constituted the Moscow intellectual elite as a sophisticated and intelligent figure who employed a number of liberal assistants. But the new spy chief quickly disappointed these hopes. In the second half of the 1960s, the Soviet surveillance budget was increased and the KGB began to step up its efforts to recruit domestic informers. By the end of the 1960s, the KGB had 166,000 domestic agents on its books.[31]

Andropov took a personal interest in the campaign against the dissidents. He approved the trials of leading human rights activists and on occasion personally interrogated prisoners. Nor was he squeamish about methods. In April 1969, Andropov expanded the use of psychiatric prisons, where what amounted to torture through the administration of harsh medication was routine.[32]

Andropov's most far-reaching move was to establish a new Fifth Directorate within the KGB with the exclusive mission of suppressing dissent. As chief Andropov appointed Filip Bobkov, a longtime counterintelligence officer whose experience stretched back to the dreaded SMERSH of the Great Patriotic War. In his first interview, Andropov told Bobkov that "a powerful psychological attack is now being unleashed against us. . . . It is nothing more than a real ideological war." Bobkov, who headed the institution throughout Andropov's tenure at the KGB, says that Andropov took a direct personal interest in the work of the Fifth Directorate, which he considered "his child."[33]

In January 1972, as the White House and the Kremlin were negotiating details of President Nixon's impending visit to Moscow, the Soviet authorities launched what was intended to be the final push to destroy the human rights movement. A wave of searches and arrests hit leading activists throughout the country. In June Pyotr Yakir and a number of other dissidents associated with the *Chronicle* were arrested. The son of Iona Yakir, a Red Army commander shot under Stalin in the 1930s, Pyotr was one of the most active and well known dissidents. But Yakir had a mercurial personality and a dependence on alcohol. Isolated and threatened with execution, he broke under KGB pressure and passed on all he knew about the *Chronicle* and the activities of former dissident colleagues. In October 1972, surviving activists managed to release the *Chronicle*'s twenty-seventh edition with a long delay and in an abbreviated format, but by the end of the year even members of the dissident community were speaking of its activities in the past tense.[34]

The Significance of the Dissident Movement

The human rights movement in the USSR never attracted more than a few thousand active participants over its fifteen or so years of existence. The absence of mass support has led some to conclude that the dissidents had only a limited impact. The reality is more complex. The dissidents failed to change the USSR of the Brezhnev era but many former dissidents played important roles in the growth of democratic activism during perestroika. In 1989, three years after Sakharov returned from exile in Gorky, he became the most prominent member of the democratic faction in the Congress of Peoples' Deputies and polls showed him to have enormous popularity across the entire country. Sergei Kovalev, one of the founders of the *Chronicle* and of the Helsinki Monitoring groups, became in the early 1990s chair of the Russian Duma's Human Rights Committee and in that capacity was one of the most vocal and courageous critics of Yeltsin's disastrous war in Chechnya. In the late 1970s, I knew Vyacheslav Bakhmin as a quiet but courageous leader of the movement to expose the Soviet abuse of psychiatry for political purposes. After I returned to Moscow in 1991, I met Slava again. This time he was serving as Russia's deputy foreign minister for Human Rights.

Harder to demonstrate but probably even more important in the long run was what might be called "dissident-guilt." Once Gorbachev lifted the fear factor, liberal intellectuals seized the opportunities for change, suddenly rediscovering the reformist dreams of their youth with an enthusiasm that might at least partly be explained by the need to compensate for their earlier silence. In the early 1990s, it was not uncommon to hear people start a conversation on politics with the slightly defensive phrase "I wasn't a dissident" and then go on to explain how they had always hoped for change in the system.

Perhaps the most telling evidence of the importance of the human rights movement comes from the Soviet authorities themselves. In 1975, in response to pleas from West European Communist parties to limit the persecution against the dissidents, KGB chief Andropov responded unambiguously. "A renunciation of active measures to terminate the politically harmful activities of the 'dissidents' and other hostile elements . . . could be fraught with the most serious consequences."[35] Relaxing the repression in Andropov's view would lead to an expansion of socially undesirable activity that could in turn call into question the existence of socialism itself.[36]

Andropov was right. Just as a tiny leak, if not plugged immediately, can eventually sweep away a massive dam, the dissidents were the earliest precursors of larger currents that only a few years later swept away the seemingly immovable edifice of Soviet rule.

When Richard Nixon resigned in August 1974, he was probably the most reviled president ever to occupy the White House. Until the end, however, the American people saw him as a capable foreign-policy practitioner. Nixon's 1972 visit to China ended a long and unnecessary hostility between two great nations. Nixon laid the basis for enduring US-Soviet cooperation in some areas and began a twenty-year process of US-Soviet strategic arms negotiations.

Yet in the two areas of foreign affairs where Nixon concentrated most of his attention, Vietnam and the USSR, his policies ultimately failed. Two years after Nixon's much-trumpeted agreement ending American engagement in Southeast Asia, the US-backed South Vietnamese regime crumbled under a renewed North Vietnamese attack. And not long after Nixon left office the broad new relationship that he forged with the USSR, which came to be called détente, although Nixon himself seldom used that term, was under such criticism that his successor, Gerald Ford, banned the word from the White House.

Nixon's foreign policy reflected his personality and operating style. Suspicious and closed by nature, Nixon distrusted the State Department and Congress and from the beginning took personal control of those areas of foreign affairs that he considered vital. Together with Henry Kissinger, his accomplished yet almost equally secretive national security adviser, Nixon negotiated skillfully across a broad range of issues. But the closed nature of Nixon-Kissinger diplomacy ultimately undermined congressional and public support needed to build a sustainable framework for the impressive structure the two created. Skilled practitioners of realpolitik, Nixon and Kissinger neglected the importance of principle and ideas in the Cold War confrontation between the two systems that Washington and Moscow represented.[1]

Linkage

Proclaimed the centerpiece of the administration's policy toward the USSR, linkage, according to Kissinger, was intended to prevent the US-Soviet relationship from being driven exclusively by crises and to block Soviet cherry-picking on foreign policy issues. Progress in superpower relations had to proceed on a broad front and the Soviets had to understand that it was unacceptable to pursue cooperation in one area while seeking "unilateral advantage" elsewhere.

Vietnam and arms control were the areas where linkage was supposed to operate with particular vigor. In his first press conference Nixon made the arms link explicit, saying that "strategic arms control talks with the Soviet Union would be more productive if they were conducted in a way and at a time that will promote if possible progress on outstanding political problems at the same time."[2]

In practice, Nixon's record on linkage was mixed. Thanks to its rigidly centralized control of foreign policy, his administration maintained a more coherent and consistent approach toward Moscow than did many others. On the other hand, the Soviets turned out to have little interest in helping the United States escape from the morass of Vietnam. And with the Soviets at last churning out nuclear missiles "like sausages," as Khrushchev had falsely said years earlier, it was far from clear which of the two capitals had a greater interest in concluding a strategic arms deal.

Linkage is a bargaining tool in any competitive relationship and the Soviets were prepared to accept the concept provided the basic trade-offs were balanced. Linkage, as the Nixon administration defined it, appeared to Moscow to be founded on the notion that the United States could grant or withhold concessions depending on how the USSR behaved in areas of importance to Washington. But by the 1970s the Soviets saw the world as basically moving in their favor and they were not about to accept a concept that seemed founded on US superiority.

The Back Channel

On February 15, 1969, Kissinger met alone at the Soviet embassy with the pajama-clad Soviet ambassador Anatoly Dobrynin, who was confined to his bed with the flu. Kissinger stressed that Nixon intended to keep the US-Soviet relationship firmly in his hands, to the exclusion of the State Department, which Kissinger said was "not particularly reliable." Over the next four years, Kissinger and Dobrynin met privately scores of times and had dozens of telephone conversations in one of the most remarkable—and controversial—

relationships in the history of modern diplomacy. The two generally met alone, although on rare occasion Kissinger would be accompanied by a note taker. The language was English, which Dobrynin spoke with colloquial American fluency.[3]

Kissinger and Dobrynin juggled an astonishingly broad range of issues, sometimes meeting or speaking on the phone several times in one day. The two never lost sight of the fact that they were representing fundamentally adversarial powers and at times the discussions could become quite heated but they developed a mutual respect for each other's abilities and a confidence in each other as reliable interlocutor. They could also engage in banter, sometimes with a pointed subtext underneath.[4]

By excluding the bureaucracy, the Nixon White House, at least in its first term, managed to avoid much of the interagency bickering on policy toward Moscow that afflicted other administrations. But the relationship between the two superpowers encompassed a huge range of issues and it was impossible for Kissinger and his team to be familiar with every one. Sometimes Kissinger's virtuoso performances led to mistakes that had to be walked back at considerable time and trouble.

The back channel offered Moscow direct access to the two top foreign policy leaders in the capital of its primary adversary. As Dobrynin said in his memoirs, "Thanks to this confidential channel the Soviet leadership had a sure and reliable connection with the president."[5] With the US ambassador in Moscow shut out from all but the most routine contacts, the United States had no such access to the Soviet leadership.

Getting Started

During his first meeting with Nixon, on February 17, 1969, Dobrynin said the Soviet government had concluded a review of its relations with the United States in light of the arrival of a new administration and gave Nixon a note setting out an agenda for future relations. The Soviets gave pride of place to conclusion of a strategic arms agreement based on understandings reached during the Johnson administration that an agreement should address strategic offensive weapons and antiballistic missile (ABM) systems. On Vietnam, the Soviets set out their own view of linkage by stating that "the complete withdrawal of the American troops from the territory of Vietnam will affect in a most positive way Soviet-American relations."

Four days later, Kissinger met Dobrynin over lunch at the Soviet embassy for the substantive beginning of their back-channel dialogue. Pulling out of his pocket the Soviet note, in the margins of which he had jotted down Nixon's comments, Kissinger laid out what amounted to a US counteragenda for the next four years. Kissinger assured Dobrynin that Nixon would pursue strategic arms negotiations but he confided frankly that there were differences within the administration and that talks would probably not begin for several months.

Kissinger also laid out a detailed description of the approach Nixon intended to take toward ending the war in Vietnam. According to Dobrynin's report (no US record was ever found), Kissinger said the president wanted to work closely with Moscow toward a settlement "honorable for all sides." The administration could not accept a settlement that would be "immediately" (according to Dobrynin, Kissinger stressed the word *immediately*) followed by a replacement of the South Vietnamese government.[6]

By October 1969, Washington and Moscow were finally able to announce the opening of SALT talks, but both sides were becoming exasperated with the lack of progress on other issues. Having just returned from Moscow, Dobrynin began his second meeting with Nixon by presenting the president with a harshly worded note stating that "Moscow is not satisfied with the present state of relations" and going on to accuse Washington of stalling on the Middle East, Europe, and Vietnam.

After listening to Dobrynin, Nixon leaned over and handed him a yellow pad saying he thought the ambassador had better make some notes. For almost half an hour, the president took the Soviets to task for failing in the US view to make any substantive steps to bring the sides closer together on any of the issues that divided them. Throughout what Dobrynin called a tirade, the president kept returning to Vietnam and at the end Nixon got down to the point. "I must state plainly and in all candor that the war in Vietnam is the main obstacle to enhancing and developing Soviet-US relations."[7] If the USSR were prepared to help the United States to end the war, Nixon would "be able to take dramatic steps to improve and develop Soviet-US relations." But if the war continued, "genuine progress in relations between the US and the USSR will be difficult."[8]

Over the next two years, US-Soviet relations stagnated. The relationship tended to be sidetracked by extraneous issues, for example, months of controversy caused in 1970 by the supposed existence of a Soviet submarine base in Cuba. But Vietnam remained the most difficult roadblock. Once it became clear that neither Hanoi nor Moscow were prepared to negotiate seriously, Nixon carried through on his threat to escalate. The Soviets, for their part, continued to supply North Vietnam with massive quantities of weaponry and saw no reason to help Nixon escape a conflict that was damaging American standing across the globe.

In November 1969, the Soviets told North Vietnamese prime minister Pham Van Dong that the correct strategy in Southeast Asia was continuation of the struggle on all fronts, including the military. The Soviets warned the North Vietnamese to be "vigilant against Washington's political and diplomatic maneuvers insofar as the actions of the Nixon administration do not testify to its intention to end aggression in Vietnam."[9]

1971: A Turning Point

Nixon described the first months of 1971 as "the lowest point of my first term as President." His gloom came from many sources: the falling dollar; the incursion into Laos, which Nixon described as a military success but a PR disaster; and the unauthorized release of classified US documents on Vietnam that came to be called the "Pentagon Papers." In the field of US-Soviet relations there was growing irritation in both capitals and a recognition that, with the Nixon administration halfway through its first term, time was running out for major progress in relations.[10]

In Moscow, Foreign Minister Gromyko and KGB chief Andropov drafted a joint memo to the Politburo that complained that the first two years of the Nixon presidency had produced only "idiosyncrasies and tactical delays." The two predicted a "historically long period" of US-Soviet confrontation, which the Soviets needed to buttress through maintaining sufficient military capability, to convince the West that it must "reckon with the interests of the Soviet Union."[11] Nevertheless, the authors concluded—and the Politburo agreed—that Moscow needed to become more actively engaged with Nixon in seeking agreements that served Soviet interests.[12]

On January 23, 1971, Kissinger saw the Soviet ambassador for a meeting he described to Nixon as "perhaps the most significant that I have had with Dobrynin since our conversations began." Dobrynin had just returned from an extensive review of US-Soviet relations in Moscow, where he had been instructed to suggest a US-Soviet summit be held in the summer of 1971 and that Moscow wanted to use the back channel to achieve breakthroughs in Berlin, SALT, and the Middle East.

After agreeing, in effect, to hit the reset button, both sides focused on getting the SALT talks, which had been largely running in place since their opening in 1969, moving toward agreement. At noon on May 20, in one of those surprise announcements he loved so much, Nixon appeared before the White House press corps to read a joint statement: "The Governments of the United States and the Soviet Union, after reviewing the course of their talks on the limitation of strategic armaments, have agreed to concentrate this year on working out an agreement for the limitation of the deployment of antiballistic missile systems (ABMs). They have also agreed that, together with concluding an agreement to limit ABMs, they will agree on certain measures with respect to the limitation of offensive strategic weapons."[13]

Behind the short and deceptively simple wording was a long and complicated negotiation that had been conducted in such deep secrecy by the White House that the secretaries of State and Defense and US SALT delegation chief Gerard Smith were unaware of it. Informed by Kissinger about the agreement two days before it was to be announced, Smith acknowledged that the statement was a turning point but warned prophetically of problems that would be caused by its imprecise wording.[14]

The joint statement provided the impetus that led to the conclusion of the SALT accords a year later but an immediate problem arose over the basic shape of the agreements the two sides thought they were negotiating. Smith took the position that the two countries had agreed to simultaneously negotiate an ABM treaty and an agreement freezing strategic offensive arms, which had been the consistent US position since the Johnson administration. His Soviet counterpart, Vladimir Semyonov, relying on the record of discussions between Dobrynin and Kissinger, to which he, unlike Smith, had some access, took the position that the parties had agreed to first negotiate an ABM treaty after which they might discuss offensive limits.

Kissinger was forced to backtrack. He told Dobrynin that the US delegation would present a draft ABM treaty early in the next negotiating round but would then insist on parallel discussions of limits on offensive systems. Dobrynin told Kissinger bluntly that the White House's approach was inconsistent with their back-channel agreement and would make "a distinctly unfavorable impression" in Moscow.[15]

As Smith had predicted, limits on submarines quickly also became an issue, not fully resolved until the final days of the 1972 summit. When the US arms control bureaucracy began to prepare specific proposals to flesh out the joint statement, they naturally included limits on missile-launching submarines, a category in which the United States had a solid qualitative edge but in which the Soviets were taking the lead in numbers. An embarrassed Kissinger then had to tell Dobrynin that Nixon, facing insistence from the Pentagon that submarines must be included in the upcoming agreement, had decided to allow the US delegation to propose such limits even though he acknowledged this approach was inconsistent with the deal achieved in the back channel. Kissinger promised that Nixon would walk the US bureaucracy away from submarine limits but the president—well aware that opposition by the US military could sink any SALT agreement—failed to do so. In the end, SALT I allowed a significant advantage in submarine numbers to the USSR, a point that became one of the chief criticisms leveled at it.

The Opening to China

On July 15, 1971, Nixon went before the nation with yet another of those dramatic announcements he cherished, telling a stunned world that Kissinger had secretly visited Beijing a few days earlier and that the Chinese had invited the US president to visit next year. Even before he became president, Nixon had laid the groundwork for relaxing US hostility toward Communist China, which he himself had done so much to encourage at the beginning of his career. In 1967 Nixon wrote an article in *Foreign Affairs* in which he proclaimed that "we simply cannot afford to leave China forever outside the family of nations." Mao read the article in a special secret summary of the world press and recommended it to Zhou En-Lai with the comment that if Nixon became president US policy toward China might change.[16]

Mao and his colleagues had good reasons of their own to relax hostility to the "American imperialists." By the end of the 1960s, Mao's Cultural Revolution had brought the country to the verge of collapse. The Brezhnev Doctrine's proclamation of a right by Moscow to discipline errant members of the "Socialist Commonwealth," demonstrated in practice in Czechoslovakia in 1968, was an ominous precedent. Sino-Soviet clashes in 1969, together with the hints of a preemptive attack from the north, brought home to the Chinese just how inferior their real military position was toward their one-time Communist ally.

During a visit to Islamabad, Kissinger and three trusted aides flew secretly to Beijing. There he held seventeen hours of intensive talks with Chinese prime minister Zhou En-Lai, whom Kissinger characterized as "ranking with Charles de Gaulle as the most impressive foreign statesman I have met." Although the Sino-Soviet split and the growing Soviet military presence to the north of China was obviously a backdrop to the visit, the USSR took up only a relatively small part of what Kissinger described as "the most searching, sweeping, and significant discussions I have ever had in government."[17] Kissinger, nevertheless, said the Chinese had demonstrated "hatred for the Russians" and were "worried about the Soviet threat to their national integrity." Kissinger promised that the United States would not allow its developing relationship with the USSR to be used against China and pledged to consult with Beijing if any aspect of the US-Soviet arms control talks touched on Chinese interests.[18]

Brezhnev Takes Charge

In Moscow, Grigory Arbatov, head of the USA Institute, recalled "an almost hysterical response" in leadership circles to the US opening to China.[19] Brezhnev's foreign policy adviser, Aleksandrov-Agentov, said that Nixon's move led Brezhnev to become personally engaged in "forcing preparations for a summit meeting" in order to prevent the Chinese from "outplaying us."[20]

Washington's display of the "China card" came shortly after what was called in Moscow a "quiet coup." For the first years after Khrushchev's ouster, Brezhnev was the first among equals on the Politburo. By the end of the 1970s, having seen off challenges by Podgorny and Shelepin and slapped down Moscow party boss Yegorychev in 1967 for unexpected criticisms in defense and foreign policy, Brezhnev was ready to make his move. In December 1969, at a regular end-of-year Central Committee session, Brezhnev unexpectedly launched a sharp criticism of the performance of the Soviet economy, which was clearly an attack on Prime Minister Kosygin.

Other members of the Politburo were alarmed by Brezhnev's sally. Ideological chieftain Suslov canvassed Politburo members and began to prepare a counterattack that was to be unleashed at a Central Committee plenum scheduled for March 1970. Learning what was afoot, Brezhnev unexpectedly postponed the plenum and flew alone to Belorussia, where Minister of Defense Grechko was leading the Soviet army in maneuvers. Brezhnev spent several days in confidential consultations with senior military leaders. No one on the Politburo knew what had been discussed but "it was obvious that the military leaders had promised him full support in case of any complications."[21]

Politburo members who had been contemplating a challenge to Brezhnev developed second thoughts. At the 1970 May Day celebrations, portraits of Brezhnev were larger than those of other Politburo members and his sayings were singled out for special prominence. In the coming years Brezhnev increased the size and expertise of his personal staff and began to take on a more prominent role in foreign affairs. In July 1971, Dobrynin told Kissinger that Brezhnev was now the "number one man" and communications from Nixon should henceforth go to him and not to Kosygin, as had been the case up to then.[22]

In his first letter to Brezhnev, Nixon reiterated US interest in working with the USSR on SALT, Berlin, and the Middle East but also pointedly noted his disappointment with the way Soviet diplomacy focused excessively on tactical advantage. In handing over the letter, Kissinger told Dobrynin that Nixon wanted to discuss matters "on a grand and global scale" and not waste time on minor issues that could be dealt with by the bureaucracy.[23] Brezhnev's reply was a litany of complaints on the US approach to Vietnam and the Middle East. It was a disappointing answer to Nixon's frank missive, which the White House had hoped would provoke the Soviets into a more thoughtful approach toward issues between the two countries.[24]

Brezhnev was cautious by nature and had limited experience in foreign affairs. The Soviet approach also reflected the influence of the dour Gromyko, who had served as foreign minister since 1957 and infuriated generations of US diplomats through his unwillingness to reach any agreement without going through endless haggling. Dobrynin acknowledges that "the collective Soviet leadership could not rapidly rally the imagination and flexibility" to deal with diplomatic strategy on a grand scale.[25]

Kissinger's Secret Trip to Moscow

On March 30, 1972, North Vietnamese forces began a long-expected spring offensive into the south. Nixon wrote that he saw the North Vietnamese invasion as a sign of desperation but over the next two months most of the desperation was in Washington. On April 15, with the North Vietnamese advancing rapidly and refusing to meet in Paris with Kissinger, Nixon contemplated the prospect that the loss of Vietnam might force him out of office and reviewed with Kissinger possible successors who might continue their foreign policy line.[26]

By late April, with North Vietnamese tanks seemingly rolling inexorably south, the White House decided to send Kissinger to Moscow for talks that were kept secret until their last day, not just from the American public but from the US ambassador as well. In a sign of how close the relationship had become, Dobrynin joined the Kissinger team on its US Air Force plane for the flight to Moscow, secretly meeting a White House car at a prearranged spot in Washington before being driven to Andrews AFB.

Kissinger left for Moscow under orders from Nixon not to discuss any issue in the US-Soviet relationship until Moscow had agreed to rein in the North Vietnamese. With the summit hanging in the balance, Kissinger disregarded Nixon's instructions and spent four days in intensive talks with Brezhnev and Gromyko. Kissinger set a positive tone at the beginning of his first, five-hour meeting with Brezhnev by referring to US-Soviet cooperation during the Second World War, which evoked an emotional reaction from Brezhnev for whom the war always remained an evocative memory.[27]

When Kissinger landed in Moscow, with the summit only a month away, the two sides were still far apart on some basic elements of the SALT package. In March Nixon had met with Dobrynin, pleading the importance of having a SALT agreement to sign at the summit and threatening that if one could not be achieved he would launch new strategic weapons programs. After Kissinger landed in Moscow, Brezhnev presented him with Soviet proposals that broke the logjam. Remarking amiably that he was agreeing to a proposal made by a member of the US SALT delegation, Brezhnev said the USSR would agree to an ABM treaty that allowed each country two sites: one to defend an ICBM field and one to defend its capital city, with no more than one hundred ABM launchers at each site. In a sign of how strained White House relations with the US SALT delegation had become, Kissinger responded sourly that "one member of the US delegation is an adviser to your delegation," but he nevertheless said he found Brezhnev's proposal "constructive."[28]

Brezhnev finally agreed to include submarines in the offensive weapons freeze but demanded that because of US geographic advantages in ocean access the USSR should have sixty-two submarines while the US would be limited to its current number of forty-one. Kissinger grumbled that it would be difficult to explain why the Soviets were allowed a larger number of land- and sea-based missiles but, nevertheless, agreed to the figures Brezhnev proposed.

Kissinger laid out US cards on Vietnam with clarity and cynicism. He told Brezhnev that the United States sought "an honorable withdrawal of all our forces" together with the return of all US prisoners and, second, "to put a time interval between our withdrawal and the political process which would then start."[29] As for the outcome of that process, Kissinger added that the United States was prepared "to let the real balance of forces in Vietnam determine the future of Vietnam."[30] Although Kissinger said the United States would never agree to "install" a North Vietnamese government in Saigon he was outlining a process that he knew would eventually lead to that outcome.

Nixon's Difficult Decision

On May 1, as Kissinger was preparing to leave for Paris to meet secretly with his North Vietnamese counterparts, the US commander in South Vietnam, Creighton Abrams, informed the White House that the provincial capital of Quang Tri had fallen. A battle for Hue was beginning, and if that city fell all of South Vietnam might collapse. Not surprising, in Paris the next day the North Vietnamese were unyielding and, after three hours of "insult and invective," Kissinger walked out.[31]

At this stage, Nixon made one of the most difficult—and as it turned out most successful—decisions of his presidency. Overriding advice from the US military, which wanted to concentrate US air power on the upcoming battles in South Vietnam, and disregarding analysis from the CIA, which advised, incorrectly, as it turned out, that the Soviets could easily shift supplies to other routes, Nixon ordered US air and naval forces to mine North Vietnamese ports and attack the delivery of supplies within North Vietnamese territorial waters. For the first time in the war, the United States was taking decisive steps to cut the flow of Soviet supplies. In addition, the United States dramatically stepped up air interdiction of the road and rail routes to Hanoi's forces in the south, attacking many targets that had hitherto been off-bounds for political reasons.

Nixon had agonized over what to do about the upcoming summit. Almost everyone expected the Soviets to cancel if the United States escalated military pressure on Hanoi. Kissinger advised Nixon to call off the summit himself in order to avoid the humiliation of being rejected by Moscow but the president chose instead to follow the advice of Texas Democrat John Connally, then serving as Secretary of the Treasury, who recommended that Nixon do what he believed necessary in Vietnam and leave the onus for any summit cancellation on the Soviets.[32]

On the battlefield, Nixon's moves had a dramatic effect. Reassured that they would not be abandoned by their US ally, South Vietnamese troops began to fight more effectively. Mining Haiphong cut seaborne imports from 250,000 tons a month to a trickle, while overland imports via the railroad from China were reduced by air interdiction from 160,000 tons to about 30,000 tons a month. US bombing destroyed much of North Vietnam's pipeline and oil storage capacity while intensified interdiction of the supply routes south reduced total shipments to North Vietnamese forces by 75 percent. By June North Vietnamese tanks were running out of gas and the tide of battle in the south was shifting.[33]

In Moscow, opposition to Brezhnev's policy of separating Vietnam from the broader agenda of US-Soviet relations precipitated what Aleksandrov-Agentov called the most difficult leadership crisis in Brezhnev's eighteen-year rule. At the end of Kissinger's April visit to Moscow, when a joint statement between Kissinger and Gromyko was presented to the Politburo, Podgorny angrily scrawled "against" on his copy.[34] A group, led by Podgorny and including Minister of Defense Grechko, wanted to cancel Nixon's visit. On the other side, supporting Brezhnev, were most of the other heavy institutional players in the Soviet leadership—Kosygin, Gromyko, Suslov, and Andropov. Just days before Nixon was due to arrive in Moscow, Brezhnev convened a meeting of the Politburo and key Central Committee members. After two days of heated debate, the decision was taken to allow the summit to proceed.[35]

Moscow Summit

Nixon arrived in Moscow on May 22, the first US president to visit the Soviet capital. The summit featured a number of US-Soviet agreements, carefully choreographed in this US election year to produce a daily signing ceremony for American evening news audiences. In addition to the SALT accords the two countries also signed a number of technical cooperation agreements including one that led to the 1975 Apollo-Soyuz mission and its well-publicized "handshake in space" between US and Soviet spacemen.

Brezhnev used Nixon's visit to upstage his Kremlin rivals. Shortly before the two delegations were due to begin their first meeting, Brezhnev invited Nixon for an unexpected one-on-one encounter. While an anxious Kissinger, unaccustomed to being excluded from such events, paced nervously outside the door, the two leaders outlined the subjects that each considered most important for the summit and established a personal rapport that lasted for the duration of Nixon's tenure. But the real reason for the private meeting was to make crystal clear to other Soviet leaders Brezhnev's preeminent position in the conduct of relations with the United States. Before the summit the Politburo had decided that Brezhnev, Kosygin, and Podgorny would conduct the negotiations from the Soviet side. By meeting alone with Nixon, Brezhnev was telling the rest of the Soviet leadership that he was the man in charge. Kosygin and Podgorny were furious but Brezhnev's position was sufficiently strong that there was nothing they could do but wait in frustration with Kissinger.[36]

SALT at the Summit

As Nixon's plane landed in Moscow, several SALT issues remained unresolved. Throughout the summit week, the White House team met with senior Soviet officials, often late at night after other business had been completed. As the two leaders were meeting, the US and Soviet SALT delegations also continued to work in Helsinki. Nixon refused to allow US delegation chief Smith to come to Moscow, lest his presence detract from the president's media limelight, but the existence of two parallel negotiating tracks led to confusion, irritation, and mistakes.

In their second meeting, Nixon and Brezhnev, accompanied only by Kissinger and Aleksandrov-Agentov, plunged bravely into the complex issues of nuclear arms control and after an exchange of arguments and banter the two leaders agreed to sensible compromises on most outstanding points. Brezhnev, after complaining that it appeared the Americans wanted the second Soviet ABM site located in China, agreed to the US position that it would be located at least 1,500 kilometers from Moscow. The leaders of the two most powerful nations in the world spent some time haggling over the meaning of the word *significant* before deciding that the agreement's ban on significant modernization meant that the dimensions of ICBM launchers—and hence of the missiles contained inside them—could not be increased by more than 15 percent.[37]

The limits on increases in silo size were supposed to put bounds on the Soviet ability to modernize its ICBM force but a few days after SALT I was signed US intelligence overheard Minister of Defense Grechko reassuring Brezhnev that SALT would not prevent the deployment of a powerful new MIRVed ICBM, called in the West the SS-19. Some in the West believed that the SS-19 was, in fact, a "heavy" ICBM, whose deployment in silos originally containing the "light" SS-11 would have been blocked by SALT, and concluded that the United States had been hoodwinked.[38]

In order to deflect growing criticism of the imbalance in submarine numbers—during the summit Kissinger's assistant Alexander Haig cabled that the Pentagon was threatening to jump ship on SALT—Kissinger insisted that as the Soviets replaced their older submarines they would have to reduce the allowed ceilings to levels closer to those possessed by the United States. Leonid Smirnov, the powerful head of the Soviet Military-Industrial Commission, whom Gromyko had brought into the talks, listened initially to Kissinger's proposals with amusement, remarking snidely that he considered them a "joke." When he realized that Kissinger was serious, Smirnov became so enraged that Gromyko had to declare a recess and walk the infuriated Soviet official into the hall for a cooling-off period.

The SALT package that the two leaders signed in Moscow consisted of two agreements. The ABM Treaty was intended to prevent either country from deploying an effective defense of its entire territory against ballistic missiles and thereby undermining the retaliatory response that lay at the heart of nuclear deterrence. It limited each country to no more than two ABM sites, each with a maximum of one hundred launchers and missiles. The treaty required early-warning radars to be located along the periphery of the country and oriented outward to prevent them from being used to defend points in the interior. It made a half-hearted stab at limiting technological improvements by banning things that the two countries did not really intend to do anyway, such as deploying launchers of multiple ABM missiles or interceptors with multiple warheads.[39]

The second component of the SALT I package, the Interim Agreement on the Limitation of Strategic Offensive Arms, was essentially a freeze on the total number of launchers of ICBMs and SLBMs (submarine-launched ballistic missiles) the two countries possessed at the time of signing. It was intended as a holding action, pending the negotiation of a more comprehensive agreement covering all aspects of strategic nuclear weapons. The Interim Agreement limited the United States to no more than the 1,054 operational ICBM launchers it possessed at the time of signing, while the Soviet Union was allowed no more than the estimated 1,618 ICBM launchers it had in service or under construction. The numerical advantages allowed the USSR in ICBM and SLBM launchers came under heavy criticism in the United States despite the fact that the accord excluded heavy bombers, where the United States enjoyed a substantial edge in numbers and capabilities.

The Interim Agreement did little to prevent the modernization of strategic forces, most notably the deployment of MIRVed missiles, which both countries did with gusto during the 1970s. When SALT I was signed, the United States had a total of 3,858 nuclear warheads on its strategic missiles. By the end of the decade, that figure had risen to 7,274. In 1972 the USSR had 2,024 warheads on its ballistic missiles, and by the end of the decade it had deployed 5,615. It is hard to disagree with the conclusions reached by a team of prestigious outside experts in a top secret Pentagon study of the US-Soviet strategic arms rivalry that the negotiations were "largely a matter of ratifying decisions on the size and basic technical composition of strategic forces which each side reached unilaterally well before formal negotiations began."[40]

Oleg Grinyevskiy, a member of the Soviet SALT delegation, said, "We won a great victory over the Americans." Within a decade, developments in the USSR and the United States would undermine this sense of Soviet confidence. But for the moment, with Washington mired in Vietnam, global developments seemed to be breaking in Moscow's favor. In the corridors of Soviet power, Grinyevskiy recalled, "there was talk that the US was losing the arms race."[41]

Vietnam at the Summit

Not until the third day of the summit did Vietnam come up. After a signing ceremony at the Kremlin, Brezhnev propelled Nixon into his limousine and sped off to his dacha, followed in a commandeered car by a frantic Kissinger and two aides who had no idea where Brezhnev was taking the president. After a hair-raising excursion on the Moscow River in a hydrofoil yacht, which Brezhnev later presented to Nixon as a gift, the Soviets sat the US delegation down at a conference table and basically proceeded to unload all of their anger over Vietnam.

Flanked by Kosygin and Podgorny, Brezhnev called the war "shameful aggression." Podgorny followed with an angry tirade in which he told the Americans, "You are murderers and on your hands is the blood of old people, women, and children." Kosygin complained that US bombs were falling close to Soviet ships and made a barely veiled threat of Soviet military intervention.[42]

The conversation dragged on until almost midnight and ended with a dinner where both delegations chatted casually as if nothing had happened. Listening to the Soviets, Kissinger gradually understood that the Americans were participants in a "charade." The tone was bellicose, but none of the Soviet statements had any operational content. It was theater to allow the Soviet leaders to vent their pent-up frustrations over Vietnam and to create a written record for display to internal critics and to the North Vietnamese.[43]

Three days later, Kissinger and Gromyko, who was not present at Brezhnev's dacha performance, had the most important substantive discussion on Vietnam at the summit, one that may have had a substantial impact on future events. Ever the methodical diplomatic tradesman, Gromyko was trying to work out some agreed language on Vietnam for the summit communiqué. In the process, he gradually plowed his way to an understanding of what he called the "rather strange" US position on Vietnam. Gromyko pointed out that President Nixon himself had said he wanted to withdraw US troops and find a political solution to the war, but at the same time the United States seemed almost "indifferent" to Vietnam's eventual status after withdrawal. At the end Kissinger, with what amounted to a broad diplomatic "wink," summed up the US position that Gromyko could communicate to the North Vietnamese: "We will not leave in such a way that a Communist victory is guaranteed. However, we are prepared to leave so that a Communist victory is not excluded."[44]

It appears Gromyko finally understood that all the United States was looking for in Vietnam was a fig leaf—a "decent interval" after the withdrawal of US troops before North Vietnam moved to end the conflict on its terms. After his meeting with Kissinger, Gromyko wrote a long memo to the Soviet leadership. Describing Kissinger's approach as going for a "military agreement" and leaving political issues to be settled by the Vietnamese themselves, Gromyko pointed out that these conditions would create a "new political reality in which it would be possible to resolve the most difficult questions of a final settlement in Vietnam."[45] After the summit, Podgorny was dispatched to Hanoi and in subsequent months the Soviets played a more active role in persuading the

North Vietnamese that if they showed some temporary flexibility Washington would later be prepared to turn away while Hanoi snuffed out the South Vietnamese government that so many lives, American and Vietnamese, had been spent fruitlessly defending.

Washington, Moscow, and Hanoi

When he took office, Nixon hoped to employ a classic "carrot and stick" approach to end the war quickly on terms favorable to the United States. But Nixon misread both the tastiness of the carrots he could offer and the strength of the sticks he was able to brandish. Toward Hanoi, the administration's stick was the threat of US escalation but domestic US opposition to the war sharply limited Nixon's options. Long after the conflict was over, Nguyen Co Thatch, the North Vietnamese foreign minister, told a US academic that Hanoi fully understood that both sides were pursuing a "talk and fight" strategy but that Nixon's ability to use a "big stick" was steadily diminishing because of the withdrawal of US troops and domestic opposition to the war.[46]

Nixon also overestimated Moscow's willingness to pressure Hanoi. The Soviets saw little reason to help the United States escape from its self-created Vietnam quagmire, especially once they realized that the Nixon administration, for all its talk of linkage, was prepared to broaden the US-Soviet relationship in ways that Moscow saw as beneficial even if Moscow failed to restrain its North Vietnamese allies. In an interview after the end of the Cold War, Colonel General Adrian Danilovich, who served on the General Staff from 1964 to 1990, acknowledged that "the Soviet military were extremely pleased to see the US tied up in Vietnam because the war represented such a large diversion of military and economic resources away from areas that were more directly threatening to the USSR."[47]

The Soviets drew two important lessons from Vietnam, both of which seemed initially to work in their favor but which eventually led to disaster. Moscow concluded that it could pursue détente in its bilateral relationship with the United States at the same time it used its growing military and political clout to pursue an aggressive forward policy against American interests around the world. For a time this approach seemed to bring important gains but eventually complaints about the one-sided nature of détente as the Soviets practiced it helped fuel the rise to power of Ronald Reagan and his renewed challenge to the USSR. The Soviets also believed that the US defeat in Vietnam was an important way station on what they saw as the inevitable decline of the world's leading capitalist power. "Blinded by Marxist-Leninist philosophy and by the conviction that the revolutionary trend of history was on their side," Soviet leaders sought to build on the triumph in Vietnam through aggressive military interventions in the Middle East, Africa, and eventually Afghanistan, where the Soviets came to grief in ways that mirrored the US experience in Vietnam but with even more disastrous consequences for the existence of the USSR itself.[48]

US-Soviet Trade Cooperation Stillborn

A US-Soviet trade agreement had been largely completed prior to the Moscow summit but, before Congress would grant the USSR the Most Favored Nation (MFN) trade status that lay at the heart of the deal, the two countries also had to agree on repaying debt Washington said that Moscow owed from World War II Lend Lease assistance. Even though the United States was only seeking repayment for materials supplied after the war ended, as had been done with other Lend Lease recipients, the issue was infuriating to the Soviets, who believed with good reason that they had already paid in blood. Many Americans found the issue embarrassing but the political realities were such that without some kind of deal no trade agreement could get through the US Congress.

Lend Lease consumed most of Nixon's session with Kosygin, the only meeting the president had in Moscow in which Brezhnev did not participate. The two came within a few tens of millions on a compromise figure, in bargaining that resembled a used-car auction, before concluding that agreement was impossible. Nixon made it clear he had little interest in the substance of the issue but simply wanted an agreement to show to the US Congress, after which he promised to provide MFN, a pledge Nixon later proved unable to deliver. Kosygin, who said he had been personally involved in Lend Lease while serving as deputy prime minister during the war, displayed little emotion but, like all Soviet leaders from Lenin onward, tried to persuade the visiting capitalists how much money they could make in the Soviet market if only they would accept Soviet terms on outstanding issues.[49]

Not until October was Foreign Trade Minister Patolichev able to visit Washington to sign a comprehensive trade deal that included Soviet agreement to pay $722 million over thirty years to close the Lend Lease debt. Despite high hopes in both countries, US-Soviet economic ties never flourished because of political intrusions on both sides and because of the difficulties in meshing two such dissimilar economic systems. Over the 1970s, total US-Soviet trade turnover rose and fell, depending largely on political developments, from $638 million in 1972 to a high of $4.48 billion in 1979. With the exception of grain sales, the Soviet Union never became a major US economic partner. At the 1979 high point, exports to the USSR amounted to only 3.3 percent of all US exports and imports less than 1 percent.[50]

The Unwanted Guest: Human Rights at the Summit

On the last day of the summit, Secretary of State William Rogers met Gromyko, his only Moscow meeting with his ostensible Soviet counterpart. When Rogers asked if Gromyko wanted to discuss the Middle East, the Soviet foreign minister, who had already had several discussions on this subject with the president and Kissinger, replied coldly that he saw no point unless the secretary had something new to say. Responding blandly that "while they were on the subject of the Middle East," Rogers said the US was pleased with the increased flow of Jewish emigration and hoped it would be allowed to rise even further.[51] Rogers then handed Gromyko, without comment, the "representation list" of people who wished to leave the USSR, whose preparation was my small contribution to the summit. Gromyko made the standard Soviet reply on such occasions, charging that the US remarks constituted "interference in Soviet internal affairs" and demonstratively handing the list to Korniyenko without looking at it, after which the meeting ended abruptly.[52]

Rogers's brief sally was apparently the only time when human rights issues were raised at the summit. Kissinger asserts he raised Jewish emigration in his back-channel meetings with Dobrynin, but there is no record of such discussion. According to Dobrynin, during the planning for the 1972 summit Kissinger passed on Nixon's assurance that he "would not make any appeals on behalf of Jewish and Zionist organizations during his Moscow visit."[53]

Disinterest in human rights was one area where realpolitik calculations failed the White House. Soft-pedaling human rights, even if motivated by the then widespread belief that nothing the West said about human rights would cause any changes in the USSR, did no service to the Nixon administration's efforts to improve the US-Soviet relationship in other areas. By ignoring Soviet human rights abuses, including the KGB's heavy-handed campaign against dissidents on the eve of the Nixon visit itself, the administration left the Soviets with the impression that such behavior could be carried out at no cost to other aspects of Moscow's relations with the United States. It also reinforced suspicions in the US that the administration's claim that it could best encourage human rights in the USSR through "quiet diplomacy" was actually a prescription for ignoring the issue. The upshot, powerfully assisted, of course, by continued heavy-handed Soviet actions, was congressional moves that forced the administration's hand on human rights and that unraveled some key elements of Nixon's strategy toward the USSR.

Summit Aftermath

Nixon returned to an enthusiastic reception from a joint session of Congress. The Soviet reaction was equally favorable. Immediately after Nixon left Moscow, a special session of the Politburo concluded that the summit had marked a positive turn in the US-Soviet relationship. "You can do business with Nixon," was how Brezhnev summed up his impressions of his American counterpart.[54]

From the Soviet point of view, the most important message of the summit was symbolic. Fifty-five years after the Russian revolution, the leader of the world's top capitalist power had visited the Communist capital and recognized the USSR as a political and military equal. Second, and almost as important, was the message to Beijing that when it came to real diplomatic heavy lifting, the field belonged to the world's two superpowers. The United States, for its part, reinforced its image as the leader of the Western coalition, demonstrating that it was still able to conduct important business with its major global rival despite the ongoing unpleasantness of Vietnam.

The mood in the White House was euphoric. Events at home and abroad seemed to be breaking in Nixon's favor. In Vietnam, Hanoi's spring offensive had run out of steam and by September South Vietnamese forces retook Quang Tri, the last provincial capital remaining in the North's hands. North Vietnamese negotiators finally seemed willing to talk seriously about a peace deal, in part because of the military setback they had suffered on the ground but also, evidently, because Soviet intermediaries had passed on Gromyko's discovery, that for all his tough talk what Nixon really wanted in Vietnam was a "decent interval" for the US to withdraw.

On the arms control front, the ABM Treaty was easily ratified by the Senate. Kissinger worked with Senator Henry Jackson, an influential Democrat with a reputation for expertise on defense matters and hard-line views on the Soviet Union, to obtain a joint congressional resolution approving the Interim Agreement. As a price for his support, Jackson insisted on a provision requiring that any future treaty provide for equality of US and Soviet forces, a concept that seemed reasonable and was in any case politically essential but one whose practical application to the very different US and Soviet strategic nuclear forces bedeviled arms control negotiations for the next two decades.

Even in the summit's immediate afterglow events with alarming implications for the future cropped up. In August 1972, the Soviet authorities suddenly and without any warning announced, in a move obviously aimed at departing Soviet Jews, that emigrants would have to reimburse the state as much as fifteen thousand rubles for the cost of their higher education, an impossible sum for most in an economy where monthly wages for most people seldom exceeded 200 rubles. Shortly after the announcement of the "diploma tax," I got an unexpected call from a then-unknown young staffer in Senator Jackson's office named Richard Perle. American groups supporting the cause of Soviet Jewry were in full-throated opposition to the diploma tax and Perle asked what I thought about linking its repeal to the US granting MFN status that was essential to the trade agreement the two countries were negotiating. It was a straightforward business proposition, Perle explained calmly. The Soviets wanted increased trade with the United States but the American people, and therefore their elected representatives, wanted to end the diploma tax. I replied that while the objective of ending the diploma tax was a good one the Soviets usually rejected any effort to link unrelated issues, especially trade from which Americans as well as Soviets expected to benefit. Obviously unimpressed by my arguments, Perle rang off, saying that the administration should expect to see a bill on the issue soon. By October, Jackson had introduced a resolution that had seventy-four senatorial cosponsors and equally strong support in the House under the guidance of Representative Charles Vanik of Ohio.

Unexpectedly, the Soviets proved willing to deal. According to Dobrynin, Gromyko understood from the beginning that the diploma tax was a "stupid political move."[55] Brezhnev commissioned a KGB study of Jewish emigration that was discussed at a special Politburo session on March 20, 1973. To the surprise of everyone, the KGB found that only 13.5 percent of Soviet Jews then seeking emigration had a higher education and only twenty-six of these individuals had doctorates. Brezhnev used the KGB study to argue that Jews should be allowed to leave the USSR more freely. Hard-liners, including KGB chief Andropov, countered that eliminating the diploma tax would be seen as appeasing the United States. Eventually, the Politburo compromised by suspending application of the diploma tax but keeping the rule formally on the books.[56]

By 1974 Kissinger had gotten Gromyko to concede that 45,000 emigrants might be a figure the Kremlin could live with. Jackson, however, kept raising the bar, seeking an ironclad Soviet commitment to allow the departure of 60,000 and, eventually, according to some sources, 100,000. Finally a formula was found by which Dobrynin, on behalf of the Soviet leadership, provided "oral assurances," after which President Ford would send a letter to Jackson conveying the administration's understanding that the Soviets had agreed not to place obstacles in the way of Jewish emigration.[57] After Jackson, by then a contender for the 1976 Democratic presidential nomination, went public with what was supposed to be a private arrangement, Gromyko wrote an angry letter, repudiating the deal and accusing the United States of distorting the Soviet position.

US-Soviet Relations in the Last Years of the Nixon Administration

Even as Watergate engulfed the administration, Nixon and Kissinger, with the latter increasingly taking a leadership role, attempted to continue the US-Soviet relationship they had worked so hard to develop. In June 1973, Brezhnev arrived in Washington, the first such visit by a Soviet leader since Khrushchev's trip to the United States in 1959 had produced the short-lived "Spirit of Camp David." I was part of a small "rent-a-crowd" of government employees assembled on the White House lawn for Brezhnev's arrival, and I recall how after the opening ceremonies the Soviet leader broke through the security barrier and plunged, beaming and hands-pumping, into the onlookers. Brezhnev was clearly a people-person in a way that his host, who proclaimed the Soviet leader "the best politician here present," was not.

The 1973 visit continued Kissinger's strategy of creating a web of bilateral linkages that, taken as a whole, would hopefully be seen by the Soviets as of sufficient importance to diminish the incentive for global mischief-making. Agreements were signed in fields such as transportation, housing, agriculture, oceanography, taxation, and civil aviation. But the two countries found little common ground in most key international areas, and it proved impossible to turn the good chemistry at the top into genuinely friendly relations between the two countries.

American participants in the summit had the opportunity to observe some of the Soviet leader's personal proclivities. During an impromptu late-evening meeting between the two leaders at Nixon's California home—fueled on Brezhnev's side by copious quantities of straight whiskey and with only Dobrynin present to interpret, the Soviet leader suddenly began to complain about Politburo colleagues who wasted his time with "all kinds of silly things."[58] Brezhnev singled out Kosygin and Podgorny as among those who were trying to undermine his authority. Nixon listened with a combination of fascination and unease as Brezhnev's revelations spilled out until, finally, the American president and the Soviet ambassador together poured the drunken general secretary into bed.[59]

Fondness for alcohol was no surprise, but Americans organizing the summit were definitely surprised by the healthy sexual appetites of the Soviet leader. After the summit was over, US security personnel described to me how an

"Aeroflot stewardess" was brought to Brezhnev's room most nights, a form of leadership amenity that interpreter Viktor Sukhodrev confirmed in his memoirs was customary during Brezhnev's travels.[60]

US-Soviet summits, by necessity, involved close cooperation between the Secret Service and the Ninth Directorate of the KGB, responsible for protecting top Soviet officials. Sometimes this cooperation went well, based on mutual respect between two professional organizations. On other occasions, when signals got crossed or egos got in the way, I saw it degenerate almost to the point of fisticuffs between respective security details. The 1973 summit witnessed what must surely have been one of the most unusual incidents involving the leaders' security detachments. On the last night of Brezhnev's stay in Nixon's San Clemente residence, Vladimir Medvedev, who later headed the security detachments for Brezhnev and Gorbachev, was on duty outside the room where Brezhnev slept. Late that night, the door to the president's suite unexpectedly opened and Pat Nixon appeared. Dressed in a white nightgown, she walked slowly toward Brezhnev's room, ordinarily occupied by daughter Tricia, and began to turn the door handle. The Secret Service, according to Medvedev, were nowhere around and when he suggested that Pat return to her room, Medvedev found that the president's wife was in a sleepwalking trance. Medvedev scooped up the still sleeping First Lady in his arms, carried her back to her room and laid her back in bed. As he left Pat's room, the Secret Service finally showed up and Medvedev told them laconically, "Everything's OK."[61]

Senator Ervin suspended meetings of his Watergate committee for the week of Brezhnev's visit but by the time of Brezhnev's departure Kissinger concluded that the Soviet leader understood that Nixon's Watergate problems were likely to be terminal. A month after the summit Kissinger gave Dobrynin a personal message from Nixon to Brezhnev, saying that "under no circumstances" would he resign and also urging the Soviets to discount any speculation that he might be impeached. Kissinger stressed that because of his special relations with Brezhnev the Soviet leader was the only foreign chief to whom he was giving such frank information. Unfortunately, Dobrynin says, Nixon's gesture may have boomeranged. Rather than demonstrating the security of Nixon's position the president's eagerness to reassure Brezhnev revealed "his growing awareness of domestic pressure" and led the Soviet leadership to understand how serious Nixon's difficulties were.[62]

CHAPTER 5

• A Tale of Two Cities
Vladivostok and Helsinki

The brief presidential tenure of Gerald Ford is primarily noted for two events in the field of foreign relations, the Vladivostok accords that established the framework for the SALT II Treaty, and the Helsinki Final Act in 1975, which turned out to be a transformational event in the Cold War. Ironically, both were widely criticized at the time, most strongly by Ford's conservative base.

Breakthrough in Vladivostok

Only hours after President Ford had taken the oath Kissinger, who had become secretary of state in 1972, brought Dobrynin to meet him in the Oval Office. The new president, in the awkward but sincere fashion he was to demonstrate repeatedly over the coming two years, told the Soviet ambassador that although he could not find "accurate and elegant wording," as president he would be more discrete and responsible in his public statements on the USSR than he had been as congressman.[1] In September Gromyko met Ford in Washington and hinted that the Soviets might be more "responsive" to the new administration, prompting a visit by Kissinger to Moscow in October 1974, which resulted in a decision that the two leaders would hold an informal meeting to get the strategic arms talks back on track in the far eastern city of Vladivostok, normally closed to foreigners since it was the headquarters of the Soviet Pacific Fleet.[2]

After opening in Geneva in late 1972, the SALT II negotiations quickly bogged down. Weakened by Watergate, Nixon was unable to resolve clashes between Kissinger and new Secretary of Defense James Schlesinger, who showed himself the intellectual and bureaucratic-infighting equal of the redoubtable Kissinger. Washington's arms control gridlock was such that the US SALT II delegation was sent off to the first negotiating round with nothing more than general instructions to develop a work schedule for future talks.

The Soviets, for their part, were in no hurry to achieve a new accord. In October 1973, the Soviets presented a draft SALT II treaty that would make permanent the 40 percent advantage in missile launchers and the twofold advantage in missile throw weight established by SALT I, while at the same time adding strict limits on heavy bombers where the US had a decisive lead. The Soviet draft would have precluded the deployment of the new US B-1 bomber and Trident ballistic missile submarine but not the modernization of the Soviet missile force and, for good measure, would require the US to eliminate all of its so-called forward-based systems (FBS) deployed abroad. First drafts of proposed treaties are generally robustly favorable to the presenting side but the Soviet draft was so self-serving that US negotiators concluded the USSR did not want a new agreement that, from the Soviet perspective, could only be worse than SALT I.[3]

At Vladivostok, Brezhnev quickly established a good rapport with Ford. He joked that if the US side made enough concessions he might let them see the city and at one point walked around to the American side of the table and made a playful effort to grab the highly classified papers of Jan Lodal, one of the technical experts on the US team.[4]

By the second day, the two sides had agreed to the framework of an agreement that formed the basis for SALT II. Each side would be limited to no more than 2,400 total strategic nuclear delivery vehicles (SNDVs), that is, intercontinental ballistic missiles (ICBMs), submarine launched ballistic missiles (SLBMs), and heavy bombers. Within that 2,400 aggregate, there was a sublimit of 1,320 MIRVed ballistic missile launchers for both sides.[5] The parties would have "freedom to mix" within these sublimits.

Both sides made concessions but what actually made the agreement possible was the fact, which both preferred to obscure, that the accord provided little real constraint on the nuclear forces of either party. The ceiling of 2,400 SNDVs was only slightly below the actual level of Soviet forces and was several hundred more than the United States possessed. And by continuing the SALT I practice of limiting only launchers of ballistic missiles, the agreement did nothing to restrict the thousands of new MIRVed warheads both countries were busily deploying on the missiles themselves.

Brezhnev seemed bothered by this paradox. In his first meeting with Ford, Brezhnev made a comment that seemed to come from the heart, even if it was somewhat ironic on the part of the leader of a country that was engaging in one of the most massive peacetime military buildups in history: "I am of the opinion that we have proceeded incorrectly, along a wrong course. We have not achieved any real limitation, and in fact we have been spurring the arms race further and further. The people don't know all the details, otherwise they would really give us hell."[6]

Despite the high levels the Vladivostok accord set, Soviet Minister of Defense Grechko angrily objected to the deal, insisting that any agreement must include British and French nuclear forces and US FBS. Brezhnev worked the phones back to Moscow, and after obtaining support from other Politburo members he overruled Grechko "in strong words," according to Dobrynin.[7]

After Vladivostok, Ford believed that "as soon as technicians had ironed out the few remaining problems we would sign a SALT II accord."[8] Brezhnev seemed to share the president's enthusiasm. Ford recounts how during a tour of Vladivostok in Brezhnev's limousine the Soviet leader reached over and took the president's hand. In emotional tones he described how much the Soviet people had suffered in the Great Patriotic War. "I don't want to inflict that upon my people again," Brezhnev said and added, "We had accomplished so much, something very significant and it's our responsibility, yours and mine, on behalf of our countries, to achieve the finalization of the document."[9]

The Vladivostok meeting was the last appearance of a healthy Brezhnev on the world scene. On the long flight from Moscow to the Soviet Far East, bad weather forced the Soviet delegation to land at Khabarovsk where Brezhnev had a mild seizure. The general secretary overruled his doctors' advice that he cancel the meeting with Ford. Shortly after the departure of the US delegation, while Brezhnev was heading for a state visit to Mongolia, he had another seizure that left him unconscious for some time, in full view of the Soviet team. His doctors managed to get Brezhnev back into shape and the trip to Mongolia and one to France shortly thereafter passed off normally. From that time, however, Brezhnev's physical and mental state began to deteriorate.[10]

Stalemate

Despite the breakthrough at Vladivostok, getting to the treaty-signing table proved impossible. When the US delegation returned, it found to its shock that "the reaction at home turned out to be not only skeptical but hostile," part of an assault on the Ford administration from both sides of the political spectrum. Brezhnev, for his part, was unwilling to consider any further modifications to the Vladivostok formula, in large part because of the personal and political capital he had invested in overruling Grechko.[11]

New developments in weaponry also continued to bedevil the negotiators. Kissinger found to his dismay that the Pentagon had decided to deploy large numbers of cruise missiles, which Kissinger claims to have rescued from the scrap heap of discarded Pentagon systems in 1973 to use as a bargaining chip. Highly accurate air-launched cruise missiles (ALCMs) flew low to hamper detection by Soviet radar and they were small enough to allow large numbers to be carried on US heavy bombers. In effect, the ALCM rescued the manned-bomber portion of the US strategic triad, as advances in Soviet air defenses made it more difficult for US bombers to fly over Soviet targets to drop their loads in classic "Twelve O' Clock High" fashion.[12]

At Vladivostok, the US team had agreed to a Soviet proposal to count every ALCM carried by a US heavy bomber as one SNDV and therefore included in the 2,400 total ceiling. With the Air Force now planning to deploy up to twenty ALCMs on its heavy bombers, this provision would have eviscerated US nuclear forces and the Americans had to spend the next two years clawing it back.

In January 1976, during a last-ditch trip to Moscow aimed at concluding SALT II before the 1976 presidential election, Kissinger and Gromyko agreed to a provision that had the effect of correcting the Vladivostok slipup by allowing 120 ALCM-equipped heavy bombers each to count as one SNDV. But final agreement on SALT continued to be stymied by differences over how to deal with ground-launched and sea-launched cruise missiles and the Soviet Backfire bomber, which the Americans claimed was capable of reaching the US under some scenarios, an assertion the Soviets angrily rejected.[13]

Helsinki

"If there was one point where the Soviet empire finally began to crack it was at Helsinki," wrote Kissinger's aide Bill Hyland in his memoir of US-Soviet relations during the 1970s.[14] Ironically, on its signing in August 1975 by thirty-five nations, the Helsinki Final Act was widely seen as a setback for the West. President Ford said, "No journey I made during my presidency was so widely misunderstood."[15] Critics charged that the Soviet Union had scored a major victory by gaining Western recognition of the post-World War II borders forcibly carved out by the Red Army. Few expected the Soviets to pay any attention to the accord's humanitarian cooperation provisions, which were generally seen as a fig leaf to cover the Soviet triumph.[16]

President Ford described the agreement as an opportunity to gain commitments from closed Communist societies in areas such as freedom of movement and information and as setting a "standard by which the world could measure progress."[17] His speech at Helsinki proved prophetic. Looking directly at Brezhnev, Ford said that the United States did not regard the principles enshrined in the accord as "empty phrases" and predicted correctly that "history will judge this conference not by what we say here today but by what we do tomorrow."[18]

Negotiating the Agreement

The push for a conference on European security was a feature of Soviet diplomacy for decades, driven by Moscow's desire for Western acknowledgment of postwar borders and also by a smarmy effort to hold a conference of "us Europeans," whose real aim was to undermine the US role on the continent. NATO and the Warsaw Pact bounced proposals back and forth for years, with the chief stumbling block being Western insistence that any conference be accompanied by efforts to reduce the massive Soviet conventional weapons advantage in Europe as well as including the United States and Canada.

At the May 1972 Moscow summit Nixon agreed to accelerate what came to be called the Conference on Security and Cooperation in Europe (CSCE), one of the chief Soviet gains from the summit, according to Brezhnev's aide Aleksandrov-Agentov. But it took three more years to reach final agreement.[19] Negotiations were complicated by the inevitable difficulty of gaining consensus among thirty-five states, by the Soviet obsessive-compulsive approach to making any concession, and the proclivity of participants to press for the inclusion of their own pet projects to placate domestic critics. Kissinger treated CSCE with barely concealed disdain, viewing it as primarily an issue of alliance management and a way to extract Soviet concessions in other areas that Kissinger saw as more important.[20]

During Kissinger's visit to Moscow in October 1974, Brezhnev made an unusual plea for the United States to be less passive and do more to reconcile the various European positions that Brezhnev believed were dragging out the talks. With Brezhnev personally committed to getting an accord and the agreed date for the signing in Helsinki approaching, Soviet diplomats found themselves in the unusual position of having to make concessions to the West on human rights, an area where they had been stonewalling for years. The senior British diplomat in the negotiations later observed, "The Russians found themselves having to make bigger and bigger concessions as the dead-line approached. As a result we achieved a text beyond our wildest expectations."[21]

The text of the accord was long, abstruse, and hedged in almost every conceivable direction by provisions intended to accommodate one country or another. It had proven impossible even to agree on a title for the agreement, leading to the slightly ominous designation "Helsinki Final Act." The ten basic principles that introduced the document, the so-called Helsinki Decalogue, included points of interest to the USSR such as the inviolability of frontiers and nonintervention in internal affairs, as well as others on which the West had insisted, such as peaceful settlement of disputes, respect for human rights, and self-determination.

Western negotiators succeeded in turning on their head many of the provisions most important to the Soviets while at the same time achieving significant concessions from Moscow in areas of importance to the West, such as human contacts. Instead of ironclad guarantees of existing borders, the accord contained more ambiguous provisions, asserting that borders should remain stable but also opening up the possibility that they could be changed by peaceful means. The document also included as the third of its four "baskets" a section on "human contacts" that included obligations with respect to travel, family reunification, and information, which were limited in scope but represented the first time the USSR had ever signed a document containing commitments in these areas.

Doubts in Moscow

As the negotiations moved toward conclusion, Brezhnev had to invest his own prestige to quash doubts within the Soviet camp. Returning to the fray after a prolonged illness following Vladivostock, Brezhnev took an upbeat tone with leaders of the Warsaw Pact in March 1975: "It looks like the cause of the European Conference is on the right track. The Americans did some work, and with our assistance they were able to find an acceptable formulation regarding the peaceful change of borders. . . . The issue of the so-called third basket, it seems to me, is being untangled as well. The excessive and obnoxious demands of some Western countries have been repelled."[22]

The head of the Soviet CSCE delegation, diplomat Anatoliy Kovalev, described two groups of Soviet officials maneuvering around the talks: "people of détente" and "people of the Cold War."[23] The head of the Soviet team negotiating basket three, Yuri Dubinin, later ambassador in Washington, was a hard-liner who acted on behalf of anti-Brezhnev forces and often disregarded Kovalev's instructions. Anatoliy Adamyshin, a distinguished Soviet diplomat who cochaired a US-Soviet working group on human rights during the Gorbachev era, said that during the Helsinki negotiations liberal-minded members of the Soviet foreign affairs establishment convinced Brezhnev that the West would never sign the Helsinki Final Act without some human rights provisions as a counterbalance to giving the Soviets what they wanted on borders. But they also believed, according to Adamyshin, that including human rights in the document was not just a concession to the West but a prerequisite for introducing long-overdue reforms into the USSR itself.[24]

Support for movement in the Helsinki talks sometimes came from unexpected quarters. KGB chief Andropov appointed senior operative Sergei Kondrashev to be his personal representative on the Soviet delegation. Andropov gave him broad latitude on what specific human rights provisions could be agreed. As an experienced KGB officer, Andropov said he assumed that Kondrashev knew the limits. "But you understand too that we must make progress on human rights—we are doomed if we don't," Andropov concluded.[25]

Nevertheless, according to Dobrynin, when "the third basket emerged in its entirety before members of the Politburo, they were stunned."[26] Conservatives, joined by many Soviet ambassadors abroad, worried that the document could allow outside interference in Soviet political affairs. N. S. Leonov, chief of the KGB's analytical branch, argued that Helsinki had a "fatal result" for the Soviet Union. He described the provisions on human rights as a "one hundred per cent loss" and even the points on borders were actually a defeat for the USSR since they opened up the possibility of "peaceful" border changes in Eastern Europe, where the Soviet hold actually rested on military power.[27]

Defending the text that had been negotiated by his own foreign ministry, Gromyko essentially took the position that the USSR could ignore the human rights provisions of the document. He asserted, "We are masters in our own house," and he was decisively supported by Brezhnev, who believed the Soviet public would view the document as assuring immutability of the borders the country had fought so hard to achieve.[28]

Helsinki Monitoring Groups

The accords had an electrifying impact on the Soviet human rights community, which had been in the doldrums since the KGB's 1972 offensive. But it was a decision by the Soviet authorities themselves that set off an explosion of interest. Shortly after the conference ended, Soviet newspapers published the full text of the accord. It is not clear what motivated this unusual step. Some believe that Brezhnev wanted the Soviet people to see what he regarded as a personal triumph. In any case, the Moscow propaganda machine seized upon publication as an example of the purported Soviet commitment to the free flow of information, noting that Western papers had somehow failed to follow the Soviet example of publishing the entire text of the long and turgid document.

The reaction inside the USSR to publication of the Helsinki accords was a surprise to everyone, perhaps most of all to the Soviet authorities. "Soviet citizens reading the text of the Final Act in the papers were staggered by its humanitarian articles—because for the first time they learned about such kinds of international obligations undertaken by their government."[29] Human rights activists in Moscow correctly saw the narrow and carefully hedged Helsinki provisions as a step back from the Universal Declaration on Human Rights proclaimed by the UN in 1948, but they also understood that since the Helsinki document, unlike the Universal Declaration, had actually been signed by the USSR it opened up the possibility of holding Soviet authorities accountable for the commitments they had undertaken—a thought that had not occurred to the Soviet leadership.[30]

Three individuals, Anatoly Shcharanskiy, Andrei Amalrik, and Yuri Orlov, took the lead in organizing what came to be known as the Helsinki Monitoring Group. Shcharanskiy, an activist in the human rights as well as the Jewish emigration movements, seems to have come up with the idea first. In March 1976, he appeared at a biweekly science symposium the physicist Orlov held in his apartment with the suggestion that "we ought to make it as difficult as possible for the Soviet Union to ignore these accords."[31]

Amalrik, a charming cynic as suspicious of the West as he was of his own government, initially regarded the Helsinki accords as "nothing more than an effort by the West to save face." Hearing Shcharanskiy, he suggested that "since the Soviet Union was the initiator of the Helsinki conference . . . the Soviet public should take the initiative in founding the first national committee" to monitor compliance with its provisions.[32] Orlov, an expert on particle physics and a founding member of the Moscow chapter of Amnesty International, had the idea of creating a committee of human rights experts whose task would be to collect information from all over the Soviet Union about the government's performance under the Helsinki accords. The new group would act openly. All members would sign its reports, which would be sent to the Soviet authorities and all other signatories of the accords. On May 18, the group issued its first report, on the arrest of Mustafa Dzhemilov, leader of the Crimean Tatars, who were seeking to return to their homeland after their expulsion by Stalin in 1944. Other comprehensive and well-documented reports followed on subjects such as unjust trials, mistreatment of political prisoners, the rights of ethnic minorities, and emigration.[33]

According to Lyudmila Alekseyeva, a founding member of the group who thirty-five years later was still fighting for human rights against the Putin regime, Orlov and other activists saw the Helsinki accords as a way to move beyond protest and try to establish a dialogue between the regime and society. Joe Presel, responsible for Embassy Moscow's contacts with the dissident community at the time the Helsinki accord was signed and later US ambassador to Uzbekistan, said none of the founders of the Helsinki group expected it to contribute to the end of the USSR. Presel believes that "few dissidents expected a fundamental change in Soviet policy but they hoped to make it a more decent place."[34]

From the beginning, the Helsinki monitors acted with one eye carefully cocked to their own authorities and the other at the West. Orlov wrote later that Western governments signed Helsinki not expecting the USSR to carry out its human rights obligations and that, "The purpose of our group was, first and foremost, to change this 'Munich' approach."[35] In the beginning, the group sent its reports to Western embassies in Moscow by mail but, when it became clear that these documents somehow never reached their destination, members began to hand them over directly to US diplomats. In the late 1970s, I met regularly with representatives of the group to receive their reports along with other documents relating to human rights violations in the USSR.

The Helsinki model inspired activists for other causes, a development the Soviet authorities found particularly alarming. In December 1976, Father Gleb Yakunin founded the Christian Committee for the Defense of the Rights of Believers in the USSR, which publicized the abuses of Soviet authorities against religious believers. In November 1976, Aleksandr Podrabinek and Vyacheslav Bakhmin founded the Working Group to Investigate the Use of Psychiatry for Political Purposes, adopting the careful style of visiting prisons and other institutions, interviewing doctors and patients, and compiling reports that were damning in their accuracy and horrifying in the abuses they documented. Most dangerous, from the perspective of the Soviet authorities, was the appearance of Helsinki groups in potentially restive republics such as Ukraine, Lithuania, Georgia, and Armenia, where they provided an intellectual center for the rise of national awareness.[36]

Counterattack

Brezhnev had trumpeted the signature of the Helsinki Final Act as a great success, and the Soviet authorities were initially slow to respond to the formation of the monitoring groups. By the end of 1976 their patience was ending. In November the KGB charged that Helsinki groups were acting in the context of "the adversary's special and propaganda services" and reported that it was "undertaking measures to compromise members of the group" and "put an end to their hostile activities."[37]

In January 1977, a bomb exploded in a Moscow metro station, killing and injuring a number of people. Shortly thereafter Viktor Louis, a notorious KGB mouthpiece, suggested that the explosion was the result of terrorist activity by dissident groups and asserted that the Soviet public demanded retribution. Although the Soviet authorities later arrested alleged Armenian terrorists in connection with the blast, the circumstances around the incident remain murky. Many suspected that even if the explosion had not been deliberately set, the KGB took advantage of the event to launch a crackdown on the Helsinki monitors and other dissidents across the country.

On January 22, Soviet television aired a documentary that portrayed Jewish refuseniks as being part of an "anti-Soviet conspiracy." On March 5, an article appeared in *Izvestiya* accusing Shcharanskiy and others of working for the CIA and naming American diplomats—none, by the way, CIA officers—as their contacts. Over the winter and spring of 1977, Moscow Helsinki group leaders Orlov, Shcharanskiy, and Aleksandr Ginzburg were arrested as were monitors in Ukraine and Georgia. Other prominent dissidents were arrested, harassed or—in a few cases, including Alekseyeva—forced to leave the country.[38]

Toward the end of 1979, with SALT II signed but its ratification uncertain and the invasion of Afghanistan looming, the Soviet authorities began what turned out to be their final assault on the Helsinki monitoring groups and virtually all other dissident activity. On November 1, 1979, the authorities arrested Yakunin and Tatyana Velikhanova, who had taken the lead in resuming publication of the *Chronicle* in 1974. Going after these key figures revealed the authorities' determination to eliminate the people most responsible for organizing dissident activity across the political spectrum.

Over the next year the Soviet authorities arrested or expelled well over 150 dissident activists, including eleven members of Helsinki groups across the country. The arrest of Tatyana Osipova and Viktor Nikipelov, the forced exile abroad of Yuri Yarim-Agayev, and Yelena Bonner's move to Gorky with the exiled Sakharov deprived the Moscow Helsinki group of its most active members. In September 1982, one of the few remaining members of the group, the aging lawyer Sophie Kallistratova, who in earlier years had defended many Soviet human rights activists, was charged with anti-Soviet slander. The group issued its last report, number 195, on her case and simultaneously announced its dissolution.[39]

An Institutional Base

Many expected that the Helsinki provisions on human contacts would vanish without trace after the document was signed. That this did not happen was primarily due to the activities of courageous individuals in the USSR, but support from the West also helped keep the issue alive.

After the meeting in Helsinki, the Ford administration began a quiet dialogue with Moscow on human rights. Jack Matlock, then serving as the Deputy Chief of Mission (DCM) at Embassy Moscow, met regularly on the subject with Deputy Foreign Minister Korniyenko or Viktor Komplektov, the head of the USA desk. The US raised specific cases on the representation lists and also touched on broader issues such as the rules governing emigration. The Soviets tended to come back with charges of US mistreatment of minorities, Indians, and other groups. The dialogue never went very far, in part because of the early demise of the Ford administration, but it was a modest first step in trying to get the Soviets to admit the legitimacy of human rights as a topic of diplomatic exchange between the two countries. After the Carter administration assumed office, Matlock sent the new National Security Council (NSC) a memo describing the dialogue and recommending its continuation but got no response.[40]

The first Helsinki review conference, held in accordance with basket four's requirement for regular meetings to review the performance of the signatories, opened in Belgrade in 1977. US delegation chief and former Supreme Court Justice Arthur Goldberg raised human rights abuses in the USSR and its Eastern European satellites in a straightforward fashion, to the outrage of the Soviets and the unease of some European delegations. The Belgrade conference ended with few results other than an agreement to meet again. But the meeting and others that followed in Madrid in 1980 and Stockholm in 1983 established the important principle that human rights were an inescapable topic on the diplomatic agenda. There was now an established and continuing international forum to ensure that repression by Soviet authorities would not go unremarked by the rest of the world.

The Helsinki accords also played an important role in mobilizing congressional engagement in human rights. Shortly after the signing of the Helsinki Final Act, a congressional delegation led by New Jersey representative Millicent Fenwick visited the Soviet capital and met with Orlov and other activists, who argued that pressure from the West could be effective in modifying Soviet behavior. Impressed with what she called the Orlov Doctrine, Fenwick returned to Washington and took the lead in establishing the Helsinki Commission, a bipartisan joint committee with the mandate to monitor and report on compliance with Helsinki obligations.[41]

The Helsinki Commission quickly became an important focal point for what was emerging as a growing political and institutional commitment to human rights in US diplomacy. Members of the Commission held hearings and provided comprehensive and balanced reports on compliance with the Helsinki accords by the USSR and other participating states. The commission assembled a permanent staff who became recognized experts in their field, visiting the USSR frequently and serving as experts on US delegations to the regular Helsinki implementing conferences.

The Scope of Repression

The extent of repression in the final years of the USSR was a matter of dispute at the time and remains so to this day. Over the course of its existence, the *Chronicle* recorded 424 political trials and 753 convictions, without a single defendant being acquitted.[42] Unofficial historian Roy Medvedev calculated that during Andropov's tenure as KGB chief, from 1967 to 1982, at least ten thousand people were arrested for violating "political" articles of the Soviet criminal codes. Several thousand additional people were imprisoned for nationalism, religious activities, for violating the internal passport regime, on trumped up charges as "parasites," and the like.[43] Another work, based on a comprehensive study of the records of the office of the Soviet chief prosecutor, found that over the period 1957 to 1985, 8,124 people were convicted of violating Articles 70 and 190–1, on anti-Soviet agitation and defaming the Soviet system.[44]

In his comprehensive history of the postwar Soviet Union, Rudolf Pikhoya, chief archivist of the Russian Federation in the 1990s, cites a 1975 KGB report to the Politburo that provides summary data on the numbers of persons it subjected to various forms of repressive measures. In the period 1967 to 1974, the KGB reported that it brought a total of 4,879 people to criminal prosecution. Of these, 753 were sentenced for "treason," in which category the KGB primarily included political offenses. An additional 729 people were sentenced for "anti-Soviet agitation and propaganda," the classic charge for dissident activity.[45]

The KGB also provided data on the numbers of people subjected to so-called prophylactic measures, which could include a wide range of extrajudicial repressive actions. In the period 1967 to 1974, a total of 128,036 people were subjected to this form of social discipline. Of this total, 70,016 experienced KGB prophylaxis for "politically harmful behavior" and 11,349 for "suspicious" contacts with foreigners. In addition, 50,690 were subjected to other forms of public disciplinary measures, which could include criticism at public meetings, being hauled before kangaroo "Comrades Courts," or "conversations with representatives of the public"—a euphemism for KGB threats.[46]

In the late 1980s, Anatoliy Adamyshin undertook a study of the misuse of psychiatry for political purposes as part of the work of a joint US-Soviet diplomatic working group on human rights. Adamyshin discovered that in 1960 a secret party instruction was issued that allowed the imprisonment without trial of "mentally ill persons who are dangerous to the public." The concept of "sluggish schizophrenia" was developed to deal with people whose threat to the public was of a political nature, on the grounds, Adamyshin dryly noted, that "only a schizophrenic would criticize Soviet power." In 1978 a special party commission under Nikolai Shvernik studied psychiatry in the USSR and found that of the 4.5 million people suffering from mental illness, 75,000 had been deemed potentially dangerous to society and confined in psychiatric hospitals. Of these, about fifteen thousand fell in the category of political prisoners.[47]

Religious believers, especially those in unregistered faiths such as Pentecostals, were subject to a wide range of repressive measures not included in these KGB reports, which might range from loss of employment, being roughed up by young hooligans, or having their children taken away from them and placed in grim, state-run orphanages. While I was in contact with dissidents and other Soviet nonconformists at the end of the 1970s, I probably met or heard about scores of such cases, and it is likely that every year hundreds if not thousands of believers were subjected to a variety of repressive measures.

In the late 1970s, I often came into contact with some of the anonymous victims of Soviet society whom the dissidents called *khodniki*, or "travelers," after nineteenth-century Russian peasants who walked from place to place seeking official or religious intercession for some personal or official problem. Sometimes such people sought me out directly on the phone or by waiting outside my apartment; others ran into me at the regular Saturday afternoon gathering of the refusenik community in front of the Moscow synagogue. Often the cases involved elderly or impoverished people who had lost a job or an apartment or suffered in some other way in a clash with local authorities. Usually they had a thick sheet of documents supporting their claims, which they entreated me to read and transmit abroad in hopes that the case would be broadcast by foreign radio stations. Sometimes affixed to the sheaf of documents was a stamp showing that the petitioner had been received at the Central Committee reception room, where thousands of Soviet citizens brought their personal complaints in the Russian tradition of subjects seeking the Tsar's intercession. One of these individuals who cornered me in front of the Moscow synagogue said that a Central Committee official had actually advised him to seek help from foreigners at the refusenik gathering—whether as a cruel joke or in sincerity I never knew.

Jimmy Carter started off badly in relations with the Soviets and ended worse. Part of the problem was the divided mind of the president, who could never decide whether his foreign policy role model was St. Francis of Assisi or Niccolò Machiavelli, and the consequent divisions within the US administration. Carter's secretary of state was Cyrus Vance, a distinguished lawyer who combined considerable foreign policy experience with the ability to see the other side of the issue, not always a wise trait to display in dealing with the Soviet Union. His national security adviser, Zbigniew Brzezinski, combined rapier intelligence with the Polish zeal for employing that or any other available weapon against Moscow.

Carter accorded human rights unusual prominence in his foreign policy but he struggled to balance human rights with other US interests in the grubby reality of the world. He could be a tough negotiator, as demonstrated by his success in the Camp David accords, the most lasting international peace settlement achieved in the Middle East. A former submarine officer, he had the abhorrence for nuclear weapons that is shared by most people who have actually dealt with them. But by trying for too much too soon in nuclear reductions, he ended by achieving less than he could have. At the end of his term, when Carter said that the invasion of Afghanistan had opened his eyes to the reality of Soviet behavior, he appeared naive to the American people who opted instead for the more confident certainties of Ronald Reagan.

Getting Started

In the 1976 presidential election, with voter turnout at its lowest level since 1948, Carter won 50.1 percent of the popular vote with 297 electoral votes to Ford's 48 percent and 240 electoral votes, one of the slimmest margins in

American political history. Democrats gained only one seat in the Senate and the House. The narrow victory and lukewarm support from some core Democratic constituencies did not bode well for policies that would require solid support in Congress.[1]

Despite its narrow mandate, the new administration adopted an ambitious international agenda. In early January, Brzezinski's National Security Council set out ten "working goals for the next four years." Some were specific, such as achieving a SALT II agreement by 1978, followed by a more ambitious treaty in 1980. Others were visionary: to weave a web of political and economic relations with emerging regional powers and "to enhance global sensitivity to human rights."[2] Taken as a whole, it was a thoughtful and ambitious set of foreign policy objectives. It reflected Carter's vision of America at its best, powerful and engaged yet seeking to use that power for global as well as American good. It also reflects astonishing hubris. At the end of Carter's term most remained unachieved. It is hard to quarrel with Brzezinski's own retrospective judgment that "we were overly ambitious."[3]

First Steps and Missteps

Grigoriy Shakhnazarov, a longtime Central Committee official who became a close adviser to Gorbachev, said the Soviets "always had high expectations of Democratic administrations and were always disappointed."[4] Almost as soon as the new administration had settled in, alarm bells began to ring across Moscow. On arms control, Carter said he did not necessarily feel bound by deals reached by previous administrations and in his first meeting with Dobrynin he floated the notion of reducing nuclear weapons to a few hundred on each side, far below levels considered previously.[5]

Carter's first letter to Brezhnev, sent toward the end of January and largely written by Vance's State Department, set a positive tone. He wrote that both countries shared a "common aspiration" for a stable peace and set out an ambitious arms control agenda. He warned that his administration could "not be indifferent to the fate of freedom and individual human rights" but couched it in terms of competition in "ideals and ideas" between the two systems, a construct the Soviets were familiar with. Carter's letter was well received in Moscow and Brezhnev's response a little more than a week later called Carter's letter "constructive and hope inspiring."[6]

In his second letter, written primarily by Brzezinski and the president himself, Carter suggested a quick SALT II agreement by exempting Backfire and cruise missiles and urged a sweeping follow-on agreement allowing no more than "the minimum number of missiles which would allow every country to feel secure from a first blow." On human rights, Carter said, "We expect cooperation in the realization of further steps toward the fulfillment of the agreements reached in Helsinki relating to human rights." He warned, "It will be necessary for our Administration from time to time to publicly express the sincere and deep feelings which our people and I feel."[7]

Deputy Foreign Minister Korniyenko described Carter's letter as "a wet rag slapped in the face of the Russian leadership."[8] Brezhnev's response accused the president of seeking "unilateral advantage" for the United States. On the same day he had written Brezhnev, Carter took the unprecedented step of sending an encouraging letter to Andrei Sakharov, and the Soviet leadership was not inclined to let that episode slip by unnoticed. Referring to "the question of so-called human rights," Brezhnev complained that Carter had written to "a renegade who proclaimed himself to be an enemy of the Soviet State. . . . The Soviet Union must not be dealt with like that," Brezhnev concluded ominously.[9]

Brzezinski described Brezhnev's letter as "brutal, cynical, sneering."[10] Even Dobrynin characterized the letter as marked by a "hard and sometimes sharp tone" and on human rights as "dismissive."[11] Vance had a different take. As Dobrynin described it to Moscow, Vance read the letter twice and replied, "Our president still approaches some international problems too lightly." Although Vance did not agree with everything in it, he said "it was important that the President get just such a letter."[12]

Carter, by contrast, received Brezhnev's letter like a "bucket of cold water," according to Brzezinski. Although the president said he would not be deflected from the pursuit of his ambitious arms control agenda, he now understood that it would take more time than he had expected. The letter also confirmed the president's inclination to pursue important foreign policy initiatives in other areas, including China where, immediately after reading the harsh Brezhnev missive, he directed an eager Brzezinski to undertake new moves.

First Moves on SALT or "Deep Cuts" Deep Sixed

Like his successor, Ronald Reagan, Carter had a deep, personal commitment to the concept of substantial reduction and eventual elimination of nuclear weapons. In his inaugural speech Carter had expressed the hope that mankind would eventually see "the elimination of all nuclear weapons from this earth," and in the early days of his administration he startled US military leaders and Dobrynin alike by floating the notion that the United States and the Soviet Union might be able to reduce their nuclear arsenals to two hundred ICBMs each.

Less than two months after taking office, Carter decided on a new SALT proposal, requiring what were then seen as deep cuts in nuclear forces. It was a radical departure from Vladivostok in many respects, most of them favorable to the United States. The Vladivostok ceiling of 2,400 SNDVs would be reduced to between 1,800 and 2,000; the subceiling on MIRVed missile launchers would be lowered from 1,320 to between 1,200 and 1,100. A new subceiling was established of 550 MIRVed ICBMs, exactly the level of three-warhead Minuteman III ICBMs the US had recently finished deploying, and the limit of 308 heavy ICBMs to which the Soviets had agreed at Vladivostok was halved to 150. The proposal would require substantial cuts in the numbers of existing Soviet forces but would leave US forces largely untouched.

The administration made a hard sell more difficult by the inept way it handled presentation of the new approach. Nervous about the Soviet reaction and divided internally, the Carter team agreed that Vance could take two fallback options with him in a March visit to Moscow, one that would essentially go back to Kissinger's January 1976 approach by accepting most of the Vladivostok package and deferring Backfire and cruise missiles for a later accord and another that would split the difference between the two approaches.[13]

A few days before his departure, Vance briefed Dobrynin on the package. The secretary of state outlined not only the preferred comprehensive proposal but also the alternative, fallback positions. Hearing this, Brzezinski, on Carter's instruction, telephoned Dobrynin with a personal message from the president, stressing the importance that Carter put on the comprehensive proposal and also conveying the president's view that he could only succeed in this ambitious approach in his first year of office. The Soviets were thus informed, even before the US team had left for Moscow, about the preferred US position and its fallbacks and were also told that if they stonewalled long enough on the comprehensive proposal even its chief proponent thought it would fail.[14]

When Vance arrived in Moscow, Brezhnev greeted him with a diatribe on the Carter administration's human rights approach and its efforts to renegotiate previous agreements. He then turned the talks over to Gromyko, never a good sign and an ominous difference from the way Brezhnev had taken personal charge of negotiations with Kissinger. Gromyko treated Vance to a long lecture on the "enormous efforts" that had been expended to achieve the Vladivostok accord and asked sarcastically whether the Soviet side should conclude that "everything that had been achieved be thrown away" just because there was a new US administration in office.[15] As was his wont in such situations, Gromyko toughened the Soviet position by resurrecting efforts to count the new B-1 bomber as three SNDVs and by going back to the original Vladivostok understanding that each ALCM on a heavy bomber would count against the 2,400 SNDV total.

After the US delegation left Moscow, Gromyko convened an unusual press conference in which he denounced the US approach as a "cheap and shady maneuver."[16] In an uncharacteristic bit of openness, Gromyko revealed all of the numbers contained in the US proposals, which Washington had not yet done in public. In his outraged insularity, Gromyko apparently thought that he would build global sympathy for his tirade against supposed US duplicity by showing how Washington was trying to depart from the Vladivostok accord but, over time, the tactic helped build sympathy for the US approach. Most people, after all, tended to believe that the fewer nuclear weapons the better.

Brezhnev was personally offended by Carter's new approach. Viktor Sukhodrev, Soviet leadership interpreter for many years, said Vance's proposals "were a disappointment for Brezhnev, who felt he had done so much hard work, personally, at Vladivostok. Suddenly this new administration was toppling the whole structure he had worked so hard to build."[17] But Brezhnev was also unhappy with the performance of his own team. When Gromyko, Ustinov, and Andropov reported on Vance's visit to Brezhnev, he reportedly said bitterly, "Here for the first time, I appointed you to conduct the talks yourselves, and you ruined them."[18]

Despite the ham-handed way it was pursued, the Carter administration's initiative represented the first serious effort by either side to actually reduce numbers of strategic offensive weapons. Viewed as an in-going negotiating position, the Carter proposal was no more one-sided than others both sides made during the decades of strategic talks. A few years later, in fact, the Soviets chose the lower end of the Carter proposal, an aggregate of 1,800 SNDVs, as the central element of their own position at the beginning of START talks with the Reagan administration.

Picking Up the Spilled SALT

After tempers had cooled, both sides moved to pick up the pieces. In Moscow Brezhnev convened a meeting of the Politburo the day after Vance's departure with only one item on the agenda: how to deal with the Carter administration. The Soviets considered the way they had handled the deep cuts episode to be the "deliberate application of an angry shock treatment to the Carter administration." But they also recognized the importance of the relationship and did not want "hostile feelings to harden" in Washington. According to Dobrynin, "it was decided to let Brezhnev write Carter a conciliatory letter" to try to get SALT back on track.[19]

The US administration put together a new, three-part package consisting of a treaty lasting until 1985, which would start with the Vladivostok numbers but provide for modest cuts by the end of the agreement; an interim, three-year Protocol covering difficult issues such as cruise missiles and Backfire; and an agreement in principle to move quickly to SALT III with deeper reductions. In May 1977, with both sides seemingly somewhat chastened by the events of March, Vance and Gromyko met in Geneva and agreed to resume negotiations on this basis.

In a September 1977 meeting in Washington, Gromyko and Carter—the president was by now the chief negotiator on the US side—achieved the outline of what became the SALT II Treaty. The United States accepted that Vladivostok would be the starting point of the agreement, with modest reductions over the term of the deal. Washington also dropped its bootless effort to exclude ALCMs and went back to the compromise Kissinger had agreed in January 1976, allowing 120 ALCM-carrying heavy bombers. On the heavy SS-18 ICBMs, which the Soviets stubbornly refused to reduce, Gromyko became uncharacteristically emotional. He drew a parallel with Stalingrad by saying that for Moscow the heavies represented "the Volga beyond which it was impossible to retreat." Carter voiced deep unhappiness, telling Gromyko he had been insufficiently flexible and complaining that the Soviets did not understand that reductions beyond Vladivostok numbers were not just a benefit to the United States but to all mankind, and tried to salvage something by insisting that the follow-on SALT III agreement should reduce nuclear weapons by 50 percent.[20]

Just six months after the deep cuts fiasco, it appeared that a SALT deal was within sight. In the event, however, it took almost two more years to conclude the agreement, in part because some of the remaining technical issues concealed political minefields that proved hard to resolve and in part because other issues introduced new difficulties into the US-Soviet relationship.

Angola

Africa was a secondary theater over most of the Cold War but for a few years in the mid-1970s it assumed center stage in the East-West confrontation in a way that initially seemed to presage a fundamental shift in the balance of power in Moscow's favor, but in the long run helped sow the seeds for Soviet downfall. The turning point in Soviet engagement in southern Africa came in 1974, after left-wing Portuguese army officers overthrew the heir to longtime dictator Antonio Salazar and moved to surrender Portuguese colonial possessions in Africa.

In Moscow Shelepin, sidelined years earlier by Brezhnev, took advantage of the general secretary's absence after his first debilitating stroke to assert that it was time for a more aggressive global course. According to some accounts, he suggested that the USSR send "volunteers" to Portugal, where the hard-line Communist party and its sympathizers among the military were making a bid for power.[21] Brezhnev beat back Shelepin's challenge. In April 1975, his departure from the Politburo was finally announced but Soviet foreign policy insiders describe heated debates around this time over how Moscow should take advantage of the opportunities the Portuguese revolution had opened up. Brezhnev was generally on the side of caution but one consequence of the internal power struggle may have been his acquiescence in a more aggressive approach in southern Africa.[22]

The critical Soviet decision to step up its engagement in Angola was made around the end of 1974, when the Politburo approved a plan to provide po-litical and "material," but not military, support to the MPLA, a faction in the three-cornered Angolan civil war that Moscow had been assisting since 1961. A few days later, however, the chief of the Central Committee International Department, Boris Ponomarev, persuaded the Soviet national security team to respond positively to a request by the MPLA for military assistance. Toward the end of March 1975, a relay of thirty Soviet cargo planes began arriving in Brazzaville, Congo, with military equipment for Angola.[23]

Cuba had long been engaged in supporting leftist African anticolonial movements, in accordance with Castro's conception of himself as the apostle of third-world revolution. After the coup in Lisbon, Cuban engagement in An-gola increased. Shipments of Cuban military equipment and Cuban personnel to operate it initially arrived in small chartered aircraft and merchant vessels. By early summer 1975, at least 250 Cuban officers were in Angola, where "they functioned as a kind of general staff for MPLA chief Neto in planning operations as well as training MPLA forces." By September significant numbers of Cuban combat troops were on the ground and "took charge of much of the fighting against the MPLA's enemies."[24]

The CIA had an intelligence collection relationship with another of the Angolan factions, the FNLA which operated out of bases in Zaire where the agency had been active since the beginning of the Cold War. In January 1975, $300,000 was authorized for covert political support to the FNLA and in July 1975 President Ford approved a plan for $25 million in covert military aid to the FNLA and the third Angolan faction, UNITA.

At about the same time the US stepped up its support for Angolan fac-tions, the Ford administration also encouraged South African intervention. By August 1975, small South African reconnaissance teams were operating in Angola and in October regular South African forces entered the battle against the MPLA, although Pretoria limited its engagement to a modest force of 2,500 troops and eight hundred vehicles.[25]

Pretoria's engagement initially seemed decisive, as the MPLA was pushed back to the outskirts of the Angolan capital of Luanda. But the involvement of the racist South African regime shifted opinion in other African states toward the MPLA and helped ease the way for a decision in Moscow and Havana to raise the stakes. Over the fall, a massive air and sea lift delivered an additional 12,000 Cuban troops and large amounts of Soviet military equipment. In November 1975, the first formal Soviet military mission arrived in Luanda, although Soviet intelligence and military personnel had been present long before this. By April 1976, 344 Soviet military personnel were in Angola and the USSR had provided twenty-two jet fighters, which were flown by Cuban pilots, over 300 tanks, and the same number of other armored fighting vehicles, along with considerable quantities of artillery, antitank weapons, heavy machine guns, small arms, and ammunition. Over the entire period of Soviet engagement in Angola, from 1975 until 1991, almost 11,000 Soviet military personnel served there, of whom 54 died.[26]

The victory of Soviet-backed forces in Angola seemed to mark a major change in the dynamics of the global US-Soviet competition. Developments in Angola unfolded as the tragic US engagement in Southeast Asia was coming to its shameful conclusion. Pictures of helicopters lifting off with terrified refugees clinging to their skids reinforced an image of American military weakness and lack of political resolve. Other traditional tools of the international struggle were also being called into question. Revelations about real and imagined intelligence abuses called into question the US ability to use covert operations, which had been a fixture on both sides of the Cold War struggle.

The way seemed open for Soviet gains elsewhere in Africa and beyond. Although Brezhnev had originally been cautious on direct engagement in Africa, "Cuban successes had convinced many that the United States lacked will in Africa."[27] The longtime head of the USA Institute, Arbatov describes a meeting outside Andropov's office where senior KGB and General Staff officers were excitedly discussing the adventure in Angola and telling themselves the USSR had nothing to fear from its capitalist rival: "The Americans will swallow it" was the view of the Soviet brass.[28]

The Horn of Africa

By the time Carter entered the White House, the Soviets and their Cuban clients were moving toward new fields of opportunity in Ethiopia. In June 1974, radical army officers known as the Dergue took power in Addis Ababa. By the end of the year, leadership had passed to Major Mengistu Haile Mariam, who combined Ethiopian nationalism and radical Marxist-Leninist socialism with a fanatical willingness to employ violence to eliminate opponents. Initially many members of the Dergue were inspired by home-grown "Ethiopian socialism," but in 1976 Mengistu introduced a new program based on Soviet experience and terminology.

Over 1975, Soviet attention to Ethiopia grew as Mengistu gained power and his sympathy for Soviet-style Marxism-Leninism became more apparent. In 1975 the Soviet ambassador in Addis Ababa compared the removal of Haile Selassie to the Bolshevik overthrow of the Romanov dynasty in 1917, a parallel reinforced by the murder of the elderly Ethiopian emperor and many members of his family. In March 1975, a secret Soviet military mission arrived in Addis Ababa, followed the next month by an Ethiopian military delegation to Moscow, which brought with it a proposal for complete reorganization of the Ethiopian military along Soviet lines.[29]

Mengistu unleashed what he called the "Red Terror," a program "to kill as many as possible of the regime's real or imagined enemies, and thereby force the population in areas held by the Dergue into obedience."[30] Amnesty International later estimated that half a million people were killed during 1977 and 1978.[31]

In addition to Mengistu's affection for Soviet ideology and demonstrated skill in the use of Soviet political methods, Ethiopia's larger size and strategic location made it easy for Moscow to switch horses when its longtime client Somalia invaded the Ogaden region in 1977, hoping to capitalize on turmoil in Addis Ababa to slice off part of Ethiopia. Decisions by Washington also provided openings for the Soviets in Ethiopia. The Ford administration had provided a modest amount of military aid to Ethiopia because of the perceived need to counter pro-Soviet Somalia and because of the importance of the major listening post the US had long maintained at Asmara. By 1977, however, the United States was cutting back operations in Asmara, which was becoming more difficult to maintain in the midst of growing violence in the region. The Carter administration stepped up its criticism of Mengistu's human rights abuses and cut off assistance, after which all US personnel were expelled from Ethiopia.

The way was now open for Moscow to move in. As early as December 1976, Moscow secretly agreed to supply military aid to Ethiopia in the amount of $100 million. After Megistu's bloody coup of April 1977 and the end of US assistance to Ethiopia, Moscow dramatically stepped up its aid. By July five planeloads of Soviet arms were arriving every week at the Addis Ababa airport. Soviet and Cuban advisers were on the scene to assemble weapons and train Ethiopians in their use. By October 1977, Soviet and Cuban assistance allowed the Ethiopians to halt the Somali advance.

In November 1977, the first deputy chief of Soviet Ground Forces, General Vasily Petrov, arrived in Addis Ababa to command an "operational group" of over one thousand Soviet military personnel, whose responsibilities included not just supplying weapons and training Ethiopian personnel in their use but the "organization of the planning and preparation of offensive operations against Somali forces."[32] Beginning in December 1977, a massive air and sea lift of military equipment and personnel unfolded rapidly. At the height of the operation, from December 1977 to January 1978, military transport aircraft were leaving airfields in the southern USSR every fifteen to twenty minutes. A sizeable sealift operated at the same time, with thirty to fifty Soviet and Bulgarian warships and freighters passing through the Dardanelles and the Suez Canal on their way to Ethiopian ports. Throughout the operation the Soviet navy maintained a continuous armed presence off the Ethiopian coast.[33]

In a three-month period, the Soviets delivered over one billion dollars' worth of equipment, including a large quantity of tanks, 600 armored personnel carriers, two squadrons of MIG 23 and sixty MIG 21 fighter aircraft, and 400 artillery pieces. The Soviets also ferried into Ethiopia several hundred East German intelligence personnel and some 17,000 Cuban combat troops and advisers. In February 1978, the Ethiopians, with Soviet equipment and technical assistance and the direct participation of Cuban combat forces, began a counteroffensive that soon had Somali forces fleeing in disarray, although guerilla warfare continued in the unhappy Ogaden for several more years. Soviet personnel in Ethiopia "took part in preparing and conducting operations (reconnaissance, developing plans, aiding Ethiopian commanders in the organization of battle); during combat operations they were at the front, often in the ranks of combat units."[34] Over the period from 1975 to 1991, more than 11,000 Soviet military personnel served in Ethiopia, of whom 89 died.[35]

The use of Soviet arms to establish Marxist-Leninist governments in Africa seemed to open up exciting new possibilities for the spread of Soviet-style socialism throughout the Third World. In the 1970s, Soviet ideologists developed a broader definition of the type of state that could be considered a candidate for inclusion into the socialist camp. Yevgeny Primakov, later head of Russian external intelligence and foreign minister, put forward four criteria for the successful pursuit of a socialist orientation, including the nationalization of state industries, education of the masses in the spirit of cultural revolution, domestic control by a "vanguard party," and the gradual shift from a "petty bourgeois" orientation toward "scientific socialism."[36] The point of the exercise was to provide a theoretical basis for encouraging Third World regimes to see themselves as the natural allies of the USSR even if they were not—for the moment at least—ruled by orthodox Communist parties. General Anatoly Gribkov, first deputy chief of staff of the Warsaw Pact, said "Ideology was present everywhere and not only in Africa; it was present everywhere there emerged states which announced they had chosen the Soviet way of development. . . . As soon as a leader in Moscow, Angola, Ethiopia, or Somalia mentioned the word 'Socialism' our leaders immediately picked up on it."[37]

The USSR paid heavily for its successes in Africa. From 1976 through 1980, Soviet arms transfers to Africa totaled almost $4 billion, vastly more than what the US supplied. By the time most aid ceased in 1989, the USSR had provided 2.6 billion rubles to Ethiopia alone, most of it military assistance. A mood approaching triumphalism could be sensed in the corridors of power in Moscow but in retrospect many Soviet national security personnel traced the beginning of Soviet imperial overreach to the engagement in Africa. In Brutents's view, the costs of the engagement "exceeded Soviet capabilities" and played a role in the "destruction of the international potential of the Soviet Union."[38] A comprehensive study of Soviet military involvement in Cold War conflicts, conducted by the Russian military after the USSR's collapse stated, "After the Vietnam catastrophe Moscow concluded that there had been a historic shift in the correlation of forces in its favor. It followed with 'expansion' into Angola, Ethiopia, and finally Afghanistan. . . . After this expansionist spurt the USSR found itself in the shadows of contradiction and finally collapsed."[39]

Low Point in 1978

In 1978, as the Soviets consolidated their gains in Africa, the Carter administration's internal battles spilled increasingly into the public domain. Eventually, senior officials began contradicting each other openly in the media. On the same day Carter was telling the National Press Club that Soviet actions in the Horn were a cause of concern and would make it more difficult to ratify any SALT agreement, Vance was informing the Senate that there was "no linkage between the SALT negotiations and the situation in Ethiopia."[40] In March, when Carter gave a speech at Wake Forest University highlighting US determination to maintain sufficient forces to prevent Soviet blackmail, Vance's chief adviser on Soviet affairs, Marshal Shulman, told the Soviet embassy—without the knowledge of the White House—that the speech was intended primarily for domestic consumption.[41]

In an effort to send a clear message about US policy to Moscow and to the warring tribes within his own administration, Carter gave a major speech on

US-Soviet relations at his Naval Academy alma mater on June 7, 1978. The president began by reminding his audience of Soviet losses in the common struggle against Nazi Germany and he concluded by stressing the US desire for a SALT agreement and cooperation across a broad spectrum of exchanges. In between, however, he was unusually blunt in describing the Soviet view of dé-tente as "a continuing aggressive struggle for political advantage" and warning that Moscow's "abuse of basic human rights" had earned "the condemnation of people everywhere who love freedom." He also pointed out that the United States had no reason to fear competition with a USSR that faced serious inter-nal problems.[42] The speech was prescient in its vision of the underlying weak-ness of the Soviet system. But to Carter's frustration it was misconstrued by both of its primary audiences, Moscow and the US public, and did little to overcome the divisions within his own administration.

While the Carter administration was wrestling itself to the ground over US-Soviet relations, Moscow was also reviewing relations with its superpower rival. The day after Carter's Naval Academy speech, the Politburo met for a major discussion of US-Soviet relations. Brezhnev warned that the USSR had to do everything possible to hinder US policy, "which is fraught with the threat of a new world war."[43] Despite the alarmist tone of Brezhnev's remarks, what he proposed was limited to public statements, a major article in the Soviet press condemning the Carter administration and a declaration on African affairs where, in classic Big Lie fashion, the Soviets would reveal how it was actually NATO that was conducting "armed intervention."[44]

SALT Endgame

Despite a growing list of divisive international issues, the two sides continued to plug away at what Vance called the "excruciatingly technical" issues of SALT. Unfortunately, just as it appeared agreement was in sight, a new issue arose that delayed the accord for months. In the late 1970s, the Soviets began to encrypt data transmitted to ground stations during the flight tests of Soviet missiles that made it difficult for US intelligence to verify Soviet compliance with key agreement provisions.

The issue proved hard to unravel and personally frustrating for negotiators on both sides, in part because of its technical complexity and in part because of its sensitivity. Dobrynin recalled that once, after listening to yet another discus-sion on encryption where specialists on both sides had recounted their diametri-cally opposite views, he asked Gromyko for enlightenment: "Tell me frankly, I don't understand what they are talking about." But Gromyko did not understand either and when the subject came up he would simply "read from his papers."[45]

Resolving the issue was not made any easier by the fact that the institutional players on both sides were among the most secretive in their respective military and intelligence establishments. The notion that they had an obligation to make information available to American intelligence was not one that leaped naturally to the minds of Soviet weapons designers. Likewise, the idea that the way to resolve the issue was for the Americans to say which specific telemetry channels they needed access to was not attractive to US intelligence personnel, who pointed out that this approach was tantamount to telling the Soviets just what the US was able and not able to intercept.

By this time, however, the process of strategic arms negotiation had acquired a momentum that could not be stopped by technical impasses. Looking ahead to the 1980 elections, Carter was increasingly eager to buff up his international credentials through a successful US-Soviet summit. Moscow conditioned the summit to conclusion of a SALT agreement but there was a limit to how far it was willing to use this linkage as a delaying tactic, since in the final analysis the Soviets had little interest in seeing the SALT process fail and thereby leaving open the prospect of unrestrained strategic competition with the United States.

Encryption was eventually settled by an exchange of letters between Carter and Brezhnev promising that telemetry relevant to verification should not be encrypted although there was little agreement on what this actually encompassed. Backfire was essentially sidestepped through an elaborate high-level pantomime in which Brezhnev would make a statement at the summit providing certain assurances on Backfire. Carter would respond with a statement expressing the US interpretation of these assurances, which Brezhnev would not contradict. By May, Vance was able to announce that Carter and Brezhnev would meet in Vienna in June to sign the treaty.

The Vienna Summit of 1979

Aside from SALT II, the Vienna summit was more about symbolism than substance. Deplaning in the rain, Carter declined the use of an umbrella lest watching journalists draw a comparison with Neville Chamberlin at Munich. The US president underlined his difference from the infirm Brezhnev by conducting well-publicized jogs around the Austrian capital.

Brezhnev was so weak that he had to be helped into meetings by burly bodyguards on each shoulder. Before each session Brezhnev's assistant, Aleksandrov-Agentov, gave his interpreter, Viktor Sukhodrev, a briefing book containing various papers keyed to possible initiatives Carter might raise. Sukhodrev was instructed to pay close attention to the substance of the president's remarks and choose the appropriate response for Brezhnev to read. In one case, when

Carter's remarks did not correspond exactly to the prepared response, Sukhodrev quickly inked out certain passages and noted in the margins where the Soviet leader should stop. Brezhnev obediently read the marked passages and then turned to Sukhodrev and asked in a loud voice, "So I don't have to read the second part?" The embarrassed Sukhodrev, with the Americans looking on replied, "That's right, Leonid Ilich."[46]

On a few occasions, Brezhnev exhibited some of his old spunk. At one point, he intervened to shut Gromyko up when the Soviet foreign minister's quibbling over previously agreed-upon arrangements threatened to cause the entire SALT II deal to unravel. As he had at Vladivostok with President Ford, Brezhnev also exhibited apparently genuine frustration with arms control agreements that did not go far enough. At Vienna he lamented that arms talks had "been marking time for years and going around in circles."[47] When the two leaders were in an elevator alone with their interpreters after a plenary session in which Carter had outlined in considerable detail what he hoped to achieve in a SALT III agreement, Brezhnev leaned over and asked the US president if he could provide more information, which prompted Carter to hand over three pages of his handwritten notes on a yellow legal pad. That night Brezhnev summoned the Soviet delegation to discuss "Carter's paper." Ustinov said the proposals were "too far-reaching" while Gromyko stalled by recommending further study and consultation with other Politburo members. Faced with a solid wall of skepticism, Brezhnev drew back and Carter's ideas vanished.[48]

After signing SALT II, the leaders got up and walked around the table. Carter later recalled, "I shook hands with President Brezhnev and to my surprise, we found ourselves embracing each other in the Soviet fashion." According to Soviet participants, it was Carter who took the initiative, to Brezhnev's initial surprise. Carter was criticized for the kiss on returning home but the gesture seemed to have been well received by the sentimental Brezhnev, who told his associates that evening that Carter was "quite a nice guy."[49]

Undoubtedly the most contentious of all the US-Soviet strategic arms control agreements, the SALT II Treaty was neither as dangerous as its many critics charged nor as beneficial as its supporters claimed. The treaty put a cap on some aspects of the nuclear arms race but it essentially permitted both sides to continue to deploy weapons they already possessed or had on the drawing boards. Despite its flaws, the SALT II Treaty made sense as a first step toward a broader agreement containing real reductions in nuclear forces. In retrospect, this is clearly how Carter saw the agreement, although he could not say this at the time. Probably the most telling argument in favor of SALT II was intangible. The treaty was a modest but important move toward increasing predictability in the strategic balance. The long hours of negotiations that lay behind the treaty began a process of increasing understanding between the national security establishments of the two nuclear superpowers, which bore fruit in the coming decade as they eventually agreed on reductions in nuclear arsenals that neither side could have imagined in Vienna.

The Dissident "Beat"

Despite the fireworks it had provoked in the early years of the Carter administration, human rights played only a minor role at Vienna. In the final session, Carter urged the release of Shcharanskiy and other dissidents and the introduction of more liberal emigration policies. When Brezhnev objected that this was interference in internal affairs, Carter replied, "You voluntarily signed the Helsinki accords which made this issue a proper item for state-state discussions."[50]

At this time, while serving in Embassy Moscow's internal political section, I was assigned to be the contact with the Soviet human rights community. In addition to Russian language, the job required a number of skills not taught in diplomatic academies, including the ability to sip endless cups of tea, or sometimes stronger liquid, while sitting around cramped Moscow kitchen tables and listening to emotional conversations, some on political topics and others on the eternal Russian questions of life and fate.

The rewards were great. Most important, of course, was the opportunity to meet a group of extraordinarily brave and thoughtful people who fought the repressive apparatus of a totalitarian state with a combination of courage, doggedness, and sometimes, inevitably, desperation. Dick Combs, one of the most outstanding of the State Department's Soviet hands, wrote that "the most rewarding aspect" of his job as chief of the embassy's internal political unit over the years 1975 to 1978 was "my extensive personal contact with leaders of the unofficial Soviet human rights movement."[51]

By the time I began to work the "dissident beat" most of the founders of the Moscow Helsinki group had been arrested or exiled. Their work was carried on by other members, including Sakharov's wife, Yelena Bonner, and Naum Meiman, a mathematician and a longtime refusenik. Perhaps the most impressive of this generation of Helsinki monitors was Yuri Yarim-Agayev, a young physicist who had attended the same school for gifted science students as Shcharanskiy. Yuri took over much of the activities of contacting Western diplomats in 1979 and 1980 and also compiled a comprehensive report on the treatment of political prisoners for which he traveled extensively in Siberia in 1980. I met regularly with him and with Vyacheslav Bakhmin, a quiet but doggedly determined compiler of the terrible experiences of those who suffered from the misuse of psychiatry to repress political dissent.

The KGB sometimes took its objections to the contacts of American diplomats with the dissident and refuseniks to extraordinarily high levels. In November 1976, KGB chief Andropov specifically singled out Combs for his contacts with Helsinki Monitoring Group chief Orlov. In February 1977, Ambassador Dobrynin was instructed—by the Politburo, no less—to complain to Secretary of State Vance about the activities of Presel.[52] As far as I am aware, my own activities never rose to the august attention of the Politburo, but on one occasion the US embassy security officer told me that the KGB office responsible for providing protection to foreign embassies had warned him that, unfortunately, they could no longer guarantee the safety of Second Secretary Sell because of his persistence in contacts with undesirables, criminals, and psychopaths.

In the steady stream of warnings KGB chief Andropov sent the Politburo on the dissidents, he highlighted the supposed role of US (generally called simply "enemy") intelligence in encouraging their supposedly hostile activities. In actuality, the CIA in Moscow stayed well away from the dissidents. According to Burton Gerber, CIA Moscow station chief from 1980 to 1982 and chief of the agency's Soviet and East European Division from 1984 to 1989, there was no policy against CIA contacts with the dissidents but "we restrained ourselves from contacts with them because we didn't want to cause them any more trouble than they might already be in, because we figured embassy personnel could quite thoroughly cover the human rights issues; and because we concentrated on Soviet targets which could provide important information not available by other means."[53]

Phones, of course, were tapped, and our apartments were thoroughly bugged. Some dissidents were unfazed by this, interjecting sarcastic messages to our unseen listeners when they called my apartment. There were also some people who preferred to try to exclude the KGB from our conversations. A jogger, I developed a pattern of running along different routes away from our apartment and stopping at random pay phones to make calls to dissident or refusenik contacts. Keeping conversations short and vague, the hope was to evade or at least discourage KGB eavesdroppers.

Harassment was an occasional feature. One frosty Moscow night, my wife and I emerged from the theater to find two tires in our car flattened. Sometimes harassment could become more threatening. On one occasion, I found two burly young men blocking my way on the sidewalk in front of our Moscow apartment, where I sometimes met unofficial contacts. They warned me in distinctly unfriendly tones how I was disturbing the tranquility of our Moscow district and affronting the sensibilities of my Moscow neighbors by meeting with "undesirables."

Sometimes my name got around at distances that were truly astonishing. Boris Perchatkin, the leader of the Pentecostal community in distant Nakhodka, violated a KGB order confining him to the Soviet Far East to travel for many days across Siberia, riding the rails and hitchhiking on trucks, to meet me. Inside our apartment, he handed over a package of documents signed by members of his parish that described in chilling fashion the repressive measures the authorities were employing against religious communities in the Far East, including imprisonment, firing from jobs, and the forcible kidnapping of believers' children.

My wife and I gave Perchatkin a meal and a chance to relax. I put him in contact with a Western correspondent interested in the problems of religious believers in the USSR and promised to forward his materials to the Congressional Helsinki Commission in Washington and then he left our small American oasis to go back into the Moscow night. In contemplating Perchatkin's saga, I could not help remarking on the paradox his story revealed. The Pentecostals were hardworking, avoided any kind of criminal activity, were teetotalers, and had large families, all traits the Soviet authorities were desperately and largely unsuccessfully trying to encourage in Soviet society as a whole. But because the Pentecostals were religious believers, they were persecuted and driven to the margins of existence. It was an example of the irrationality of the Soviet system, which in a small way helps explain why it eventually crashed of its own perverse weight.

In addition to working with dissidents, I also backed up my colleague Judyt Mandel in contacts with Jewish refuseniks. In the late 1970s, the Moscow refusenik community consisted of several thousand people. Some had been waiting a decade or more—often these were people who had been denied exit permission on security grounds—while others had only recently put in their applications to leave, encouraged by the rise in emigration that accompanied the conclusion of the SALT II arms accord.

The most important commodity keeping the refuseniks going was hope, which they nurtured in a variety of ways, listening to American and Israeli radio, avidly following US-Soviet relations for signs of movement on emigration, endlessly speculating on how to manipulate the system either to gain an exit visa or at least some kind of employment, and immersing themselves in things that would help once they finally began a new life in Israel, such as studying Hebrew, Jewish religion, and Israeli politics. Hope sometimes led the refuseniks into touching acts of affirmation. The wife of a leading member of the refusenik community once showed my wife and me a mural she had drawn in the kitchen of her Moscow apartment of the Jerusalem that existed in her mind as a beacon for the future. Covering all four walls was a lovingly detailed charcoal depiction of a walled city whose towers and crenellated battlements bore a strong resemblance to the ancient Hanseatic capitals of her native Baltic region but little to modern-day Jerusalem.

The central institution of the refusenik community was a regular gathering every Saturday afternoon in front of Moscow's synagogue. On a fine summer afternoon, several hundred refuseniks might congregate on the sidewalks in front of the synagogue, sometimes spilling over into the street. On a chill Moscow winter day, the number might dwindle to a few dozen hearty souls.

People came to the gathering for a variety of reasons, to exchange information about who had gotten a treasured exit visa and who had gotten another denial, to pass on information and rumors about what the Soviet authorities were doing or likely to be doing, to speculate about the latest developments in US-Soviet relations and what impact they might have on the refusenik community. Gossip was always a feature: who was sick, who was well, who had fallen in love and who was getting a divorce. Some people came for personal reasons: to ask if anyone had leads on finding a job, even a menial one, which was necessary to avoid the possibility of being prosecuted for "parasitism." Others had services to sell: Hebrew classes, help with correspondence and translations, or even tennis lessons.

The dissident beat led naturally into contacts with other members of Moscow's nonconformist community, such as artists who worked outside the officially sanctioned Artists Union. In 1974 Soviet authorities earned worldwide condemnation when they bulldozed the works of unofficial artists who had organized an open-air show in Moscow's Izmailovsky Park. By the end of the 1970s, the authorities had worked out a compromise, permitting the artists to hold informal exhibits roughly twice a year in the basement of a school. Although no publicity was allowed, the exhibits were regularly thronged by crowds of Soviets and foreigners. The evening before the opening, officials from the Ministry of Culture would visit the hall to inspect the works on display and decide which would be allowed to appear and which were deemed unsuitable for the tender sensitivities of the Soviet public. Another regular visitor, the artists told me, was Interior Minister Shchelokov, who reportedly patrolled the exhibits and took away pictures that caught his fancy, though whether this was a commercial transaction or a kind of tax the artists paid to keep on the right side of the authorities was unclear.

My wife and I attended the exhibits regularly and got to know some of the artists. We had an interest in Russian history and folk art and we found the bright and cheerful scenes of prerevolutionary Moscow painted by Aleksandr Tumanov to be irresistible. Sasha and his parents, with whom he then lived, became close friends of our family, sometimes babysitting for our young children. In those days, Tumanov painted in a small spare room adjoining his parents' kitchen, in a typical Soviet apartment building overlooking Leninsky Prospekt. Now, he has permanent exhibits in Venice and Paris as well as Moscow. There was nothing anti-Soviet about Tumanov's work or indeed any political content at all, which was apparently what kept him outside of official favor. He was unwilling to paint scenes that sugarcoated contemporary Soviet life while his fanciful, almost fairytale depictions of prerevolutionary Russia showed a side of life under the Tsars that the Soviet authorities could not acknowledge.

Very different from the gentle Tumanov was Ilya Glazunov, probably the most well known—some would say notorious—of the artists we got to know during our first tour in Moscow. Glazunov was famous for his romantic depictions of scenes from Russian history and for his portraits of foreign leaders such as Indira Gandhi and, it was rumored, Soviet leaders such as Brezhnev, Gromyko, and Suslov, whose patronage Glazunov was said to enjoy. Glazunov's works, which were heavily influenced by Russian Orthodoxy, generally told a story, sometimes of village life and sometimes of Russian history. Art critics tended to sniff at Glazunov's depictions while others decried his flirtation with Russian nationalism.

A visit to Glazunov's apartment-studio included an intensive introduction into the life and work of the artist, a demonstration of the rituals of Russian hospitality, and a generous dose of performance art by Glazunov himself. A visit typically began with a film about the artist's life and work. After the film, visitors toured the studio, ending with a viewing of a picture still in progress at the time of our first visit, which Glazunov considered one of the major works of his life: *The Mystery of the Twentieth Century*, a wall-sized painting that included capsule portraits of great or notorious figures ranging from Lenin to the Beatles, with the artist himself in one corner. *The Mystery* was banned by the Soviet authorities because Glazunov included a portrait of Solzhenitsyn wearing his gulag garb.

After visitors had a chance to absorb *The Mystery*, they were escorted downstairs to a dinner served by attractive young female art students and joined by Glazunov's artist wife, whom he once described to me as his "Minister of Security." During the dinner, Glazunov, asserting that his experience as a portrait painter allowed him to read a person's inner thoughts, gave capsule summaries of his guests' reactions to the visit. (About me, he said I kept my real thoughts hidden but observed Glazunov and the events of the evening like a spectator might watch the performance of a trained bear.)

In the early 1990s, Rudolf Pikoya, head of the Russian archives under Yeltsin, and retired Lieutenant-General Dmitri Volkogonov, who supervised the USSR presidential archive, found a handwritten paper headed, "On the Situation in Country A." It contained five short sentences that indicated "approval of the considerations and measures put forward by comrades Andropov, Ustinov, and Gromyko."[1] At the bottom of the page was Brezhnev's ragged, old-man's signature followed by that of every Politburo member. This scrawled note, which the authors had obviously intended never to see the light of day, constituted authorization for the Soviet invasion of Afghanistan.

Invasion

With Brezhnev unable to work more than a few hours a day, Minister of Defense Konstantin Ustinov, KGB chief Yuri Andropov, and Foreign Minister Andrei Gromyko met on December 8, 1979, in deep secrecy, not just from the world outside the Kremlin walls but from their own Politburo colleagues as well. On the agenda was the deteriorating situation in Afghanistan, a rapidly growing insurgency that controlled up to 70 percent of the country, and the unreliability of the current Afghan leader, Hafizullah Amin, who had murdered the pro-Soviet Nur Muhammad Taraki only days after Taraki had visited Moscow in September. But what most concerned the participants in the Kremlin meeting was the fear that the United States was somehow poised to exploit the situation if Afghanistan slipped out of Soviet control. Even though the US position across the region was rapidly crumbling—only a month earlier Iranian militants had seized the US Embassy in Teheran and taken its diplomats hostage—the elderly Soviet leaders managed to persuade themselves that they faced a looming American offensive. The Kremlin barons took two fateful decisions. They agreed to "remove" Amin from power and replace him with the more pliant Babrak Karmal. In fact, this was a decision to murder Amin, who had already survived at least one unsuccessful KGB effort to kill him. The second decision proved even more fateful, not just for Afghanistan but for the future of the USSR itself. The participants decided to dispatch a "certain quantity" of Soviet troops to Afghanistan.[2]

Two days later, Ustinov summoned Marshal Nikolai Ogarkov, the chief of the Soviet General Staff. Ustinov ordered Ogarkov to prepare to send 75,000 troops into Afghanistan for a "temporary" intervention. Surprised at this "reckless" decision, Ogarkov replied that 75,000 troops were not enough. Ustinov asked Ogarkov whether he was presuming to "teach the Politburo" and told him his only duty was to carry out orders.[3]

Once the decision to invade Afghanistan was made, the Soviet military carried it out loyally and skillfully. On December 25, Soviet aircraft began landing at Bagram airport near Kabul in an operation that over the next forty-eight hours would bring in 8,000 airborne troops and 800 vehicles.

Amin had ensconced himself, his family, and several hundred heavily armed bodyguards in a palace that looms on a hill overlooking Kabul. Reportedly in a state of euphoria over the news that Soviet forces were coming to what he thought was his assistance, Amin told guests, "Soviet divisions are already on the way here. Everything is going wonderfully. I am constantly on the phone with Comrade Gromyko." During dinner many of the guests became ill, victims of poison concealed in a soup prepared by a KGB agent who had infiltrated Amin's entourage as a cook. Amin's aides called the Soviet ambassador who, apparently unaware of the KGB plot, sent Soviet doctors to treat Amin.[4]

After a specially assembled unit of Soviet soldiers from Central Asia, the so-called Moslem battalion, had surrounded the palace to block any assistance from Afghan forces loyal to Amin, two special KGB detachments moved inside. A sharp firefight swirled through the corridors of the palace. The Soviet troops were dressed in Afghan uniforms with white armbands for recognition but in the confusion of the night assault the Soviets found that healthy doses of Russian swearing was the best form of identification.[5]

The Soviet doctors found Amin bleeding and dressed in his underwear. They bandaged his wounds and took him into a sheltered barroom, where he slumped against the wall, his arms around his eight-year-old son. Amin ordered his adjutant to call the Soviet commander in Kabul to request assistance in repelling the attack. As the adjutant was telling Amin that it was, regrettably, Soviet troops who were attacking the palace, the KGB detachment burst into the room and, allegedly in the course of a firefight, Amin and his son were killed.

The Soviet people learned about the invasion at the end of December, when *Pravda* announced that Soviet authorities had responded positively to a request by a new Afghan government headed by Babrak Karmal to render "political, moral, and economic aid, including military aid." *Pravda* also reported that a revolutionary court had sentenced Amin to death but failed to note that the sentence had actually been carried out by KGB forces before the court had the opportunity to meet. On December 31, when most Soviets were preparing their New Year's festivities, an article appeared in *Pravda* under the authoritative pseudonym "A. Petrov," which reported that the "limited Soviet military contingent" would be used exclusively to repel armed interference from abroad.[6] For the next several years, this was all the information the Soviet people received from their own government about a war in which thousands of their sons were fighting and dying.

Although the Soviet media remained silent on the subject of casualties for years, people whispered among themselves about friends or relatives who had been informed that a loved one had perished "while performing his patriotic duty." After the invasion, junior officers at the American embassy were instructed to visit Moscow cemeteries to look for fresh graves. One day in late winter, toward the back of a cemetery, I came upon a section where several young men had been laid to rest in newly dug graves. In the Russian fashion, the wooden burial markers had pictures of the young victims. All had died in the first months of 1980 and on the markers was the simple inscription "For the Fatherland."

A few months after the invasion, the Politburo rejected a proposal that the families of soldiers killed in Afghanistan be given one thousand rubles to purchase a headstone. Ideological chieftain Suslov remarked, "Is it politically desirable at this moment to raise memorials and write the whole story on headstones?"[7] Sometimes there would be a sealed coffin that relatives were ordered under no circumstances to open, or sometimes there was simply a letter that meant that a loved one was never coming home.

Background to Invasion

Afghanistan's position as playing field in the "Great Game" of nineteenth-century geopolitical competition between Great Britain and Russia is well known but after the Second World War, when London gave up its subcontinent empire, influence in Afghanistan was mostly left to Moscow. In the 1960s, the United States provided substantial amounts of development aid and numbers of young Afghans studied in America but the Soviet position was always predominant.

In April 1978, Afghan president Daoud was overthrown by army units loyal to the Peoples Democratic Party of Afghanistan (PDPA), the Afghan communist party. The new regime, under the leadership of Mohammad Taraki, who had been a KGB agent since 1951 and who reportedly kept a picture of Stalin on his desk, proclaimed the objective of creating a Soviet-style socialist system. Whether the Soviets instigated the April Revolution remains a matter of dispute, but once it was successfully concluded in the traditional Afghan fashion, with the murder of Daoud and his family, Moscow quickly embraced the new regime. But the Soviets overlooked one key factor according to Peter Tomsen, an American diplomat with long experience in Afghanistan and the USSR: "The PDPA had seized power in the capital but most of Afghanistan had never been ruled from Kabul."[8]

In Moscow it was a heady time for ideologues. Pro-American regimes were collapsing across Africa and the Middle East and many believed that the revolution in Afghanistan was just the latest in a line of dominos falling in Moscow's direction. Party officials such as Central Committee International Department chief Boris Ponomarev and ideological chief Suslov began to regard Afghanistan as "another Mongolia," ready to jump directly from feudalism to Socialism.[9] When Deputy Foreign Minister Korniyenko ventured to remark that rural, poverty-stricken Afghanistan hardly seemed ripe for socialism, he was sharply challenged by R. A. Ulyanovskiy, Ponomarev's "right hand" for the Third World, who said with the confidence that was then reverberating throughout Moscow, "In the world today there is no country which is not ripe for Socialism."[10]

Taraki introduced sweeping programs of land reform, education, and women's rights. He also moved swiftly and ruthlessly to forestall resistance from traditional forces in Afghan society through a "reign of terror: landowners, mullahs, dissident officers, professional people, even members of the Communist Party itself, were arrested, tortured, and shot in large numbers."[11]

Taraki's radical agenda provoked immediate resistance. Members of the moderate Parcham faction of the PDPA were pushed aside. Within Taraki's more extreme Khalq faction serious infighting began between him and Amin, who became prime minister in April 1979. In the countryside, the regime's policies triggered armed resistance by local leaders who saw their traditional positions threatened.

Despite Soviet assistance, the Afghan military was unable to counter the insurgency. In March 1979 insurgents, supported by mutinous army factions, seized control of Herat, killing hundreds of government supporters and also reportedly murdering dozens of Soviet military advisers and their family members, whose bodies were said to have been paraded through the streets.

The Herat uprising provoked a panicked appeal by Taraki for Soviet intervention. When Prime Minister Kosygin, who was delegated by a divided Politburo to telephone Taraki, asked what had happened to the hundreds of Afghan officers trained by the USSR, Taraki replied, "Most of them are Moslem reactionaries. We are unable to rely on them." Kosygin reported that "without realizing it, Comrade Taraki responded that almost nobody does support the government." Kosygin's assessment, together with news that the situation around Herat was improving, pushed the discussion away from intervention. Originally a hawk, Andropov now concluded that it would be inadmissible to "suppress a revolution in Afghanistan only with the aid of our bayonets." Gromyko pointed out that an invasion of Afghanistan would make impossible the upcoming summit between Brezhnev and Carter and, for good measure, said an invasion would not be justified under international law since "Afghanistan has not been subject to any aggression." Brezhnev added sarcastically but wisely, "Their army is falling apart and we are supposed to wage war for them!"[12]

Moscow rejected Taraki's request for Soviet combat troops but stepped up its supply of weapons and advisers. Nevertheless, the situation in Afghanistan continued to deteriorate. Insurgents were killing Soviet military advisers at a high rate and the in-fighting between Taraki and Amin grew worse.[13]

In September, at the insistence of Soviet ambassador Puzanov, who said he had a message from Brezhnev demanding that the two Afghan leaders end their conflict, Amin agreed to meet Taraki. On the way into the president's office, gunfire broke out. The prime minister escaped, mobilized supporters in the Kabul garrison, and seized power himself. Despite a personal appeal from Brezhnev to spare Taraki's life, it was announced that Taraki had died "after a severe illness," an affliction which it later transpired had been brought about by being smothered with a pillow.[14]

The situation in Kabul was rich in grimly baroque irony. Amin had seized power in a regime dependent for its existence on Soviet support despite the awkward fact that the Soviets had been complicit in at least one effort to murder him. Amin quickly resumed his predecessor's requests for the dispatch of Soviet forces to help fight the insurgency, which did not prevent the Soviets from coming to the conclusion that Amin might well be a CIA stooge who was actually seeking to turn the country over to the United States. According to

Leonid Shebarshin, then KGB resident in Teheran and later chief of the KGB's foreign intelligence directorate, the Soviets suspected Amin of plotting to "do a Sadat on us."[15]

Washington Watches

While Washington might well have been pleased to see Amin replicate Egyptian leader Sadat's 1972 expulsion of Soviet advisers, the realities of Afghanistan pointed to much more modest US objectives. In February 1979, US ambassador Spike Dubs was kidnapped by a group of militants and held in a Kabul hotel. Despite entreaties by US personnel, an Afghan assault group acting on the advice of KGB personnel on the scene stormed the hotel and in the shootout Dubs was killed. After the assault, the KGB planted weapons to make it appear that the kidnappers and not Afghan commandos had killed Dubs, and murdered captured kidnappers to prevent them from talking. Angry with the failure of the Afghan regime to provide an accounting of the incident or an apology for Dubs's death, Washington cut back its presence in Afghanistan.[16]

US diplomats in Kabul at the time strongly denied suggestions that Amin was about to switch sides. J. Bruce Amstutz, the US chargé immediately after Dubs's murder, said that in his five meetings with Amin over 1979 the Afghan leader had never suggested in any way that he was interested in allying with the United States. Archer K. Blood, US chargé in the fall of 1979, met only once with Amin, who reaffirmed his desire for US aid but would do nothing to satisfy US insistence on an apology for Dubs's death.[17]

The notion that the United States—preoccupied in 1979 with watching its investment in Iran go down the tubes and locked in another bitter regional dispute with Pakistan because of Islamabad's nuclear weapons program—would somehow have either the capability or the will to supplant the Soviets in Afghanistan verges on the otherworldly. In a triumph of understatement, Stansfield Turner, CIA director at the time, told a conference years later, "The suggestion that NATO was talking about bases in Afghanistan or that we were talking about short-range missiles in Afghanistan . . . or listening posts in Afghanistan is way beyond the scope of our thinking in those days."[18]

The Invasion Unfolds

The real threat that the pro-Soviet regime in Kabul faced was from domestic insurgency. By the fall of 1979, the Soviets estimated that 70 percent of Afghanistan was outside of government control and that Mujahedin forces had grown to at least forty thousand men.[19]

In early December, Andropov sent Brezhnev a handwritten note warning that "the situation in Afghanistan began to take an undesirable turn for us." Andropov's alarmist information found receptive ears in Brezhnev, who was personally offended by Amin's murder of Taraki after Brezhnev had embraced him, literally and politically, as the leader of a fellow Socialist state. Brezhnev also saw his credibility on the line. "How should the world be able to believe what Brezhnev says if his words do not count in Afghanistan?" he told his aides.[20]

Soviet decision-making was not helped by conflicting and sometimes misleading advice from its representatives on the ground in Afghanistan, where there were at least four separate reporting chains going back to the Soviet capital: the KGB, the GRU (Soviet military intelligence), diplomatic reporting from the embassy, and party representatives who reported to the Central Committee International Department. Visiting Kabul in July 1979, Brutents observed how Moscow got different information from these channels and how the competition among the different Soviet structures sharpened conflicts within the Afghan leadership.[21]

After the invasion, Soviet forces initially had only a limited mission to establish control of the cities, roads, and infrastructure and back Afghan government forces, which were expected to do most of the fighting. But after the invasion the Afghan army shrank from 100,000 to 25,000, and Moscow soon discovered that it was impossible to avoid combat operations.[22]

Soviet actions helped stimulate the resistance. In February 1980, two months after the invasion, protest gripped Kabul for three days. An estimated 400,000 people gathered on the rooftops of the capital, chanting "God is great." Afghan security forces deserted their posts and belligerent but largely unarmed crowds occupied the streets and gathered near Soviet facilities. The Soviet commander declared martial law and ordered his troops to shoot, killing over three hundred civilians.

Washington Responds

When US intelligence informed Carter of the Soviet airlift into Kabul, he sent Brezhnev what he described as "the sharpest message of my Presidency." Via the hotline, Carter said that the invasion of Afghanistan was "a clear threat to world peace" that could lead to a "long-lasting turning point in our relations." Carter's message evoked what the president described as a "devious" reply, that the Soviets had intervened at the request of the Afghan leaders and that Soviet troops would be withdrawn as soon as the reasons prompting the Afghan request had disappeared.[23] The president noted sarcastically in the margins of Brezhnev's message that "the leaders who requested Soviet presence were assassinated."[24]

Carter was determined to make the Soviet invasion "as costly as possible."[25] At a special NSC meeting on Afghanistan, there was broad agreement that the US objective had to be to "ostracize and condemn the Soviets." Even the hawkish Brzezinski, who said Washington should do what it could to turn Afghanistan into "Soviet Vietnam" by supplying money, arms, and technical advice to the rebels, also told the president it was unrealistic to expect to drive the Soviets out of Afghanistan.[26] US measures against Moscow included limits on grain sales, stricter controls on the export of US high technology, reduction of Soviet fishing in US waters, and the suspension of exchange programs. In a measure particularly painful to Carter, who saw nuclear arms limitations as one of his legacy issues, the president withdrew SALT II from Senate ratification but promised that in the interim the United States would continue to observe the treaty's terms. Later, the United States also announced that it would not participate in the 1980 summer Olympics in Moscow.

Unmentioned publicly was a decision to step up covert assistance to Afghan forces fighting the Soviet invaders. In July 1979, as Soviet military, economic, and political assistance to the PDPA regime was escalating, Carter had signed an intelligence "finding" authorizing $500,000 to the Afghan rebels for the purchase of radios and medical supplies. After the invasion, the Carter administration allocated $30 million for the supply of weapons. The goal of the program was described as harassment of the Soviet forces and arms were restricted to handheld infantry weapons, initially ancient British bolt-action rifles and later Soviet-style AK-47s and rocket-propelled grenades.[27]

Cover-Up and Criticism

Moscow initially expected that its troops would only remain in Afghanistan for a brief period. In January 1980, as Ambassador Dobrynin was preparing to return to Washington after New Year's leave, Brezhnev told him not to worry about Afghanistan: "It'll all be over in three to four weeks."[28]

Skepticism about the invasion was widespread. Early in 1980, two of the capital's prestigious think tanks, Arbatov's USA Institute and the Bogomolov Institute, sent separate memos to the Central Committee raising serious questions about the invasion. Sergei Tarasenko, later a close aide to Gorbachev's foreign minister Eduard Shevardnadze, said that the first news the MFA's USA desk received about the Soviet invasion was when the note taker returned from a meeting in which US ambassador Watson had protested the act to Foreign Minister Gromyko. As Tarasenko described it, "Absolutely everyone in our department was outraged and spoke against this action. Everyone agreed it was stupid, that it should not have been done, that it was a blunder, and that it would have serious consequences."[29]

When Andropov became general secretary, the supposed desire of the new leader to end the Afghan conflict—which he himself had done so much to instigate—was part of the public relations boomlet that accompanied his accession. In 1983, shortly after Andropov took office, the Soviets scaled back their offensive operations and concluded a truce with Ahmad Shah Massoud, known as the Lion of Panjshir for his fierce resistance to repeated Soviet efforts to control that strategic valley north of Kabul. But the Soviets were unwilling to make the difficult decisions that would have made withdrawal possible. When UN secretary general Perez de Cuellar met Andropov in Moscow, the general secretary, reading from notes, said that if there was a cessation of "interference" in Afghanistan—that is, if outside aid to the Afghan resistance forces was stopped—it would "not be difficult to settle other issues, including the withdrawal of Soviet troops." Departing from his notes, Andropov added that if the interference did not stop, "Soviet troops would stay in Afghanistan as long as necessary because this is a matter which concerns the security of the Soviet Union's borders."[30] It is difficult to see any window of opportunity in these remarks other than one of surrender by the Afghan forces fighting the occupation of their homeland.

Olympics in Fortress Moscow

Moscow's physical preparations for the 1980 Olympics were more or less what could have been expected from the Soviet regime: massive, expensive, and superficially glitzy but shoddy underneath, a Soviet practice Putin seems to have followed in preparations for the 2014 winter Olympics in Sochi. Moscow's defensive preparations, by contrast, set the gold medal standard against which all other efforts by totalitarian Olympic hosts would subsequently be judged.

The first sign I saw of the storm that would shortly sweep Moscow came in the spring of 1980, when I was driving to Moscow's Sheryemetyevo Airport, in those days well outside Moscow's urban area. The road was lined with charming if decrepit wooden peasant huts. Some retained the carved window decoration and stylized fence ornaments characteristic of traditional Russian peasant architecture. More than a few had operating wells in their yards. They presented a picturesque if somewhat seedy panorama for the visitor driving into the city.

That day I noticed that all of the huts lining the road had disappeared, replaced by burned ruins. Some still smoldered and others had people, presumably former inhabitants, picking through the rubble. It was immediately obvious what had happened. Worried that arriving Olympic visitors would not get the proper impression as they drove into the Soviet capital, the authorities had executed a quick and brutal form of urban renewal by burning the old wooden buildings, leaving the visitor it should be added with unobstructed views of grimy industrial complexes belching dark smoke into the sky, which had been screened by the offending huts. Later I learned from my dissident friends that the authorities had provided almost no warning to the inhabitants, who had to scramble to remove belongings before their homes were torched. In some cases, it was rumored, people who happened to be away returned to find their homes and everything in them destroyed.

As the date of the Olympic invasion approached, the authorities intensified their efforts to sanitize the city for the benefit of foreign visitors. As might be expected in the country that invented the term *Potemkin village* much of the preparation was superficial. The smell of paint and disinfectant hung like a sickly sweet cloud over those parts of Moscow where foreigners were expected to penetrate.

In the weeks before the Olympics, Moscow was emptied of a substantial part of its population. Hundreds of thousands were essentially ordered out of the city—in some cases people were given tickets for desirable tourist destinations or in other cases they were simply told to vacate their apartments. The authorities also took steps to block the thousands of Soviets who came to Moscow every day for business, tourism, or to shop in the stores of the capital that were better supplied than in any other part of the country. Declaring the city closed to all Soviet visitors, the authorities suspended the sale of plane or train tickets into Moscow and established three concentric rings of police barriers at distances of up to 100 kilometers on all the roads leading into the city.

During the Olympics, Moscow became a virtual ghost town. On a normal day, given the dense crowds and the Soviet proclivity for bodily contact, walking on Moscow's major streets was something like trying to ram through an NFL front line. During the Olympics, by contrast, the streets were so empty that the experience of strolling along the sidewalks would have been enjoyable had they not been so eerily empty.

Of course, not even the KGB could expect to remove all Moscow habitants. Those who remained were lectured at their schools, workplaces, and residential areas about how to handle the invading foreigners. People were enjoined to be polite, to respond courteously to even the most ridiculous questions—for example, why is there no toilet paper in any public restroom—and to avoid offensive behavior, such as shoving on the metro, a second-nature survival reflex for most Muscovites. Since the city was expected to be flooded with desirable goods in the days before the Olympics, to give the foreigners something on which to spend their hard currency and also to ensure that they got the correct impression about the state of socialist abundance that Muscovites enjoyed, the lectures also included warnings against jumping into line just because some "deficit good" had suddenly appeared, an admonition akin to telling a fish to stop swimming.

Other lectures warned of the dangers ahead. At least some of the foreign visitors were, presumably, sports fans but Muscovites were also warned that the "enemy" would try to take advantage of the Olympics to send in spies and provocateurs. Citizens were enjoined to ensure that visitors did not get away with taking unauthorized photos. They were also warned against accepting any of the forbidden fruit that some foreign visitors would undoubtedly try to bring in, such as works by Solzhenitsyn or other banned Soviet authors or—heaven forbid—the Bible. Even more dastardly possibilities were also exposed. One of my dissident friends told me that his children were lectured at school about the dangers of consorting with superficially friendly foreigners, including a warning against accepting seemingly innocuous gifts such as candy or chewing gum, which his children were told might be infected with syphilis.

After Munich in 1972, protection against terrorism was an unfortunate necessity for every Olympic city and Moscow in 1980 saw the deployment of a massive armed presence. Even in ordinary times, Moscow was a heavily policed city, but during the Olympics it took on the characteristics of an occupied fortress. At every intersection groups of at least four policemen were deployed who, since almost all traffic had been banned, had little to do but stand around. Military police vehicles cruised the streets nonstop. Hundreds of military police personnel were deployed at key points inside the city while entire divisions were camped outside.

Reservists were also called up. One of my nonconformist artist contacts told me that he was mobilized a week before the Olympics and sent to a remote part of the Moscow region where he was given the mission of guarding the village well. We wondered whether the KGB had really persuaded itself that enemies might try to embarrass the USSR by poisoning village wells during the Olympics or had the authorities simply decided to mobilize a certain number of men, leaving some poor officer on the scene to try figure out what to do with them, which was my friend's opinion. In any case, despite his dissident proclivities, my friend assured me that he had loyally protected the village water supply against any threat although, as it happened, none had actually arisen.

Crisis in Poland: The Unseen End of the Brezhnev Doctrine

The invasion of Afghanistan represented the high-water mark of the Soviet empire, although it was not evident at the time. Less than a year later came another crisis, this time in Poland, at the other end of the empire, that marked the beginning of the retreat of the Soviet system, although once again it was not visible at the time. In Afghanistan the USSR found itself bogged down in a war it could not win. In Poland the Soviets came within days of invading but backed off and left the job of crushing the independent Solidarity trade union to Polish security forces. Unbeknown to the world beyond the Kremlin, the Soviet leadership was so reluctant to use its own troops in Poland that they were even willing to contemplate the loss of the country to the Socialist camp if Polish forces had proven unwilling to act.

The Rise of Solidarity

Poland always sat uneasily in the Soviet empire. Poles considered themselves part of the Western world and tended to disdain their Soviet overlords as barbarians from the East. Communist Poland never erupted in full-scale armed rebellion as did Hungary in 1956, but the country experienced repeated instances of unrest that were often suppressed with considerable violence.

By the end of the 1970s, the Polish economy was in serious trouble. Foreign debt had risen from $1.2 billion to $20.5 billion; debt service payments were taking up all of Poland's export earnings. Government subsidies to keep food prices low rose from 19 billion zlotys in 1971 to 166 billion zlotys in 1979. Food subsidies were an unsustainable burden on the inefficient Polish economy yet low food prices were an essential part of the implicit bargain that the Polish authorities struck with their own people to tolerate the Communist system.[31]

Another element in the steamy brew was the election in 1978 of a Polish pope. In 1979, during his first visit to Poland, the articulate and thoughtful John Paul II delivered thirty-two sermons that were heard by over twelve million Poles. The pope's visit was a political earthquake. For a few days, one observer wrote, "There had been a temporary displacement of the Communist state."[32]

In July 1980, as rumors circulated that Polish goods were being sent to Moscow for the Olympics, the Polish government introduced price increases on meat. A wave of strikes erupted, and on August 14 a recently fired worker climbed over the fence of the shipyard in Gdansk and assumed control of the strike committee. Lech Walesa proved to be a charismatic leader and a shrewd negotiator. By the end of August, the entire Polish Baltic Coast was on strike.

Workers controlled Gdansk and were deciding which enterprises should be allowed to produce necessities for the people. From Rome, the pope assured the strikers that he supported them "with all my heart and prayers." Solidarity quickly assumed the character of an alternative authority structure across much of Poland.

Caught between the anger of their own people and the intractable reality of economic disaster, the Polish authorities decided to negotiate. On August 31, Walesa and Prime Minister Jagielski signed the Gdansk Agreement, which provided for the right of workers to organize free trade unions, the right to strike, access to mass media, and the release of political prisoners.

Response

The Soviet authorities watched developments in Poland with alarm. On August 25, the Politburo established a special commission on Poland, headed by Suslov and including the troika that had instigated the invasion of Afghanistan: Ustinov, Andropov, and Gromyko. The Soviets interpreted the Gdansk Agreement as a capitulation to Solidarity and over the coming months urged the Polish authorities to walk it back. The Soviets also said that "if circumstances warrant it would be advisable to use the contemplated administrative means," that is to crush the striking workers by force.

Soon after the strikes erupted, a special Polish internal security task force had been set up and on August 29 its commander assured the Polish Politburo that his forces could "exterminate the counterrevolutionary nest in Gdansk" if so ordered. At about the same time, the Suslov Commission authorized the mobilization of up to 100,000 Soviet troops to support Polish forces in an internal crackdown.[33]

Throughout the fall, preparations for armed action continued. Plans for an invasion of Poland were secretly drawn up, using as cover a Warsaw Pact exercise scheduled for December 8. On December 1, Soviet chief of staff Ogarkov informed the Polish military leadership that fifteen Soviet, one East German, and two Czechoslovak divisions would enter Poland under pretext of participating in the exercise. On December 5, with their troops assembling around Poland, Warsaw Pact leaders gathered in Moscow. In a one-on-one meeting with Brezhnev, the head of the Polish party, Stanislaw Kania, warned that if the Soviets continued with the invasion "socialist ideas would be swimming in blood." Brezhnev replied, "OK, we will not go in, although if complications occur we would."[34]

Moscow had given up on the option of invading Poland but it had by no means abandoned its determination that Solidarity had to be crushed. Throughout 1981, the Soviets alternatively bullied and cajoled the Polish leadership to move on its own. Plans were drawn up to introduce a state of emergency at the end of March, timed to coincide with another Warsaw Pact exercise, but the Polish leadership lost its nerve after a four-hour general strike brought the entire country to a standstill.[35]

The Politburo decided to send Andropov and Ustinov to a secret meeting with Kania and Defense Minister Jaruzelski, who had also become prime minister in February. It occurred on April 9 in the dead of night in the traditional venue for Soviet officials to lecture errant satellite leaders, a railroad car parked on the border. Jaruzelski asked to be allowed to step down but the Soviets brusquely told him to stay put. Andropov had thoughtfully brought along documents declaring martial law for Jaruzelski's signature, with the date left blank, but the Polish leader declined to make use of them. The Soviets told the Poles in no uncertain terms that they expected them to honor their commitment to crush Solidarity but left without any understanding when this would happen.[36]

In September Solidarity held its first national congress. In a triumphalist mood, the delegates adopted a "Message to the Working Class People in Eastern Europe," which urged "all the nations of the Soviet Union" to establish their own independent trade unions, a barely disguised appeal for a Solidarity-style uprising in the USSR itself. The Soviet leadership denounced the statement as "a summons to counterrevolution," and Brezhnev vowed to crush the "hooliganistic stunts of Solidarity's leaders."[37]

In October Jaruzelski took over as Party leader from the hapless Kania, who seems to have privately come to the conclusion that Poland's best hope lay in cutting a deal with Solidarity, as in fact happened eight years later. While all this was going on, Soviet military and KGB personnel were assisting Polish counterparts in preparations for an armed crackdown. By December 1981, the Polish authorities were finally ready to move, but at the last minute Jaruzelski tried to condition the introduction of martial law on the promise of armed intervention by the Soviets if Polish forces proved unable to do the job themselves.

Meeting to discuss Jaruzelski's plea, Politburo leaders, who two years earlier had secretly committed the USSR to invade Afghanistan with hardly a doubt expressed, now concluded unanimously that Soviet troops could not be sent to Poland, even if that meant the loss of Poland to the Socialist camp. Andropov said the operation "must entirely and unequivocally be decided by the Polish comrades themselves. Whatever they decide will be." The Soviet Union could not take the risk of sending troops into Poland: "We do not intend to introduce troops into Poland. . . . Even if Poland falls under the control of Solidarity, that's the way it will be." Andropov said the USSR needed to look after its own interests and saw the chief danger to be Western economic and political sanctions that would be "very burdensome for us" if Soviet troops invaded Poland. Gromyko agreed, "There cannot be any introduction of troops into Poland." Restoration of order would have to be a matter for the Polish party alone. Even the hard-line Suslov agreed that there could be no introduction of Soviet troops. "World public opinion will not permit us to do so," he declaimed.[38]

Jaruzelski recovered his nerve, bucked up by Soviet advice on the planning of the crackdown and promises of assistance short of troops. On the morning of December 13, Poles woke to a somber Jaruzelski announcing that "our country is at an abyss" and that martial law had been introduced. For the moment, it appeared as if the Soviets and their Polish clients had won their gamble. An overconfident Solidarity allowed most of its leaders to be arrested overnight and in the next few days Polish riot police broke up the scattered strikes and factory occupations that constituted the only overt opposition to the crackdown.

Why Moscow Failed to Roll the Tanks

The decision not to send Soviet troops into Poland even if that meant the end of Communist control, unknown outside of a very narrow circle of top Kremlin officials until after the Cold War, amounted to the secret repudiation of the Brezhnev Doctrine years before it was publicly abandoned by Gorbachev. Over the thirty-five-year history of Soviet rule in Eastern Europe, Moscow had used force on three occasions to crush unrest. And during the previous decade, an increasingly confident Moscow had shown itself willing to employ military force in southern Africa and other places far removed from traditional Soviet zones of influence. For a brief time over 1980 and 1981, I sat on a State Department working group to consider responses to the crisis in Poland and I do not recall anyone doubting that the Soviets would invade Poland if they believed it to be necessary.

By 1980, however, a number of factors were pushing the Soviets away from intervention. A conflict in Poland, with its thirty-five million inhabitants and large military would require a major campaign. The USSR would undoubtedly prevail but the consequences in Eastern Europe, in the USSR itself, and in the broader Cold War confrontation with the West would be dangerously unpredictable. The sanctions the Carter administration undertook in response to the invasion of Afghanistan had surprised Moscow and the prospect of additional sanctions in response to an invasion of Poland was cited by Politburo members as one reason Soviet troops could not be dispatched.

The ongoing war in Afghanistan, a drain on Soviet resources and deeply unpopular among the population and the leadership itself, was likely the most important factor discouraging Soviet intervention in Poland. In December 1979, Brezhnev had unquestioningly accepted the precooked decision to invade Afghanistan presented to him by Andropov, Ustinov, and Gromyko. Brezhnev soon developed second thoughts and he was not inclined to go along with those pushing him toward another armed adventure.

Opposition to an invasion of Poland seems to have been strong at the upper levels of the Soviet military, as it was prior to the invasion of Afghanistan. A few years after the crisis, Chief of Staff Ogarkov told Volkogonov that he had been worried during the Polish crisis about a possible Soviet invasion. "Another war, this time in Europe, could have become an insupportable burden for our country," Ogarkov said. Even Warsaw Pact commander Kulikov, by all accounts one of the leading hawks on Poland, seemed to harbor doubts about whether an intervention might lead to a repetition of the Afghanistan misadventure. Volkogonov accompanied Kulikov to Poland in August 1980 and sat in on his meetings with Jaruzelski. When Volkogonov alluded to Afghanistan and asked Kulikov if the Soviet Union was about to commit another "fatal mistake," the marshal replied that such a "mistake must not be allowed to happen."[39]

Leadership politics also played a role. By 1981 Andropov was positioning himself for a run to succeed Brezhnev as general secretary. He had taken great care to conceal knowledge of his leading role in the decision to dispatch troops to Kabul and he certainly understood that being tagged as the instigator of yet another conflict was not likely to be a winning ticket in the general secretary sweepstakes.

Silently present for the Soviet leadership's deliberations on Poland was one promising younger member, Mikhail Gorbachev. A little less than eight years later, Gorbachev faced the question of how to respond to a Solidarity-backed figure becoming Poland's first non-Communist prime minister since the end of the Second World War. There are many reasons why Gorbachev did not use force to block the fall of Communist regimes in Poland and the rest of Eastern Europe in 1989 but one is likely Gorbachev's memory of how Soviet leaders in the Brezhnev era, when Moscow's domestic and international position was in most respects stronger than in 1989, saw the use of force in Poland as imposing unacceptable costs.

The US Response to the Polish Crisis

The Reagan administration's policy toward the imposition of martial law in Poland was hammered out in four emotionally charged meetings over December 19–23, which included only a few of the president's top advisers. The meetings resulted in a decision to impose sanctions, a presidential letter to Brezhnev, and a tough speech by Reagan on December 24.[40]

Despite the administration's tough rhetoric, the sanctions it adopted were, in most respects, weaker than those adopted by the Carter administration after the Soviet invasion of Afghanistan. Negotiations for a new long-term grain-sales agreement were suspended, although the existing agreement, unilaterally restored by Reagan in April after Carter had suspended it, remained in force. Restrictions were imposed on US sales of gas and oil-pipeline equipment, which promptly involved the United States in a major row with its European allies, and most remaining détente-era scientific and technical agreements were ended.

Behind the scenes, the Reagan administration began a program of covert support to Polish opponents of Communist rule. When NSC Soviet adviser Richard Pipes raised the possibility of covertly funding Solidarity, his suggestion was opposed by Vice President Bush and Secretary of State Haig, who reportedly exploded, "That's crazy; . . . The Soviets would never tolerate it. Solidarity is lost." Reagan, however, bought Pipes's suggestion and instructed CIA chief Casey to go ahead.

Casey produced a plan for supplying Solidarity with money, communications equipment, and shared intelligence information, in cooperation with the Vatican and the AFL-CIO, which had been funding Solidarity since 1980. The amount of money involved in the Reagan administration's covert action program in Poland was not large. At its peak, $8 million annually was being transferred to Solidarity, and according to Robert Gates, then Casey's deputy at CIA, the program did not really get rolling until late in 1982. Most of what flowed from the CIA to Solidarity consisted of printed material, communications and office equipment, and other supplies to allow Solidarity to wage an underground political struggle. No lethal equipment was supplied.[41]

The most effective measure the US took to aid Solidarity and other independent actors in Eastern Europe was the administration's decision to step up support for Radio Free Europe (RFE), which broadcast news and commentary in the languages of all of the Eastern European satellite regimes. RFE became, in effect, the media arm of Solidarity, depriving the Polish Communist regime of the most important tool in the totalitarian arsenal, the monopoly of information. When Walesa, during a visit to the United States shortly after Solidarity had taken over the government of Poland, was asked how important RFE had been to the cause of Polish freedom he replied, "Would there be earth without the sun?"[42]

CHAPTER 8 · Interregnum: Andropov in Power

Death of an Old Man

At 9:00 AM, November 10, 1982, Vladimir Medvedev, Brezhnev's chief body-guard, entered his boss's bedroom to wake him as usual. Three days earlier, Brezhnev had stood for several frigid hours atop the Lenin mausoleum, presid-ing over the annual Revolution Day display of military might the USSR had accumulated during his eighteen-year rule. Before retiring the previous night, Brezhnev had complained of a "terrific headache" and now Medvedev found him lying unconscious. Within an hour, Minister of Health Chazov told An-dropov, who had arrived immediately after being informed of what was hap-pening, that Brezhnev was dead. Not until then was Brezhnev's long-suffering wife, Viktoriya Petrovna, allowed into the room.[1]

Brezhnev's death immediately set off intense maneuvering behind the se-cretive walls of the Kremlin but only in the evening did the external world sense that something was amiss. A TV program in honor of the "Day of the Militia Men" was replaced by a film on Lenin, which was followed by Tchai-kovsky's *Symphonie Pathétique* and other somber music. Not until 11 AM the next day, over twenty-four hours after Brezhnev's death, was the public in-formed that Leonid Ilich was no more. The Soviet people, who had reacted in 1953 with seemingly genuine grief at Stalin's death, met with indifference the death of Brezhnev, whose long incapacitating dotage had become a source of embarrassment. The basic reaction could be summed up by a quip in which one person, told that Brezhnev has died, replied coolly, "How could they tell?"[2]

The USSR at the End of the Brezhnev Era

By the end of the Brezhnev era, the chronic diseases of the Soviet system could no longer be hidden. The country faced a material crisis. The economy was slowing and shortages were increasing. Even more important in some ways was the crisis of belief. The gap between ideology and reality was huge and few took seriously the official line mouthed by leaders and repeated endlessly in the media.

In his comprehensive history of the USSR from the end of World War II to its final collapse, historian Rudolf Pikhoya gives a good snapshot of the situation:

> The beginning of the 1980s became a time of crisis. This was not a subject of learned argument by economists: the consequences of the crisis were evident to every citizen of the country. The USSR had been sucked into the Afghan war, in cities and villages terrible tales circulated about the Afghan "Basmachs" who were killing our soldiers. The television told stories about "international aid" while in the country funerals were being held. The stores sold goods. But they could not be bought; they had to be "scored" (dostat). Goods had become "deficit." One had to "score" shoes and cakes, shirts and books, cars and washing machines, televisions and medicine. One could only dream of "scoring" imported tape recorders or food. . . . In many cities meat and butter could only be obtained through ration cards.[3]

Many Soviets interviewed by US scholar Donald J. Raleigh in his oral history project saw the second half of the Brezhnev era as a turning point in the development of their own consciousness. Over the 1970s, it became clear to the interviewees that the USSR was not really building socialism, that the myths that lay at the root of the Soviet system had become meaningless. Outwardly compliant, these Soviet "baby boomers" questioned the command's economic system as shortages of basic consumer items grew. Sympathetic to the human rights movement—at least as they described things years later—but unwilling to risk their lives or careers by joining it themselves, they were undermining the Soviet system from within their own consciousness, almost without realizing it, and "thereby demonstrating how late socialism lost the allegiance of its most educated, and in some ways, most privileged class."[4]

As Brezhnev became increasingly incapacitated, the troika of Ustinov, Andropov, and Gromyko took responsibility for directing Soviet national security policy while on domestic affairs the inner circle included Suslov, Chernenko, and Prime Minister Tikhonov, who took over after Kosygin's departure

in 1980. These groups met informally outside the Politburo to decide important issues, after which Brezhnev duly endorsed them. Only then were they
presented to the Politburo for rubber-stamp approval. It was an example of
the phenomenon that was occurring at lower levels in many parts of Soviet society: the replacement of regular institutions of party and state authority with
informal networks of patronage, influence, and corruption. These unofficial
links helped the increasingly creaky Soviet system function in its later years
but they also contributed to the decline in respect for established institutions,
rules, and leaders that was growing throughout society. And with the benefit
of four decades' hindsight, it can be seen that the phenomenon also helped the
rise of the corrupt "crony capitalism" that sabotaged Yeltsin's efforts at democratic reform in the 1990s and laid the basis for Putin's twenty-first-century
"kleptocracy."

At a different social level the late Brezhnev era saw the appearance of groups
who deliberately organized their life to have as little contact with the system as
possible. These were tightly knit networks of friends who shared some interest
or occupation—sports, nature, archeology or the like—that they turned into
the central organizing focus of their lives. Members of such groups might be
indifferent or even scornful of the official order but were also uninterested in
active opposition. They read Solzhenitsyn and other samizdat writers but did
not emulate his example of fighting the system.[5]

In May 1980, on the twentieth anniversary of Boris Pasternak's death, my
wife and I met one such group at the charming village of Peredelkino, outside
Moscow, where Pasternak had lived and where he is buried in the local cemetery.
We found a collection of about twenty neatly dressed young people sitting
under the trees, taking turns reading aloud Pasternak's poetry. Full of infectious enthusiasm, the young people had dedicated themselves to keeping alive
the memory of Boris Pasternak, who at that time remained a nonperson in the
official Soviet world.

Every year on the anniversary of his death, they came to his grave site and
spent the entire night reciting his poetry. I did not see a single printed volume
with the group. One young man proudly showed me a thick sheaf of pages on
which he said he had copied out by hand all of Pasternak's poems. He added
that he had memorized every one and from the way he began to spontaneously
recite the verses I could certainly believe it.

Their life and their future, one said, was Boris Pasternak. All they wanted
to do was to continue to read his poetry and preserve his memory. Nothing
in the comments or the behavior of the young Pasternak enthusiasts was

overtly political or critical of the Soviet system and the young people said they had experienced no problems from the authorities nor did they seem to expect any.

The Kremlin Pot Begins to Boil

The final year of Brezhnev's life was marked by signs, obscure to most people but unsettling to Kremlin insiders, that the freeze on factional infighting that had prevailed during the last half of Brezhnev's rule was thawing. Someone was stirring the pot of Kremlin intrigue, and that unknown person seemed to have access to highly secret levers of power and information.

In December 1981, Brezhnev's seventy-fifth birthday was marked by celebrations and an outpouring of media praise. Little noticed was an article, published intriguingly on page seventy-five, in the Leningrad literary journal *Avrora*, about a supposedly imaginary writer who "lives and doesn't think of dying to general amazement. The majority think of him as having died long ago. . . . But I don't think we'll have to wait long." The anonymous author's allusion to Brezhnev was evident but it was far from clear how a satire aimed at the Soviet leader had managed to escape the usually sharp eyes of Soviet censors. Someone—almost certainly highly placed—wanted to send a message to Brezhnev and his supporters.[6]

In the same month stolen diamonds were discovered in the apartment of circus performer Boris Buryatia, known as Boris the Gypsy, the sometime lover of Galina Brezhnev, the daughter of the general secretary himself. The theft lifted the veil not just on a large-scale diamond smuggling business with tentacles throughout the Moscow demimonde but also a broader network of corruption that included senior government and police officials, highly placed individuals in Moscow's literary and cultural society, and the director of Moscow's Gastronome Number 1, where the elite went to receive goods available only to the upper reaches of Soviet society.[7]

The investigation into what came to be known as the "Diamond Affair" was put in the hands of Semyon Tsvigun, deputy chairman of the KGB, who was also the general secretary's brother-in-law, having married the sister of Brezhnev's wife Viktoria Petrovna (or her cousin, according to some accounts) when both men were rising young officials. During his career at the KGB, Tsvigun had been entrusted with a number of delicate missions. He was also something of a man-about-Moscow, having written an espionage novel that was later turned into a movie, and he served as consultant on spy films to Moscow studios.

About a month after Boris the Gypsy's detention, still unknown outside a narrow circle of officials, the Soviet media reported Tsvigun's death. Conspicuously absent from his obituary was Brezhnev's signature, which immediately set informed Moscow tongues wagging. Andropov presided over Tsvigun's funeral, at which Brezhnev and others associated with him were nowhere to be seen. In a striking departure from the usual Soviet obsession with secrecy, the entire KGB leadership attended the funeral.

Soon afterward, rumors began to circulate that Tsvigun had committed suicide. According to one version, he killed himself out of depression brought on by the fact that he was being blocked from acting against the high-level corruption revealed by the Diamond Affair. Other accounts say that when Tsvigun told Brezhnev about his daughter's connection with the Diamond Affair, Brezhnev responded, "Prosecute her to the full extent of the law," then turned to the wall and wept.

Whatever its reason, Tsvigun's death opened up new room for maneuver by Andropov. He took personal charge of the investigation into the Diamond Affair and soon Boris the Gypsy, along with much of the leadership of the Moscow Circus, found themselves in Butyrka prison, where they began to tell tales of corruption reaching into the very top of the Soviet leadership. In late January, a senior official of the Ministry of Culture was arrested after diamonds and other questionable goods were found in his apartment and the head of the country's visa office was arrested for taking bribes. Shortly thereafter, Svetlana Shchelokova, wife of the Minister of Internal Affairs, committed suicide after being questioned in connection with the Diamond Affair, whose origins according to some accounts may stem from a corrupt deal that Galina and Svetlana concocted in 1981 with the director of Moscow's largest jewelry store. Learning about an impending rise in the state-controlled price of diamonds, the two women bought a number of large and expensive items, which they later sold back to the store at the new, higher price, sharing the proceeds from the insider deal with the director.

As KGB chief, Andropov had accumulated power and prestige along with information about the true state of affairs in the country and the personal peccadillos of its leaders. But it would have been virtually unthinkable for him to move directly from the KGB to the the general secretary position. When Mikhail Suslov died in May—according to some accounts from the aftereffects of a stroke brought on by a shouting match with Tsvigun over the Diamond Affair—Andropov overcame resistance from some in the Brezhnevian old guard to take Suslov's job as second secretary in the party apparat, thereby positioning himself as the lead contender in the succession sweepstakes.

The Enigmatic Yuri Andropov

Andropov brought a number of strengths to the race. He was widely acknowledged to be intelligent and honest, a strong asset in view of the growing disenchantment with the public sleaze associated with the last years of Brezhnev's rule. As KGB chief, he had solid experience in international and domestic affairs. Andropov also had a broad network of loyal former aides among the liberal Soviet intelligentsia going back to his days as chief of the Central Committee department for relations with foreign Communist parties. They were not themselves players in the Kremlin power game, but they had broad contacts at home and abroad and were capable, as the world soon saw, of an impressive job of image-building.

Even in 1981, signs were appearing that Andropov was seeking to expand his horizons beyond the confines of the KGB. Shortly after US diplomat Shaun Byrnes, an experienced Soviet hand, arrived in the summer of 1981 to assume his new position in the political section in the US embassy in Belgrade, a Soviet diplomat sought him out at a reception. "I am one of Andropov's guys," said the Soviet, who was in fact the KGB chief in Belgrade. At roughly this time, several other KGB officers in various parts of the world also sought out US officials to establish a dialogue. "I am prepared to work with you" was the message Byrnes's contact said Andropov wanted to pass on to the US leadership. The emissary assured Byrnes that Andropov understood that in order to reduce nuclear arsenals and return US-Soviet relations to where they had been during the time of détente both sides would need to modify their positions. Over the next two years, until Byrnes left Belgrade for a new assignment, he met regularly with his Soviet contact in a dialogue that was known only to the very top officials in the State Department and the White House.[8]

There are few Soviet leaders about whom so much contradictory and misleading information has been written as Yuri Andropov. The man, who as Soviet ambassador to Budapest was an active participant in crushing the 1956 Hungarian uprising and who presided over the persecution of the Soviet human rights movement during the fifteen years in which he led the KGB, was also touted as a closet liberal who read Shakespeare, listened to Frank Sinatra, and sometimes wrote poetry. Undoubtedly a man of intelligence and discernment, Andropov encouraged subordinates to provide him information on all sides of the issues. He was respected by the KGB rank-and-file for his integrity, for increasing the institution's professionalism, and for his ability to use his position on the Politburo to increase the resources available to the KGB. Typical of many former KGB officials are the views of Rem Krasilnikov, for many years the head of KGB counterintelligence against the US, who wrote in his memoirs, "The time of Andropov is truly considered the golden era of the KGB."[9] Yet at the same time, many KGB insiders describe the KGB in the Andropov era as riddled with corruption and sycophancy toward superiors. On Andropov's watch the KGB systematically fed the Soviet leadership with misleading and politically motivated intelligence that had a disastrous impact on Soviet policy making in crises such as Czechoslovakia and Afghanistan. Capable of clear thinking and coldly rational analysis, he was also prone to belief in conspiracy theories, including the conviction that the United States was actively preparing to launch a nuclear first strike against the USSR, which led to what even his loyal KGB subordinates acknowledged was a years-long wild goose chase to find the nonexistent evidence to fit Andropov's preconceived notions. Andropov was one of the few members of the Soviet leadership under Brezhnev to understand that the USSR was slipping into crisis, yet the solutions he proposed in private memos to Brezhnev never went beyond the banal. In post-Soviet Russia, Andropov is often seen as a moderate, who if he had lived might have introduced gradual reforms that could have saved the Communist system. Yet Andropov is also the man who put Gorbachev firmly on the road to the top of Soviet politics and it was essentially Andropov's recipes that Gorbachev pursued in his first two years in power.

Andropov Takes the Helm

The evening of November 10, a few hours after Brezhnev's death, the Politburo gathered behind the firmly closed walls of the Kremlin. Andropov was the first to speak. Asking all to rise for a minute of silence, he delivered an effusive eulogy almost as if Leonid Ilich was still there. After a characteristic warning that "our enemies" will do everything possible "to shake our ranks," Andropov announced that on the agenda was the question of the new general secretary. Looking around the table, he asked, "What are your proposals, comrades?"[10] Chernenko immediately took the floor. After adding his own even more effusive—and probably more sincere—praise of the dear departed, Chernenko proposed that Andropov become the new party chief. With no further discussion all present agreed.

Despite the surface unanimity, Andropov enjoyed only a slim majority on the Politburo and behind the scenes were hints of a struggle between him and Chernenko, who represented a faction apparently worried that Andropov might upset the cozy relationships that had developed under Brezhnev's long tenure. The next day—before Andropov's elevation had been publicly announced—Chernenko backers spread rumors intended to discredit Andropov, including the insinuation that he was part Jewish, in hopes that his candidacy might be questioned by the Central Committee. Andropov enjoyed powerful support from fellow national security dons Ustinov and Gromyko. Arkadiy Shevchenko, Gromyko's aide, who defected to the United States in 1978, reported that Gromyko and other senior members of the Politburo resented Chernenko's rapid rise into the leadership and considered him basically a "senior clerk and by no means their equal." Ustinov, according to some accounts, played a key role in Andropov's victory by telling his Politburo colleagues that military leaders "would not understand any other choice" but Andropov. The day after Brezhnev's death, Western correspondents reported that the army and the KGB had set up roadblocks on all avenues leading to the Kremlin. John Parker, for decades one of the US government's foremost analysts of Kremlin politics, described Andropov's group, which largely controlled the country's main security organs, as having in effect "captured Moscow." At the end of the day on November 11, five hours after the announcement of Brezhnev's death, Andropov was publicly identified as heading the commission organizing the late leader's funeral, a sign to Kremlin watchers that the struggle was over.[11]

Andropov Takes Charge

Andropov made a number of moves intended to differentiate himself from his predecessor. He closed the large "Secretariat of the General Secretary," which had been created under Brezhnev, and dismissed most of Brezhnev's personal aides, retaining only the dryly professional Aleksandrov-Agentov as his foreign-policy adviser. Arriving at his Kremlin office precisely at 9 AM every morning, Andropov brought a new pace to the relaxed work style that had developed under Brezhnev. "All the workers in the Central Committee apparatus as well as the workers in the state and economic organizations quickly sensed that the former flabby approach to governing from now on was over."[12]

Andropov's accession was greeted warmly by most Soviets, who saw his initial activism and candor as a welcome change from the embarrassing decrepitude of Brezhnev's last years. *Washington Post* correspondent Dusko Doder remarked that in the beginning of 1983 Moscow took on a different mood. Beneath the drab winter surface "there was a ferment of anticipated change. Moscow's political life bustled as never before." New decrees appeared almost every week and there was a new style of work.[13]

In his first public remarks as general secretary, Andropov adopted a refreshing new tone by acknowledging that there were problems in the economy and admitting that he had no "ready recipes" for improvements. He took an implicit swipe at his predecessor by pointing out that "you cannot get things moving by slogans alone."[14] Andropov hinted at personnel changes to come by stating that if people in responsible positions did not know how to do their jobs, "Thought should be given to the help that must be accorded such comrades." A week after the speech, the kind of help Andropov had in mind became clear when longtime Minister of Railways Pavlovskiy, whose chronic mismanagement of the ailing Soviet rail system had earned him a rebuke by Brezhnev in 1979, was fired.[15]

Andropov was a man in a hurry. As KGB chief, he was better informed than most Soviet leaders about the problems the country faced and he also understood that for health reasons his time at the helm was likely to be limited. Andropov stayed late in his office every night, meeting a broad range of officials and calling for endless files. "It seems clear now that he was looking for miracle clues and ways to resuscitate the dying system, to reassure the population, breathe new life into the Party and launch the 'final ascent' to Communist heights."[16]

Discipline

In January 1983, less than two months after taking office, Andropov found the remedy he was looking for, convening a meeting of party, government, and trade union leaders to demand more stringent workforce discipline. Soon the new policy took on the trappings of a major campaign aimed at cracking down on laxness across all aspects of society. Police checked the documents of people they found on the street during working hours and launched well-publicized raids on restaurants, movie theaters, and bathhouses where Russians loved to relax, usually with the aid of plentiful supplies of vodka. People who could not explain their presence in these places during working hours often found themselves hauled off to police stations where they might be fined or receive short jail sentences.

Absenteeism, rule-breaking, and pilfering were major problems throughout the Soviet system. But much of this behavior was part of the survival strategy by which Soviet citizens navigated through daily life. In many workplaces, there was a well-practiced system whereby one or two members of the group would be dispatched to wait in line and buy for themselves and other members of the collective treasured "deficit goods" that might suddenly have become available. Everyone understood that waiting until the end of the workday would be futile since the goods in question would almost certainly be long since sold out.

Andropov's stress on discipline was seen by Soviets as violating one part of the state's implicit social contract with its people, sometimes encapsulated by the phrase "the state pretends to pay us and we pretend to work." As the campaign unfolded, the tightening extended to the arts and other fields of cultural and social life. Some began to sense a whiff of return to the Stalin era, when being ten minutes late for work could earn the offender a stint in the Gulag.

In January 1983, Andropov paid an unannounced visit to the vast Ordzhonikidze machine tool factory in the outskirts of Moscow. He walked through the facilities, stressing to the workers that bringing discipline and order to the country would be the chief tasks of the coming months. Standing before a large crowd in the factory's club, Andropov said, "Without the necessary discipline—labor, plan, and state, we cannot move forward." But "the workers listened in silence" as Andropov "talked to them like a foreman about order, discipline, and absenteeism—the all too familiar slogans of Soviet industrial life. They were more interested in wages, housing, local transportation, empty shops, and endless queues."[17]

Eventually popular unhappiness became so strong that Andropov had to end the document checks and police dragnets. He did not, however, abandon other aspects of his discipline campaign, which in some respects represented an effort by the new general secretary to introduce into society rules he had learned to appreciate in fifteen years as KGB chairman. In March 1983, new KGB chief Chebrikov, with Andropov's obvious blessing, proposed to the Politburo a sweeping set of measures to increase the role of the KGB in preventing "state crimes and politically harmful acts."[18] Chebrikov's measures toughened the legal climate around the daily lives of Soviet citizens, including the adoption in January 1984 of a law on "state crimes" that broadened the definition of disclosing state secrets to the point where Soviets faced the possibility of criminal charges for providing even the most innocuous information to foreigners.[19]

Andropov resumed the drive against corrupt officials who had been caught up in the Diamond Affair and other scandals. In November Yury Sokolov, director of the Yeliseyev Gastronome, was arrested and later shot. The director of Gastronome Number 2, located just across the street from the MFA and considered, together with a somewhat less-frequented gastronome located in an alley behind the KGB's Lubyanka Headquarters, as the next best-supplied food store in Moscow, reportedly committed suicide when he learned of Sokolov's arrest. In December 1982, Interior Minister Shchelokov was removed from his post and was reported to have committed suicide rather than face arrest.

The upright and ascetic Andropov also moved against the network of privileges that cocooned the lives of top Soviet leaders. He authorized an investigation into the luxurious state dachas that surrounded Moscow and lined the most exclusive sections of the Black Sea coast, finding that the Brezhnev family alone claimed ownership of eight dachas in the Moscow region. Andropov's moves against privilege came to an end with his death but they might have had more serious consequences had he remained on the scene longer.[20]

Pikhoya describes the country as "freezing up" under the influence of Andropov's discipline campaign.[21] Censorship, whether imposed from the top by the authorities or self-censorship exercised by writers and artists themselves, became the rule in all publications and artistic productions. The gray conformity of the Brezhnev era was replaced by an even grimmer climate of hopelessness about the future.

Andropov and the Economy

Andropov understood the need for change in the Soviet economy, but his brief tenure at the top allowed little time for real reform. In a January 1983 meeting of the Secretariat, Andropov acknowledged that the Soviet economy suffered from 50 billion rubles' worth of unsatisfied consumer demand. Andropov raised the prices on some goods, although he avoided the sensitive issue of price rises on food and other necessities. He also lowered the price of cheap vodka, which came to be called "Andropovka," possibly one reason for his enduring popularity in post-Soviet folk memory.[22]

Andropov's brief time in office was marked by considerable ferment among Soviet economists. The most sensational example to surface publicly was the so-called Novosibirsk Memorandum, written in 1983 by sociologist Tatyana Zaslavskaya. Her report portrayed an economic system that was wasteful, riddled with corruption, and hostile toward innovation. Zaslavskaya pointed out that the Soviet economy had worked well as a vehicle for transforming a peasant society into an industrial behemoth but in the contemporary era the system itself was becoming an obstacle to further development.[23]

In July 1983, Andropov announced the introduction of a new experiment in economic management, aimed at increasing enterprise autonomy and tying income more closely to the quantity and quality of output. Only a few ministries and republics were included in the scheme, which resembled Kosygin's abortive 1965 economic reform, but some believe Andropov intended to expand it to the entire country in the twelfth Five Year Plan, beginning in 1986.[24]

The Soviet economy enjoyed a modest uptick during Andropov's short time in office. In 1983 Soviet national income grew by approximately one percent more than the previous year. Given Andropov's emphasis on tightening discipline, Soviet workers and managers may have found it expedient for a time to work harder and reduce absenteeism. But cooking the books could be another element in Andropov's apparent initial economic success. Soviet economic statisticians often "gifted" incoming general secretaries with a tweak of the data to make the new leader's first year look better. As one leading Western student of the Soviet economy observed, "The Soviet authorities, in economic matters, preferred secrets to lies; but they were not dogmatic about it."[25]

Struggles for Power and the Country's Future Direction

Throughout the interregnum between Brezhnev's death in November 1982 and Gorbachev's accession in March 1985, a behind-the-scenes struggle for power and influence roiled the top ranks of the Soviet leadership. In the last and in some ways most personal of the numerous books Gorbachev wrote about his life, he said that without understanding the intrigues of the era of Andropov and Chernenko it was impossible to understand his own rise to power.[26]

At the December 1987 Washington summit, Raisa Gorbachev, on seeing a photograph of Andropov, remarked, "We owe everything to him." When Andropov was chosen general secretary in 1982, Gorbachev ranked last in the Politburo pecking order and played no role in the choice. But Andropov recognized that Gorbachev was one of the leadership's most able figures and the person best placed to assist him in carrying out his vision of cautious reform. Immediately after he returned from inspecting Brezhnev's body, Andropov pulled Gorbachev out of a meeting, and in the coming days, Gorbachev was "constantly at Andropov's side," a close association that eventually propelled the younger man into the top slot himself.[27]

Across 1983 Andropov, with Gorbachev's assistance, made a number of important personnel moves at the sub-Politburo level. In June Andropov appointed Yegor Ligachev, until then the party chief in the Siberian center of Tomsk, to head the critically important Central Committee department that supervised top-level party personnel decisions. Ligachev, who had a reputation for integrity and discipline that must have endeared him to Andropov, began the process of removing many of the long-serving regional party bosses of the Brezhnev era, which he continued in 1985 after Gorbachev's accession. In August 1983, Vadim Medvedev, later a key Gorbachev aide, replaced the reactionary Sergei Trapeznikov as chief of the Central Committee Department for Science and Academic Institutions.

Chernenko and his Old Guard supporters were not without resources. They managed to delay until mid-1983 Andropov's assumption of the largely ceremonial position of head of the Supreme Soviet and his identification as chair of the Defense Council. In June 1983, the hard-line Leningrad party boss, Grigoriy Romanov, was brought to Moscow to head the Soviet military-industrial complex, an appointment that could not have been to the liking of

Andropov, given Romanov's reputation for self-serving and corrupt behavior. Romanov, roughly the same age as Gorbachev, quickly assumed a visible public role, seemingly intended as a counterpoint to the prominence accorded to Andropov's new protégé.

In July Chernenko took advantage of Andropov's absence from the Politburo to propose a gesture that was sure to resonate with party conservatives: readmission to the party of Stalin's former foreign minister, the ninety-three-year-old Vyacheslav Molotov, and the rehabilitation of other aged Stalin henchmen Georgy Malenkov and Lazar Kaganovich. Chernenko's initiative set off a fascinating discussion in the Politburo. First to speak were the elderly Ustinov and Tikhonov, who strongly supported Chernenko's move and took the occasion to unload on Khrushchev, whose "ugliness" toward Stalin, said Ustinov, had done more harm to the USSR than any acknowledged enemy. Only Gorbachev and KGB chief Chebrikov ventured cautionary notes. Gorbachev supported the rehabilitation of all three old Stalinists but questioned whether it needed to be announced publicly. Chebrikov warned that the action would elicit critical letters from Gulag victims, although he later added that many had been "illegally rehabilitated."[28]

Andropov's Illness

At the beginning of 1983, only a few weeks after he had taken over as general secretary, Andropov's kidneys ceased functioning. A secret facility was set up at the Kremlin hospital where Andropov underwent dialysis twice a week, and the general secretary soldiered on with his regular work schedule. In September Andropov departed for vacation in the Crimea, where another special hospital facility had been set up at the so-called First Dacha. At the end of September, after a long walk in the lovely grounds of the estate, Andropov's condition took a dramatic turn for the worse. He entered the special Kremlin hospital in Moscow, never to leave.[29]

Andropov's body was failing, but his mind remained clear, and he continued, in a fashion that is both pathetic and moving, to try to rule the country from his hospital bed. Aides would read him papers for decision and Andropov would signify his assent or disapproval by nodding his head or sometimes by blinking his eyes. As Volkogonov wrote, "It is impossible not to give him credit for his courage. Critically ill, he was still trying to summon up a fresh breeze, to move the ship from its deathly calm."[30]

In the waning days of his life Andropov, like Lenin before him, apparently attempted to anoint his successor, but his wishes were successfully, although temporarily, subverted. Arkadiy Volskiy, an aide who regularly saw Andropov in the hospital, said that Andropov prepared a long message for the December 1983 Central Committee Plenum. Andropov acknowledged that he was unlikely to be able to resume leading the party and asked that the Central Committee entrust Gorbachev with the direction of the Politburo. Volskiy gave Andropov's message to those responsible for preparing the session but to his surprise, when the general secretary's "Testament" was presented to the plenum, its recommendation on Gorbachev had been deleted—at Chernenko's initiative, Volskiy assumed.[31]

Andropov's Death and Chernenko's Accession

Andropov finally slipped away from this world on February 9, after being in a coma for at least two days. Following what was by now a familiar routine, news of his death was not released for almost twenty-four hours, while the leadership decided on his successor. Midmorning the next day, February 10, Soviet broadcast media switched from regular programming to classical music and later that afternoon the Soviet public was informed about the death.

The choice of Chernenko is often cast as a battle between him as the candidate of the Brezhnevite old guard and Gorbachev as the representative of the younger generation. After it was over, however, Ustinov told Chazov that he had proposed Chernenko as general secretary to head off a bid by Gromyko, whom Ustinov believed would have been supported by Prime Minister Tikhonov. Ustinov was visibly downcast at this turn of events. Gorbachev had carefully cultivated the powerful minister of defense who, in turn, seems to have grown to respect his able younger colleague. In an earlier meeting, Ustinov had told Chazov that Andropov wanted Gorbachev to succeed him as general secretary and that Ustinov agreed with this. "We need a young, clever leader, who knows the Party . . . and who would continue the work begun by Andropov." Now he told Chazov, "There was no choice." Speaking of Gromyko, Ustinov said, "You understand that to put him in that position could not be allowed. You know his character."[32]

The new general secretary was already terminally ill with emphysema. Most of his thirteen months in office were spent at his dacha where he was kept alive through oxygen and heavy doses of medication. His rule passed almost unnoticed except for the embarrassment evoked by his few halting appearances in public.

During his first administration, President Reagan was often criticized for not meeting with his Soviet counterparts, a charge he deflected by pointing out "they kept dying on me." This type of perfidious behavior by Kremlin leaders confirmed some hard-line Reaganites in their belief that the Soviets would stop at nothing to frustrate their hero but, more seriously, it also symbolized an important shift in the underlying dynamics of the US-Soviet relationship as the Cold War entered its final decade. If throughout the 1970s many international trends seemed to favor Moscow, during the first half of the 1980s the transitions through four general secretaries in three years, all but the final one aging and ailing, served as a metaphor for the increasingly evident Soviet decline. On the other side, by contrast, the advent of a new US president highlighted the enduring strength and growing confidence of the Western democracies.

Election

Ronald Reagan began running for president almost as soon as he left the governor's mansion in California in 1975. By March 1976, however, his campaign for the Republican nomination had run out of money, and many expected him to concede. But when Reagan shifted the focus from domestic to foreign issues, his campaign took off. Reagan won primary after primary amid attacks on the supposedly one-sided policy of détente pursued by President Ford and Secretary of State Kissinger. Reagan and Ford went neck and neck into the Republican convention in the summer of 1976, but the president controlled the party's machinery and he emerged as the candidate.[1]

The 1980 election occurred during one of America's periodic bouts of "declinism," and Reagan's confident assertion of America's continued greatness struck a chord among many voters troubled by what seemed to be a string of foreign policy setbacks and who took little comfort in Carter's seemingly pessimistic vision of the future. "I find no national malaise. I find nothing wrong with the American people," Reagan proclaimed in his election eve speech.[2]

Reagan won 489 electoral votes representing forty-four states, handing Carter the most lopsided defeat suffered by any incumbent president. He captured a majority of independents and ran surprisingly strong among union and Democratic voters. Reagan had long coattails, with the Republicans taking control of the Senate for the first time in twenty-six years and cutting heavily into the Democratic majority in the House. It was the most sweeping mandate for change the United States had seen in decades.[3]

Who Was Ronald Reagan?

Few recent presidents have elicited such contrasting evaluations as Ronald Reagan. To his detractors, he is a cowboy, with a simplistic view of the world and a reflexive anticommunism that threatened to provoke nuclear holocaust. His supporters see Reagan as an inspirational figure who single-handedly saw off Communism and ended the Cold War with a US victory.

None of the senior officials who worked most closely with President Reagan shared the simplistic image of him that is widespread among the president's detractors. Typical is Colin Powell, who served as national security adviser at the end of the Reagan administration: "Reagan was a more complex man than the one-dimensional figure his critics tried to paint. He was confident and comfortable in his own skin, more than anyone I have ever known."[4] At a NATO summit in March 1988, Powell found that the talking points the president had received from the bureaucracy had been overtaken by presentations of other speakers. Powell told his boss that he would have to "wing it" and Reagan spoke without notes about what the United States was seeking to achieve with the USSR in a way that showed his complete grasp of the historic changes taking place and that "obviously moved the other heads of state."

With eight years as the chief executive of the nation's most populous state, followed by another eight years as president of the world's most powerful nation, Ronald Reagan accumulated sixteen years of reasonably successful experience in leading large, complex, and highly charged political entities. It is hard, therefore, to take seriously the image spread by his detractors that he was out of his depth in dealing with difficult issues and manipulated by his aides on matters of substance. On the other hand, even in the area where Reagan demonstrated his greatest success—foreign affairs—his record as manager is definitely mixed. Reagan's administration was probably more deeply divided on matters of policy and personality than any postwar US administration. Decision mechanisms in the field of national security proved so dysfunctional that senior officials interested in moving forward had to simply bypass them if they wanted to achieve anything at all.

The words of the man himself provide some of the best tools for understanding the reality of Ronald Reagan. After stepping down in 1975 as governor of California, Reagan began a series of nationally syndicated weekly radio programs. The drafts of these short broadcasts, written by Reagan in longhand on yellow legal pads as he crisscrossed the nation in pursuit of the Republican nomination, were published after his death, and they show him summoning up data, citing historical precedents, and drawing on the arguments of a range of sympathetic scholars. The five-minute format was not a vehicle for deep analysis, not something Reagan ever paid much attention to in any case, but the broadcasts illustrate the core elements of Reagan's worldview, which to a large extent he put into practice once he entered the White House.[5]

Another source of insight into Ronald Reagan is the diary he kept throughout his presidency. Reagan's diary entries are not long; nor do they reveal much evidence of profound thinking about the great issues of the day. But they show the president grappling seriously with the full range of problems that came across his desk. The diaries also reveal that what really grabbed Ronald Reagan, in US-Soviet relations as in all other matters, were things that affected people. After meeting Avital Shcharanskiy, a beautiful and powerful advocate who touched many American officials over the years of her husband's confinement, Reagan exploded, "D—n those inhuman monsters. . . . I promised I'd do everything I could to obtain his release & I will."[6] But Reagan was not inclined to follow Carter's example by making a public show of his concern for human rights. After meeting Sakharov's US relatives and publicly signing a petition on his behalf, Reagan told his diary that he was "kind of sorry." Quiet diplomacy was better in Reagan's view because "this kind of public demand puts the Soviet politics in a corner where they lose face if they give in."[7]

The New Administration

Reagan's first secretary of state, Al Haig, was replaced in 1982 by George Shultz, who remained until the end. Shultz, who compiled distinguished careers in government, business, and academia, was one of the greatest secretaries of state of the Cold War era. He had an enormous capacity for work, absorbed large amounts of information while quickly getting to the heart of any issue, and was a shrewd judge of people. He was not one of Reagan's longtime, inside advisers and it took him some time to develop a relationship with the president, but once he did it was effective. Shultz was frustrated and occasionally angered by Reagan's proclivity to listen sympathetically to the views of his conservative friends and even more so by the president's unwillingness to end the bickering over foreign policy that afflicted the Reagan administration almost until the end. Shultz respected and made good use of the Soviet specialists at State but he grew increasingly skeptical about the intelligence community, which he saw as lagging behind the pace of change in the USSR.

For secretary of defense, Reagan chose an old colleague and friend, Caspar Weinberger, who had been Reagan's director of finance in California. Weinberger wanted to be secretary of state, but Reagan slotted him for defense because Weinberger was deeply committed to Reagan's plan to rebuild US military strength.

Reagan chose the flamboyant and devious William Casey to head the CIA. In his campaign, Reagan had promised to "unleash" the CIA and Casey brought a major infusion of funding and confidence, which helped raise the agency's morale and operational effectiveness after the bruising investigations of the 1970s. Casey found working with the CIA bureaucracy frustrating and preferred to operate outside of regular channels. He was fascinated by the covert-action side of the intelligence business. Robert Gates, who served as Casey's deputy, wrote that Casey came to the CIA in order to "wage war" against the USSR.[8]

Reagan promised that he would limit the role of the National Security Council chief, a pledge the president kept to the detriment of his administration's national security functionality. Reagan's first NSC adviser, Richard Allen, was largely shut out of the policy process. His successor, William Clark, was one of Reagan's closest associates, but he lacked the intellectual depth and foreign policy experience to take charge of the NSC portfolio and was unable to rein in the increasingly bitter disputes between Shultz and Weinberger. The next two NSC advisers, Robert F. "Bud" MacFarlane and Rear Admiral John Poindexter, were experienced in the ways of the Washington bureaucracy, and MacFarlane at least demonstrated a capacity for sound judgment, but they tended to bypass rather than coordinate the administration's acrimonious national security process, a tactic that ultimately had disastrous consequences in the Iran-Contra affair. Not until 1986, when Frank Carlucci took over the NSC position with Powell as his deputy, did Reagan get an NSC team capable of providing effective coordination and sound policy advice.[9]

Reagan's Tough Public Approach toward the USSR

A new rhetorical tone was evident from the first days of the Reagan administration. At his first press conference, Reagan asserted that "so far détente's been a one-way street." In pursuit of their goal of world revolution, Reagan charged that Soviet leaders "reserve unto themselves the right to commit any crime, to lie, to cheat, in order to attain that."[10]

Reagan's response was widely criticized by the punditocracy but it had the virtue of truth, as even a cursory review of Soviet history reveals. But Reagan's views on the Soviet Union were grounded on more than a well-justified skepticism about Soviet motives. He was also convinced that the USSR suffered from inherent internal weaknesses and was confident that democracy's enduring strength would allow it to prevail in its long, twentieth-century contest with totalitarianism. These themes came together in Reagan's address to the British parliament in June 1982, which deserves to go down as one of the greatest delivered by any Cold War president. Updating Winston Churchill's 1946 "Iron Curtain" speech, Reagan intoned, "From Stettin on the Baltic to Varna on the Black Sea, the regimes planted by totalitarianism have had more than 30 years to establish their legitimacy. But none—not one regime—has yet been able to risk free elections." He provided a cogent analysis of the difficulties facing the contemporary USSR, concluding "In an ironic sense Karl Marx was right. We are witnessing today a great revolutionary crisis. . . . But the crisis is happening not in the free, non-Marxist West but in the home of Marxism-Leninism, the Soviet Union. It is the Soviet Union that runs against the tide of history by denying human freedom and human dignity to its citizens."[11]

In March 1983, the president traveled to Florida to speak to a meeting of the National Association of Evangelicals. Seeking to persuade the audience not to endorse the nuclear freeze movement then sweeping the country, Reagan urged the evangelicals to refrain from ignoring the "facts of history and the aggressive impulses of an evil empire."

The media seized upon the phrase as an example of Reagan's supposedly simplistic view of the USSR. But if the Soviet Union—a country whose rulers were responsible for the deaths of millions of their own citizens and uncounted more abroad—was not an evil empire, then the words had no meaning. Reagan's characterization of the USSR as "the focus of evil" was more questionable. No country has a monopoly on evil. Yet even here many commentators ignored the fact that in his speech the president had recognized that the United States had "a legacy of evil with which it must deal" and urged his listeners to fight "hate groups preaching bigotry and prejudice."[12]

Criticism of Reagan's rhetoric was often driven by partisan politics and a kind of smug intellectual laziness that refused to look at the facts of Soviet behavior. It is, however, legitimate to ask whether a leader should adopt such a tone, however truthful or cathartic it might be, at the same time he is also trying to improve relations with the target of his rhetoric. Unknown to almost everyone, less than a month before Reagan made his "evil empire" speech he had invited Dobrynin to a private meeting at the White House, where he emphasized his desire to begin a dialogue between the two countries. According to the ambassador, the Soviet leadership saw Reagan's behavior as "deliberate duplicity," although he also admits that the "thin-skinned" Soviet leadership was "forgetting that they also engaged in the same kind of propaganda against the United States from time to time. He was giving them a dose of their own medicine."[13]

NSDD-75

When distinguished professor of Russian history Richard Pipes left Harvard in 1981 to become the chief Soviet expert at the NSC, he found that the president "knew what he wanted but could not articulate his feelings in terms that made sense to foreign policy professionals." Pipes decided to take "it upon myself to do so on his behalf."[14] The result was NSDD-75, a blueprint for dealing with Moscow that has become exhibit A for those who claim that Reagan executed a carefully conceived plan to overturn the USSR.

Blandly titled "US Relations with the USSR," NSDD-75 was signed by the president in January 1983, after a bruising internal battle. It sets out three basic tasks for US policy toward the USSR: (1) To contain and reverse Soviet expansionism, (2) to promote pluralistic change in the USSR, and (3) to engage in negotiations that enhance US interests. The nine-page document reflects the tendency to give something to both sides in a bureaucratic battle, with the hard-line stances preferred by the NSC and DoD balanced by cautious modifiers inserted by State. In the end, however, it concluded that "the U.S. must demonstrate credibly that its policy is not a blueprint for an open-ended, sterile confrontation with Moscow, but a serious search for a stable and constructive long-term basis for U.S.-Soviet relations."[15]

In diplomacy, as in war, plans seldom survive the first engagement with the other side. NSDD-75 reflected an internal correlation of forces in the early years of the deeply conflicted Reagan administration. Once US-Soviet dialogue got under way, the attitudes that underlay NSDD-75 and the bureaucratic players that drove it became weaker. In large part this was because one important player, Ronald Reagan himself, was strongly committed to dialogue with Moscow, something hard-liners in the administration did not understand. By the time I took over as the chief of the US-Soviet Bilateral Relations office (Bilat) in 1985, NSDD-75 was a dead letter, and many of the people who crafted it were no longer in the administration. Veterans recalled with a shudder the bureaucratic battles around NSDD-75, but the United States had moved on in its relationship with the USSR.

Economic Warfare

In the early 1980s, French intelligence obtained access to a KGB official, code-named Farewell, who provided massive amounts of data about Soviet theft of Western technology. Using information obtained from Farewell, US agencies worked with cooperating businesses to send doctored information and goods back to the USSR. In the most spectacular operation, doctored software alleg-edly led to an explosion at a Siberian pipeline so massive it was initially thought a possible nuclear blast.[16]

Officials behind the program claimed there were no casualties in the blast. Nevertheless, sabotage activities of this nature, capable of causing significant material damage and loss of life, seem to go well beyond anything that Soviet intelligence carried out in the United States. They could easily be considered an act of war, not perhaps the most sensible move to undertake against a powerful and unscrupulous nuclear-armed adversary without a clear evaluation of the risks and benefits involved.

The Farewell campaign is unlikely to have had more than a marginal impact, but another move in the Reagan administration's campaign of economic mea-sures against the USSR may have had a much more damaging effect. Beginning in May 1982, CIA director Casey made several secret trips to Saudi Arabia. High on Casey's agenda was an effort to persuade the Saudis to drive down the world price of oil and thereby deal a body blow to the Soviet economy.[17]

In the early 1980s, Saudi Arabia performed the role of "swing producer," adjusting its oil production to support the predetermined OPEC price. By 1985 the cost to Riyadh of this role was growing as global oil consumption dropped and other OPEC members covertly produced more oil than their quotas al-lowed. In September the Saudis announced what became a threefold rise in production. Global oil prices plunged and remained low throughout the 1980s.

It remains uncertain what role US entreaties aimed at damaging the USSR played in the Saudi decision. Secretary of Defense Weinberger, as committed as Casey to undermining the USSR, described the move as "an internal Saudi de-cision" but one "they knew would sit very well with the United States."[18] What is certain is the catastrophic effect the decline in oil prices had on the Soviet economy. By the 1970s, exports of petroleum products had become the USSR's leading source of hard currency. In the year after the drop in prices, the Soviet trade balance fell into a substantial deficit from which it never emerged.[19]

The Mini-Thaw of 1983

On February 12, Washington was assaulted by a blizzard that dumped almost two feet of snow. With the city paralyzed, the president invited Shultz and his wife Obie for dinner in the White House family dining room. During a long and relaxed evening, Shultz found that Reagan was eager to move forward in relations with the USSR. Noting that he was planning to meet Dobrynin in a few days, the secretary suggested that he bring the Soviet ambassador over to see Reagan, and the president immediately agreed. Reagan said the meeting should be kept secret and in his diary he wrote that Shultz "sneaked" Dobrynin into the White House.[20]

When Dobrynin arrived at the State Department for what he expected to be a routine meeting with Shultz, he found himself bundled into the secretary's limousine and driven in secrecy to the White House for an extended discussion with President Reagan. It was the first time the usually well connected Soviet ambassador had a private meeting with the president and also apparently the first time Reagan ever had an extended conversation with a senior Soviet functionary. The president told Dobrynin that "if Andropov is willing to do business, so am I." He made a special appeal on behalf of the Pentecostal family that had taken refuge in the Moscow embassy in 1978, urging that "kindness to these people would make it easier for us to do something for his government and we'd never mention it as an exchange or concession."[21] Dobrynin astutely recognized this was for Reagan a "personal test of the Soviet government's goodwill."[22]

Despite feelings in the Soviet leadership that it was "distinctly odd, even suspicious" that this was the one concrete issue the president had raised, Moscow responded.[23] Shortly after the meeting, one of the Pentecostals, who had left the embassy in 1982 because of illness, was told by local authorities in her hometown to apply for an exit visa. In April, after she had arrived safely in the West, the other Pentecostals left the embassy. By July all were out of the USSR, completing what Shultz called "the first successful negotiation with the Soviets in the Reagan administration."[24]

Gradually, the hard-line White House phalanx began to fall away. Clark, always uncomfortable at the NSC, escaped to become Secretary of the Interior, replaced by the pragmatic MacFarlane. Jack Matlock, the most outstanding State Department Soviet specialist of his generation, took over as Reagan's chief Soviet adviser. MacFarlane explained the situation to Matlock by saying that the president, "satisfied that he had restored enough momentum to our defense programs to deal with the Soviets effectively," had decided that it was now "time to pursue negotiations aggressively."[25]

Over the spring and summer, the dialogue proceeded with cautious steps by both sides. In April Reagan announced his willingness to negotiate a long-term grain agreement, suspended after the 1981 imposition of martial law in Poland. By the end of the summer, US and Soviet diplomats had agreed to open new consulates in Kiev and New York and to revive US-Soviet cultural exchange agreements.[26] This briefly promising interlude, unknown to most outside the bureaucracy, came to a crashing halt thanks largely to a tragedy that occurred over Sakhalin Island, in the remote Soviet Far East.

Tragedy over Sakhalin

The morning of September 1, 1983, I opened the locked leather pouch containing top secret, "code-word" intelligence material that was delivered every morning to the office of the chairman of the US START delegation, Ed Rowny. On top of the pile was an unusual document: the intercepted transcript of radio conversations between Soviet air defense ground controllers and fighter pilot Gennadi Osipovich, as only hours previously he had shot down an unarmed civilian airliner. All 269 passengers and crew died on Korean Air Lines flight 007 after Osipovich fired two missiles into their Boeing 747, on a flight from Anchorage to Seoul.

What Happened

For years after the shoot-down, arguments raged about how the aircraft managed to wander so far off course while being flown by a crew that had made the same flight many times before. A 1993 report by the International Civil Aviation Organization (ICAO), using information from the flight recorders that Yeltsin handed over after they had been concealed for years by the Soviets, showed conclusively that crew errors caused the deviation. In the dry words of the ICAO report, "The crew inadvertently flew virtually the entire flight on a constant magnetic heading . . . and the resulting track deviation was due to the KE 007 crew's failure to note that the autopilot had either been left in a heading mode or been switched to INS when the aircraft was beyond the range (7.5 km.) for the INS to capture the desired track."[27]

When KAL 007 first entered Soviet airspace over Kamchatka, Soviet air defense forces in that region categorized it as a US RC-135, an intelligence aircraft built on a Boeing 707 airframe. But the transcripts of conversations among Soviet air defense personnel never reveal any moment when the Soviets conclusively identified the aircraft. One Soviet officer worried "that the unidentified intruder might be a passenger aircraft."[28]

Earlier that evening, a US RC-135 had been flying a routine mission known as Cobra Ball, whose purpose was to monitor Soviet missile tests. The Cobra Ball flight that night orbited over the ocean well away from Soviet airspace, waiting for a test that never occurred. Soviet radars routinely monitored Cobra Ball flights and this is likely the reason why Soviet air defense in Kamchatka initially categorized KAL 007 as a RC-135. Cobra Ball and KAL-007 never got closer than 150 kilometers to one another and by the time the Soviets shot down the civilian aircraft Cobra Ball was taxiing toward its hanger on Shemya Island in the Aleutians.

As KAL 007 neared Sakhalin, Major Osipovich approached it from behind. He was ordered to "interrogate" the intruder with a Soviet "friend or foe" signal, to which the Korean aircraft gave no reply, not surprising since it could not pick up that frequency. The Soviets made no effort to contact the intruding craft on the international distress frequency, which is standard procedure around the world. After Osipovich reported the intruder was displaying navigation lights and a flashing beacon—not exactly standard practice for intelligence penetration flights—the senior Soviet commander ordered Osipovich to flash his lights and force the intruder to land at a nearby Soviet airbase, which is normal procedure and also happened to be what was required by Soviet law. A few seconds later, he ordered Osipovich to reinforce the point by firing a warning burst from the cannons on his SU-15. Osipovich fired several hundred rounds but, as he expected, these had no effect, since his aircraft was loaded with armor-piercing ammunition that did not include the bright tracer rounds that might have been visible to the Korean crew.

At about the time Osipovich fired, KAL 007 made a shallow turn, which its cockpit recorders later showed was a routine course shift but which convinced Soviet ground controllers that it was trying to escape. Osipovich received the order, "Destroy the target," although as the ICAO report states, "apparently some doubt remained about its identity."[29] One missile hit the rear of the fuselage and the stricken plane spiraled downward. In a few seconds its lights disappeared. "The target is destroyed," Osipovich reported and headed home to a hero's welcome.

After the shoot-down, Osipovich gave varying accounts of what he actually saw that night. In 1991 he told *Izvestiya*, "I had no idea it was a passenger aircraft." He also said he could not identify the type of the plane since, "Soviet pilots did not study foreign civilian aircraft." Four years later, he said in an interview with the *New York Times,* "I saw two rows of windows and knew that this was a Boeing. I knew this was a civilian plane."[30]

Cover-up in Moscow

As news spread across the world that the USSR had shot down an unarmed civilian airliner, the Soviet leadership dug itself into a position of angry denial. When Korniyenko found Gromyko working on a stonewalling press statement, he remonstrated that it would be impossible to hide the truth in the era of radar and other electronic devices. Gromyko told him to telephone General Secretary Andropov, whom Korniyenko found inclined to act "honorably" but also firmly convinced that the incident was the result of "Reagan's machinations." Andropov telephoned minister of defense Ustinov while Korniyenko waited on the other line, where he heard, along with angry imprecations toward himself, assurances from Ustinov that "everything will be OK; no one, nowhere, no how will be able to prove anything."[31]

The next day, the Politburo met to review the incident. Gromyko reported that the downed plane had been a civilian airliner and that transcripts were available in the West showing the conversations of the Soviet pilot with ground control during the shoot-down. He warned that Reagan's "rude anti-Soviet statements" were rallying the international community against the USSR and concluded that Moscow needed to prove it had acted legally and, possibly a hint of sarcasm, to show that the shoot-down had actually been a piece of "brilliant work."[32]

Gromyko's remarks were too much for Ustinov, who asserted that the USSR had acted correctly in downing the craft and made a number of false assertions to his Politburo colleagues, including the claim that KAL had penetrated 500 kilometers into Soviet territory and that the plane had flown without warning lights. KGB chief Chebrikov reported that the aircraft had actually been downed over international waters, that KGB data did not show the Korean aircraft had had any contact with US aircraft, and that in general it had flown "as if it were blind." Despite urgings by Gromyko and Korniyenko that the USSR at least admit that the shoot-down occurred, Chernenko concluded with a statement approving the shoot-down and authorizing continuation of the cover-up.[33]

Not until September 6, almost a week after the intrusion, did the Soviets finally acknowledge that Soviet fighters had fulfilled an order "to stop the flight" after concluding that it was "a reconnaissance plane performing special missions." The Kremlin repeated earlier lies that the downed aircraft was "flying without aerial navigation lights," that the Soviet pilot had fired tracer warning rounds, and that the "intruder" had tried to escape. There was no indication of regret for the deaths of 269 victims.[34]

Anger in Washington

Late in the morning of September 1, with Moscow still silent, Shultz held a televised press conference. Speaking with "controlled fury," Shultz said, "We can see no excuse whatsoever for this appalling act."[35] President Reagan rewrote almost all of the draft speech on the incident to "give my unvarnished opinion of the barbarous act." Despite his anger, Reagan was cautious in his policy response, telling NSC chief Clark, "Let's be careful not to overreact to this. We have too much going on with the Soviets on arms control. We must not derail our program."[36]

In Madrid a meeting between Shultz and Gromyko turned "brutally confrontational." Korniyenko later wrote that there was one moment when "both of them jumped up and it seemed would grab each other by the shoulders."[37] Tom Simons, then chief of the State Department Soviet desk, recalled two "red-faced and angry old men" stalking out of the meeting.[38]

Andropov, like Reagan, initially seemed reluctant to allow the KAL controversy to derail US-Soviet relations. He summoned Dobrynin from vacation in the Crimea and told him to return immediately to Washington "to dampen this needless conflict." Although he left Dobrynin with the impression that he sincerely believed the incident had been a US intelligence probe, the general secretary also told Dobrynin that the Soviet military "made a gross blunder by shooting down the airliner."[39] Whatever sentiments Andropov may have been willing to express about the incident in private, a harsh statement issued in his name on September 28 basically took the position that it was impossible to work with the Reagan administration and pushed relations toward the deep freeze that followed the Soviet walkout from Geneva arms control negotiations at the end of the year.

Soviets Find the Black Boxes

Unknown to the West, about a month after the shoot-down the Soviets found the wreckage of the KAL craft and recovered its black boxes from the ocean floor. In December 1983, Ustinov and Chebrikov sent Andropov a memo reporting what Soviet technicians found when they analyzed data from the black boxes. The Soviet military and intelligence chiefs acknowledged that they "did not succeed in obtaining outright proof that the flight was on an intelligence mission." This unfortunate lapse did not, however, stop them from concluding that KAL "deliberately intruded into Soviet airspace" as part of a "major dual-purpose political provocation carefully organized by the US special services."[40]

Buried in annexes to the memo sent to Andropov were conclusions by Soviet technical experts that the KAL crew were completely unaware of being off course, had no inkling of the presence in their vicinity of Major Osipovich's aircraft, and did not see the warning rounds he fired. Soviet technicians also pointed out with a certain delicacy that the black box data could be used to argue that there were, in fact, crew errors in using the aircraft's navigational equipment and that the flight had actually been shot down outside of Soviet airspace. Not surprisingly, Ustinov and Chebrikov said it would be "inadvisable" to hand over the black boxes to ICAO.[41]

Yeltsin Ends the Deception

In October 1992, nine years after the shoot-down and a millennium later in terms of political change, Boris Yeltsin finally ended the deception. In a Kremlin ceremony before representatives of the families of the victims, he called the incident "a Cold War catastrophe" and expressed "regret that we are not capable of undoing the wrong."[42] Yeltsin handed over the black boxes, wrapped in heavy orange containers, and released transcripts from the Korean airliner's cockpit recorder as well as numerous other documents recovered from Soviet archives. All of the information was given to ICAO, which used it as the basis for its report issued the following year, which closed the file on KAL 007.

I represented the US embassy at the ceremony, one of the most moving of my foreign service career. Yeltsin's courageous decision to release all of the documents despite the damning picture they painted and the simple dignity he displayed in embracing family members of the victims was a sign of the determination of the leaders of the new Russia to put the Kremlin's dark Communist past behind them. Afterward, Russian officials who had been senior figures at the time of the shoot-down embraced me, saying how relieved they were to be able to stop living a lie.

The War Scare That Wasn't: Operation RYAN

In May 1981, senior Soviet intelligence officials gathered at the new KGB headquarters at Yasenovo, in the suburbs of Moscow. After Brezhnev opened the session with a routine denunciation of the Reagan administration, Andropov brought the intelligence barons to astonished attention. "The new American administration," he declared, "was actively preparing for nuclear war. There was now the possibility of a nuclear first strike by the United States."[43] The

Politburo had decided that Soviet intelligence's top priority was to collect information on the threat of US nuclear attack, in a global operation given the code name RYAN (Raketno Yadernoye Napadenie [Nuclear Missile Attack]).

Shortly thereafter, instructions were sent to KGB residencies abroad. "Not since the end of World War II has the international situation been as explosive as it is now," the center intoned. KGB personnel were instructed to "organize a continual watch" for political, military, and intelligence signals of a US decision to use nuclear weapons against the USSR. In carrying out this new mission KGB officers were told to monitor the difference between normal activity and crisis situations in government institutions—including such things as "the number of lighted windows." They were also charged with identifying people associated with "preparing and implementing RYAN," monitoring routes used regularly by leading military and political figures, identifying evacuation routes and organizing a watch on civil defense installations, and monitoring the "increased purchase of blood from donors."[44]

Few Soviet intelligence personnel took seriously the notion that the United States was actively preparing to launch a nuclear strike against the USSR. Arriving in mid-1982 to assume his new position as the number two at the KGB's London residency, Oleg Gordiyevsky, who had been recruited as an agent by the British several years earlier, found that most of his colleagues viewed RYAN with skepticism. In Washington, Ambassador Dobrynin learned about RYAN from the KGB chief in his embassy, who like Dobrynin was dubious about the threat but who nevertheless sent back to Moscow what information he could obtain, mostly "rumors and guesses," according to Dobrynin. The chief of the East German service, the formidable Markus Wolff, found the exercise "a burdensome waste of time" but he formed a separate staff, which had to undergo special military training, to uncover plans for a surprise nuclear assault.[45]

Over the next several years, Soviet intelligence agents wasted countless hours in such activities as counting lighted windows as they cruised past the Pentagon and State Department and their equivalents in other Western capitals. The East Germans built a round-the-clock situation room with a special communications link to Moscow to monitor political and military indicators of an impending NATO attack. "RYAN created a vicious circle of intelligence collection and assessment. Residencies were, in effect, required to report alarming information even if they themselves were skeptical of it. The Centre was duly alarmed by what they reported and demanded more."[46]

The center's paranoia was not limited to uncovering nonexistent moves toward a Western nuclear strike. In 1983, at the height of RYAN, Andropov ordered the KGB's Department 8 to make preparations for attacks on US, British, and NATO targets in Europe. Plans were made for letter bombs to be sent to British prime minister Thatcher's office and to other prominent US and NATO representatives. At about this time, the KGB also established a series of dead drops in bars and restaurants near US bases in Germany, intended to conceal explosives that would be used to give the impression of a terrorist campaign against US forces.[47]

Able Archer

In November 1983, NATO held its annual Able Archer command-post exercise to practice procedures for the use of nuclear weapons in Europe. The Soviets had for years watched Able Archer, which involved no troop movements. Lt. General Gelii Bateinin, first deputy chief of staff at the time, said that thanks to sources within NATO and the high quality of its signals intelligence the Soviet military was confident that it would discover any moves by NATO to use nuclear weapons: "We would detect mating warheads to missiles, uploading nuclear bombs and artillery. We listened to the hourly circuit verifying signal on your nuclear release command system and we believe we would recognize a release order."[48]

Despite the abundance of information the Soviets had available on the real nature of Able Archer, they reacted to the 1983 exercise somewhat differently than in the past. On the day that Able Archer began, a senior British intelligence official wrote later, it "seems certain that Soviet Chief of Staff Ogarkov moved for a time to his wartime bunker deep beneath Moscow. At the height of the exercise, a flash telegram went out to all KGB stations in the West, reporting, incorrectly, that US bases had gone on alert and holding out the possibility that this step might be the beginning of preparations for a nuclear strike."[49]

In May 1984, largely as a result of the concern among senior US officials about the information Gordiyevsky was providing, the CIA undertook a special study to look at the possibility that the Soviets genuinely feared the outbreak of war. Analysts found signs that Soviet air units in Poland and East Germany had been placed on a higher alert status, but the only concrete indications of actual military movements involved about a dozen Soviet fighter aircraft. US intelligence concluded that although the Soviet reaction to Able Archer was somewhat greater than usual, "by confining heightened readiness to selected air units Moscow clearly revealed that it did not think that there was at this time a heightened possibility of a NATO attack."[50]

Some accounts of the supposed "war scare" of 1983 have asserted that aggressive NATO naval exercises in the maritime approaches to the USSR and an

increase in the number of air probes close to Soviet borders helped stoke Soviet anxieties about an impending US attack.[51] In fact, while US air and naval
probes doubtlessly provoked anger in the Soviet military, they did not lead
senior officials in Moscow to conclude that conflict was imminent. The Soviet
military was familiar with US probes, which did not begin—or end—with
the Reagan administration. Although they certainly did not like these actions
and understood that, in addition to their testosterone-driven posturing, they
were intended to practice for nuclear conflict, they also understood the difference between exercises and war.

Moscow, moreover, had a special reason for confidence unknown to the US
at the time. Thanks to John Walker's long spying career, the Soviets possessed
detailed knowledge about the operations of US naval forces, including nuclear
missile submarines. Boris Solomatin, who was KGB resident when Walker was
recruited in 1967, boasted, "For more than 17 years, Walker enabled your enemies to read your most sensitive military secrets. We knew everything!"[52]

In Moscow: Tension but No War Scare

There is no doubt that in the early 1980s escalating rhetoric on both sides of the
ocean led to mounting concern in the Soviet capital. When Pavel Palazhenko,
later Gorbachev's interpreter and adviser, returned to Moscow in December
1983 after the Soviets had walked out of the Geneva arms talks, he found that
the massive propaganda campaign against the deployment of US missiles in
Europe "had created an almost pre-war atmosphere."[53]

Senior national security officials reflected the mood of tension. In September 1982, Ogarkov told Warsaw Pact general staffs that the United States had
"in effect already declared war on us."[54] Bateinin said, "There was a great deal of
tension in the General Staff at that time. . . . I don't recall a period more tense
since the Caribbean crisis in 1962." Vitaliy Katayev, a longtime senior official
in the Central Committee Defense Department, recalled that the early 1980s
were "considered a pre-crisis period, a pre-war-time period. We organized
night shifts so there was always someone on duty."[55]

Nevertheless, most senior Soviet military and civilian officials dismiss the
notion that the actual outbreak of war was considered imminent. Marshal Sergei Akromeyev, deputy chief of staff in 1983, told a US military interviewer that
Gordiyevsky's allegations were "self-serving fabrications." Akromeyev pointed
out that "Gordiyevsky did not know what the General Staff was doing. . . . War
was not considered imminent." Colonel General Andrian Danilovich, a senior
general staff officer and the author of Soviet strategic war plans, agreed that the

1980s were a "period of great tension" but there was never a "war scare" in the general staff, because "no one believed there was a real likelihood of a nuclear strike from the US or NATO."[56]

Civilian officials also dismissed the notion that war was imminent. Gorbachev's foreign affairs aide, Anatoliy Chernyayev, who in 1983 was the deputy head of the Central Committee International Department said, "In the highest levels of the Soviet government there really was no serious fear that this situation might provoke a nuclear conflict or a large-scale international conflict."[57] KGB professionals held similar views. Viktor Cherkashin, a senior KGB officer who recruited some of the most damaging agents Soviet intelligence ever developed, said fears ran high during Able Archer. But, "despite the tensions, reports that Washington and Moscow came close to nuclear war are exaggerated."[58] It is hard to quarrel with Matlock's assessment that "there was no evidence then, and none has emerged subsequently, to suggest that the United States and the Soviet Union were at any time in the 1980s close to war."[59]

CHAPTER 10

Eagle vs. Bear
US and Soviet Approaches to Strategic Arms Control

Negotiating from Strength

The first step in the Reagan administration's strategy toward the USSR was to rebuild US military forces. Reagan's program included major upgrades for all elements of the US nuclear triad. The B-1 bomber, canceled by Carter, was built in an updated version; development of the new Stealth bomber was accelerated, and thousands of ALCMs would be deployed on existing B-52s. Construction of the new Trident submarine was speeded, which for the first time would have the yield and accuracy to attack hardened Soviet missile silos from invulnerable undersea sites. The president said the United States would go ahead with the new MX ICBM, intended as a counter to the massive Soviet SS-18, but he planted the seed of future trouble by rejecting Carter's planned basing system without coming up with any alternative of his own.

In dealing with the Soviets, it was necessary to stand Clausewitz on his head, for Moscow politics was a continuation of war by other means and it was, therefore, not possible to successfully negotiate with the Soviets from a position of weakness. To shift the analogy, negotiating with the Soviets was a game of high-stakes poker. A poker player needs chips, and accumulating chips was to some extent what the Reagan administration was about in its first term.

A successful poker player also needs to gain the respect of his opponent. Reagan did this with the Soviets in a variety of ways, some of which had little to do with US-Soviet relations directly. Secretary Shultz, no mean diplomatic poker player himself, once observed that Reagan's 1981 decision to fire air traffic controllers after they violated federal law by going on strike was the most important foreign policy move Ronald Reagan ever made. The Soviet leaders saw that the toughness of the president's words would, if necessary, be backed by action.[1]

What Reagan also understood, although some in his administration did not, was that for negotiations with the USSR to succeed a second factor was also necessary, trust between the leaders of the two countries. To a large degree, the practical working out of these two principles explains the distinction between the first Reagan administration, marked by tough rhetoric and hard-nosed action, and the second, dominated by a broadening agenda of negotiation and capped by a solid record of agreements.

Strategic Defense Initiative

The evening of March 23, 1983, Ronald Reagan achieved two things almost unknown in Washington: he unveiled a truly revolutionary proposal and he launched it to the surprise of virtually everyone. Speaking from the Oval Office the president shared "a vision of the future": "What if free people could live secure in the knowledge that their security did not rest upon the threat of instant U.S. retaliation to deter a Soviet attack, that we could intercept and destroy strategic ballistic missiles before they reached our own soil or that of our allies?"[2]

Many have claimed paternity over what the Reagan administration dubbed the Strategic Defense Initiative (SDI), but its real origins are in the president's deeply held aversion to the nuclear balance of terror. Reagan said, "I came into office with a decided prejudice against our tacit agreement with the Soviet Union regarding nuclear missiles. I'm talking about the MAD policy. . . . It was like having two Westerners standing in a saloon aiming guns at each other's head—permanently. There had to be a better way."[3]

During the first two years of the Reagan administration, ballistic missile defense (BMD) was quietly studied by an unusual group consisting of retired military personnel; scientists close to Edward Teller, the father of the American H-bomb; and some of Reagan's conservative backers. Conspicuously absent was anyone from either the Defense or State Departments.

In December 1982, Reagan surprised the Joint Chiefs of Staff (JCS) by asking "what if we began to move away from our total reliance on offense to deter a nuclear attack and moved toward a relatively greater reliance on defense?" In early February, the chiefs replied that new technologies warranted taking a closer look at whether defensive systems could allow the US to "deal with a Soviet attack." Listening closely, Reagan said, "I understand; that's what I've been hoping."[4]

Reagan's SDI proposal exploded across the US national security community with the force of a tactical nuclear device. Not until two days before Reagan was scheduled to deliver his speech did Secretary of State Shultz learn about the new initiative. For once both State and Defense were united in opposing drafts of the speech, which pledged a nuclear-free world by the end of the century. Shultz succeeded in getting some of the rhetoric toned down but he also recognized the depth of the president's personal commitment.[5]

As a member of the US START delegation, I sat through numerous briefings by the head of the SDI program, General Abrahamson, in which arrays of sensors, weapons, and control systems were displayed for our consideration. Unfortunately for Reagan's vision, the task of detecting the launch of thousands of ballistic missiles, reliably discriminating thousands of real warheads from a much larger number of decoys, and then directing interceptors to destroy the in-coming weapons—all within less than thirty minutes—was simply beyond technological capabilities, and remains so even now more than thirty years after Reagan's speech.

The Soviet Response to SDI

Like the rest of the world, the Kremlin was surprised by Reagan's initiative. In public the Soviets sought to use SDI to build up European opposition to the deployment of US missiles and to encourage US opponents of Reagan's nuclear policies. Internally, the Soviet defense establishment was torn between the conviction that the program described by Reagan could not work and worry that the Americans with their more advanced computing and sensor technologies might be onto something.[6]

Immediately after Reagan's speech, Soviet minister of defense Ustinov and Academy of Sciences chief Aleksandrov commissioned a study of the US programs that would likely go into SDI as well as Soviet measures to counter it. Soviet military engineering circles concluded that SDI was "an extraordinarily complicated and expensive program and could hardly be expected to be accomplished in the 20th century." Nevertheless, Soviet specialists also believed SDI posed a significant challenge to the Soviet Union, in part because for the USSR to create its own SDI was "unrealistic because of financial difficulties which the defense industry was experiencing."[7]

While the Soviet propaganda machinery castigated SDI, some saw it as an opportunity. "Unlike the political and military leadership, the defense industry was quite enthusiastic about the U.S. initiative, seizing the opportunity to advance its projects."[8] In July 1985, a party-state decree launched a long-term research and development program whose goal was "to create by

1995 the technical and technological base in case the deployment of a multi-layered missile defense system would be necessary."[9] Work proceeded under two "umbrella" programs. One amounted essentially to upgrading the existing Moscow ABM system. The second, which bore some resemblance to SDI, concentrated on space-based missile defenses and antisatellite systems.

By 1987 pursuing these programs seemed less urgent as the climate of US-Soviet relations improved, as Soviet economic difficulties grew, and as arms-control agreements reduced some of the threats these programs were designed to counter. Soviet attention shifted to developing SDI countermeasures to be installed on offensive ballistic missiles, a significantly cheaper and technically less daunting approach than trying to develop an SDI lookalike system. In July 1987, the Politburo approved a program of countermeasures, including improved missile engines to shorten the vulnerable boost phase of flight, protecting missile bodies with heat-absorbing material, and deploying penetration aids and maneuverable warheads to counter future US sensors and interceptors.

In the end, the Soviet defense establishment concluded that the USSR did not need to undertake the expense of trying to duplicate SDI. The most expensive and realistic programs, such as upgrading the existing Moscow ABM system, were already included in the Soviet long-term military budget and did not require additional resources. The countermeasures included in the asymmetrical response to SDI adopted in 1987 were far less expensive than SDI. According to one source they cost about 6 billion rubles and it is not clear how many of these were actually implemented before the Soviet collapse in 1991.[10]

The Nuclear Freeze

In 1982 the *New Yorker* published a three-part series by Jonathan Schell called "The Fate of the Earth," a chilling depiction of the human and ecological consequences of nuclear war. Later published as a book that was nominated for a Pulitzer Prize, *The Fate of the Earth* became the centerpiece of the broad wave of antinuclear activism known as the "nuclear freeze" movement for its central demand: a halt to the production, testing, and deployment of nuclear weapons. By 1982 activists were collecting millions of signatures on profreeze petitions; initiatives in favor of the freeze were appearing on local and congressional district ballots, and polls showed large numbers of Americans to be in sympathy with the movement's aims.

Statements by some close to the Reagan administration helped stimulate anxiety about nuclear conflict. T. K. Jones, a former SALT delegation adviser who became Deputy Under-Secretary of Defense in the Reagan administration, earned his allotted fifteen minutes of fame as well as an appearance in the

Doonesbury comic strip when he explained to a congressional committee that nuclear war was not nearly as devastating as Americans had been led to believe. Saving the population was just a matter of shelters. "Dig a hole, cover it with a couple of doors and then throw three feet of dirt on top," Jones explained. "If there are enough shovels to go around, everybody's going to make it."[11] Most in the Reagan administration who actually had their hands on nuclear weapons policy had responsible views. But there were definitely some, especially in its early days, whose views bordered on the extreme. After the 1980 Reagan election victory, the SALT backstopping office where I was serving got an infusion of political appointees. One of our new colleagues—who clearly regarded government officials as suspicious, if not actual Communists—placed on his office door a large, full-color picture of a nuclear mushroom cloud with a greeting card taped underneath displaying the logo "When You Care to Send the Very Best."

A vigorous public debate is a prerequisite for a flourishing democracy. In the case of the freeze, however, the debate was confined to one side of the Iron Curtain. In the early 1980s, when some of the antinuclear propaganda material written by Soviet civilian specialists for the use of Western activists made its way back to the Soviet Union, it was sharply criticized by the Soviet military for undermining the morale and fighting spirit of Soviet armed forces.[12]

Had the freeze succeeded and the US unilaterally halted its nuclear programs, it is hard to imagine the Soviets having much incentive to accept the sweeping arms control agreements of subsequent years. On the other hand, freeze supporters were certainly correct to highlight the dangers of nuclear war. In my experience, almost everyone who worked with any aspect of nuclear weapons has some kind of epiphany moment about the underlying horrors of the subjects we became accustomed to dealing with in routine fashion. Mine came in the early 1980s, when the US START delegation visited the naval base in Norfolk, Virginia. Near the office of the commander was a huge, room-length and highly classified wall map that used small balls of different colors to depict US nuclear attack plans against the USSR. Weapons delivered by ICBMs were shown by balls of one color, by submarines another, and bombers by a third. Vast numbers of these balls spread across the entire USSR but what caught my eye was Moscow. The area around the city was covered by a small mountain of balls representing strikes against the city by every element of US nuclear forces. I had lived in Moscow and in my mind's eye I could visualize the city that was buried under those gaily colored little balls. At the time of the briefing, I was living with my family in Washington and I knew that somewhere in the USSR there was probably a similar map showing the US capital buried under a mountain of nuclear explosions. Looking at the map, it was clear that after the nuclear conflict it depicted the only question about Moscow—and Washington—was just how virulent would be the vast radioactive craters, which had once been historic and heavily populated cities. The experience brought home the ultimate absurdity of a nuclear conflict. It did not lead me to doubt that a strong US deterrent was the best way to avoid such a tragedy.

Intermediate Nuclear Forces

Reagan's first priority in the field of national security was rebuilding US defenses. But NATO politics did not allow delay with respect to talks on US and Soviet intermediate nuclear forces (INF), that is, systems with ranges shorter than intercontinental weapons but greater than tactical battlefield weapons, which had begun in the waning days of the Carter administration.

Driving the urgency was the appearance of new Soviet SS-20 missiles targeted on Western Europe and a 1979 NATO decision to meet this threat by deploying US INF missiles in Europe if negotiations with the Soviets did not succeed. NATO had always relied on US nuclear weapons to counter Soviet superiority in conventional weapons, but the deployment of the SS-20, a mobile, solid-fuel missile, carrying three highly accurate warheads, raised the prospect of "decoupling" Europe from the protection of the US nuclear umbrella. According to General Bateinin, "The SS-20 had a very low vulnerability, high accuracy, and a great range not only over Europe but over the Middle and Near East and much of the Mediterranean. Under the roof of the SS-20 it was possible to think about deep operations."[13]

On December 12, 1979, NATO adopted what came to be known as the "dual-track decision." The alliance would deploy 108 Pershing II (P-II) ballistic missiles and 464 ground-launched cruise missiles (GLCMs). The P-IIs would be based in Germany while the GLCMs would be deployed in other NATO countries, to assure that the burden, and political heat, was shared. During the several years before the new missiles were ready to take the field, NATO offered US-Soviet negotiations aimed at making the US INF deployments unnecessary.

The battle over INF was actually a battle over the future of the NATO alliance. If the Soviets had succeeded in blocking US deployments, it would have meant a decisive shift in the European political-military climate. For the United States, the task was to demonstrate to its European allies that it was capable of maintaining a credible defensive capability in Europe while at the same time remaining sensitive to the need many Europeans felt to avoid unnecessarily provoking their powerful neighbor.

In November 1981, the Reagan administration brought a controversial new proposal to the talks. The president announced, "The United States is prepared to cancel its deployment of Pershing II and ground-launched cruise missiles if the Soviets will dismantle their SS-20, SS-4, and SS-5 missiles."[14] It was what became known as the "zero option": the US would give up all of its planned INF deployments if the Soviets would eliminate all of their equivalent missiles.

The zero option was simple, straightforward, and would dramatically reduce the nuclear threat hanging over Europe. There was, however, one issue with the US proposal that immediately attracted critics on both sides of the East-West divide, its negotiability. By the time President Reagan made his proposal, the Soviets had deployed approximately 250 SS-20s with 750 highly accurate nuclear warheads. Together with the remaining SS-4s and SS-5s, the Soviets had over 1,100 INF missile warheads targeted on Western Europe. The United States was offering to forgo the future deployment of 572 warheads on its P-II and GLCM systems, assuming that Western European governments resisted the rising pressure to cancel the deployments altogether, in return for the Soviets' agreeing to destroy larger numbers of existing systems. The proposal was breathtaking in its audacity but critics charged that it was intended to string out negotiations while the United States proceeded with its own deployments.

The genius of the zero option was its simplicity. The idea of no INF weapons appealed to all European audiences: policy wonks who understood that decoupling was not something that happened to runaway railroad trains, conservatives who worried about the growing strength of the USSR, and even those in left-leaning "peace" movements who might occasionally be willing to mouth concern about nuclear weapons on the other side of the Iron Curtain but whose real objective always seemed to be to prevent the deployment of American missiles in their own backyard. In the words of Maynard Glitman, the US INF negotiator when the agreement was signed in 1987, "The zero option, as its proponents had predicted, gave us the initiative and the high ground inside, and as importantly, outside the actual negotiations."[15]

When the US and Soviet delegations met in Geneva, predictions of stalemate quickly proved accurate. The US delegation, headed by the redoubtable Paul Nitze, formally proposed the zero option and the Soviets, as expected, promptly rejected it. In early 1982, the Soviets presented their own proposal, a "moratorium" that would allow both NATO and the Warsaw Pact to have 300 INF missiles in Europe with no limits elsewhere. The Soviet proposal was even more one-sided in Moscow's direction than the much-maligned zero option was in US favor. It would have allowed the Soviets to complete all of their planned deployments of SS-20 missiles in Europe, giving them 900 accurate and powerful SS-20 warheads, while at the same time blocking any US INF missiles, because the Soviets included the minimal British and French deterrent forces in the 300 missiles that NATO would be allowed. At the same time, the Soviets could deploy unlimited numbers of SS-20s in the vast stretches east of the Urals, where they would threaten China and Japan, and because of their mobility could be quickly redeployed to Europe. Even Soviet chief negotiator Yuliy Kvitsinskiy acknowledged that the Soviet proposal was "not a very impressive act."[16]

By early 1982, both sides were dug into maximalist negotiating positions. This situation was not much different from the early phases of most other US-Soviet arms-control talks, where eventually the two sides would find some way to begin inching in each other's direction. What distinguished the INF talks—and what blocked any progress for several years—was that each side was pursuing incompatible objectives outside the talks. For Moscow the overriding objective was to block any US INF deployment while giving up no SS-20s. Kvitsinskiy says that the only instructions he got at the beginning of the talks were to "do everything possible to prevent the deployment of new American missiles in Europe." The US, by contrast, if it could not secure the elimination of all SS-20s, was determined to go forward with the planned deployment of its INF missiles.

In early 1982, Kvitsinskiy suggested to Moscow that the Soviets modify their one-sided proposal by offering to reduce the numbers of INF warheads to the levels of 1978, in the early stages of the SS-20 deployment. Kvitsinskiy, who was getting tactical advice from his friends in the German Social Democratic Party (SPD), told Gromyko that his proposal would undermine support in Bonn for the deployment of US INF missiles. But no one in the Soviet leadership wanted to take a stance that could open themselves up to charges of being "soft on Americans," a potentially fatal handicap in the post-Brezhnev succession sweepstakes that all understood were drawing near. As the Soviet delegation prepared to return to Geneva in early 1982, Gromyko's instructions to Kvitsinskiy were simple, "Curse the Americans more strongly and step up the pressure on them."[17]

The Walk in Woods

US negotiator Nitze also believed that his country's position needed to be modified if an agreement was ever to be reached. On his own authority and outside regular channels, Nitze proposed to his Soviet counterpart a package deal involving major modifications to the positions of both countries. The so-called walk in the woods became the most well known, and controversial, episode in the history of nuclear arms control negotiations between the two superpowers.

On July 16, 1982, Nitze and Kvitsinskiy spent two and a half hours walking along a forest path near Switzerland's Jura mountain border with France. Once the two negotiators found a comfortable resting place on a recently cut log, Nitze pulled out his new proposal: a ceiling for both sides of no more than 225 INF aircraft and missiles in Europe, with a sub limit of 75 INF missile launchers. The United States would agree to deploy only cruise missiles, giving up the P-II ballistic missiles that were Moscow's primary concern, while the Soviets, in return, would agree to have no more than 75 SS-20s, a significant reduction from what they possessed at that time.[18]

When Nitze informed Washington about his initiative, the Pentagon argued that it would be wrong for the United States to give up the right to deploy P-IIs while allowing Moscow to maintain SS-20s in Europe and Asia. Others feared that the Soviets would "pocket" the US P-II concession and then ask for more, a tactic Kvitsinskiy wanted to pursue but was blocked by policy paralysis in Moscow. Even State was unwilling to endorse the Nitze proposal, largely out of concern that it might undermine alliance solidarity over INF deployments. What settled the argument was opposition from President Reagan himself. When Nitze warned at a September NSC meeting that if there were no changes the Soviets would find the formal US position unacceptable, Reagan replied, "Well, Paul, you just tell the Soviets that you are working for one tough son of a bitch."[19]

When Kvitsinskiy made the rounds of the Soviet national security establishment, he found an even more skeptical reaction. At a meeting of the Soviet arms control backstopping group, the "Big Five," the senior military representative Marshal Sergei Akromeyev sympathized personally with Kvitsinskiy's desire for movement but was overruled by Chief of Staff Ogarkov, who described the walk in the woods as an "American provocation."[20] Akromeyev confided to Kvitsinskiy that Ogarkov and other senior Soviet military planners were worried that the Western edge in precision-guided weaponry might allow NATO to destroy the bulk of Soviet nuclear weapons in a conventional strike, which meant that the Soviets needed to deploy even larger numbers of SS-20s. Akromeyev also told Kvitsinskiy that senior Soviet officials were unwilling to give any serious consideration to Nitze's initiative because it would require changing positions that Brezhnev had already staked out publicly.[21]

Nitze's plan was an honest effort to get some kind of an agreement that would meet US and Soviet interests. Nitze feared—fortunately incorrectly—that without an agreement Germany would reject any deployment of US INF missiles, which would have led to the complete collapse of the US INF position and likely the NATO alliance as well. The greatest weakness of the walk in the woods was that it treated the zero option as an in-going negotiating position and not as an achievable final outcome, which is what Ronald Reagan thought it was, a judgment that events proved to be correct.

The Start of START

In May 1982, at Eureka College in Illinois, where he had graduated fifty years earlier, President Reagan laid out principles that shaped the US approach toward strategic arms control until the successful conclusion of an agreement nine years later. The president said the US delegation would propose "a practical, phased reduction plan. The focus of our efforts will be to reduce significantly the most destabilizing systems, the ballistic missiles, the number of warheads they carry, and their overall destructive potential."[22] Reagan's speech, with its pledges to reduce nuclear forces to enhance stability, signaled a significant change from previous strategic arms-control regimes, which were actually followed by increases in the number and destructive power of nuclear weapons on both sides.

The centerpiece of the initial US proposal in what the Reagan administration called START (Strategic Arms Reduction Talks) to distinguish it from SALT, which the president and his allies had been criticizing for years, was a ceiling of 5,000 warheads on ballistic missiles with no more than 2,500 allowed on ICBMs. It also established a ceiling of 850 ballistic missiles but did not include any limits on heavy bombers or cruise missiles. The US proposal would have required significant cuts in the numbers of US ballistic missiles and warheads but placed few constraints on future programs such as the MX ICBM and the D-5 submarine-launched ballistic missile (SLBM). It would have required much greater reductions in the Soviet ICBM force and by completely eliminating heavy bombers from limits the United States was, in effect, attempting to return to the position under SALT I ten years before. There was pretty clearly never going to be an agreement based entirely on the US proposal but it was a sensible ingoing position to take with a tough negotiating partner.

In August the Soviets presented the outlines of their initial START proposal—a 1,800 ceiling on strategic nuclear delivery vehicles (SNDVs, that is ICBMs, SLBMs, and heavy bombers) with no sub-limits at all on any categories of missiles, which meant in theory that the Soviets could have deployed their entire force as heavy SS-18 ICBMs. The Soviets included US heavy bombers and weapons based overseas (so-called forward based systems or FBS) in their proposed limits and for good measure proposed to ban all cruise missiles with a range over 600 kilometers, thereby renouncing the compromise agreed at Vladivostok in 1974. The ingoing Soviet START position was at least as imbalanced as its US counterpart, although vociferous critics of the US approach somehow managed to overlook this fact.

By the summer of 1983, despite the barrages of public rhetoric volleying back and forth, both sides were beginning to modify their initial positions in a way that offered hope for serious negotiations ahead. In June 1983, the United States presented a draft START treaty that contained ceilings of 1,200 deployed ballistic missiles, whether land- or sea-based, and 5,000 warheads on ballistic missiles. It also included a separate limit of 400 heavy bombers.[23]

Later, the Soviets presented their own treaty, which proposed phased reductions to 1,800 SNDVs, with sublimits of 1,080 MIRVed ballistic missiles and 680 MIRVed ICBMs but no separate limits on heavy ICBMs. It was the first time in the history of US-Soviet arms control that Moscow had ever proposed actual reductions in its own forces. Ironically, the new Soviet START position resembled in some respects the Carter administration's "deep cuts" proposal that the Soviets had so harshly rejected in 1977. Unfortunately, the Soviets also conditioned their new proposal on the United States giving up Reagan's newly announced SDI program, a stance that blocked agreement for the next several years.

Although the two countries remained far apart in many respects, their evolving positions were close enough to see the outline of a possible compromise. In their draft treaty, the Soviets had for the first time accepted the concept of limits on warhead levels. In the end, the Soviets proved willing to accept a ceiling of 6,000 warheads, only one thousand above the initial US proposal. The two sides continued to argue vociferously about the danger presented by heavy ICBMs but they were beginning to move closer on actual numbers. At this stage the US was signaling a willingness to allow the Soviets to retain about one-third of their current heavy ICBM force while the Soviets in the end agreed to a one-half cut, a not insurmountable difference of about fifty missiles. The US had abandoned its bootless effort to keep heavy bombers completely out of any deal while the Soviets, for their part, had returned to the SALT II compromise position of allowing 120 ALCM-carrying heavy bombers. The US proposal of 1,200 ballistic missiles and 400 heavy bombers amounted to an implicit SNDV ceiling of 1,600, not that far from the 1,800 SNDV ceiling proposed by the Soviets.

Street Theater in Geneva

As the November 1983 deployment of US INF missiles approached, activists of almost every conceivable antinuclear, antiwar, and green persuasion converged on Geneva. Although most of the protestors claimed to be in favor of peace everywhere, it was hard not to notice that every demonstration featured banners and chants against "Pershing" and "Cruise" but few if any calling for the removal of SS-20s.

The focus of the demonstrators' attention was on INF but, to the average street-level antinuclear activist, one US arms control delegation probably looked about the same as any other and the START delegation, going about its business in Geneva at that time, came in for its share of attention. Most of the demonstrators seemed peaceful by nature and the Swiss police generally did a good job of keeping protestors away from the delegations. Sometimes, however, precautions broke down.

One evening, as I was accompanying the US START negotiator Rowny in his car back to his Geneva apartment, our driver made a wrong turn in the darkness and we found ourselves cruising among a marching column of protestors. This group seemed more militant than most, at least judging by the pounding of drums and clashing of metal garbage can lids that came from somewhere ahead. It was difficult to predict the reaction of the protestors had they discovered that the US START negotiator had unexpectedly joined their demonstration, but it seemed unlikely to be one we would want to put to the test. Rowny was reading with the aid of a small lamp above his seat and had not noticed what was happening. I advised him to turn out the light and our car crept along with the column of demonstrators until we came to an unblocked intersection and the driver was able to turn away.

The End

On November 22, the German parliament approved the deployment of P-II missiles and the next day the first units arrived in Europe. When the US INF delegation arrived at the Soviet mission for the next regular session, Kvitsinskiy announced that the USSR "declares this round of negotiations discontinued, without setting any date for resumption." Members of the Soviet delegation thought they had come up with an elegant way to execute Moscow's instructions while leaving the door open "just a little" for eventual resumption. The next day, as they were packing their bags to return home, they watched with dismay as Andropov, by then in the final stages of his fatal kidney disease, said the talks could only resume when US missiles were withdrawn from Europe.[24]

Moscow was wagering that public opposition would force European governments into reversing INF deployments and that in the 1984 elections the American people would vote Ronald Reagan out of office. It was a dead end that reflected the paralysis at the top of the Soviet system.

Two weeks later, an uncomfortable-looking Soviet delegation told us they could provide no resumption date for the START talks. Fifteen months passed before the two sides sat down again for nuclear arms talks and when they did it was with new leaders at the table and in Moscow.

The Soviets and Arms Control

From the days of Peter the Great, when specialists sent West to learn shipbuilding decided not to return home, rulers of the Kremlin looked with suspicion on subjects entrusted to deal with the outside world. Brezhnev was no exception. When the general secretary met the Soviet SALT delegation in 1969 as it was preparing to leave for its first meeting with the Americans, Soviet arms negotiators did not hear any noteworthy advice on the thorny issues of nuclear diplomacy, but none ever forgot Brezhnev's ringing last words of warning to be sure to preserve Soviet secrets as they left to do battle with the Americans. "Don't forget about Lubyanka," KGB headquarters, Brezhnev told them.[25] The general secretary's admonition had a paralyzing effect for some time on the Soviet delegation, especially its military members, who were not particularly happy to be discussing arms limits with the Americans anyway.

There was only a limited amount that civilian members of the delegation could have spilled in any case. Dobrynin said foreign ministry personnel "knew very little about what was going on in our military thinking. . . . All we knew about nuclear war we knew from American sources."[26]

Soviet determination to keep secrets within the military sometimes assumed absurd dimensions. The first US SALT negotiator, Gerard Smith, recalled that the Soviet military seemed "uneasy about starting down a road . . . that required Soviet civilians from the Ministry of Foreign Affairs to get involved in weapons matters from which they had largely been excluded in the past."[27] This uneasiness assumed startling dimensions when Soviet military representatives asked that US counterparts stop talking about Soviet military systems so openly in front of civilian members of the Soviet delegation. The Soviet military understood there would have to be discussions of weapons systems on both sides but they preferred these be handled strictly between uniformed officers.

One consequence of the tight Soviet approach toward information was that for many years both sides used US data in the negotiations, not just in discussing US forces but Soviet as well. Not until SALT II, in 1979, did the Soviets provide a list of their strategic forces subject to the agreement and this database, although officially part of the treaty, was not made public in the USSR until the end of the 1980s.

The Soviets were able to get away with this approach because of the imbalance in information between the two societies. Simply by reading the media or following congressional debates the Soviets could obtain detailed information on the numbers and characteristics of US weapons systems, data the CIA would have paid millions to obtain about Soviet forces. The practice of relying on US data gave significant advantages to the Soviets, who were able to learn what the United States knew about Soviet forces before deciding themselves what information they would reveal to the Americans.

But there were also costs to the practice, as Dobrynin pointed out after the end of the Cold War. The Soviet ambassador, who handled some of the most sensitive discussions on arms control with senior US officials, said that when he went into negotiations he generally had no background information to help him steer the discussion in a direction that Moscow wanted. When he posed questions to his American interlocutor, "I was trying to find out what was going on." The Soviets were gradually drawn into using American strategic concepts, Dobrynin said. "Little by little we began subconsciously to think that you really knew more than we, because we used your terminology, we used your designations for our missiles."[28]

The Big Five: Soviet Arms Control Backstopping

Soon after the beginning of the SALT talks in 1969, a Politburo commission, dubbed the Big Five, was established under the chair of Dmitry Ustinov, then Central Committee Secretary in charge of the defense industry. Other members were Defense Minister Grechko, Foreign Minister Gromyko, KGB chief Andropov, and Military-Industrial Commission (MIC) chief Leonid Smirnov. In preparation for the 1974 Vladivostok meeting the Big Five principals appointed trusted deputies to follow the negotiations more closely and to take whatever decisions needed to be made at the working level. This body became known as the Little Five, although its members were all senior figures in the Soviet national security bureaucracy. Not until 1979 did the ministries of Defense and Foreign Affairs establish offices for arms control, headed respectively by General Nikolai Chervov and Ambassador Viktor Karpov.[29]

The MFA drafted instructions to the arms control delegations but the defense establishment maintained a monopoly of information on all military aspects of the negotiations and it is unclear how much real coordination there was. Korniyenko said, "There was no system according to which the Defense Ministry would inform on a continuing basis the Foreign Ministry about the facts of its position."[30]

In the United States, arms control was something of a cottage industry, with nongovernmental specialists often moving into official positions as the wheels of party power rotated. Professionals sometimes found this irksome, but it provided valuable intellectual leavening. In the closed Soviet system, outsiders had little role. When Marshal Shulman, Secretary of State Vance's chief adviser on Soviet affairs, told a post–Cold War conference on SALT that he had the impression that leading Soviet academics, many of whom met regularly with Shulman and other Americans, had been influential in the Soviet arms control process, Dobrynin and other Soviet officials hastened to correct him. "Unfortunately," Dobrynin said, "the scientific community, from the very beginning was not very much involved in the practical work of the negotiations." A few well-known individuals such as USA Institute director Arbatov had access to the Soviet leadership and some influence on the general character of US-Soviet relations, "but they did not know any concrete details of the negotiations."[31]

Despite its constrictive approach to information-sharing the Soviet backstopping system seems to have functioned relatively effectively. It certainly operated with more continuity over the years than its messy and sometimes downright dysfunctional US equivalent. Closed throughout its existence to all but a handful of long-serving bureaucrats—Sergei Tarasenko, an aide to Gorbachev's foreign minister Eduard Shevardnadze, said that "no more than ten or twelve people were involved in the process"—the Soviet backstopping system also had the effect of protecting institutional interests, especially those of the defense establishment.[32]

Just Say No

The Soviet military's attitude toward strategic arms negotiations with the United States was at best one of intense skepticism and more commonly downright hostility. Defense Minister Grechko "believed that the talks were nothing but deception by the United States in an attempt to achieve unilateral American advantage," perhaps one reason why defector Arkadiy Shevchenko described him as "permanently apoplectic during SALT."[33]

The Soviet military viewed talks with its American adversary as a classic zero-sum game. According to Nikolai Detinov, a longtime military participant in the arms talks, "The Defense Ministry saw its main task as preserving and strengthening Soviet military might, which in this case, included weakening the potential chief enemy—the United States—by means of negotiations."[34] This combative stance toward the negotiations was justified in Soviet eyes by the conviction that the United States was pursuing a similar approach. "During SALT I and SALT II the interlocking leadership believed that through arms control talks, the US sought to achieve unilateral advantage over the USSR and . . . to deceive the Soviet side."[35]

The Soviet military was almost viscerally opposed to giving up any weapons through negotiations. It only went along with SALT II's modest reduction of 150 SNDVs because it had already decided to cut its ballistic missile launchers by that much. The opposition of some senior Soviet military officers to arms control seemed at times to verge on the irrational. According to General Danilovich, the Soviet military opposed every US-Soviet strategic arms agreement because "the concessions that we made outweighed the benefits by two, three, four times." It was a Shakespearean tragedy: "We were forced to sign something our hearts were against."[36]

Winning a Nuclear War?

Soviet nuclear specialists were as aware of the devastating consequences of nuclear war as their American counterparts. In 1954, after the explosion of the first Soviet thermonuclear device, Academician Igor Kurchatov, the scientist in charge of the Soviet H-bomb project, and V. N. Malyshev, the head of the Ministry of Medium Machine Building which was responsible for building Soviet nuclear weapons, warned in a secret memo to the Soviet leadership that "use of atomic weapons on a mass scale would lead to devastation in the warring countries . . . a huge threat which could obliterate all life on Earth hangs over mankind."[37]

In the 1960s and 1970s, "many of the best and brightest minds of the Soviet scientific community were working in uniform within the General Staff in the area of analysis and planning" for nuclear warfare, according to a General Staff officer, who directed many of these studies. They were ordered to focus only on military aspects of the issue without addressing broader social or economic consequences. Nevertheless, the conclusions of the studies were that "nuclear use was operationally counter-productive and generally self-destructive." Senior Soviet military leaders were briefed and fully understood that "nuclear use at any level by either side would be catastrophic for Soviet armed forces and the Soviet state." But once it became clear that these studies contradicted some of the most fundamental premises of Soviet military and political doctrine, they were suppressed by giving them such a high level of classification that dissemination became impossible.[38]

Soviet military exercises showed that a nuclear exchange would for all practical purposes mean the elimination of both the United States and the Soviet Union as functioning societies. In a study conducted in the early 1970s, in which the US was assumed to have struck the USSR first and then to have been hit by a Soviet retaliatory blow, the conclusions were that eighty million Soviet citizens would die, the armed forces would be reduced to one-thousandth of their former strength, 85 percent of the Soviet economy would be destroyed, and the European part of the USSR would be contaminated by lethal levels of radiation. Brezhnev and Kosygin were "visibly terrified" by the results of the study and one of its authors said it was never disseminated because it was judged "too psychologically detrimental to morale and resolve."[39]

Even though no one on the Soviet, as on the US, side ever seems to have come up with a convincing picture of a victorious nuclear war, Soviet military professionals saw warfare as the continuation of policy by other means and, since the policy of the USSR was the global victory of socialism, nuclear war had to be considered as something that would end in final triumph of the socialist side.[40] In Danilovich's view, "to officially acknowledge that nuclear war was senseless and basically catastrophic would require several changes in the entire Soviet political-military-economic system, that were completely unacceptable to the senior officers who were the products and beneficiaries of that system." Acknowledging that victory was impossible in a nuclear conflict would undermine Marxist-Leninist dogma, open up the way for deep reductions in Soviet military forces, and raise questions about the sanctity of the military in the Soviet system. Danilovich concluded that by the 1970s the Soviet civilian and military leadership understood that the large-scale use of nuclear weapons was no longer rational, yet at the same time the Soviets continued to believe that they could win in a nuclear conflict "by striking at the Americans and then using our general superiority to bring the nuclear war to victory."[41]

Dead Hand?

Throughout the Cold War the United States and the USSR worried about their ability to communicate with their nuclear forces during an attack—with blast, heat, debris, radiation, and electromagnetic waves sweeping across a tortured landscape—in order to ensure that even if the other side struck first, it would still face a devastating retaliatory response. The United States created an airborne command system designed to lift off the runway on fifteen-minutes warning and capable of remaining aloft continuously during a crisis. It also deployed the Emergency Rocket Communications System (ERCS), silo-based Minuteman II ICBMs and smaller mobile missiles capable of being deployed to remote sites in a crisis, which could be launched in case of necessity to relay a nuclear launch command during their twenty- to thirty-minute flight times.

During the Cold War US satellites observed silos in Soviet ICBM fields that seemed to contain missiles that had a function similar to ERCS. After the end of the Cold War some evidence appeared that the Soviets may have gone beyond this to create a "Strangelovian" system called "Dead Hand," which would automatically launch Soviet missiles even if no senior civilian or military official survived to actually push the button. Col. Valery Yarynich, a leading specialist in the command and control of nuclear weapons, described the Soviet "Perimeter" system in which preselected officials based in secret and heavily protected facilities would be able to launch Soviet nuclear missiles even if the country's leadership had been wiped out in a US strike. Varynich said, however, that the Perimeter system would only work under three conditions: if Soviet leaders had first activated it, if contact had been lost with all three of the nuclear "briefcases" that authorized the launch of Soviet nuclear weapons (under custody of the general secretary, the minister of defense, and the chief of the General Staff), and if nuclear detonations were confirmed on Soviet territory.

According to some Soviet specialists, however, the system also contained a Dead Hand feature that could automatically trigger the launch of the nuclear missiles without any human intervention once sensors had detected the light, blast, earth movement, or radiation associated with a nuclear explosion. Col. Gen. Varfolomei Korobushin, deputy chief of staff of the Strategic Rocket Force (SRF), said any US first strike would have been futile because Dead Hand would "automatically launch all missiles remaining in our arsenal even if every nuclear command center and all of our leaders were destroyed."

Other Soviet officials, however, have cast doubt on whether the Soviets actually deployed the Dead Hand system in a fully automatic mode. Soviet weapons specialist Viktor Surikov said his design bureau had created the Dead Hand system but that Chief of Staff Akromeyev had rejected its deployment. Yarynich wrote that "the system has no capability for preparing a launch order automatically without participation of the center's crew." Vitaly Katayev, a longtime senior Central Committee defense official, who toward the end of the USSR served as Gorbachev's arms control adviser, confirmed that the Soviets had developed a system for automatic launch of retaliatory missiles if the central command was eliminated but added that "introduction of this system meant that the fate of humanity would be passed to computers, so it was abandoned."[42]

Continuity in Government, or You Are Now the Secretary of State

Preparations for fighting a nuclear war were not, of course, limited to the USSR. The Reagan administration invested considerable resources in upgrades to the US system of nuclear command and control and other programs designed to enhance the ability of the US government to survive a nuclear conflict.

In the mid-1980s, I was drawn into one of these programs, known as Continuity in Government. My involvement began when I was instructed to attend a meeting on a subject that could not be mentioned. Participants learned that we had been selected for teams that would serve as the nucleus of the US government's national security operations in the event of nuclear conflict.

We had been chosen, so they told us, because of our backgrounds, current positions, and language ability, and we would be joined by counterparts from other national security agencies. This was not something to be taken lightly, we were rather sternly informed when some began to smirk at the notion of continuing the Washington interagency process after a nuclear holocaust. We were also told to be ready to move at short notice and advised to keep a small suitcase with all we needed for a quick departure from Washington. (This instruction raised for me the issue of what reading matter to take along for a nuclear conflict, a question I never resolved and perhaps one reason I never got around to assembling my nuclear war kit bag.)

Some of the leaders did not exactly inspire confidence. The man in charge of State Department preparations for the program once tried to buck up his troops for the coming war by telling us how lucky we were to have been selected. He pointed out that after a nuclear conflict US military capabilities would likely be somewhat diminished. This development, while regrettable no doubt, would make the diplomatic skills we State Department types possessed even more valuable he assured us.

For two years, until I left Washington for a new assignment in Belgrade, I participated in a number of training sessions and exercises, one of which involved spending days deep inside a mountain. In that exercise, we were told excitedly that we would be using the actual state-of-the-art computer and communications equipment that we would deploy if we ever had to sally forth to do real nuclear battle. Confidence was not increased when shortly after we had deposited our things in underground bunks and sat down to carry out what we were told would be an exercise involving real US and Soviet war plans, all the computers froze up and refused steadfastly to perform for the rest of the exercise. We were reduced to fighting the war through yellow tablets, trading options with our pretend Soviet adversaries who, we later learned, had enjoyed their nuclear war in comfortable aboveground facilities.

On December 25, 1991, our family was preparing Christmas dinner in our town-house on the grounds of the US embassy in Moscow together with several other embassy families. It was a happy group, the holiday atmosphere enlivened by the presence of young people home from school and by the prospect of a full day off from work, unusual in the dramatic pace of events that had unfolded in Moscow since the failed August coup, when I had arrived to assume my new duties as head of the political section at the embassy. Our festivities were suspended when I got a telephone call from a friend in the Kremlin advising me to turn on my television. Mikhail Gorbachev would soon announce his resignation as president of the USSR and his place in the Kremlin would be taken by Boris Yeltsin as president of Russia.

It had been clear for some time that Gorbachev's days in office were numbered although Gorbachev himself seemed reluctant to recognize this fact. As late as December 20, he told German chancellor Helmut Kohl that his resignation was not imminent. Nevertheless, real power in Moscow had shifted to Yeltsin after the August coup, when the future Russian president had famously climbed on a tank in front of the Russian White House, whose massive bulk gleamed through the snowy Moscow twilight only two hundred yards behind our house. Three weeks before, the final blow had come when Yeltsin, meeting secretly in a remote nature preserve with the leaders of Ukraine and Belarus, had announced the end of the USSR and the creation of a new association called the Commonwealth of Independent States (CIS). Gorbachev's irrelevance was humiliatingly demonstrated by the fact that he was not even invited to the meeting and, that after it was over, the first leader a triumphant Yeltsin had telephoned was US president George H. W. Bush.

Gorbachev was justly angry but there was nothing he could do. After six eventful years as Soviet leader his time had run out. Abroad, Gorbachev had won renown for his courageous efforts to promote change. At home the picture was different. The enthusiasm that had greeted his efforts to reform the ossified system he took over in 1985 had long since been replaced by despair at political chaos, economic decline, and ethnic violence.

Behind the scene in the Kremlin the transition from Gorbachev to Yeltsin was marked by anger and petty posturing on both sides. The Soviet system never developed a mechanism for the transfer of power and Gorbachev and Yeltsin, bitter personal and political rivals, bickered through several days of negotiating the changeover. On December 23, Gorbachev and Yeltsin met, the last time they ever saw each other face-to-face, to negotiate Gorbachev's departure. Over several hours, with Aleksandr Yakovlev, the intellectual godfather of perestroika, as referee, the two eventually hammered out what amounted to Gorbachev's severance package. Gorbachev had to break off the session with Yeltsin for a farewell call with British prime minister Major, and after the call was over Yakovlev found Gorbachev on a sofa in his private office with tears in his eyes: "You see Sasha, that's it."[1]

Gorbachev's final speech to the citizens of what used to be the USSR was delivered with dignity, but he could not conceal his bitterness. Gorbachev cited with justifiable pride the achievements of the past. "Free press, freedom of worship, representative legislatures and a multi-party system . . . An end has been put to the cold war and to the arms race." Not until the final words of his half-hour address did Gorbachev acknowledge "there were mistakes made" but he took no responsibility for these failings and his account of the past seemed impersonal and disconnected from the harsh realities that his fellow citizens were facing and which many blamed on him.[2]

As Gorbachev was speaking, the famous Soviet hammer and sickle banner came down from the Kremlin, replaced by the red, white, and blue Russian flag. In Red Square, only a few chance passersby observed the final lowering of the flag that for much of the twentieth century had symbolized both hope and fear for millions. Watching the event, a drunk suddenly shouted, "Why are you laughing at Lenin?"—whose embalmed body still rested nearby in the shuttered mausoleum. The drunk was silenced by others, who warned that foreigners were watching and that he should not embarrass the new Russia. Another passerby laughed, "Foreigners? Who cares? They're the ones who are feeding us these days."[3]

Comrade Gorbachev Goes to Moscow

Mikhail Sergeyevich Gorbachev was born in 1931 in the remote village of Priv-olnoye, in the southern Russian steppe country near Stavropol. The last leader of the USSR was also the first to be born and live his entire life under Soviet power, a fact that is not irrelevant in understanding why Gorbachev's reforms ultimately failed. Gorbachev vigorously attacked many of the problems of the Soviet system. Yet when it became clear that the real issue was not reform of the system but its replacement, Gorbachev could not bring himself to aban-don the Socialist order under which he had been born, grown, and prospered.

After graduation from Moscow University's law faculty, Gorbachev returned to Stavropol and climbed the ranks of the local party apparat becoming in 1970, at the relatively young age of thirty-nine, the first secretary of the Stav-ropol regional party organization, joining the elite group that constituted the backbone of Communist rule. One of Gorbachev's colleagues in this group, Boris Yeltsin, who served as first secretary of the major industrial region of Sverdlovsk (now Yekaterinburg) described "the first" as "a god, a tsar—master of his province."[4]

In 1978 Gorbachev made the critical transition from regional overlord to central apparatchik, becoming the Central Committee secretary responsible for agriculture. Gorbachev was an unknown figure when he arrived in Moscow but, more than a decade younger than any other figure on the aging Soviet leadership team, he enjoyed obvious actuarial advantages. The agricultural portfolio had been the graveyard for many political ambitions and during his early years in Moscow Gorbachev kept a low profile. He seldom entered into the Politburo's discussion of policy issues, and when he did it was generally to support whatever consensus position had developed around the table.

Even before Gorbachev moved to the Soviet capital he had quietly signaled his loyalty to Brezhnev. Gorbachev reported many years later that Brezhnev had formed a sort of "rapid reaction group" consisting of regional first secre-taries who enjoyed his special trust and who worked to further his interests. In one of his first visits to Moscow after becoming Stavropol first secretary, Gorbachev was invited to meet the group, which he had never heard of before. Typical for the Brezhnev era, the first test was to hand Gorbachev a large glass of vodka. Frowns followed when the man who later became known as the "lemonade general secretary" took only a sip, but the mood changed when Gorbachev replied positively to questions about Brezhnev. After this Gor-bachev says he was invited to join the group, whose efforts at that time were directed toward furthering Brezhnev's agenda and diminishing the influence of his rivals.[5]

Against this backdrop, it is not surprising that Gorbachev had a sharp dispute with Kosygin during his first year on the Secretariat, one that apparently permanently spoiled his relationship with the prime minister. As he describes the incident in his memoirs, Gorbachev reported to the Politburo that a disastrous harvest would have to be met by grain purchases from abroad. Kosygin complained that Gorbachev had brought the subject to the Politburo without first checking with the government. The prime minister said there was no money to buy grain and the right response was to simply be firmer in demanding that state production quotas be fulfilled. Gorbachev shot back that Kosygin should in that case simply instruct farmers to produce the necessary grain. Kosygin was not used to being sassed this way, especially by younger colleagues, and a deathly silence followed this rare interruption of the usually tightly scripted Politburo sessions.[6]

Fifteen minutes after the Politburo adjourned, Brezhnev telephoned Gorbachev to offer his full backing. Two hours later, Kosygin called Gorbachev to surrender, telling the younger official to send his paper forward. Gorbachev noted coyly that "some in the Soviet leadership regarded the incident with approval as evidence of my tough stand against Kosygin."[7] Frosty relations between the general secretary and the prime minister had been a feature of Kremlin insider politics for years. Gorbachev had effectively sided with Brezhnev, a good career move.

Gorbachev Becomes General Secretary

On March 11, 1985, the world learned that Mikhail Gorbachev had been chosen general secretary of the Soviet Communist Party, after the death of Brezhnev crony Konstantin Chernenko. Gorbachev's quick accession seemed to have gone smoothly. Behind the scenes, however, there had been considerable skirmishing. Just hours before the Politburo gave Gorbachev the nod, it appeared that the decision might actually have to be made by the Central Committee, something that had never happened before.

Gorbachev, young, vigorous, and occupying the second secretary slot that was the traditional stepping stone to the top, had been an obvious candidate for general secretary for several years. But Chernenko's accession a year earlier had revealed the lingering strength of the aging Brezhnevite old guard and, as Chernenko slid toward death, the factions gathered their forces for another struggle. As he received regular reports on Chernenko's condition from

Minister of Health Chazov, Gorbachev used Yegor Ligachev to mobilize the network of supporters the two had been developing among the party apparat since the time of Andropov.

On the other side, Moscow party boss Viktor Grishin was maneuvering. In February 1985, the USSR held so-called elections for the rubber-stamp parliament, the Supreme Soviet. One aspect of the ritual was for top leaders to hold well-publicized meetings with the voters of the constituency that had been given the honor of selecting them. As the election approached, Chernenko was in the hospital. Gorbachev was surprised to get a call from Grishin, who said he had gotten the ailing general secretary's permission to organize a meeting with the voters in which Grishin would read Chernenko's remarks. The performance was televised and the entire country saw Grishin acting on behalf of the absent general secretary. On election day a ballot box was set up next to Chernenko's hospital room, in such a way to appear as if it were an ordinary polling place. That night TV viewers saw Grishin walking solicitously beside Chernenko, who shuffled vacantly to the box and duly deposited his ballot. Gorbachev, who aptly described these maneuvers as the "apotheosis of cynicism," understood that behind Grishin stood other aging conservative figures and what was going on was an effort to "stop Gorbachev."[8]

When Chazov telephoned Gorbachev with the news of Chernenko's death, Gorbachev convened a meeting of Politburo members present in Moscow. Conveniently for Gorbachev, some of his likely opponents were absent. Nevertheless, this session ended inconclusively. Grishin reportedly surprised participants by saying, "Everything is clear. Let's appoint Mikhail Sergeyevich."[9] But possibly fearing that Grishin's move was some kind of a ploy, Gorbachev deferred a decision until the next day.

After the session ended, Gorbachev, Ligachev, and KGB chief Chebrikov worked the phones in the Kremlin until 4 AM, dragging Central Committee department chiefs, ministers, and heads of agencies out of their beds. Once they arrived in their offices, according to Gorbachev's chief of staff Boldin, "we gave them their assignments."[10] By the next day, Gorbachev and Ligachev felt they had a majority of the Central Committee, but they were still concerned about what might happen when the full Politburo met later in the day.

That morning, just hours before the impending Politburo session, Gromyko unexpectedly telephoned Ligachev. The foreign minister said he would like to be the first to nominate Gorbachev. Behind Gromyko's move was a blatant political horse trade between the aging diplomat and the rising party official. Gorbachev and Gromyko had secretly agreed that Gromyko would back

Gorbachev for general secretary in return for Gorbachev's promise to install Gromyko as chairman of the Supreme Soviet, which would allow Gromyko to close out his long career as the titular Soviet head of state.

Initiative for the deal seems to have come from Yevgeniy Primakov, an influential foreign-affairs specialist with close ties to the KGB. Primakov approached Aleksandr Yakovlev, whom Gorbachev had recently installed as chief of the prestigious Moscow think tank IMEMO (Institute of World Economy and International Relations), and the foreign minister's son Anatoliy, with the suggestion that the two senior figures combine forces to prevent the fiasco of another Chernenko-like appointment. Anatoliy raised the issue with his father, who authorized his son to discuss the proposed deal with Yakovlev, who went immediately to Gorbachev. Pacing about his spacious Central Committee office, Gorbachev debated the pros and cons. Finally, Gorbachev told Yakovlev to convey his acceptance, saying "I know how to keep my promises." Many years later Gorbachev wrote that on learning of Chernenko's death he had promptly telephoned Gromyko at the airport and proposed that they "unify their efforts" but in this account he did not mention any deal.[11]

At Last We Have a Leader

In his first major speech, at the April 1985 Central Committee plenum Gorbachev demonstrated a refreshing candor. "Unfavorable tendencies have strengthened in the economic development of our country in recent years," he acknowledged.[12] It was a breath of fresh air in comparison with what had generally been heard from the Kremlin over the past two decades. Moreover, Gorbachev specifically rejected the notion that Soviet problems might be the result of natural difficulties or external interference. The source of the current difficulties lay in the failure to undertake major changes in the way the economy had been managed.

Gorbachev projected an image of vigor and receptivity that was intended to contrast with the behavior of the aged leaders who had preceded him. In seemingly unscripted visits to ordinary Moscow and Leningrad neighborhoods in April and May, he listened to the complaints of people thronging around him and showed himself capable of improvisation and humor. When a woman shouted out, "Just get close to the people and we'll not let you down," Gorbachev laughed back, "Can I be any closer?" Stage-managed events had been a feature of Kremlin politics at least since the time of Potemkin, but in these early days Gorbachev's forays into the crowds seemed genuine.

Other, less public initiatives also showed his determination to present a new image. At an April 4 Politburo meeting, Gorbachev urged that party leaders adopt a simpler style in public: shorter speeches, less jargon, avoidance of showy optimism. Gorbachev called in top newspaper editors to tell them that he did not want to be cited each day as a font of wisdom. "You can quote Marx and Lenin if you have to have quotations," he enjoined.[13]

Gorbachev tapped into a wellspring of hope across Soviet society. Leaving the Kremlin after their first meeting with the new leader, Chief of Staff Akromeyev and Defense Minister Sokolov told each other, "Now it seems, we can work. Finally we have a leader."[14] Leon Onikov, a senior official in the Central Committee, said that initially "many workers in the party apparat regarded the idea of revolutionary perestroika, put forward by Gorbachev, as the salvation of the country and displayed a sincere wish to aid its fulfillment."[15] In Gorky, after watching Gorbachev speak on television, Andrei Sakharov told a fellow patient in the hospital where he was recovering from forced feeding during a hunger strike, "It looks like the country has gotten lucky this time; the new leader is an intelligent man."[16]

Gorbachev Cleans House

The first job of any new leader in the USSR was to secure his own power base, and Gorbachev managed the task in a way that showed him to be a skilled practitioner of old-fashioned Kremlin power politics. Within a few months, Gorbachev moved decisively to eject opponents from key slots, appointing a new generation of younger officials in what amounted to a purge of the Brezhnev machine.

In April, at the first Central Committee plenum since Gorbachev's accession, KGB chief Chebrikov and Central Committee secretaries Ligachev and Ryzhkov—the team that had engineered Gorbachev's victory—were rewarded with full Politburo membership. At the July Central Committee plenum, Gorbachev dispatched former Leningrad party boss Romanov, who retired from the Politburo for "health" reasons, thereby eliminating his youngest and potentially strongest conservative challenger. At the same plenum, two regional barons were brought to Moscow to serve as Central Committee secretaries: Lev Zaikov, who had taken Romanov's place in Leningrad, and Boris Yeltsin, from Sverdlovsk, about whom much more would be heard later.

The day after the July plenum, Gorbachev carried out his part of the bargain with Gromyko, who was elevated to be chairman of the Supreme Soviet. Gorbachev announced that Gromyko's replacement as foreign minister would be Georgian party boss Eduard Shevardnadze, a rude surprise for Gromyko, who had expected that his successor would be his longtime deputy Korniyenko. The move showed Gorbachev's political astuteness; he had carried out his part of the bargain, but he had done so in a way that effectively sidelined the conservative Gromyko and enhanced his own personal control over the foreign policy portfolio.

In September, eighty-year-old Prime Minister Tikhonov, who had to be held up by Gorbachev when he tripped in public, resigned at his doctors' insistence. Ryzhkov, at fifty-four the same age as Gorbachev, replaced Tikhonov, thereby putting a Gorbachev ally at the head of the Soviet government. At roughly the same time, Nikolai Baibakov left Gosplan, which he had headed since the Stalin era, allowing Gorbachev to appoint a sympathizer to lead the Soviet central planning apparatus.

In December 1985, the last of the Brezhnev coterie fell, when Yeltsin replaced Grishin as head of the Moscow party organization. Gorbachev also moved decisively to get his people installed at lower levels. Georgi Razumovskiy, who had impressed Gorbachev while heading the Krasnodar region near Stavropol, took over the key Central Committee department in charge of personnel and Yakovlev was brought in to head the ideology department. By the end of 1985, Gorbachev had taken firm control over all of the traditional levers of power in the USSR, with the exception of the military, which was not inclined to challenge the new leader who, for his part, was careful in the early years of his tenure not to rattle the generals' cages.[17]

Acceleration

One of the ironies of the Soviet system, supposedly founded on central planning, was how little actual planning was done. Vadim Medvedev, who became one of Gorbachev's closest aides, wrote, "There was no program carefully worked out on all points . . . There was a sum of ideas on the basis of which was gradually formulated a new political course."[18] Another close adviser, Georgi Shakhnazarov, agrees that Gorbachev had "no complete and carefully worked out program." Still less did Gorbachev have any intention of completely transforming the existing system. Rather, "He simply wanted to make it better and more perfect."[19]

Gorbachev's early programs are associated with the term *acceleration*— essentially do what the country was already doing, but do it better and faster. Andropov adopted the notion of acceleration during his brief tenure, and Gorbachev quickly picked it up once he took office. Acceleration emphasized growth in traditional Soviet industrial sectors, increasing discipline through attacks on drunkenness and corruption, and efforts to apply in the civilian-sector approaches derived from the military-industrial complex, which was thought to be one branch of the Soviet economy that worked well.[20]

On the economic side, acceleration centered around the machine-tool-building sector, where in June 1985 Gorbachev called for investment to rise by 80 percent. By the end of the upcoming five-year plan in 1990, according to Siberian economic guru Abel Aganbegyan, who was emerging as a key adviser to the new Gorbachev team, half of the current industrial equipment of this type would be replaced by new.[21]

Gorbachev drew on the model of the Military-Industrial Commission (MIC), which united supervision of all elements of the Soviet military industry under one roof, to create similar bodies in other important branches of the economy. In an effort to improve quality, he introduced into the civilian sector the military practice of stationing officers in plants with the power to reject unsatisfactory items, with disastrous results when such large numbers of goods were rejected that planned targets could not be met, leading to near rebellion among managers and workers alike.

The "Lemonade" General Secretary

In April 1985, less than a month after he had become general secretary, Gorbachev chaired a meeting of the Politburo to tackle Russia's age-old problem of drink. A commission, established under Andropov and chaired by the head of the Russian republic, Mikhail Solomentsev, produced data showing the disastrous effect of this traditional Russian woe. Soviet citizens consumed an average 8.3 liters of pure alcohol per person every year. Alcohol abuse caused an economic loss of at least thirty billion rubles per year, and the human cost was even more staggering. In 1984 almost twenty million people were arrested or received some form of administrative punishment for drunkenness or abuse of regulations governing alcohol. The commission proposed a broad range of measures, including cuts in production, price increases, stiffened punishments for drunkenness, and educational measures in party organizations, schools, and workplaces.

After hearing the commission's sobering report, Gorbachev called for comment. What he got was a stark warning. First Deputy Finance Minister V. V. Demichev produced a detailed set of figures showing that cutbacks in the sale of alcoholic beverages would cause a sharp drop in state revenue and send the budget into deficit. Gorbachev dismissed Demichev's warnings, coldly reminding the unfortunate official that he was speaking before the august majesty of the Politburo. Undeterred, L. A. Voronin, First Deputy Chief of Gosplan, predicted that cutting back sales of alcoholic beverages would increase inflationary pressures and lead to immediate shortages in goods such as sugar, used in the production of samogon, the potent Russian version of moonshine.[22]

Despite these warnings, in May Gorbachev launched the USSR's most stringent antialcohol campaign since the Bolsheviks tried to ban it altogether in 1919. Gorbachev's efforts produced some positive results. Russia's crude death rate fell by 12 percent. Crime, industrial accidents, and domestic violence declined. But the campaign also had negative consequences that contributed to its relaxation in 1987 and complete abandonment by 1988. As alcohol sales fell, state revenue also declined, and the Soviet budget went into a deficit from which it never emerged. In 1985 the state budget was estimated to be in deficit by eighteen billion rubles; by 1988 the deficit had risen to an estimated ninety billion rubles.[23]

Soviet officials, long-practiced in the display of zeal in executing the center's periodic propaganda campaigns, reacted with the usual excesses. In winegrowing regions, vineyards were uprooted. Beer production facilities, some only recently purchased abroad, were dismantled or allowed to rust in unopened packing crates. Soviet citizens also reacted in predictable ways. Sugar disappeared from the shops as Soviet men turned to producing samogon, exactly as had been predicted. Some switched to less conventional sources to slake their thirst. Supplies of antifreeze, aftershave, and perfume, not exactly abundant in any case, also disappeared. Deaths from drinking poisonous alcohol rose markedly.

Another consequence was a rise in jokes. A famous example has two friends standing in an interminable line to buy vodka. Losing patience, one storms off saying he is going to shoot the SOB who started this campaign. After a while he returns, complaining that the line waiting to take a shot at the general secretary is even longer. Gorbachev initially took the criticism in stride, even telling Western leaders some of the jokes directed at him, but when the political heat became too great and the economic consequences too obvious, Gorbachev sought to shift the blame to subordinates.

Had the antialcohol campaign been undertaken more gradually and with greater attention to economic side-effects, it might have succeeded. Instead it became an embarrassing setback, what Yakovlev called "the most serious mistake of our rule."[24] The episode revealed important elements of Gorbachev's personal style that became even more obvious in later years: an eagerness to tackle long-standing problems but also an arrogance that sometimes translated into refusal to listen to those who questioned his views. Gorbachev was willing to adopt outside-the-box solutions, but when these ran into difficulties his inclination was to hesitate, maneuver, and eventually move on to some other problem, leaving behind an accumulating train of half-filled measures and unresolved issues.

The Twenty-Seventh Party Congress

Opening on February 25, 1986, thirty years to the day after Khrushchev delivered his famous "secret speech" denouncing Stalin, the 27th Party Congress was Gorbachev's opportunity to unveil a program to implement the changes he had been calling for in well-publicized forays across the country. Yet what Gorbachev proposed was far from a complete overhaul of the system. "What we had in mind," Gorbachev said, "was not a revolution but a specific improvement of the system, which we then believed was possible."[25]

Gorbachev opened with an unprecedented acknowledgment of problems in the party. "For many years," according to Gorbachev, "the practical actions of party and state organs had lagged behind the demands of the times." On the economy, Gorbachev called for "radical reform" and floated phrases that seemed to hint at serious change: market forces, financial incentives, local autonomy.[26] The five-year plan adopted at the congress, by contrast, hardly seemed to envision any kind of reform. It called for an 18–22 percent increase in capital investment and an 80 percent increase in machine-tool building, the heart of Gorbachev's acceleration strategy but clearly unattainable in view of other commitments. Spending on the consumer was supposed to increase due to a sharp rise in overall national income, which in fact was actually falling. One-third of all capital investment would go to agriculture, continuing its drain of the Soviet economy.[27] Real spending on the military was, as always, carefully concealed, but years later Gorbachev acknowledged that in this, the last five-year plan formally implemented by the USSR, military spending grew one and a half or two times as fast as did overall national income.[28]

Personnel moves at the 27th Congress consolidated changes that Gorbachev and his team had made at all levels of the party's leading organs. By March 1986, over 60 percent of Politburo members and Central Committee secretaries had taken their posts after Gorbachev's accession. Of the 307 full Central Committee members chosen at the Congress, 41 percent were new, the highest rate of turnover since the 22nd Party Congress in 1961. Five of the fifteen republican leaders were new and of the 157 regional first secretaries, 50, or almost one-third were replaced after Gorbachev took office, coming on top of the substantial changes in this key pillar of the Soviet establishment begun under Andropov.[29]

Gorbachev was eager to use the momentum of the congress to step up the pace of reform. Meeting on March 10 with top party officials, he enthused that the congress had created a "new atmosphere of party frankness." Yakovlev also emerged from the 27th Congress filled with hope. Earlier, Gorbachev had only been willing to discuss some of his more ambitious plans in private, but now he was going public with speeches about "democracy, about law and order, about the equality of all before the law." But Gorbachev proved unable to transform his stirring phrases into practical steps. Underlying the problem, Yakovlev acknowledged, was a deeper one. Gorbachev and his team, including at that time Yakovlev himself, saw the issue as one of a "return to some kind of Leninist principles." But this concept of reforming the system from within could not succeed, Yakovlev eventually concluded, because what was needed was "to demolish the entire system without any equivocations."[30] In any case, Gorbachev's ambitious plans for following up the 27th Congress were soon put on hold by an unexpected tragedy in a small Ukrainian town.

Chernobyl

On April 28, 1986, I was at my State Department desk when Swedish nuclear power plants began reporting high levels of radiation in the atmosphere over their country. Analysis of radiation and the prevailing wind patterns pointed to the likelihood of a serious nuclear accident in the western USSR, a conclusion reinforced by airline pilots who observed a massive smoke column. Soviet authorities remained silent but it appeared that something had gone seriously wrong at a nuclear power plant whose name would soon reverberate around the world—Chernobyl.

The Accident

At approximately 1:20 AM on April 26, during an exercise intended to test an emergency procedure considered so risky that other Soviet nuclear power plants had refused to do it, the massive Chernobyl complex began to shake with the violence of an earthquake. Technicians tried to slow the reaction by ordering control rods to descend into the reactor but it was too late. Steam and hydrogen gas accumulating in the stricken reactor room triggered explosions that blew a hole in the roof and sent flames and radioactive debris cascading across the grounds. Not immediately understanding what had happened, technicians rushed to the reactor floor, where they found massive concrete blocks and heavy equipment tossed about like pebbles and fires raging through the corridors of the complex. Their heroism and that of firefighters soon on the scene, who fought the blaze without any radiation protective gear, saved three nearby nuclear reactors, a feat for which many paid with their lives. But no one could get close to the reactor core, which was spewing highly radioactive smoke from burning graphite in an amount equivalent to many times the mass of radioactive substances released by the Hiroshima bomb.

During the incident, the plant's operators made a number of mistakes: disconnecting key safety systems before the exercise began and responding inappropriately to problems once the procedure began to go off course. But there were deeper causes to the Chernobyl catastrophe. Over the previous two decades, there had been at least a dozen serious nuclear power accidents in the USSR, some of which caused numerous casualties, but none had ever been reported in the Soviet media.

Soviet RBMK nuclear power reactors used ordinary water for cooling, graphite for moderating the nuclear chain reaction, and natural, nonenriched uranium for fuel, features that made it possible to build the reactors cheaply and in large size. But they contained design flaws that made them unstable at low levels of power and the Soviets neglected to surround them with containment vessels to prevent the release of radioactive material in the event of a catastrophic accident, a routine feature in Western reactors. The International Atomic Energy Agency (IAEA) concluded that the accident at Chernobyl stemmed from "deficient safety culture, not only at the Chernobyl plant, but throughout the Soviet design, operating and regulatory organizations for nuclear power."[31]

Initial Responses

There was naturally some initial confusion about what had happened and how best to respond but the plant's senior staff and local officials in the area also concealed the truth. Chernobyl station director Viktor Bryukhanov, later jailed for misconduct, initially told Moscow that the reactor was intact. When the plant's civil defense chief reported that his dosimeter was showing radiation levels "off the scale," Bryukhanov told him to "toss that garbage aside."[32] The Energy Ministry's first report, about three hours after the explosion, said, falsely, that the fire had been extinguished and that measures were being taken to deal with the consequences of the accident and to investigate its causes. It concluded that "special measures including evacuation of the population from the cities are not required."[33]

Despite efforts on the ground to conceal the facts, information about the incident began flowing back to Moscow almost immediately. By 2:30 AM, little more than an hour after the explosion, Chief of the General Staff Akromeyev had been informed and was on his way to his office. At 6 AM on April 26, Minister of Energy Bois Mayorets called Prime Minister Ryzhkov at home to say there had been an explosion followed by a fire at Chernobyl. Ryzhkov ordered Mayorets to go immediately to Chernobyl and telephoned Gorbachev. By 9 AM that morning, uniformed civil defense personnel were measuring radiation in the vicinity of the plant.

By midday on Saturday, an emergency governmental commission had been formed in Moscow. Much remained unclear but personnel and resources were flowing toward the scene. What was not happening were any steps to inform the public, even those in the immediate vicinity.[34]

Pripyat

Pripyat, a town of about fifty thousand, located almost literally in the shadow of the Chernobyl plant, enjoyed fine spring weather the morning after the accident. Many people were outside preparing their gardens for planting. Older children went to school and younger ones were in the playgrounds. Fishermen lined the banks of the streams that meander through the low-lying terrain. Some had witnessed the accident, which they later described as sounding like a huge rush of steam followed by a thunderous explosion and a fireball surging skyward. Women did their Saturday laundry, hanging the clothes to dry on their balconies, where they accumulated large doses of the radiation silently descending on the town.

Many of the nuclear plant's 4,500 workers lived in Pripyat and word that some kind of an accident had occurred spread quickly. Initially, few inhabitants thought anything serious was amiss. Accidents had occurred before and the authorities were not saying anything about danger. As the day progressed people became more worried. The authorities remained silent but the cloud of smoke intensified. The air took on what inhabitants described as a metallic smell. Those lucky enough to have cars packed their families into them and fled. As night fell, the remaining inhabitants closed their windows and drew their curtains, overcome by a grim sense of foreboding.

Finally, late in the evening of April 26, the government commission that had arrived on the scene that afternoon ordered Pripyat to be evacuated, over the objections of Bryukanov and the chief of the local party committee, who continued to insist that everything was under control. Deputy Minister of Health Vorobyov made an impassioned plea, "The air is full of plutonium, cesium, and strontium.... Everyone's thyroid glands, including those of the children, are packed with radioactive iodine." Overnight 1,100 buses lined up on twelve miles of highway outside of town. Guards were assigned to each building and by the next evening all inhabitants of Pripyat had left their homes, never to return.[35]

Heroism and Loss of Confidence

Over the next several weeks, government personnel on the scene at Chernobyl coordinated efforts to deal with the immediate consequences of the accident. Ultimately several hundred thousand personnel, many of them military, were detailed to fight the problem. Helicopter crews and ground personnel ventured into the hot zone for minutes at a time to drop sand on the fires. Among these "Chernobyl liquidators" instances of heroism were frequent, if largely unsung, for example, nuclear engineers who donned scuba gear and descended into fiercely radioactive water in the depths of the plant to close valves that were spewing contaminated water. Yakovlev described another instance that he learned about later from Minister of Defense Yazov. A unit of construction troops was sent urgently into the hot zone to build a barrier to prevent radioactive water from flowing into the Pripyat River. Yakovlev asked where radiation suits for the soldiers had been found on short notice and Yazov replied that the troops were sent in without any protective gear. "They were soldiers and had to do their duty," he said.[36]

Eventually the Soviet system—slow, cumbersome, sometimes heroic and sometimes brutally insensitive—managed to contain the Chernobyl tragedy. But the way it did, marked by delays, inefficiencies, and most of all by the failure to provide the truth about the incident to an increasingly alarmed population, had a powerful effect on the confidence of the Soviet people in the system and the people at its top. The process that only five years later brought about the end of the Communist system began in earnest at Chernobyl.

Pavel Palazhenko returned to Moscow from a foreign assignment shortly after the accident. He found the Soviet capital "close to panic. The city was rife with rumors and few people believed the official version of events." The mood in Moscow was gloomy, angry, and deeply distrustful of the authorities. According to Palazhenko and many other contemporary observers, Chernobyl caused a rift between the people and the government that never closed. It was the beginning of "the loss of legitimacy of the country's leadership in the eyes of the people."[37]

Official Prevarication

Only late on April 28, more than sixty hours after the explosion and after information had appeared in the West, did the Soviet authorities issue their first cryptic announcement: an accident has occurred, measures are being taken, a government commission has been created. The next day, the authorities released another short statement that added mendacity to obfuscation by concluding that "the level of contamination somewhat exceeds allowed norms but not to that degree which would require special measures for the protection of the population."[38]

Not until May 6, nine days after the accident, did *Pravda* report that an explosion followed by a fire had destroyed "structural elements housing the reactor." *Pravda* acknowledged that "radioactivity was partially discharged," but it stressed that the situation was "under control not only near the NPS [nuclear power station] but also in the surrounding areas."[39] No information was provided about levels of radiation that had been released, the dangers that people might be exposed to, or what steps people might reasonably take to protect themselves.

On May 14, Gorbachev finally spoke to the Soviet people. He provided more information about Chernobyl than previous leaders had about other Soviet accidents, but what he said was incomplete or at best a half-truth. Gorbachev said casualties totaled nine dead and 299 hospitalized for radiation sickness.[40] Listening to Gorbachev's speech, General Valentin Varennikov, who had been recalled from Afghanistan to direct the efforts of the Soviet military at Chernobyl, felt a sense of disappointed surprise. He knew that the actual number of deaths was larger and he was especially critical of Gorbachev's assertion that there would be no serious consequences from the Chernobyl accident, something that Varennikov could see with his own eyes was false.[41]

More than half of Gorbachev's speech was devoted to an attack on foreign reactions to the accident, using language reminiscent of the Soviet cover-up following the KAL 007 shoot-down. The Soviets had rejected US offers of assistance and now Gorbachev chose to accuse the "ruling circles of the USA" and other Western nations of exploiting the accident to create obstacles to East-West dialogue. I recall watching the speech in my office—where we had spent much of the past two weeks trying to collect information about the accident and coordinating the many offers of assistance that began to flow in as soon as the US public became aware of the disaster—and wondering what it said about the real intentions of the Soviet leader who for the past year had been proclaiming his intention to introduce positive change in the USSR.

The leaders of Ukraine, the republic in which Chernobyl was located, provided the worst example of high-level insensitivity. Within hours of the explosion the wind had brought radiation drifting over Kiev, only sixty miles from Chernobyl. Top Ukrainian officials sent their families out of Kiev but party boss Shcherbitskiy insisted on going through with the May Day celebrations as if nothing had happened.

Despite the official silence, word about the accident could not be completely concealed. Within days of the explosion, something like mass panic infected the Ukrainian capital. Arriving in Kiev on his way to Chernobyl a week after the accident, nuclear engineer Grigoriy Medvedev noticed the streets were unusually empty. Midlevel Ukrainian officials told Medvedev that in the week since the explosion about one million people had left the city. Medvedev heard rumors that in the first three days after the explosion radioactivity in Kiev had been as high as one hundred milliroentgens per hour, which Medvedev said was approximately two thousand times the World Health Organization (WHO) norm.[42]

At the time of the Chernobyl accident, I was in charge of preparations to open a new US consulate in Kiev. In October 1986, after repeated stalling by the Soviets, we were finally allowed to send a radiation assessment team to Kiev, headed by Bill Courtney, then designated to become our first consul general in Kiev and later ambassador in Kazakhstan and Georgia. By the time of the visit to Kiev, the Ukrainian authorities had been washing the city for months. The US team, which included scientists from government and private institutions, collected radiation samples from around the city and bought food in the local markets. Courtney also surreptitiously collected fallen leaves which had been on the trees at the time of the accident and which revealed lingering traces of the radiation that had descended on the city after the accident. Nevertheless, analysis of the data brought back by the US team showed radiation in the fall of 1986 to be essentially at background levels.[43]

The failure of the Soviet authorities to release radiation information was not due to a lack of data. The State Committee for Hydrometeorology regularly collected information about radiation levels that was transmitted to the Politburo on a daily basis, but there it was classified secret and remained unavailable to the public.[44]

Alla Yaroshinskaya, a reporter from the town of Zhitomir, about 130 kilometers from Chernobyl, was elected to the Congress of People's Deputies in 1989, where she managed to obtain access to the records of the Politburo commission established to deal with the accident. She found that data the commission received on the number hospitalized because of the accident was consistently higher than the figures it released to the public. Early in May, the commission recorded that the Soviet Ministry of Health had secretly adopted new allowed levels of radiation that were ten times higher than those previously in effect.[45]

The deception continued for years. In the spring of 1989, Soviet authorities published maps revealing that large areas of the country, previously declared safe, had actually been contaminated. People were belatedly evacuated from these areas amid a general attitude of "panic and disbelief."[46]

SOUL SEARCHING

Loren Graham, one of the foremost US experts on Soviet science and technology, described Chernobyl as "a disaster waiting to happen." The Soviet approach toward nuclear power was based on minimizing construction and operating costs over all other considerations. Atommash, the Soviet organization responsible for building nuclear power plants, operated under an assembly-line approach, building large plants as quickly and as cheaply as possible, putting as many as six of these giants together in one spot, and locating them near cities to reduce the cost of transmission.[47]

At the June 3 session of the Chernobyl commission, with Gorbachev present, Deputy Prime Minister Shcherbina provided a reasonably accurate summary of the causes of the accident, which he said lay in serious mistakes by the staff and problems with the design of the reactor. After listening to Shcherbina, Gorbachev accused the nuclear industry of putting into operation a "half-completed" reactor and demanded to know who had made the decision to locate the Chernobyl station near a populated area.[48] The longtime head of the Soviet nuclear power industry, Yefim Slavskiy, who had received the first of his three Hero of Socialist Labor awards in 1949 for his work on the first Soviet A-bomb, was not about to take Gorbachev's accusations lying down. Replying that he was "astounded" by Gorbachev's remarks, Slavskiy placed all the blame for the accident on the failures of the operators. He defended the RBMK reactor, which he claimed worked well everywhere and pointed out, correctly enough, that decisions on locating the reactor and building it without any containment vessel had been made at the highest levels of the Soviet government.[49]

Slavskiy's remarks precipitated an emotional response by Academician Valery Legasov, deputy director of the famed Kurchatov Institute for Nuclear Physics, who had been at the scene of the accident from its earliest days. Legasov said the RBMK reactor did not meet international or Soviet norms. Its weaknesses had been known for ten years and he pointed out that the Finns, who had been pressured to buy one, had replaced all of its control equipment with Western devices and installed a containment vessel.[50]

Two years after the Chernobyl accident Legasov hanged himself in the stairway of his Moscow apartment building, reportedly out of remorse because he had not been allowed to tell the whole truth. Before he died, Legasov recorded a TV interview with himself in which he lamented that in the Soviet system technology had been allowed to trump morality. Earlier generations of Soviet scientists, Sakharov, Pyotr Kapitsa, and Kurchatov, had a "correct moral sense" in part because they had been educated in the tradition of the giants of Russian culture. But the connection with Russian prerevolutionary traditions had been broken, and "Soviet man was technically developed but morally stunted."[51]

Gorbachev and Chernobyl

Gorbachev wrote later that his life could be divided into two parts—one before and one after Chernobyl.[52] He concluded that Chernobyl "shed light on many of the sicknesses of our system as a whole" and served as a "convincing argument in favor of radical reforms."[53] Chernobyl marked, in some ways, the switch from Gorbachev as Andropov, the cautious tinkerer with the more obvious symptoms of the country's problems, to Gorbachev the radical reformer as the world remembers him.

But Chernobyl also revealed flaws in Gorbachev's personality that became more evident as his tenure in office continued. Within the closed structure of the Soviet leadership, Gorbachev insisted that top officials get personally involved and he supported Ryzhkov's determination to visit the scene when the prime minister concluded that accurate information was not reaching Moscow. But Ryzhkov also asks why Gorbachev himself never visited Chernobyl. Somehow he did not seem to realize, as Ryzhkov put it, "how much human sympathy he would have gained from even a short, several hour appearance at Chernobyl."[54]

Gorbachev consistently argued for providing information to the public but what he actually said was not always truthful. Supporters of Gorbachev's view were a minority on the Politburo, and he had to engage in a kind of balancing act over Chernobyl. It was not the last time Gorbachev would be forced into this kind of maneuvering, but it is impossible not to agree with Palazhenko's rueful conclusion that "he sometimes continued to balance even when it was time, as they say, to fish or cut bait."[55]

An Unexpected Phone Call

In December 1986, Sakharov and his wife Yelena Bonner were surprised to hear a knock at the door of their Gorky apartment. A visitor of any kind was a rarity for the two exiles but surprise turned to astonishment when the callers turned out to be repairmen who said they had come to install the Sakharovs' new telephone. The Sakharovs had not actually ordered a phone, but after seven years of isolation they were not about to object, and they watched with interest while the technicians silently went about their business. After they left, the Sakharovs tried the phone but found the connection was dead. Suspecting it was some kind of KGB trick, they left the new instrument sitting in splendid silence on their kitchen table.

The next morning, the Sakharovs were surprised when the phone rang. On picking up the receiver, a brusque voice asked if this was the residence of Andrei Dmitriyevich Sakharov and if their phone was working satisfactorily. On receiving an affirmative answer to both questions, the unidentified caller slammed down the line. A few minutes later the phone rang again but this time a pleasant young woman identified herself as the Kremlin operator. She asked courteously if Andrei Dmitriyevich was at home. On learning that she was speaking to Sakharov himself, she asked him to wait and a few seconds later Gorbachev was on the other end of the line, with the message that Sakharov was free to return to Moscow to resume his "patriotic work."[1]

When the two exiles arrived on December 22, on the platform to interview them were representatives of Soviet and foreign media. The next day, when Sakharov returned to his home institute of nuclear physics, he was greeted by a standing ovation.

Stepping Up the Pace of Change

Sakharov's return was a sign that Gorbachev had decided to step up the pace of change. In January 1987, he opened a Central Committee plenum with an impassioned three-hour speech. Central Committee members listened "in tense silence" as the general secretary delivered a plea for fundamental changes in the way the party operated. Gorbachev acknowledged "the problems that have accumulated in society are more deep-rooted than we had thought." The solution was to deepen democracy throughout the Soviet system, including in the party itself.[2]

Gorbachev's speech set off a vigorous debate. Although no one expressly challenged him, the resolution adopted at the end of the plenum was silent on a number of Gorbachev's specific proposals. Despite Gorbachev's impassioned rhetoric actual changes in party practice were small. During the rest of 1987, 120 party secretaries across the entire USSR were chosen by secret ballot but none were higher than a city party committee and all of the multiple candidates were chosen from above by the next higher party organization.[3]

Around the time of the January 1987 plenum, a sensational film began appearing in cinemas across the USSR. *Repentance* is an allegorical portrayal of a small Georgian town where the corpse of a mayor responsible for numerous crimes keeps reappearing despite repeated efforts to bury it. The film attracted intense excitement because of its unmistakable allusions to Stalin. It had been created in 1984 under the patronage of Eduard Shevardnadze, then the party boss of Georgia. After Shevardnadze came to Moscow as foreign minister, he brought the film to the attention of Yakovlev and Gorbachev, who overruled Politburo conservatives and released the film for general viewing.[4]

Glasnost Opens Up

Gorbachev aimed to use glasnost to mobilize the power of public opinion to outflank his conservative opponents but it took some time to get started. Accompanied by Ligachev and Yakovlev, Gorbachev met in June 1986 with leading writers to seek their support against "the apparat which broke Khrushchev's neck." The general secretary acknowledged that "clashes" in the Politburo had had the effect of putting off change: "Now, we want to act. . . . We have to make the process irreversible."[5]

Soviet intellectuals at first reacted cautiously. Vitaliy Korotich, editor of the weekly magazine *Ogonyok*, which became one of the driving forces behind glasnost, described his initial reaction: "When Gorbachev proclaimed glasnost it first seemed like giving an old trollop a sponge bath and putting clean clothes on her, assuming that this would restore her virginity."[6]

Slowly at first, but with increasing speed glasnost picked up. In 1987 Soviet readers were rocked by Anatoly Rybakov's novel *Children of the Arbat*, whose hero is a Komsomol activist exiled unjustly and which featured some unflattering portraits of Stalin and his chief lieutenants. Rybakov's work was more noteworthy for its political impact than literary merit. But the next year a novel appeared that portrayed Soviet reality in a fashion worthy of the classics of Russian literature. Vasily Grossman's *Life and Fate* described with Tolstoyan sweep the trajectories of an extended family through some of the grimmest episodes of the Second World War. Grossman drew an explicit parallel between the totalitarianisms of Stalin and Hitler—no doubt why Suslov reportedly told Grossman, after the KGB had confiscated his manuscript, that it could not be published in the USSR for hundreds of years.[7] Finally, in 1989, to the astonishment of almost everyone, Solzhenitsyn's *Gulag Archipelago* was published in the USSR, fifteen years after its appearance in the West.

Filling in the Blank Spots

Once it became clear that the constraints of fear were loosening, people plunged headlong into the new world. Dreary Soviet publications turned overnight into interesting purveyors of contemporary news and sensational sources of information about the past. People argued passionately in the streets, on the metro, and in offices. "Lines to newspaper kiosks—sometimes huge crowds around the block—formed at 6 AM and the daily allotments were often sold out in two hours."[8]

The history that glasnost turned up was not pretty. Yuriy Afanasyev, the rector of the Moscow Institute of History and Archives, said, "No country and no people has had a history as falsified as ours."[9] In 1988 the poet Yevgenii Yevtushenko, who in his youth had warned against the dangers posed by Stalin's heirs but had mostly fallen into uneasy silence under Brezhnev, reemerged with a warning, saying, "We must know our history—all of it to the last hidden bit. Otherwise the blank spots in history become blank spots on the national conscience."[10] In November 1988, Roy Medvedev for the first time informed the Soviet public about the true scope of Stalin's crimes. During 1937 and 1938 five to seven million people were arrested, of whom only one million were party members, taking the story beyond the revelations of Khrushchev, who had focused on Stalin's actions against the party and military elite.[11]

As history's blank spots began to be filled in, glasnost turned to contemporary Soviet reality. Soviet citizens learned that the USSR ranked seventy-seventh globally in per capita consumption, behind every European country except Albania. As many as fifty million people, 17 percent of the total population, lived in communal apartments or workers' dormitories. Expenditure on health care amounted to 3 percent of GDP, the lowest figure for all developed countries, perhaps one reason why 35 percent of Soviet hospitals had no hot water and one-sixth had no water at all.[12]

Against this backdrop, it came as no surprise that economic growth over the period of Soviet rule turned out to be far lower than the authorities had claimed. Growth had been higher in the 1920s during Lenin's more relaxed New Economic Policy (NEP) than during the Stalin era and economists concluded that the USSR could actually have developed faster without the brutalities of Stalinism. Radical economists wrote, "We can never escape the tragic fact that the price (the country paid) was in no way commensurate with the results," or in other words, "millions of people had died for nothing."[13]

In unleashing the creative energies and moral outrage of the Soviet people, Gorbachev got more than he bargained for. Glasnost shattered virtually every myth on which the Soviet system was founded. For many intellectuals these revelations were another argument in favor of moving toward a truly democratic system, but for Gorbachev, who could never bring himself to support change beyond the "socialist choice," glasnost became a dilemma. Gorbachev mobilized a large and vocal segment of the intelligentsia but in doing so he ended up undermining belief in the system he wanted to rejuvenate, not destroy.

Donald J. Raleigh's oral history of Soviet baby boomers from Moscow and Saratov provides good insight into the reaction of ordinary people to glasnost. Many of the participants in the study recalled that their first reaction to the sudden and unexpected openness of glasnost was one of euphoria. Moscow chemist Lyubov Kovalyova said, "At first it was very interesting, everyone simply lapped up this information. People stayed glued to their television sets, avidly read newspapers, and discussed everything." Marina Bakutina, a teacher at Moscow's Institute of Foreign Languages, described the outpouring of glasnost as "like a clap of thunder on a clear day." But as glasnost revelations unfolded, many said it forced them to reconsider their understanding of Soviet history and eventually destroyed their belief in the system. Olga Gorelik, a professor of physics at Saratov University, recalled how unpleasant it was "to know that you had been deceived for a long time on so many questions." Others said simply, "We lost our anchor."[14]

Economic Reform Stumbles

During the first two years of Gorbachev's tenure the Soviet economy enjoyed a modest uptick. At the beginning of 1987 production began to decline and difficulties arose in the critical metalworking sector. Some of the problems stemmed from Gorbachev's own actions. The budget deficit associated with the antialcohol campaign was ballooning. The Andropov economic "experiment" was expanded under Gorbachev. But even though the number of plan targets was cut by half, managers still received a "tremendous number of plan assignments" and could be penalized for not meeting them.[15]

Political changes Gorbachev introduced also helped undermine the economic system. With the emergence of a new generation free from the fear complex, the command-style economic system lost its essential political underpinning. Labor discipline plunged and a general apathy and inertia set in.[16]

Gorbachev summoned economic officials and academic economists to a four-hour discussion on how to get reform moving again. All agreed that the piecemeal approach pursued up to then was not working and that a comprehensive strategy to simplify planning mechanisms and allow greater initiative by enterprise managers was needed. Unfortunately, beyond consensus on these few principles, agreement broke down. Prime Minister Ryzhkov believed that fundamental reform could not be undertaken until the next five-year plan and that central planners should retain key levers of state control. Academic economists wanted to reduce the scope of central planning but after that they divided into liberals who believed in "market socialism" and a quantitative school that followed the econometric approach developed by Leonid Kantorovich. Gorbachev was sympathetic to the latter group, largely because at this stage any flirtation with the market was still considered out-of-bounds.[17]

Gorbachev decided that the June Central Committee plenum should be devoted to economic reform. Unfortunately, preparations were handled by two separate working groups. Academic economists and Central Committee experts were given the task of drafting Gorbachev's speech, while a team of government officials, led by Ryzhkov, worked on a packet of decrees to implement the new program.[18]

Inevitably, the plenum was a disappointment. Gorbachev warned that the Law on Enterprises, which was supposedly the centerpiece of the plenum, could suffer the same fate as Kosygin's reforms if it was encircled by "a palisade of numerous instructions which could emasculate its essence." Unfortunately, despite the fact that thirty-two speakers trudged to the podium after the general secretary finished, as Gorbachev noted later, "there was no serious discussion of reform."[19] In a clear sign of pique, Prime Minister Ryzhkov, the most senior official responsible for the economy, failed to speak at all.

Formally, the plenum seemed to give Gorbachev a victory. It approved the Law on Enterprises and established the principle that all enterprises would eventually move to self-financing. At the same time, many elements of the old system were retained, including "the rationing of producer goods, price controls . . . and resource distribution through the ministries." The resolutions adopted by the plenum raised the prospect of competition and even bankruptcy. But the basic framework of a planned economy based on state ownership was retained. "Not a single word was said about the transition to market relations."[20]

Gorbachev and his advisers, recognizing they could not get what they wanted on economic reform, decided to attack "the main brake—the conservative political system" and turn back later to the economy.[21] Unfortunately, while Gorbachev focused on his political agenda the Soviet economy continued its downward spiral, ensuring that when Gorbachev turned his attention to economic reform two years later it was amid a deepening crisis that made change even more difficult.

The Yeltsin Uprising Begins

On October 23, 1987, Secretary of State Shultz saw Gorbachev in Moscow for what should have been a routine meeting. Gorbachev, however, was unexpectedly pugnacious, even at one point asking sarcastically how much the United States had paid for the pension of the pilot who flew KAL 007. Shultz, who had always viewed Gorbachev as "super-sure of himself," like a fighter who has never lost a battle, was surprised. Shultz told his aides, "This boxer has been hit."[22]

The secretary was right. Two days before he met Shultz, Gorbachev had faced an unusual challenge. At the end of a Central Committee plenum convened to approve Gorbachev's speech on the occasion of the seventieth anniversary of the Bolshevik revolution, Boris Yeltsin unexpectedly rose to speak. In a rambling presentation that was part an attack on perestroika and the party leadership, part an admission of personal failings, and in some ways a cri de coeur from a troubled soul, Yeltsin first astonished and then enraged Gorbachev.

Yeltsin began by attacking the work of the Secretariat and its chief, Ligachev, and then took on Gorbachev for allowing glorification of the general secretary. But Yeltsin quickly broadened his assault. People felt they were getting nothing from perestroika, he said. Their mood was souring and they were becoming increasingly skeptical about the length of time it was taking to fulfill leadership promises. Yeltsin concluded that "evidently, my position on the Politburo is not working out."[23]

After Yeltsin had finished, Gorbachev—his face "purple with rage"—invited other Central Committee members to give their opinion. In time-honored show-trial fashion, twenty-four participants, including many who liked to portray themselves as liberals, trouped to the podium to lambaste Yeltsin. At the conclusion of what amounted to a public lynching, a chastened Yeltsin said how difficult it had been for him to listen to the criticism, including from some whom he had previously thought of as friends. But he also told Gorbachev, "Regarding perestroika, I won't tremble before you." The mood of the people was changing and there had been too much wavering by the leadership, Yeltsin concluded.[24]

In his two years at the helm of the Moscow party machine, Yeltsin had developed a populist public persona based on raids of Moscow stores and factories, where he put top officials on the spot for abuse and corruption, and his practice of traveling on some well-publicized occasions by subway instead of leadership limousines. Yeltsin's remarks at the 27th Party Congress, where he had questioned the privileges enjoyed by the leadership, were applauded by the delegates. According to Ambassador Matlock, Yeltsin "quickly became a legend and to Muscovites was the most tangible proof that perestroika was not a sham." Yet Yeltsin was rarely mentioned in the central media despite the flowering of glasnost. Political insiders told the US embassy that orders to keep Yeltsin's "antics" out of the media came directly from Gorbachev.[25]

A few days after the Central Committee meeting, the Moscow party committee duly criticized Yeltsin's actions but also said he should be allowed to stay on as first secretary of the capital's party committee. It was an unusually courageous move and a striking demonstration of the respect Yeltsin had gained during his relatively brief time in the Soviet capital. The city's "mayor" was delegated to present the committee's decision to Gorbachev, who refused to meet him.

Two days later, Yeltsin was hauled by KGB guards from a hospital bed. Dazed by medication, Yeltsin was taken to a meeting of the Moscow party committee. In Gorbachev's presence, twenty-three speakers rose to attack their former chief in another orchestrated assault. At the end of the repulsive performance, Yeltsin went haltingly to the microphone, with Gorbachev steadying him at the elbow. The general secretary silenced a claque in the first rows shouting "Down with Yeltsin." His career seemingly at an end, Yeltsin made an abject recantation after which he returned to his seat and put his head down on the table.[26]

In Ambassador Matlock's view, "October 1987 marks the first of Gorbachev's major political blunders." Gorbachev acted in part because of personal reasons—"envy blinded his judgment"—but he also saw popular and charismatic figures like Yeltsin as potential rivals. Gorbachev would have done well to heed the advice of adviser Anatoliy Chernyayev, who warned that Yeltsin's dismissal "would be received as a victory for conservative forces" and be especially resented in Moscow.[27]

The Nina Andreyeva Letter: Party Conservatives Counterattack

In March 1988, I found myself at the foreign ministry in Belgrade for a briefing on Gorbachev's just-completed visit to Yugoslavia. Trading on their traditional balancing position between East and West, the Yugoslavs habitually provided Americans with informed briefings on the state of affairs in the USSR. On one point the usually well-informed Yugoslavs acknowledged some perplexity. Throughout the visit, they said, Gorbachev seemed preoccupied and distracted. He spent considerable time on the phone back to Moscow and often came late to meetings. The Yugoslavs speculated that the Soviet leader felt under heavy pressure from events at home.

The Yugoslavs, as usual, were perceptive. The day Gorbachev left for Yugoslavia the conservative paper *Sovetskaya Rossiya* published a letter from a previously unknown teacher in Leningrad, Nina Andreyeva, which amounted to the most dangerous public challenge Gorbachev had yet faced. In a long and densely argued essay, Andreyeva charged that perestroika was undermining verities of the Soviet system, including the class struggle, dictatorship of the proletariat, and socialist realism in the arts. Glasnost had led to a situation where problems were being discussed at the prompting of "Western radio voices." Andreyeva descended into the pit of anti-Semitism by charging that the views of liberals were characterized by "cosmopolitan" tendencies.[28]

Filled with densely argued dialectical reasoning as well as references to works published abroad that were not generally accessible to ordinary Soviets, Andreyeva's article was clearly something more than a polemical opinion piece by an obscure teacher. An investigation later established that the article had been put together during a secret visit to Leningrad by an editorial team from *Sovetskaya Rossiya* on the basis of two much longer submissions by Andreyeva. There also seemed to be solid circumstantial evidence of support by Ligachev, who praised the article in a meeting with the editors of leading Moscow media organs. Party organizations were instructed to give Andreyeva's article favorable study and it was reprinted in papers around the country.

Alarm spread among perestroika supporters. The editor of *Izvestiya*, Ivan Laptev, who had turned that former government mouthpiece into one of the leading organs of perestroika, told close associates after he returned from meeting Ligachev, "The time to choose has arrived. Personally I am for Gorbachev but I am getting ready to retire. The youngest of you here must make your own decisions, knowing what the risks and the stakes are."[29]

After returning from Yugoslavia, Gorbachev sent assistants to Leningrad to investigate Andreyeva, and he also received a detailed report on Ligachev's activities. But the situation within the Politburo was complex, and Gorbachev evidently felt that he had to tread carefully. Not until March 23, ten days after the article appeared, did Gorbachev launch a counterattack. That evening, Politburo members taking a break in the VIP lounge of the Kremlin Palace of Congresses began to praise the Andreyeva article. When Gorbachev broke in coldly with "I have a different opinion," an awkward silence ensued while the assembled leaders looked uneasily at one another. Gorbachev continued angrily, "This smells of a split . . . The article was against perestroika."[30]

At a Politburo meeting the next day, "Gorbachev was in a fighting mood." The stance of "some comrades," he said, had caused alarm. The article questioned the need for perestroika and was aimed at returning Soviet society to the 1930s. Ligachev countered with a complaint that the Soviet media was blackening the past and even raising such unacceptable issues as a two-party system. Ligachev also acknowledged that the editor of *Sovetskaya Rossiya* had visited him and that he liked the Andreyeva article. Yakovlev went through a point-by-point criticism of Andreyeva, concluding that those who supported the article were acting against Gorbachev and the policies the leadership had hitherto endorsed. After another day's discussion in which support for Andreyeva withered, Yakovlev was authorized to prepare a riposte for *Pravda*. Ten days later, *Sovetskaya Rossiya* issued a humiliating recantation.[31]

Gorbachev used his victory to solidify his position at the top of the party. Ligachev was effectively sidelined, as were almost all other members of the Politburo who had the temerity to defend the Andreyeva article. After Yakovlev's reply appeared, reformers heaved a sigh of relief and resumed the charge with even more intensity. According to Pikhoya, "The condemnation of the publication of Nina Andreyeva's article in the eyes of wide layers of the intelligentsia was the last step on the path toward the condemnation of the entire history of the party and of Soviet socialism as a system."[32]

The 19th Party Conference

The Nina Andreyeva affair brought opposition to reform out into the open, but it also changed the atmosphere in the Soviet "street." The fear factor that had hovered like a gray cloud over Soviet society since the 1930s began to lift.

In the spring of 1988, David Remnick, one of the most talented in a long line of distinguished American journalists reporting from the USSR, met a young woman collecting signatures on Moscow's historic Arbat for a new group called "Memorial," which wanted to build a monument to the victims of Stalin's repression. Throughout the spring, Memorial and its circle of prominent intellectual leaders organized demonstrations in the streets of Moscow, Leningrad, and other Soviet cities. People "took obvious delight in their freedom to chant slogans and carry signs" with messages such as "No to Political Repression" or "Death to Stalinism" that only a short time earlier would have landed them in jail.[33]

The drive for change produced street theater but it also had a solid intellectual component. A few weeks before the conference, a book called *No Other Way* appeared, a collection of thirty-five essays by leading pro-perestroika intellectuals. It included contributions on the persistence of Stalinism, environmental catastrophes, and other long-concealed problems of Soviet society, and a piece by economist Gavril Popov, who in two years would become mayor of Moscow, on the absurdity of the centrally planned economic system. Also included was an article by Sakharov on "The Necessity for Perestroika." In earlier years, Sakharov's essays had circulated in samizdat. This one appeared in a volume printed in 100,000 copies by the state-run Progress publishing house that was distributed to every delegate to the 19th party conference.[34]

In May 1988, Ambassador Matlock was in Helsinki to brief President Reagan, who had stopped there on his way to the 1988 Moscow summit. Matlock scanned a copy of the just-released "theses" for the upcoming 19th party conference to see what, if anything, he should tell Reagan. As he read, Matlock's excitement grew. Never before in a Soviet document had he seen such extensive language on protecting the rights of citizens, judicial independence, and the like. Indeed, some of the theses seemed paraphrased from the US constitution. Briefing Reagan, Matlock said that if the theses "turned out to be real, the Soviet Union could never again be what it had been in the past."[35]

The image Gorbachev presented to the world at this time was one of confidence and authority. Despite setbacks, he seemed to be delivering on the political side of his agenda for change. The vibrant and exciting Soviet Union of 1988 was a radically different place from the sullen country Gorbachev had taken over in 1985. Glasnost had been eagerly embraced by the liberal intelligentsia and, if changes in the structure of the Soviet system had been less sweeping than promised, most Soviets were probably still willing to give the general secretary the benefit of the doubt.

Within the party, however, the situation was different. From the very beginning, the apparat had acted behind the scenes to retard Gorbachev's efforts. After Gorbachev's groundbreaking trip to Leningrad in May 1985, local party organizations received instructions to ignore what the new general secretary had said to citizens gathered in the street. In 1986 workers in the Central Committee General and Organizational Departments had quietly removed provisions from Gorbachev's proposed new party statutes that would have fundamentally changed the way the party operated.[36]

When the changes sought by Gorbachev in the run-up to the 19th conference seemed to threaten the party's hold on power, unease and quiet subversion turned into open and angry opposition. Gorbachev may have cowed the Politburo but the critically important regional first secretaries seemed to be slipping outside of his control. Brezhnev had made a practice of personally interviewing and approving every regional first secretary candidate and he always remained attentive to their views. Under Gorbachev, these appointments seem to have been handled by Ligachev. Most were in the Ligachev mode, supportive of reform that would make the system more efficient but hostile to anything that might undermine party traditions or threaten control over their own local fiefdoms.

Over the week of April 11–18, Gorbachev held three meetings with regional party leaders from around the country. When Gorbachev charged that the Nina Andreyeva article had been against perestroika, he ran into such a buzz saw of criticism that he eventually burst out, "if any one of you preaches that philosophy—it would be better to leave."[37]

When the 19th conference opened, Gorbachev's keynote address began with what he later described as an invocation based on Hamlet's "To be or not to be" soliloquy—"how to deepen and make irreversible revolutionary perestroika."[38] He called for term limits for party officials, separation of powers between party and governmental bodies, a reduction in the size of the party apparat, and freedom of debate. He also proposed that the current rubber-stamp Soviet parliament, the Supreme Soviet, be replaced by a new Congress of People's Deputies, many of whose members would be chosen through elections allowing multiple candidates.

In his memoirs, Gorbachev describes the 19th party conference as a personal watershed, when he gave up wavering and decided to push decisively for real reform "without fear of being torn from ideological propositions that had outlived their time."[39] The conference featured dramatic debates and sharp criticism of the leadership, including Gorbachev himself. The general secretary, nevertheless, remained firmly in charge throughout the show, frequently eliciting applause, and generally managing to portray himself as the confident balancer between extremes. He denounced the "abuses" of democracy and rejected creation of a multiparty system but also nodded toward Memorial's proposal to commemorate Stalin's victims.[40]

The conference adopted, virtually unchanged, most of Gorbachev's proposals. In the end, however, it was Boris Yeltsin—to Gorbachev's obvious annoyance—who once again provided the most memorable performance. Yeltsin was silent until the last day, when he walked to the podium and waved his delegate's card until Gorbachev was forced to recognize him. Yeltsin called for transparency in party financing, downsizing the apparat, and once again raised the need to reduce privileges for the party elite.

Contrition was never Yeltsin's strong point. He asked that the Central Committee resolution condemning him be rescinded, but the only mistake he admitted was in raising problems with perestroika on the eve of the seventieth-anniversary celebration. After a break, in what had all the hallmarks of another stage-managed political show trial, ten speakers criticized Yeltsin.

But much had changed in the eight months since Yeltsin's October 1987 outburst. Ligachev harshly criticized Yeltsin, as he had months earlier, but this time his performance was broadcast over Soviet television for the entire country to see. When Ligachev leaned over the podium and said, "Boris, you are wrong," using the familiar Russian form of address, it came across as condescending. Yeltsin's later political campaigns made ironic use of the incident. "Boris is right" or "Yegor, you are wrong" became frequent posters at pro-Yeltsin rallies.

To no one's surprise, the conference rejected Yeltsin's appeal for rehabilitation, but television had allowed millions to see his criticism of party privilege and arbitrary power. Yeltsin's feisty reemergence onto the political scene was a clear sign that he intended to play a role in the future and the sympathy his performance evoked showed that there was support for taking perestroika farther than it had gone so far.

CHAPTER 13 · New Kid on the Block

Gorbachev Emerges in US-Soviet Relations

Reagan's reelection and the deployment of US INF missiles in Europe showed Moscow that its 1983 arms negotiation walkout had failed. In January 1985 Shultz and Gromyko met in snowy Geneva with the unstated but clearly understood objective of finding some face-saving way to resume the talks.

Sack-Pig Does Geneva

Shultz's instructions for the meeting in Geneva took up sixteen densely typed pages whose content reflected more the balance of power within the administration than any realistic roadmap to agreement. Confronted with seemingly irreconcilable divisions, Shultz decided to take the entire interagency circus with him to Geneva. In what was later called "the ship of feuds," Shultz's plane when it lifted off for Geneva included the entire Senior Arms Control Policy Group (SACPG), known, and not particularly affectionately, as "Sack-Pig."

Shultz met several times with Gromyko over two days, accompanied only by MacFarlane and Nitze, who had emerged as Shultz's chief arms control adviser. Before Schultz met the Soviets the US team would debate options with suggestions often scrawled in handwritten notes that aides would collate and copy to be passed around and critiqued. Discussion among the US delegation was intense but largely polite as the discipline of having to decide complex issues in a face-to-face setting, with the Soviets sometimes literally waiting outside the door, had its effect.

Finally, late that night the two countries announced an agreement. What emerged was an awkward hybrid called the "Nuclear and Space Talks" (NST), one umbrella delegation with three separate negotiating components: START,

INF, and a new forum called Defense and Space (D&S). The ostensible purpose of this last group was to discuss the benefits of a regime in which defensive strategic weapons would over time replace the supposedly outmoded concept of deterrence based on strategic offensive arms. But in fact, according to Bill Courtney, Deputy Chief of the D&S delegation, there was never any real expectation of achieving agreement on missile defense, and no effort was ever made to work out a treaty text. The real point of the D&S exercise was to keep the Soviets from linking limits on SDI to conclusion of treaties on INF and START or, in other words, "to hold up a cross and keep Dracula away" from the other two negotiations.[1]

Gorbachev Appears on the International Scene

At the end of the January Geneva talks, Shultz told Gromyko that Vice President Bush would like to meet with Mikhail Gorbachev, who only the month before had made a well-publicized visit to London, after which British prime minister Margaret Thatcher had declared, "I like this man Gorbachev. We can do business together."[2] Gromyko, who had reprimanded Soviet ambassadors for reporting too extensively on the enthusiastic Western media coverage of Gorbachev's visit, claimed that for Bush to meet someone who until recently had been an obscure member of the Politburo was "nonsense."[3]

Only two months later, Shultz accompanied Bush to Chernenko's funeral, where they were the first US officials to meet Gorbachev as general secretary. Gorbachev quickly threw away his prepared notes and seemed to be thinking out loud. The substance of what he had to say broke no new ground but he demonstrated an unusual confidence and freshness. Shultz concluded that the new Soviet leader was "tough and his manner was aggressive" even if the "spirit was different." There was already a Gorbachev boom in the air but Shultz found himself recalling Gromyko's remark: "Gorbachev has a nice smile, but he has iron teeth"—a judgment Gromyko himself soon had reason to confirm.[4]

Gorbachev's first public foray into foreign policy as general secretary, his speech to the April 1985 Central Committee plenum, was largely a rehash of standard Soviet positions. But when Dobrynin, back in Moscow for the plenum, had his first meeting with the new Kremlin chief he found Gorbachev to be "like a gust of fresh air in the dense fog of recent years." Gorbachev instructed Dobrynin to avoid sterile arguments over ideology and "to spare no effort to reverse the hostility in our relations." Casually disregarding Gromyko's reserve toward the idea of a meeting between the leaders of the two countries, Gorbachev told the Soviet ambassador that his "first task was to arrange a summit with Reagan."[5]

Aleksandr Yakovlev and "New Thinking"

The seeds of Gorbachev's trademark "new thinking in international affairs" began to sprout in 1983, when Gorbachev first made connection with the man who was to become known as the intellectual godfather of perestroika: Aleksandr Yakovlev. Gorbachev met Yakovlev during a visit to Canada, where Yakovlev had been exiled as ambassador in 1973 for publishing an article that warned against dangers of "great power chauvinism, local nationalism, and anti-Semitism" in conservative journals and the upper level of the party. Gorbachev brought Yakovlev back to head Moscow's prestigious Institute of World Economy and International Relations (IMEMO), which soon became the center of an informal Gorbachev brain trust.

Aleksandr Yakovlev's life could be seen as a metaphor for the liberal Soviet intelligentsia of his generation. When the Nazis invaded the USSR in 1941, the eighteen-year-old Yakovlev volunteered for the marines and was severely wounded in a landing below Peter the Great's famous palace outside Leningrad. For the rest of his life, Yakovlev walked with a limp from this wound earned in defense of his country, which did not prevent his conservative opponents from calling him a traitor. In 1958 Yakovlev, by then already working in the Central Committee apparat, spent a year at Columbia University in the first group of Soviet exchange students to the United States. Yakovlev spent many years in the Central Committee department of propaganda, ending as its acting chief.

Back in Moscow, Yakovlev set IMEMO staffers to reading the works of Western economists and thinkers with whom he had become familiar during his time in Canada: John Kenneth Galbraith, Daniel Bell, and Wasiliy Leontieff, among others. "Soon IMEMO was producing studies that proposed the creation of Soviet-Western joint ventures and warned that without economic reform the country would sink to the status of the third world in 15 years."[6]

Yet even as Yakovlev was positioning himself at the forefront of the coalition for change that was already beginning to take shape under Gorbachev's auspices, he published a number of articles that stood out for their vicious criticism of the United States. In the aftermath of the KAL shoot-down, Yakovlev authored some of the most outrageous charges against Reagan, including the assertion that the president had "openly proclaimed his support for all fascist and terrorist regimes," a charge Gorbachev repeated a year later in a speech at Smolensk.[7]

I got to know Yakovlev late in his career, working with him to arrange a memorable 1994 speech by President Clinton at Moscow's Ostankino television tower, which Yakovlev then headed and which had become a symbol of resistance to a bloody and near-successful armed attack by hard-liners attempting to overthrow Yeltsin in October 1993. At that time, Yakovlev still professed to be hopeful about the possibilities for the development of democracy in Russia, for which he had fought so valiantly in many ways, but there was also an air of sadness about him.

Yakovlev moved slowly with the effects of age and his war wounds, but his mind was sharp. He was outspoken in his determination to safeguard the newly won freedom of the media in Russia, a stance that not long afterward earned his dismissal. But he had a conflicted view of the turbulent era that he had lived through. In one long discussion, we touched on the changes in relations between our countries he had seen: a war in which we were allies, the Cold War, and now as the host of an American president speaking to the people of Russia. Yakovlev said his anti-American articles reflected a different era, when people in certain positions simply had to say some things. Now people knew more, he said, speaking with pride mixed with anger. His work as the head of a commission to document the victims of Stalin's repression, he said, had destroyed the remnants of his belief in the Soviet system.

Eduard Shevardnadze

In foreign as in domestic policy, Gorbachev understood that his first task was to put into key positions people who shared his vision for change. In June Gorbachev told an astounded Georgian party boss, Eduard Shevardnadze, that he intended to appoint him foreign minister. Gorbachev quickly dismissed Shevardnadze's objections that he was not a Russian and that he had no experience in foreign affairs. Gorbachev said lack of experience was actually a plus: "Our foreign policy needs fresh viewpoints, bravery, dynamism, and an innovative approach."[8]

Shevardnadze first met Gorbachev when the two were serving as Young Communist leaders. Gorbachev and Raisa had frequently visited neighboring Georgia, to observe the somewhat freer atmosphere in the southern republic. According to Shevardnadze, he and Gorbachev agreed on all questions of global policy and also understood that in order to begin the process of democratization within the country it was necessary to "renew" Soviet foreign policy.[9]

When Gorbachev, after elevating Gromyko to the Supreme Soviet, announced that his replacement as foreign minister would be Shevardnadze, no one was more surprised than "Dr. Nyet," who had expected the job would go to his longtime deputy, Grigory Korniyenko. Aleksandr Bessmertnykh, then serving as chief of the MFA USA department and later foreign minister, recalled that when Gromyko and Korniyenko returned to the ministry after Shevardnadze's appointment was announced, "Gromyko's face was flushed with rage and Korniyenko's white as a sheet."[10]

Dobrynin did not bother to hide his disappointment. "Our foreign policy is going down the drain. They have named an agricultural type," Dobrynin replied when Shultz asked him about the new appointment.[11] Other senior Soviet diplomats were also baffled, even if they also cautiously welcomed the possibility of change. Shevardnadze, who had assumed his Georgian party post in 1972, was viewed as one of "Brezhnev's men" and had a reputation for extravagantly sycophantic remarks in the Caucasian style.[12]

Within Georgia, Shevardnadze was respected for honesty, courage, and a modest lifestyle. He had reduced the corruption that traditionally plagued that republic. The story of how shortly after taking office he called for a vote on a routine issue and then sacked everyone whose raised arm displayed an expensive foreign watch may have been apocryphal but was nevertheless widely told.

Foreign ministry insiders soon noticed a welcome new personal style. When Kvitsinskiy returned from the first round of NST talks in Geneva in the summer of 1985, Shevardnadze actually listened to what he had to say instead of following Gromyko's practice of giving him a lecture on the history of US-Soviet nuclear arms negotiations and then dismissing him.[13]

In September 1985, I was sent to New York to greet Shevardnadze, who was arriving to address the UN General Assembly. The task was purely protocol; it was Shevardnadze's first visit to the US, and he would have intensive meetings with Shultz and Reagan in Washington after his UN speech. But it was immediately evident that the new Soviet foreign minister was a very different personality from the dour Gromyko, who never bothered to hide his disinterest in anyone below the very top. Shevardnadze seemed pleased that the first American diplomat to greet him on US soil did so in Russian. His manner was spontaneous and friendly, and he made it clear that he was looking forward to a full exchange of views when he arrived in Washington.

"Fireside Summit" in Geneva

Given the interest of both leaders in meeting and with Gromyko out of the way, it proved relatively easy to agree on a "get acquainted" summit in Geneva in November 1985. As the date approached, both sides made small gestures to improve the atmosphere. The Soviets released a number of people on the State Department's representation lists. Reagan, for his part, "made a conscious decision to tone down my rhetoric." On the eve of the summit, Shultz traveled to

Moscow to iron out final preparations. Shultz said he found Gorbachev "filled with anti-American, anti-capitalist propaganda." Pondering Shultz's report, Reagan came to the conclusion "in Geneva I'll have to get him in a room alone and set him straight."[14]

The summit began with what was supposed to be a fifteen-minute private session between the two leaders that stretched to over an hour. Reagan used the talk to try to establish a personal rapport with his Soviet counterpart. He and Gorbachev had both come from humble beginnings in small farming communities, the president pointed out, and now they were the only two men who had it in their power to start global conflict or to bring lasting peace to the world. Gorbachev tried to continue the positive tone by noting that the two countries had cooperated in the past and stressing his conviction that the two could change their relations for the better.[15]

When the two leaders rejoined their aides for the first plenary session, Gorbachev launched into a long polemic aimed at countering "delusions on the part of the American ruling class" that the USSR was facing economic difficulties, lagged behind the West in technology, or could be pressured through an arms race. When Reagan finally got his turn he took "Gorbachev through a long history of Soviet aggression, citing chapter and verse of the Soviet Union's policies of expansion from 1917 onward."

After this, both sides were understandably eager to break for lunch, during which Gorbachev told his Soviet colleagues that Reagan appeared to be "not simply a conservative but a political dinosaur." When they resumed, Gorbachev picked up where they had left off by rejecting the "primitive approach" he said Reagan had taken during the morning. He then marched through a long discussion of the USSR's own "principled approach" toward regional conflicts across the world, including Afghanistan, where for the first time he said that the USSR would like to withdraw—as soon as Soviet forces had achieved what amounted to victory. He next turned to US actions that fueled the nuclear arms race and finally got to the heart of his disquisition with an attack on SDI, which he described as an offensive weapon, which if not banned, would force the USSR to "rethink" its entire approach toward nuclear arms talks. Reagan replied with a treatise on the Soviet nuclear arms buildup since SALT began and then launched into a point-by-point rebuttal of Gorbachev's remarks that started with Yalta and continued through virtually every subsequent crisis.

When Reagan finished, Gorbachev said, "It looks like a dead end." An uneasy silence fell over the room until other members of the US and Soviet delegations took the floor. Given the tenor of the discussion so far, it hardly seems surprising that when Reagan suggested the two leaders break away for some fresh air and another fireside talk, "Gorbachev leaped out of his chair almost before I finished," according to the president.[16] Reagan began this second one-on-one meeting by handing Gorbachev a nine-point proposal on nuclear arms negotiations. Gorbachev quickly agreed to the centerpiece of the US proposal, a 50 percent reduction in strategic offensive arms. He also asked a number of constructive questions that at least showed his willingness to consider arms-control deals along the lines the US was suggesting.

When the first day's session was over, Gorbachev climbed into his limo accompanied only by Shevardnadze and drove back in silence to the villa where he and Raisa were staying. When Raisa asked how the talks had gone, Gorbachev replied by instructing his foreign minister to prepare the Soviet delegation's plane for an early return to Moscow. "It's impossible to negotiate with this American government," he said. Shevardnadze and Raisa argued that he could not allow the talks to collapse in this fashion and after an hour Gorbachev, who may have simply needed to vent, agreed to return to the table the next day.[17]

The second day of the summit began with another one-on-one session between the two leaders, this time on human rights, which Reagan did in private to avoid putting his Soviet counterpart on the spot. Gorbachev said he would consider individual cases as a good-will gesture but the two emerged from the session unsmiling.

While the leaders debated, the diplomatic pick-and-shovel work of drafting a joint statement was entrusted to a senior working group led by Bessmertnykh and Assistant Secretary for European Affairs Roz Ridgeway. Shultz was dismayed but not necessarily surprised to be called away from a joint dinner the second night of the summit by Ridgeway, who had walked out of the working group when the Soviets stonewalled on every comma of the thirty-point statement. Before the summit Reagan had publicly unveiled an ambitious program of people-to-people exchanges between the two countries, an idea he also pushed hard with Gorbachev. The Soviets concluded that the exchange program was the central US objective and were, in classic Gromyko style, holding it hostage to agreement on every other issue on Soviet terms.

Shultz angrily accused Korniyenko of reneging on points the general secretary had already decided. Gorbachev called a time out and while both sides huddled, a US interpreter heard Gorbachev lecture Korniyenko that "We don't go back on our agreements." Gorbachev also hauled Minister of Civil Aviation Bugayev out of bed in Moscow to find out whether the objections the Soviets were raising in Geneva to a US-Soviet aviation deal were really important, only to hear that as far as the minister was concerned his negotiations with the Americans were going fine.[18]

The public message at summit's end was mixed. At a press conference, neither leader tried to hide disappointment. Gorbachev said the talks had "failed
at solving the most important problems concerning the arms race." Reagan,
who threw out of his statement three negative paragraphs written by hard-line
White House speechwriters, said the relationship was now "heading in the right
direction" although there were "important disagreements on matters of principle that remain between us."[19]

Despite the two leaders' unhappiness at the absence of a decisive breakthrough, the joint statement issued at the end of the summit recorded a modest
amount of progress and laid out a roadmap for the future. On strategic arms,
the statement established a joint goal of 50 percent reductions in the strategic
nuclear arsenals of both sides, a far cry from the outrage that had greeted Jimmy
Carter's far more modest "deep cuts" proposal of 1977 and a sign that arms control under the Gorbachev administration would be handled differently. The
statement called for "effective verification" of arms agreements, a term of art
that had come to stand for onsite inspections hitherto anathema to Moscow.
The Soviets also made a small step toward the notion that human rights were a
legitimate part of the relationship between the two countries by acknowledging
the "importance of resolving humanitarian cases in the spirit of cooperation."[20]

The two leaders viewed the Geneva summit as a kind of personal breakthrough. Gorbachev recognized, "Something important had happened to each
of us."[21] Despite everything, "Somewhere in the backs of our minds a glimmer
of hope emerged that we could still come to an agreement." When Gorbachev
briefed the Politburo, he said there was an opening for better relations under
Reagan that the USSR should explore.[22]

As for the US leader, flying back from Geneva, Reagan said, "I think I'm
some judge of acting and I don't believe Gorbachev was acting. I believe he is
as sincere as we are in wanting an agreement." Reagan's press spokesman, Larry
Speakes, came away with the "impression that the two had decided they could
do business." Speakes said, "I believe they genuinely liked each other."[23]

The Four-Part Agenda

The Geneva summit marked the moment when the US and Soviet national
security bureaucracies began tentatively to work together in a problem-solving
mode across the range of issues where the two superpowers touched. The
United States had long resisted the Soviet practice of emphasizing the over-
arching importance of arms control in the dialogue and thereby reducing the
attention given to other issues, especially human rights. At the insistence of
Secretary Shultz, the Soviet desk had begun dividing the agenda of issues to be

discussed at high-level meetings into four parts: arms control, human rights, regional issues, and bilateral matters, to ensure that all four were addressed at high-level US-Soviet meetings. The Geneva joint statement followed this framework and in the summer of 1986 Bessmertnykh suggested holding experts' meetings on all four agenda topics in preparation for a meeting of the two foreign ministers in September. According to Tom Simons, "It was the American formula; we accepted immediately."[24]

Soon, meetings between senior officials of the two countries were routinely structured around the four-part agenda, in what amounted to a joint cooperative framework for managing the relationship. By 1987 Secretary Shultz was taking with him to meetings with Shevardnadze large numbers of experts in the key fields to be discussed. These officials would meet together in informal working groups, in what Simons described as the "boiler room of the new relationship," with the objective of coming up with practical solutions to recommend to the two ministers.[25]

The Soviet Military Discovers the Uses of Arms Control

Two months after Geneva, Gorbachev announced the most extensive Soviet arms control proposal since Khrushchev's offer of "general and complete disarmament" twenty-five years earlier. When Shultz called his top arms control advisers into his office for a quick analysis of the Soviet proposal, Nitze asked, "I wonder whose work of art on the Soviet side this is?"[26] Nitze might have been surprised to learn that the author of the sweeping proposal was the Soviet General Staff, which had concocted the offer as a way to head off the danger that the new general secretary might push for an arms deal that could actually require reductions in Soviet nuclear weapons.

By the mid-1980s, the Soviet military faced challenges from two directions. On the one hand, the Reagan administration's arms buildup threatened to force the USSR into even more spending, which enlightened military leaders understood could no longer be supported by the faltering Soviet economy. At the same time, the new Soviet foreign-affairs tandem of Gorbachev and Shevardnadze was demonstrating an alarming willingness to consider real nuclear reduction agreements. On December 30, 1985, Gorbachev and Shevardnadze met with Soviet civilian arms negotiators. Citing confidential information that 40 percent of Soviet industry was devoted to military purposes, Gorbachev said this burden had to be reduced in order to satisfy domestic consumer needs and to gain international support for Soviet foreign policy initiatives. Perhaps emboldened by the unusual absence of military officials, the Soviet civilian negotiators urged radical changes to long-standing Soviet positions.

Veteran strategic arms negotiator Viktor Karpov urged acceptance of Reagan's "zero option," and Oleg Grinyevskiy, chief of the Soviet delegation at Stockholm talks on European security, called for cutting nuclear weapons by half.[27]

Desperate to forestall real negotiations, Akromeyev and General-Colonel Nikolai Chervov, the chief of the General Staff's arms-control department, came up with the idea of developing a comprehensive plan for the phased elimination of all nuclear weapons that would contain enough plausible details to appear realistic but would have the effect of putting off any prospect of agreement until some never-never land in the future. Gorbachev gave his "instant approval" to the new plan when Chervov presented it to him during a New Year's vacation at the Black Sea. The military was relieved that the general secretary seemed not to understand that "such a declaration hardly could lead to any practical results in the foreseeable future."[28] And in the unlikely event that the 1986 Soviet proposal would actually come to pass, the result would have been to leave the USSR with a massive superiority in conventional weapons. As veteran Soviet arms negotiator General-Lieutenant Viktor Starodubov said, "If the USSR and the Warsaw Pact had not exceeded the West in conventional weapons the Soviet Union would have hardly put forward this initiative."[29]

At first blush, the Soviet military's tactic seemed to have worked brilliantly. President Reagan's first reaction was "Why wait until the end of the century for a world without nuclear weapons?"[30] The Soviet military believed they had regained the political initiative, but the proposal, which showed a rhetorical willingness to walk away from some cherished Soviet negotiating positions, ended up working against them. Eventually, the "authors of this idea became entrapped by their own gambit."[31] The highly secretive Soviet military found that it had given Gorbachev the information and the confidence he needed to craft his own proposals and later to accede to US proposals that cherry-picked elements of the January 1986 offer acceptable to the West.

Afghanistan: War and Withdrawal

During their first years in Afghanistan, the Soviets mounted large-scale offensives in which heavily armed units slogged across the Afghan countryside, preceded by massive artillery barrages. Soviet forces could generally capture whatever objective they chose but, with much manpower tied up protecting lines of communication, they had insufficient troops to hold ground for long.[32]

Beginning in 1984 the mobility and aggressiveness of Soviet forces increased dramatically. Massive armored sweeps were replaced by deeper forays into Mujahedin territory, with airborne and special forces units used to cut off the retreat of the enemy. The Soviets made more effective use of their techno-logical advantage, for example, scattering remote acoustic sensors along paths used by the Mujahedin, which allowed devastating and demoralizing artillery or gunship attacks on infiltrating guerillas even at night.

Mao Tse-tung described the guerilla fighter as swimming among the people like a fish swims in the sea. In Afghanistan the Soviets sought to dry up the sea of the people through terror tactics that depopulated large swaths of the Afghan countryside. Indiscriminant artillery and air attacks on towns and villages, scattering millions of antipersonnel mines along roads and paths used by the civilian population, and the deliberate destruction of crops and supplies, drove people out of their homes and into refugee camps. Mujahedin forces found it harder to operate in the empty countryside. "Early in 1986 the morale of the Mujahedin was clearly lower and the civilian population, which had re-sisted remarkably well, was becoming exhausted by the war and the exodus of millions of people."[33]

Stingers Turn the Tide

In 1985, under prodding from Casey and congressional backers such as flam-boyant Texas Congressman Charlie Wilson, Reagan dramatically stepped up US assistance to Afghan rebels. By 1986 the US and Saudi Arabia were together providing assistance worth approximately one billion dollars. The CIA was al-lowed to use "all available means" to support the Afghan rebels and was autho-rized to act separately from the Pakistan intelligence service, the ISI, through which the CIA had channeled assistance up until then.[34]

The Soviets' undisputed control of the skies over Afghanistan remained the Mujahedin's chief vulnerability. In early 1985, Mort Abramowitz, then direc-tor of the State Department's Bureau of Intelligence and Research and later ambassador to Thailand and Turkey, was asked to begin one of Shultz's regu-lar Saturday-morning information sessions with a briefing on the situation in Afghanistan. Abramowitz described the Afghan resistance fighters as "in seriously bad shape." The Soviet military offensives of 1984 and 1985 had made deep inroads and "the spetsnaz and the helicopters were decimating the Muj." Abramowitz told Shultz that unless something was done to reverse the Soviet helicopter advantage, "prospects for the Muj were gloomy."[35]

Later that year, Abramowitz visited the region together with DoD officials Rich Armitage and Mike Pillsbury. They met with Afghan resistance leaders, senior Pakistan officials, and CIA personnel involved in the US assistance mission. The Afghans pleaded with the US visitors for some way to deal with

Soviet air power and Abramowitz and the others came back "beating the drums" for Stingers, handheld antiaircraft missiles deadly up to an altitude of 12,000 feet. In Washington, the Pentagon opposed supplying Stingers to the Afghan resistance, arguing that the United States did not have sufficient stocks for its own use and worrying that the missile might fall into Soviet hands. CIA headquarters also opposed the provision of the Stingers, for reasons Abramowitz said he could never understand.[36]

Finally, in January 1986 President Reagan decided to allow Stingers to be supplied to the Afghan rebels, under carefully controlled conditions.[37] On September 25, 1986, after a week of trekking through the mountains, a team of resistance fighters fired four Stinger missiles at Soviet helicopters near the Jalalabad air base, downing three. Within a week, Milt Bearden, the CIA officer in charge of supplying aid to the Mujahedin, had a film of the downing on its way to Washington, carefully edited to eliminate footage of the triumphant Mujahedin mutilating the bodies of the dead Soviet crews.[38]

The Stingers had an immediate impact. In July 1986, just before the Stingers appeared, Bearden described Mujahedin morale as waning. Other observers have reported that at this time the Pakistanis often had to pay the Mujahedin to get them to venture into Afghanistan. By January 1987, Bearden reported a dramatic turnaround: "Before [Stingers] all these guys were walking around waiting to be martyred. Now they were heading into Dodge City on purpose, looking for trouble."[39]

Helicopter gunships could no longer strafe Afghan positions with virtual impunity and the accuracy of close air support declined dramatically as fighter pilots lost their taste for low-level attacks. The morale and effectiveness of the Mujahedin rose while that of the Soviets plummeted. A young Soviet journalist in Afghanistan, Aleksandr Prokhanov, who later became one of the leading hard-line nationalist opponents of the Yeltsin government, described the change. Helicopter pilots "used to be Kings of Afghanistan and everyone saluted them. But after the Stinger they took to flying very high to keep out of range. They had little value up there and the ground troops began referring to them as cosmonauts."[40]

The Soviet 40th Army in Afghanistan calculated that in its first year of combat the Stinger had a success rate of 20 percent. In the cautious words of Soviet military historians, "Use of helicopters was severely limited later by the introduction of man-portable Stinger air defense missiles. This appreciably decreased the results of operations and combat which frequently did not achieve their projected goals."[41] In the early 1990s, I had the opportunity to ask Russian vice president Aleksandr Rutskoy about the Stingers. A decorated su-25 pilot who had been shot down over Afghanistan, Rutskoy had no doubts: "It was the Stingers; they made the difference."

Gorbachev and Afghanistan

Gorbachev understood that he could not achieve fundamental change in either the domestic or the international arena while the war in Afghanistan raged. His initial strategy for ending the war built on the surge in Soviet offensive capability that had begun before he became general secretary. Two new special forces brigades were sent into Afghanistan, long-range bombing from bases in the southern USSR was increased, and fighting on the ground rose to the highest levels of the war. Gorbachev appointed a new commander in Afghanistan and according to some accounts gave him "a year or two to win."[42]

Aggressive Soviet tactics inflicted severe losses on the Mujahedin, but the Soviets themselves suffered heavy casualties without fundamentally changing the military situation. Soviet military leaders began to raise serious questions not just about the possibility of victory but also about the basic effectiveness of Soviet forces. General Valentin Varennikov, in overall charge of the Soviet war effort in Afghanistan, reported to Minister of Defense Sokolov that in Afghanistan "it was acknowledged by all that it was impossible to save the April revolution by military means alone."[43] Even as he increased the military pressure, Gorbachev was also contemplating a political solution to the war. Soon after he took office, Gorbachev instructed the Politburo to undertake a review of Soviet policy "aimed at the withdrawal of Soviet troops from Afghanistan and the resolution of the problem of Afghanistan by political means."[44] But as other leaders in similar circumstances have discovered it is not easy to turn around a major power and exit a conflict gone sour.

According to Shevardnadze, even before Gorbachev became general secretary the two men had agreed that Afghanistan was the most serious problem facing the USSR and that it needed to be ended one way or another. Once Gorbachev took charge of the Kremlin he became more cautious. The night before the 27th Congress, in February 1986, Shevardnadze got a final copy of the keynote speech Gorbachev was to deliver. Shevardnadze was surprised to find no mention of Afghanistan. He immediately called Gorbachev to demand restoration of a passage on the conflict that had earlier been agreed. Failing that, Shevardnadze said he would bring it up himself. The next morning, as Shevardnadze was in his office preparing to leave for the opening session, he got a call from Gorbachev saying ironically that he had carried out the foreign minister's instructions. Nevertheless, despite Gorbachev's desire to end the war, Shevardnadze says it took a couple of years for the internal situation at the top of the USSR to change sufficiently to allow real movement on Afghanistan.[45]

Not until the end of 1986, after the Stingers had shifted the military balance in Afghanistan, did Gorbachev begin seriously to map out a strategy for withdrawal. At a November 13 Politburo meeting Gorbachev said, "We have been fighting in Afghanistan for six years already. Unless we change our approach we shall continue to fight for another 20–30 years." Evidently referring to the recently introduced Stingers, Gromyko added that in Afghanistan "the situation is worse than half a year ago." Marshal Akromeyev, in what Gorbachev aide Chernyayev described as a "brilliant" statement, acknowledged that the Soviets had "lost the battle for the people." The majority of Afghanistan remained in rebel hands and, although Akromeyev said that the Soviet military could maintain the situation at the current level, he called for a neutral Afghanistan as a way to facilitate Soviet departure.[46]

Over the next year, as even conservatives such as Ligachev acknowledged that "We have suffered a defeat in this cause," Gorbachev dithered, to the growing frustration of those who saw the need to bring the war to a quick close.[47] In a February 1987 Politburo meeting, Gorbachev said the USSR could not afford to "leave quickly, not thinking about anything," which would be a blow to the authority of the USSR in the "national liberation movement."[48] In May 1987, Gorbachev bemoaned the lack of progress in the policy of "national reconciliation" by which the Soviets hoped to weaken support for the insurgency. Varennikov replied bluntly, "The policy of national reconciliation is dying," and Akromeyev urged creation of a "bourgeois" government to be supported for about a year by Soviet "bayonets."[49]

At the December 1987 Washington summit, Gorbachev agreed that the USSR would announce a specific date for the withdrawal of its troops and on February 8, 1988, he stated publicly that Soviet troops would begin pulling out of Afghanistan in May. Once the Soviets had declared their intention to leave, the two countries became locked into a bitter argument about what would happen after Soviet withdrawal. The United States rejected Pakistan's pleas that it insist on the removal of the Soviet-backed Najibullah regime as a price for concluding an international accord, but Washington was also unwilling to go along with Gorbachev's entreaties that the two countries cooperate to create a neutral nonaligned state. Hard-liners in the Reagan administration believed this would be tantamount to accepting a thinly disguised pro-Soviet regime and were convinced, like most in Moscow, that Najibullah would quickly fall once the Red Army departed.

Even more painful was the issue of continued aid to the two sides' respective clients. Although the State Department had earlier been willing to go along with the suspension of US military assistance to the Mujahedin once the Soviets withdrew, pressure from Congress and from executive-branch hardliners led to a last-minute change. Washington insisted that both sides should adopt the same position regarding assistance to their respective clients: if the Soviets were unwilling to end aid to the Najibullah regime, the US would continue to supply the Mujahedin. The United States was unyielding, despite an appeal from Gorbachev, who according to Dobrynin felt "betrayed" by the US position, and an emotional three-hour personal presentation in Washington by Shevardnadze, who said that the USSR had done everything the United States had wanted in Afghanistan and now asked for a simple yes or no to his request that the US stop supplying weapons to the insurgents. After a pause, the US team returned with a negative reply. Shevardnadze "paled and threw up his hands."[50]

In retrospect it is hard not to have a certain degree of sympathy for the Soviet view that the United States had, in fact, moved the goalposts on the issue of postwithdrawal aid. In part the problem arose because of a disconnect in Washington between positions taken by negotiators in the UN channel and those in the high-level and closely held US-Soviet bilateral talks. But there was an inherent political and military logic to the US view that it could not simply leave the Mujahedin, whom it had been backing for years, to the mercy of Afghan opponents who would continue to be well supplied by Moscow.

Consequences

The Soviet military conducted a skilled withdrawal from Afghanistan, with as much dignity and pride as could be mustered under the circumstances, although it was marred by an unnecessary spasm of heavy bombing along the Salang valley withdrawal route in the final weeks, which caused many civilian casualties. The final Soviet commander in Afghanistan, General Boris Gromov, was the last Soviet soldier to leave, walking across the bridge into Uzbekistan on February 15, 1989. No one from the Moscow political or military leadership met the withdrawing forces, a source of enduring bitterness to Afghan veterans.

The Soviets officially acknowledged 13,833 combat deaths in Afghanistan but most observers believe the real total was considerably higher. In May 1991, General Varennikov told the press that "18,826 Soviet citizens placed their lives on the altar of the Fatherland" and that more than 50,000 had been wounded. The authors of a General Staff study of the conflict stated that the war "took the lives or health of 55,000 Soviet citizens."[51] Afghan casualties were far higher, with estimates of those killed during the fighting ranging from 600,000 to 2.5 million.[52]

The war in Afghanistan opened wounds in the Soviet body politic that played an important role in the collapse of the Communist system and the dissolution of the USSR itself. A watershed came in the summer of 1987 with the appearance of a three-part series on the Afghan war by Artyom Borovik, a courageous young reporter who spent his time with Soviet forces in the field and for the first time showed the Soviet people what their sons were experiencing. Nothing about the war, the Soviet military, and indeed the Soviet system itself would ever be the same after Borovik's grippingly honest portrayal of the brutality of the war on both sides.

The epitaph of the Soviet adventure in Afghanistan was written by the Soviet military itself: "On 15 February 1989 the last unit left the territory of Afghanistan. Thus those forces returned to their people, having been sent to another country on the whims of a few Kremlin politicians. Their history is written in the blood of thousands of people on the soil of Afghanistan."[53]

After the Soviet Withdrawal

The 2001 terrorist attacks and the subsequent US involvement in Afghanistan led some to condemn US assistance to the Afghan rebels fighting the Soviet invaders. It is certainly possible to question aspects of the US program of aid to the Mujahedin, particularly the delay in providing truly decisive assistance. But carried too far this process can become an exercise in the rewriting of history from back to front.

In retrospect, the critical failure in US policy toward Afghanistan came in the years immediately after Soviet withdrawal. At the December 1989 Malta summit Gorbachev said, "We can't order Najib out, but if they [the Afghans] decide he should go, so be it." A policy of US-Soviet cooperation aimed at creating some kind of government of national unity might have ended the internal Afghan bloodletting that eventually led to the Taliban takeover. US leverage on the ground in Afghanistan was at its height after its success in forcing a Soviet withdrawal, and in this era Washington and Moscow were successfully working together in many areas where cooperation would have once been unthinkable. Failure to halt the fighting by political means meant that the people of Afghanistan were exposed to three additional years of civil conflict, which set the stage for the turmoil of the subsequent two decades with all its terrible consequences for Afghanistan and the world beyond.[54]

US policy toward Afghanistan after the Soviet withdrawal was riven by internal conflicts. Instead of seeking a negotiated outcome, the US threw the bulk of its support to a Pakistani plan aimed at beefing up the Mujahedin, defeating the Najibullah regime, and installing a new government that would almost certainly have been dominated by the fundamentalist elements that received the bulk of assistance channeled through ISI. Other elements wanted to move US assistance toward more moderate groups. The US envoy to the Afghan resistance, Ambassador Peter Tomsen, put forward a plan that envisioned negotiating with Moscow to establish an end to all outside military assistance and the creation of a broad-brushed transition government presided over by the still respected king Zahir Shah as symbolic head.

In the event, Afghan resistance groups backed by the ISI proved unable to defeat the Najibullah regime. The Soviets continued to provide military assistance, and the bulk of the traditional Afghan population distrusted the fundamentalists and their Pakistani backers. US leverage declined as its assistance to Afghan resistance groups fell and eventually ended in 1992, while other players, including the Saudi government and independent actors such as Osama bin Laden, stepped up aid to radical Islamic groups. The weak government that took power in Kabul in 1992 after Moscow cut off aid to Najibullah was unable to control Afghanistan's regional, ethnic, and religious factions. It proved an easy victim to the radical Taliban, who in 1996 swept out of the refugee camps in Pakistan promising order and peace and quickly captured Kabul, reportedly with considerable covert help from Pakistan.[55]

CHAPTER 14

· "I Guess I Should Say Michael"
The Turn in US-Soviet Relations

The Geneva summit seemed to have launched US-Soviet relations on a promising new path. Unfortunately, over the next year the relationship stagnated, in part because of Gorbachev's preoccupation with internal issues such as Chernobyl and in part because of events in the murky world of US-Soviet espionage.

Spy Wars

In the 1970s and 1980s the US obtained a number of Soviet agents who provided valuable insights into the tightly closed Soviet military and intelligence world. Burton Gerber, who presided over the recruitment of many of these agents, described this era as a disaster for the KGB.[1]

Beginning in 1985, the pendulum seemed to tilt in the opposite direction. John Walker and members of his family were arrested after a long career of spying for the USSR, in which he handed over the most sensitive US Navy codes. FBI official Richard Miller was convicted of cooperating with the Soviets, and in the following year NSA employee Ronald Pelton was arrested after a six-year career of spying in which he betrayed a US underwater wiretap that allowed the United States to read much of the Soviet navy's operational traffic.[2]

Aldrich Ames

In the spring of 1985, Viktor Cherkashin, KGB counterintelligence chief at the Soviet Embassy in Washington, sat down to a lunch in a Georgetown riverfront restaurant that "may have done more harm to US intelligence than any other single incident" in the Cold War. Cherkashin's luncheon date, Aldrich Ames, a midlevel official in the CIA's Soviet division, produced a yellow note pad and began writing down names. When he had finished he handed the list to Cherkashin, who described it as "a catalogue of virtually every CIA asset in the Soviet Union."[3]

According to an assessment undertaken by the CIA after Ames's arrest in 1994, over thirty US operations could have been compromised by Ames, who acknowledged providing the Soviets with information on over a hundred Soviet and East European cases. Ten of the US agents betrayed by Ames were shot and many others were arrested. According to congressional investigators, "The compromise of the identities of these intelligence agents amounted to a virtual collapse of the CIA's Soviet operations."[4]

Ames was not arrested until 1994 although the consequences of his treason quickly became evident as the CIA's agent network began to unravel. But there were more public events in the "Year of the Spy." In June 1985, a young CIA case officer at Embassy Moscow was arrested on a Moscow sidewalk on his way to meet one of the most valuable agents the US ever recruited: Adolph Tolkachev, a scientist at a secret design bureau that developed new technology for Soviet fighter aircraft. Tolkachev was betrayed by Edward Lee Howard, a former CIA recruit who had been in training to go to the US embassy in Moscow until his drinking problems led the agency to fire him. Using his CIA skills, Howard escaped FBI surveillance and traveled secretly to Moscow, where he provided valuable information on CIA operations.

The Spy Who Went Home

In August 1985, Vitaly Yurchenko, a KGB veteran of many years, telephoned the CIA station chief in Italy and offered to defect. Yurchenko provided information that led to the discovery of Howard and Pelton and he also warned that Gordiyevsky was under suspicion in Moscow. In November Yurchenko was allowed to go to dinner at an expensive French restaurant in Georgetown, despite Gerber's orders that he was to be kept well outside Washington. After obtaining assurances from his inexperienced American escort that he would not be shot if he tried to escape, Yurchenko simply got up and walked into the night. He turned up at the Soviet embassy, where he claimed the CIA had drugged and kidnapped him. The Soviets pretended to believe Yurchenko's tale and demanded that he be allowed to return to the USSR.

During my time as head of Bilat, I found myself involved in one of the minor features of the US-Soviet intelligence game: meetings between defectors and representatives of the Soviet embassy. These meetings were voluntary, but defectors were encouraged to participate to avoid giving the Soviets an excuse to deny access to Americans who might find themselves in custody in the USSR. Usually held in an anonymous meeting room on the ground floor of the State Department building, the meetings followed a well-rehearsed routine. The agency would bring the defector into the State Department through the basement and the Soviet embassy representatives, brimming over with concern for the fate of their errant citizen, would be escorted into the room. I would tell the embassy representatives that they could speak as long as the defector agreed to talk to them but that if any threat was made I would immediately have them ejected from the building. If the defector had left his family behind, as many did for various reasons, the Soviets would say how much the family missed the defector and wanted him home, to which I would reply that we would be happy to consider expedited visas for the grieving family if they wished to join their beloved relative in his new home.

I was told to get ready to hold a similar meeting with Yurchenko, but at the last minute plans changed and I learned that the meeting would be held at a slightly higher level, to wit, by the secretary of state himself. Yurchenko and his Soviet embassy escort drove up to the diplomatic entrance of the State Department building, where I met them and took them to the secretary's seventh-floor suite. Once there, it turned out that the interview would be conducted by Assistant Secretary Ridgeway in the presence of two CIA representatives. Roz went through the drill in her usual forthright style. Yurchenko, for his part, voiced outrage over his supposed kidnapping and said that all he wanted to do was go home immediately. Yurchenko seemed to be on an emotional rollercoaster, accusing the CIA of behaving in an amateurish fashion and objecting to the pistol that he claimed one of the CIA representatives had surreptitiously packed into the meeting.

After the charade was over, I escorted Yurchenko back downstairs. As platoons of reporters shouted questions from behind the police line and cameras flashed, I walked Yurchenko to the waiting Soviet limousine. As he slid into the rear seat, Yurchenko's mood seemed to deflate. Not knowing what else to say, I wished him good luck and he replied softly, "I'll need it."

Spy Dust

On the Soviet desk, one of the first events in the Year of the Spy was the appearance of something that came to be called "spy dust." Shortly after I took charge of Bilat the CIA informed the State Department that the Soviets were using a chemical to monitor the movements of foreign personnel in the USSR. Sprayed onto cars, door handles, and furniture, it allowed the movements of people who touched these things to be tracked. Called NPPD (nitrophenyl pentadien), the compound was dubbed spy dust by the media. The agency said it was likely that significant numbers of people in the US embassy community had been exposed.

Many on the Soviet desk at the time spy dust came to light had also served in the US embassy during the 1970s, when it was revealed that the State Department had for years concealed the fact that the Soviets were beaming microwave radiation at the embassy. This time around, we were determined to do better. We informed all current and former embassy Moscow employees about spy dust and since NPPD belonged to a class of chemicals that were possible carcinogens we enlisted the medical branch of the State Department to commission a scientific investigation into it. These studies found no evidence that exposure to NPPD caused any risks to human health. But they did determine that for unknown reasons the compound caused laboratory mice to grow copious amounts of hair, leading some wags to suggest the possibility of a joint venture with the KGB to market the stuff as a cure for baldness.

The Bugged Embassy

Spy dust was quickly replaced by a more sensational affair. In the summer of 1985, the story that the State Department had allowed Soviet workers building the new US embassy in Moscow to install sophisticated eavesdropping devices splashed across the US media and set off a political firestorm that complicated US-Soviet relations for decades.

The saga of the "bugged embassy" may go back to a day when, according to Moscow legend, Stalin looked out of his Kremlin office and in one direction saw the US flag flying from the top of the American embassy, then located near the Kremlin. Looking in the other direction, Stalin saw the Union Jack flying from the British embassy, directly across the Moscow River. The dictator supposedly ordered that the imperialists be moved away from the Kremlin forthwith.[5]

Unlike the British, who remained in their lovely, if cramped, prerevolutionary embassy until the end of the twentieth century, the United States jumped at the opportunity to leave its crowded building. In 1953 the US embassy moved into an apartment building on Moscow's misnamed Garden Ring road. This was supposed to be only a temporary expedient until the two countries agreed on permanent sites for their respective embassies. But the one-time apartment building remained the embassy chancery for almost fifty years.

In 1972 the two countries signed an agreement establishing reciprocal conditions of construction for their new embassies. Under its terms, the host country would be responsible for building the foundation and framework of the embassy in its capital while the possessing country would do all of the interior work above the fourth floor. Construction was to proceed in parallel and neither embassy could be occupied until both were completed.

After ground was broken for the new US embassy in 1979, Soviet workers, supervised by Americans from the State Department's Foreign Buildings Office (FBO), completed the foundation, frame, external walls and rough interior floors of what was called the New Office Building (NOB). As they worked the Soviets—many of them, of course, KGB—also covertly installed eavesdropping systems that snaked through the columns, floors, and walls of the NOB.

It did not come as a surprise that the Soviets would try to bug the NOB. Unfortunately, the United States underestimated the determination and technical sophistication that the Soviets would bring to the effort. It is also sadly true that the steps the US took to block the Soviet penetration were poorly coordinated and riddled with mistakes.

The US firm designing the NOB hired a recent Soviet émigré with impressive architectural credentials to serve as interpreter and adviser only to find that once the planning phase was over the individual vanished back to Moscow taking with him a complete set of blueprints. Supervision of the Soviet workmen on the construction site was obviously ineffective. Burton Gerber, who observed the situation himself as CIA Moscow station chief in the first years of the project, described the US monitoring as "a joke."[6] The United States also permitted the Soviets to use concrete construction elements that were fabricated off-site. This was standard Soviet construction practice but it allowed the KGB to install sophisticated electronic equipment inside prefabricated materials where there was no possibility of monitoring.

In the spring of 1982, a team of CIA technical specialists covertly employed MRI and other sophisticated technology to peer inside the structural members being built by the Soviets. They discovered that the Soviets had installed metal rods and other apparatus in the columns supporting the NOB that had the potential, some asserted, to turn the whole building into an antenna.

After a sharp internal debate, a decision was taken to allow construction to proceed using Soviet workers until the frame was completed, as was called for in the US-Soviet agreement. In retrospect, this decision was clearly a mistake but, as usual, it was likely a trade-off between several different priorities. The State Department wanted the NOB finished quickly and within its planned budget. The intelligence community, worried about how the Soviet measures might affect its operations from the new US embassy, wanted tougher measures to impede Soviet actions.

Arthur Hartman, US ambassador at the time, said no one came out looking good. The United States underestimated the Soviets, assuming they would put listening devices in bricks as had been done in the past. But Soviets found other ways. "We never figured how the system was supposed to work," according to Hartman. It was also a time of bureaucratic inefficiency and bickering. Ambassador Hartman described the embassy, FBO, the State Department, and the intelligence community as "working on parallel tracks and not together."[7]

In the summer of 1985, the Soviet desk succeeded in getting approval to remove all Soviets from the site, although not until we had overcome bureaucratic opposition from FBO which was concerned that throwing Soviet workers off the site could expose the department to breach-of-contract lawsuits.

After the discovery of the Soviet devices, the CIA had continued a secret and sophisticated campaign to monitor what the KGB was doing. At night, after Soviet workers had been escorted off the site, a team of CIA specialists used sophisticated detection gear to go secretly through every inch of what had been built that day. Sometimes members of the team rappelled down the sides of the NOB in the dark to get access to exterior construction elements. By the time the Soviet workers were expelled, the United States had a relatively good idea of what the Soviets had installed, although how it was supposed to operate was uncertain—and indeed remains so to this day.

At about this time, I accompanied Ambassador Hartman to a building in Rosslyn that served as the headquarters for the CIA team monitoring what the Soviets were up to. The enthusiastic head of the office called up a sophisticated three-dimensional computer image of the NOB that depicted in different colors the components the Soviets had secretly installed throughout the building. Interlocking systems ran through the frame in a kind of multicolored tinker-toy pattern as seen on the screens.

Once the Soviets were expelled from the NOB site, it was planned for American technical experts to extract samples of what the Soviets had inserted and either remove them or take other steps to neutralize their actions, for example, by cutting the connections of the components running up columns or through floors. Once that had been done all of the top floors of the NOB would be completed by American workers using only American materials brought in under escort from abroad. Secure rooms using a variety of electronic countermeasures to prevent penetration would be the only places where any classified work would be allowed. As Ambassador Matlock said, "There was no reason to believe that planned countermeasures were not adequate to foil any attempt to extract sensitive intelligence from secure areas of the new embassy."[8] Unfortunately, in view of the political firestorm that had erupted around the incident, sensible approaches were not on the table and it was not until almost fifteen years later that the completely rebuilt structure was able to be occupied and used as the new embassy offices.

Cutting Soviet Spies

By the early 1980s, the FBI estimated that about 40 percent of the approximately one thousand Soviet officials in the United States had intelligence connections, meaning that there were more Soviet spies in the United States than all American officials in the USSR. The mood among Soviet intelligence personnel around this time can be seen by a remark one Soviet reportedly made to an FBI official. Speaking of the three US cities where the Soviets had diplomatic establishments, he said, "New York belongs to us; San Francisco is yours, and we'll fight you for Washington."

Revelations of Soviet intelligence activity during the "year of the spy" increased pressure to correct this imbalance, and in March 1986 the United States ordered a reduction in the size of the Soviet Mission to the UN (SMUN) from its then level of about 270 to a maximum of 170 over a two-year period, in tranches of twenty-five every six months. In September Washington ordered twenty-five specific SMUN officials, all identified by the FBI as intelligence operatives, to leave the country. Moscow replied by expelling five American diplomats. The Soviet action led Washington to take a step for which many had long been arguing: a reduction in Soviet diplomatic personnel to a number equal to that of US diplomats in the USSR. Enforcing this decision required the expulsion of an additional fifty-five Soviet diplomats, all also identified by the FBI as spies. The Soviets countered with what amounted to an "own goal," pulling all Soviet employees out of the US missions in the USSR, which initially caused hardship but which over the long run deprived the Soviets of a valuable intelligence tool.

Like many foreign service Soviet hands, I had tended to believe that the FBI routinely classified Soviet diplomats as spies, even if they were only doing work that might normally be expected of any diplomat, just as the Soviets tended to treat all US diplomats as if they were spies. As the issue of cutting back Soviet intelligence activities in the United States played out, I ended up in close contact with FBI officials responsible for countering Soviet spies. Bob Wade, then in charge of the FBI's Soviet counterintelligence department, discussed, with what I believe was unprecedented frankness, the voluminous files the FBI maintained from surveillance on all Soviet diplomatic personnel in the United States. It was a sobering lesson in just how egregious the actions of many of the so-called Soviet diplomats were. I came away with respect for the professionalism of the FBI team, whose resources for combating Soviet intelligence in the nation's capital were probably less in terms of money and personnel than what the Soviets deployed in their intelligence attack on the United States.

The reductions Washington ordered in the official Soviet presence in the United States amounted to the largest round of diplomatic expulsions between the two countries during the entire Cold War. In an earlier time, they would have probably led to a prolonged deep freeze in relations. In the new era, the only surprise was how little impact the reductions had on the broader course of relations.

Sometimes a sense of humor even managed to break through. I was at Dulles airport as the first tranche of expelled Soviet diplomats boarded planes to return home. Watching the Soviet officials and their families file toward the gate, with the wives carrying flowers given by friends remaining behind, one of the younger members of the Soviet consulate staff came up to me. "I have a complaint to make," he told me. As the young Soviet, probably at least six feet six, loomed over me, I braced myself for a fruitless discussion but instead he said, "Couldn't you check with us before you put people on your hit list?" The next weekend, he explained, would see the annual basketball game between the Soviet embassy in Washington and SMUN in New York. "Your guys wiped out our team," he said pointing to the line of people filing onto the Aeroflot plane. "We are going to lose big time."

Sometimes, also, there was a form of tacit cooperation to work out bureaucratic problems arising from the expulsions. To no one's surprise, it turned out that a large number of Soviet personnel assigned to replace those expelled were also known intelligence agents. Some of their visa requests we refused outright and some we just sat on. The Soviets were doing roughly the same thing in Moscow, where the CIA station chief had been among the smaller number of Americans expelled. When the CIA came to my office to complain that the new station chief had been waiting for some time for his Soviet visa, I pointed out that the Soviets probably knew exactly who he was and were unlikely to jump to fulfill his application with us holding up visa requests for Soviet intelligence types. "Just get him in" was the response I got.

After checking up the chain, I called the Soviet consul general Kuleshov and asked him to come to my office alone. I pointed out that this official had been waiting for his visa for some time and said his travel was a matter of urgency for the United States. Kuleshov, as expected, was unimpressed by our desire to get this particular individual on a plane quickly, but he began to listen more closely as I continued that if he got his visa we would find a way to be helpful in return. I pointed out that, sadly, we had noticed that a certain Soviet official had also been waiting some time for his visa. Although I did not say so, the individual had been identified as the new KGB resident in Washington. Kuleshov thought for a minute, smiled and said "understood." Shortly thereafter both men had their visas.

Marine Security Guard Fiasco

At the 1986 Christmas party at the US Embassy in Vienna, Clayton Lonetree, a Marine security guard who had formerly served in Moscow, approached Jim Olson, a veteran of CIA operations in the USSR, to confess that in Moscow he "got into something with the KGB." Lonetree had fallen victim to the honey trap. Young and alone, he had an affair with an attractive Soviet employee of the US embassy. Eventually her "Uncle Sasha" appeared and the not-so-sweet part of the honey trap unfolded. Uncle Sasha, in reality KGB officer Aleksey Yefimov, demanded information about people and activities in the embassy and Lonetree complied. When Lonetree was transferred to Vienna, he was turned over to a new KGB officer who made such heavy demands that he drove Lonetree to seek help.[9]

In the spring of 1987, at about the same time the story of Lonetree and other Marine security guards supposedly suborned by the KGB was splashing across newspapers, it also became known that the Soviets had inserted devices in some US embassy typewriters that allowed them to intercept the documents typed on these machines. Shultz wisely rejected calls by many in Congress and the media to cancel a planned visit, but with the US embassy reduced to writing its diplomatic messages in longhand on yellow tablets, Schultz had to bring with him a planeload of self-contained communications equipment. All classified work done by the Shultz delegation was conducted in tents that were set up in the underground parking garage of the new embassy and draped in metal screens that supposedly blocked Soviet eavesdropping. Portable military generators were installed in the garage to power the equipment. It is possible that these measures hampered Soviet eavesdropping but, as I can testify personally, the noise, fumes, and claustrophobic dimness made many of the working stiffs on the Shultz delegation physically sick.

Over time the case against the Marines began to unravel. One supposed Marine culprit withdrew his confession, which had been improperly obtained after three days of nonstop interrogation. Careful examination revealed that Lonetree could not have allowed the Soviets to gain unauthorized access to the secure areas of the embassy. "Lonetree was just a poor unfortunate," Ambassador Hartman concluded. Nevertheless, the publicity given to the incident—photos of Marines supposedly compromised by the KGB appeared on the covers of major papers and news magazines—and the inevitable congressional grandstanding threatened to derail the US-Soviet relationship just when it was finally beginning to show signs of improvement. It also may have had a deeper role in the hidden world of spy versus spy.

Yevgeny Primakov, who headed the post-Soviet successor to the KGB's foreign-intelligence operations, told Hartman after the end of the Cold War that the Marines had not been very important as intelligence sources and that the Soviets had used the affair to block suspicion falling on Ames. Gerber is confident that Lonetree was in fact a "genuine" Soviet agent but according to Gerber the damage that Lonetree could have done was exaggerated. According to Gerber, "at no time did we ever conclude that Lonetree was responsible for what was happening to the CIA in 1985–1986," when the damage done by Ames was unfolding.[10]

End of the Cold War

On August 23, 1986, while I was vacationing at our family cottage on the Maine coast, I read to my surprise that the FBI had arrested Gennady Zakharov, a Soviet employee of the UN Secretariat. Zakharov did not have diplomatic immunity and instead of being released into the custody of the Soviet mission, which would have immediately loaded him onto a plane for Moscow, he was held for trial. As Bearden wrote, "The KGB interpreted this operation as a profound breach of etiquette." During my first tour in Moscow, when the FBI had arrested two UN Secretariat employees, the Soviets detained US businessman Jay Crawford on trumped up charges. After reading about Zakharov's detention, I called my office and told them to expect trouble, which was not long in coming. On August 30, Nicholas Daniloff, the Moscow correspondent for *US News and World Report,* was arrested in Moscow when he met "Misha," a long-standing contact who was almost certainly working for the KGB. A fluent Russian speaker, Daniloff was one of the most active US correspondents in the Soviet capital. Over several years, Daniloff had been meeting Misha, who among other things supplied him with grainy photos of Soviet troops in Afghanistan. This time, among the materials Daniloff received from Misha, who it later turned out had been sentenced for murder before he met Daniloff, were military maps of Afghanistan marked secret.

There was worse to come. A few years earlier Daniloff had been contacted by someone identifying himself as "Father Roman," who claimed to be a member of a "quasidissident" organization of Orthodox youth. Father Roman, who like Misha was almost certainly working for the KGB, had contacted Daniloff in January 1986 and said he would be giving him a packet of material. Two days later, Daniloff found an envelope in his office mailbox. Inside was a letter addressed to Ambassador Hartman. Daniloff took it to Ray Benson, the chief of the press and culture section at the embassy. Inside the envelope to Hartman was another document that neither Daniloff nor Benson, also a fluent Russian speaker, could decipher but that appeared to deal with Soviet missile programs.

The mysterious document turned out to be in the handwriting of one of the most important sources the CIA ever had whose information on Soviet strategic weapons "held the promise of being one of the most highly prized sources the CIA might ever obtain on the Soviet nuclear target." In 1981 an unidentified scientist had approached a US journalist in Moscow and handed him a package that turned out to be an intelligence windfall: 250 pages of revealing data on Soviet strategic weapons programs. For years after that tantalizing contact, the agency had tried vainly to reach the unknown source. Now he seemed to have surfaced again. Daniloff met the CIA station chief and passed on to him Father Roman's telephone number and physical description. In Washington, numbers crunchers at the NSA matched a likely address in Moscow with the phone number and the CIA sent a rising operative to try to establish contact. He telephoned someone believed to be Father Roman with a message intended for the mysterious scientist. To establish his bona fides, he said he had obtained the information from their mutual friend "Nikolai," thereby identifying Daniloff as the intermediary.[11]

US leaders responded angrily to Daniloff's arrest. Shultz said, "We had arrested a real spy in a sting operation and the Soviets had taken a reporter to use in bargaining." President Reagan sent Gorbachev a letter saying that the reporter was not a spy. When the Soviets nevertheless charged Daniloff with espionage, Reagan used the hotline to warn of "serious and far-reaching consequences."[12]

Reagan's initial inclination was to go for a quick swap, Daniloff for Zakharov. Shultz argued for a better deal, seeking the release of some prominent Soviet dissidents as well as Daniloff. I was told to prepare a list of twenty-five leading Soviet human-rights activists whose release the US should seek as part of a Daniloff deal, a task my office completed with alacrity, putting Sakharov at the top.

Not until Daniloff had been in jail for over a week did the facts about Father Roman reach senior US policy makers, which somewhat undercut the case for US moral outrage. The State Department's chief lawyer told Shultz that a Soviet journalist who had acted similarly in the United States could be prosecuted here. The revelations accelerated pressure in Washington for a deal, as did concern that the deeper Zakharov descended into the US legal system, the harder it might be for the State Department to extract him as part of a deal based on foreign policy interests.

As the State Department negotiated with the Soviets for Daniloff's release, the CIA opened the "Gavrilov channel" with the KGB, a secret communications line established in 1983 to deal with potential crises between the two intelligence agencies. Burton Gerber and Gus Hathaway, both former CIA station chiefs in Moscow, met Arkadiy Kireyev, the chief of counterintelligence for the KGB's First Directorate, in Vienna. Gerber had a simple message: "Daniloff was not a spy and had nothing to do with the CIA." Professionals such as Kireyev presumably understood that fact but it was not really the point. Daniloff was being used as hostage. The Vienna meeting did not go well but at its end Kireyev remarked, seemingly casually, that Father Roman was a "pain in the rear," which Gerber took as a confirmation that the mysterious priest had likely been a KGB informant who was being used to track and possibly provoke Daniloff.[13]

On September 12, Daniloff and Zakharov were released to the custody of their respective ambassadors. Shortly thereafter, Shevardnadze had a one-hour meeting with Reagan from which the Soviet foreign minister "could not conceivably have emerged without knowing that the president was truly angry." Amid the shouting over Daniloff, Shevardnadze delivered a personal suggestion from Gorbachev that the two leaders meet for an impromptu session in either London or the Icelandic capital of Reykjavik. At a time when "every aspect of superpower relations seemed to have become like an exposed nerve," the Reagan team took the proposal as a sign that Gorbachev wanted to find a way out of the morass.

Finally, on Sunday, September 28, after a three-hour negotiating session, the two foreign ministers reached agreement. Daniloff would leave the USSR, and twenty-four hours later Zakharov would depart the United States after he had pled nolo contendere to the charges against him. Washington would state that Yuri Orlov would be allowed to leave the USSR, and the two sides would jointly announce that the two leaders would meet in Reykjavik on October 10.

In summing up the outcome of the Daniloff affair, Reagan concluded, "In the final analysis we stood our ground and the Soviets blinked." In fact, of course, both sides compromised, but Gorbachev gave up more than he acknowledged publicly, largely to gain US agreement to a meeting at Reykjavik. In order to avoid the appearance of a one-for-one swap, the US insisted the Soviets release a larger number of human rights activists over time as an unpublicized part of the deal. President Reagan went to the extent of instructing the US embassy in Moscow to ask Daniloff's wife whether she had anyone to add to the US list.

In Moscow the decisive step toward resolving the issue was taken at a Politburo meeting on September 22. Shevardnadze reported from Washington that Reagan had agreed to meet Gorbachev in Reykjavik but only if the Daniloff affair was resolved satisfactorily and if there was movement on the twenty-five. Like Reagan, Gorbachev had taken a tough public stance, calling Daniloff "a spy who was caught in the act." Now, however, Gorbachev made clear to the Politburo that his desire to meet Reagan in Reykjavik, where he was preparing a proposal he hoped would lead to a breakthrough in the nuclear arms talks, made it imperative to end the Daniloff affair.

Gorbachev outlined for the Politburo the deal that would make Reykjavik possible. The United States would receive Daniloff in trade for Zakharov; Orlov could be released within a month while the others on the list of twenty-five would be released later. The Soviet leader's concessions on Daniloff and the others to be released were intended "to force Reagan to go to the meeting which was necessary for the resolution of a task vital to the success of perestroika— to reduce the burden of arms," according to Chernyayev.[14]

Feeding Frenzy in Reykjavik

The meeting in Reykjavik, the most unusual ever between the leaders of the two superpowers, began with a surprise Gorbachev proposal for sweeping nuclear reductions, passed through what one participant described to me on returning from Iceland as a "feeding frenzy" of proposal and counterproposal that came close to a deal involving the complete elimination of all nuclear weapons, and ended with angry personal recriminations between the two leaders. But Reykjavik also laid the foundation for the groundbreaking INF and START accords only a few years later. As Ambassador Matlock said, "Reykjavik was the psychological turning point in the US-Soviet negotiations that subsequently ended the Cold War."[15]

After Gorbachev had thrown out two efforts by the Soviet national security bureaucracy to come up with a sweeping new arms-control proposal, the general secretary instructed his aide Chernyayev to put together a package himself that would "stun" Reagan. After Gorbachev unveiled his new proposal in a one-on-one meeting with Reagan, Shultz described Gorbachev as "heading dramatically in our direction. He was laying gifts at our feet." Nitze described Gorbachev's offer as "the best Soviet proposal we have received in twenty-five years."[16]

After the first day's meetings, as had by now become traditional, a working group of senior US and Soviet officials labored on arms-control issues through the night. With Chief of Staff Akromeyev in the chair, the Soviet working group was for the first time headed by someone with knowledge about Soviet forces and the authority to make decisions affecting them. After several hours of intensive negotiations, the working group had agreed to a package that incorporated 50 percent reductions in the strategic nuclear forces of both sides and essentially contained the central elements of the INF accord concluded the following year and of the START I treaty finally signed by Gorbachev and Bush in 1991.

At about 4 AM, the working group turned to "defense and space (D&S)." And here, as Akromeyev said, "the scythe hit the stone." Nitze told the Soviets that the United States insisted on continuing research and development of SDI but also promised that it would share the results of this research with the USSR, a guarantee it was willing to write into the ABM treaty. Akromeyev said the Soviets simply did not believe the US would really be willing to share research into advanced military technology with its major adversary. And even if Reagan proved sincere, the Soviets had no confidence that a succeeding administration would make the same commitment. Bleary-eyed US and Soviet working group members walked out of the session expressing mutual frustration at how close they had come to a breakthrough.[17]

While the arms-control teams debated all night, a second working group on bilateral issues, chaired by Ridgeway and Bessmertnykh, had managed to finish its work by midnight, and in the process achieve a stunning breakthrough, almost completely unnoticed in the furor over the arms-control talks. The Soviets agreed "to recognize human rights issues as a regular, open and legitimate part of our agenda," or, as Roz said later, the Soviets "discovered that the words human rights did translate into Russian."[18]

On Sunday morning, the two leaders and their respective foreign ministers reconvened for what was supposed to be their last meeting. As the haggling continued, the discussion became heated, and both leaders began to dredge up accusations from earlier stages in the relationship. Eventually, the two agreed to hold one last session later in the afternoon and instructed their foreign ministers to craft a statement to bridge the differences on SDI while preserving what had been agreed elsewhere.

Shultz began that meeting by saying he hoped to clear up the minor issues remaining from the morning sessions of the two chiefs, perhaps understandable from a tactical point of view but still an astonishing flight of optimism. Shevardnadze brought the discussion down to earth by replying curtly there was only one issue: "The period of time during which the United States is willing not to withdraw from the ABM treaty."[19]

While Shultz and Shevardnadze debated, the NSC's chief arms-control expert, Air Force Colonel Robert Linhard, conferred with Richard Perle and began scribbling on a yellow legal pad. Linhard resuscitated a proposal the US had made earlier at Pentagon instigation, that both sides agree to eliminate all strategic ballistic missiles, the so-called zero ballistic missile approach. Now, Linhard suggested that during the second half of the ten-year reduction phase for strategic offensive arms, which the two sides had already agreed on, they would eliminate all ballistic missiles, in return for which the United States would sign on to the Soviet proposal to keep all SDI research within the limits allowed by the ABM treaty for ten years.

Specialists on both sides understood the zero ballistic missile proposal for what it was, a pure propaganda ploy. It would eliminate the ballistic missiles that were the heart of the Soviet strategic force but leave untouched heavy bombers and cruise missiles where the United States enjoyed a substantial advantage. General Starodubov described it as "a typical American proposal, advanced so that it could be rejected." Watching the Soviet reaction at the table, Nitze, who had earlier described the Pentagon's proposal as voodoo arms control, saw to his surprise that Shevardnadze, who was still learning his way in the arcane field of nuclear arms control, simply said he would pass the proposal on to Gorbachev.[20]

At 3:30 PM, with masses of impatient journalists waiting, the two leaders reconvened for the climactic bargaining session. The US presented a draft statement based on Linhard's proposal. When Gorbachev, by now fully briefed on the implications of the ballistic missile ploy, insisted that bombers also had to be eliminated, Reagan seemed surprised. He said he had been told that ballistic missiles were the Soviets' primary concern. When Gorbachev disabused him of this notion, Reagan remarked, "Evidently we have misunderstood you. But if that's what you want, all right."

This led to a long discussion between Gorbachev and Shultz about how to limit various types of nuclear systems. Listening, Reagan became impatient and interjected, "All this could be sorted out." The president asked Gorbachev whether in the deal under discussion "we would be reducing all nuclear weapons—cruise missiles, battlefield weapons, sub-launched and the like." He added, "It would be fine with him if we eliminated all nuclear weapons." Gorbachev replied quickly, "We can do that. We can eliminate them." Hearing this, Shultz said simply, "Let's do it."

It was perhaps the most astounding moment in the history of US-Soviet arms negotiations. In a few quick words, the two leaders had dismantled the military strategy the West had followed since the end of the Second World War, which relied on US nuclear weapons to counterbalance Soviet superiority in conventional forces. Having blithely turned the world upside down, Reagan suggested they hand the details over to negotiators in Geneva with Gorbachev coming to the United States to sign the deal.

Gorbachev agreed but then said the words that brought everything crashing back to earth. "He now wanted to turn to the ABM treaty." Having just agreed to eliminate all nuclear weapons, there was no longer much point to either SDI or the ABM treaty, but neither leader seemed to be capable of climbing out of his deeply entrenched position. Reagan acknowledged, "We may not build SDI in the end; it might be too expensive," but he insisted that he would not "destroy the possibility of proceeding with SDI." As it became clear that Gorbachev was prepared to block the deal that loomed so close, Reagan "blew my top."[21] Gorbachev, for his part, complained that "the President had not made a single, substantial, major step in Gorbachev's direction."

At this point, it is difficult to understand what was going on other than to assume that the better judgment of both leaders had been overcome by the heat of combat. The US note taker for the session, Deputy Assistant Secretary of State Tom Simons, said that by the end of the session he was not certain if the two leaders truly understood the significance of the proposals on the table. Simons added that he really didn't know what was going on in the hearts and minds of the two leaders.[22]

As the meeting came to a close, emotions were high. The Soviet record shows Reagan saying, "It's too bad we have to part this way. We were so close to an agreement. I think you didn't want to achieve an agreement anyway." Gorbachev expressed regret but added that "I did everything I could if not more." In his memoirs, Reagan describes a parting exchange that has become emblematic of the failed opportunity. Gorbachev said, "I don't know what else I could have done," to which Reagan replied, "I do. You could have said yes."[23]

There has been confusion about what was on the table when the talks collapsed. Coming out of the final meeting, Shultz told other Americans that the deal had been to eliminate all ballistic missiles and Reagan took the same line in his speech to the nation. The two were apparently articulating the proposal contained in the paper the US presented at the beginning of the climactic session with Gorbachev, but the record clearly shows that on several occasions Gorbachev said he would insist on the elimination of heavy bombers as well as ballistic missiles and that Reagan agreed to this proposition. Gorbachev outlined that position in his speech on October 14 to the Soviet people. On the plane back from Reykjavik, Matlock consulted with the US interpreter Dmitry

Zarechnak, who confirmed that Reagan had spoken of eliminating all nuclear weapons and that Gorbachev had never accepted the idea of eliminating only ballistic missiles without including bombers.[24]

US allies were appalled when they learned what had happened at Reykjavik. Prime Minister Thatcher was typically forthright: "When I heard how far the Americans had been prepared to go it was as if there had been an earthquake beneath my feet." The president's proposal meant that "the whole system of nuclear deterrence which had kept the peace for forty years was close to being abandoned." Thatcher and German chancellor Kohl rushed to Washington to register their objections. Reykjavik also elicited an unprecedentedly negative reaction from the US military leadership. JCS chief Admiral Crowe told the president that "the proposal to eliminate all ballistic missiles in ten years time would pose high risks to the security of the nation."[25]

Despite initial perceptions of failure, Reagan eventually came to see Reykjavik as "a major turning point in the quest for a safe and secure world." Two days after returning from Reykjavik, Shultz told the president "you smoked the Soviets out and they are stuck with their concessions. . . . We should instruct our Geneva team to move the positions up to reflect what Gorbachev has given."[26]

The roller-coaster negotiations left behind an emotional bond among the participants. Before Reykjavik, Reagan and Gorbachev had been slowly moving toward building trust in their ability to work together. After Reykjavik, the two men began to develop not just mutual confidence but a sense of shared affection. Chernyayev says that Gorbachev often cited Reykjavik as the time where he became convinced that "he and Reagan could work together" and that the president "intuitively felt the challenge of the times."[27]

Gorbachev knew he could not continue domestic reform without reducing the burden of international competition. He was determined to preserve the changes in Soviet arms-control policies he had forced through on the eve of Reykjavik, telling the Politburo after his return that "the options which we advanced in the past are now buried." Soviet negotiators in Geneva should be instructed to introduce elements of the Reykjavik package into the talks, and the general secretary added for good measure that it was time to look at new approaches in military doctrine and structuring Soviet armed forces.[28]

Gorbachev and the Generals

Under the sympathetic rule of Leonid Brezhnev, Soviet military leaders became comfortable operating in a system where they received practically unlimited resources and only a handful of political leaders had access to military decision-making. Soviet military leaders, like most of the rest of the Soviet elite, welcomed Gorbachev's advent, but they also felt uneasy at the prospect of working under a general secretary who had never worn a uniform or fought in the Great Patriotic War.[29]

Like most senior Soviet officials, Gorbachev understood that military spending needed to be cut. On one occasion an exasperated Gorbachev described the military as "spongers" to Minister of Defense Dmitry Yazov but he also understood that given the encrusted interests involved, any changes had to be carefully prepared. Gorbachev's aide Shakhnazarov pointed out that Gorbachev "had to conduct in a certain sense a diplomatic game with the military." The generals, for their part, demonstrated a "refined experience in reporting to the political leadership one thing and thinking and executing something completely different."[30]

The decisive breakthrough in Gorbachev's approach to the military came on May 28, 1987, when a young German named Mattias Rust landed his small Cessna aircraft on the cobblestones of Red Square. An enormous embarrassment to the Soviet armed forces, Rust's feat proved to be a heaven-sent opportunity for Gorbachev to move against the military establishment, where he claimed "there had already been signs of trouble." Possibly convinced by Raisa's purported view that it was "an attempt by the military to humiliate her husband," Gorbachev told the Politburo that the Rust incident was "a blow against the leadership of the country and all of its policies." Defense Minister Sokolov resigned on the spot and after a short break the Politburo accepted Gorbachev's proposal that Yazov become his successor.[31]

By the 1980s, problems with the Soviet military went far deeper than difficulties in detecting low-flying private aircraft. The war in Afghanistan had exposed poor discipline, low morale, drug abuse, and violence within its own ranks and against unarmed civilians. Soviet soldiers in Afghanistan routinely experienced shortages of clothing, food, and medical supplies. They suffered far higher rates of illness and infection than was common in modern twentieth-century armies.

There was an underlying problem that almost no one wanted to acknowledge let alone address. The Soviet military had become a deeply corrupt institution. According to Shakhnazarov, senior Soviet officers had become accustomed to living in comfortable luxury that was even greater than the top party-state leadership enjoyed. In addition to the privileges that always went with top positions in the USSR, spacious apartments, luxurious dachas, personal cars and drivers, and access to scarce foods and consumer goods, Soviet commanders found ways to profit personally from their positions. One widespread practice was selling the labor of their conscript soldiers to nearby factories or collective farms, what Shakhnazarov called "the trade in living goods." In Afghanistan Soviet soldiers routinely sold weapons to their opponents and the practice spread to the USSR itself as ethnic conflict unfolded there.[32]

Gorbachev used the Rust incident to carry out the most sweeping purge of the Soviet military establishment since Stalin, although his methods were of course less draconian. Approximately 150 officers, mostly in the air defense forces, were tried and retired in the immediate aftermath of the Rust affair. Over the next two years, about 50 percent of the top managerial personnel in the Ministry of Defense was changed. "Gorbachev had moved a younger generation into leadership positions and also made room for the Afghan war generation of officers to advance."[33]

Unfortunately, Gorbachev seems to have made little effort to put supporters of perestroika in key places or to try to educate the military on the long-range value of the painful changes he was proposing. The men he chose for top positions in what turned out to be the most difficult period for the Soviet military since the early days of the Great Patriotic War were for the most part "mediocre careerists who would follow orders, any orders" and who ended up trying to overthrow him in August 1991. In the words of one of the foremost US students of the Soviet military, "Gorbachev had intimidated his generals, he had not convinced them to undertake radical military reform."[34]

Around this time, Gorbachev also moved to take personal control of another area long dominated by the military: the arms-control process. Gorbachev had revitalized the "Big Five" policy backstopping group, which had fallen into desuetude after Ustinov's death in 1984, by appointing as its chief Lev Zaikov, whom Gorbachev had brought from Leningrad to head the Central Committee department responsible for supervising the military-industrial complex. Energetic and intelligent and with strong backing from the general secretary, Zaikov took personal charge of the Big Five, which came to be called the Zaikov Commission. According to Vitaly Katayev, a longtime Central Committee Defense Department official, Zaikov brought a broader range of specialists into the decision-making process, which had the effect of reducing the tight control the uniformed military had formerly exercised over all defense issues. The result, according to participants, was that Soviet arms-control policies became more thoughtful and better coordinated, with key conceptual moves being debated at the senior policy level before being sent down to the backstoppers for staffing. They were also, of course, more in tune with Gorbachev's preferences.[35]

Some Soviet military leaders still hoped they could minimize change by delay and obfuscation. In 1988 Yazov sought to give Soviet commanders gathered in Warsaw the impression that the changes Gorbachev was publicly advancing were primarily rhetorical, saying that "Gorbachev was a very clever fellow in advancing slogans that put the imperialists off balance and divided the Soviet Union's enemies." Similarly, in the summer of 1988 the Soviet military sent Gorbachev material for remarks he would be expected to give as host of the Warsaw Pact political leaders. The text contained all the appropriate political phrases but, when Gorbachev saw a draft of the remarks Pact commander Kulikov would give to the assembled generals once the political chiefs had departed, a very different picture emerged. Kulikov intended to tell the brass that the danger of war in Europe had increased, that it was necessary to continue the modernization of all weapons, and that military expenditures would likely have to rise in the future.[36]

Despite such equivocations, by 1988 Gorbachev seemed to have assumed a commanding position toward the military. He was ending the "running wound" of Afghanistan. He had installed figures personally loyal to him, or at least so it appeared at the time, in the key positions of minister of defense and chief of staff. With the talented Akromeyev working directly for Gorbachev and the energetic Zaikov in personal control of the Big Five, the general secretary seemed to be in a position to drive forward his security agenda with the West.

INF Agreement

Even before Reykjavik, some senior Soviet figures had suggested that it would be in Soviet interest to conclude a separate deal on INF in order to eliminate the threat posed by US P-II missiles, which Katayev once described to Gorbachev as "a pistol aimed at the forehead of the country." When in February 1987 Yakovlev suggested to Gorbachev that the Reykjavik package be unbundled and that the Soviets seek an early INF agreement, even conservatives like Gromyko and Ligachev agreed.[37]

Signed on December 8, 1987, during Gorbachev's first visit to Washington, INF was the first US-Soviet arms-control treaty to eliminate an entire category of offensive nuclear weapons. During the three-year reduction period established by the treaty, the two countries destroyed a total of almost 2,700 missiles. The most striking aspect of the treaty was its comprehensive verification provisions. In scores of pages, the treaty's mutually agreed database provided detailed information on the technical characteristics and location of every missile and its associated support equipment. For the first time, Moscow had consented to American inspectors on Soviet territory, where they could witness the destruction of weapons, monitor production facilities, and conduct short-notice "challenge" inspections when questions arose.

Despite its political importance, the actual military significance of the INF treaty was rather limited. The parties gave up no more than about 4 percent of their total nuclear arsenals and both retained more than enough strategic nuclear weapons to attack targets in Europe or Asia that had been covered by shorter-range missiles eliminated under the INF treaty. In practice, it was the United States that actually sacrificed more in purely military terms. Elimination of the P-IIs and GLCMs removed highly accurate systems capable of attacking targets throughout the western USSR with little warning time. These US INF systems considerably complicated Soviet planning for a ground attack on Western Europe and also raised Soviet fears about the possibility of "decapitating" US nuclear strikes on Soviet command and control facilities.

A decision Gorbachev made to include certain shorter-range Soviet missiles in the treaty's limits, over the advice of his national security bureaucracy, and the fact that the Soviet Union would have to destroy more weapons than the United States aroused resentment among the Soviet military. Despite such reservations, "there were no serious conflicts either within the leadership of the USSR or among experts of the Five" when it came to signing the INF treaty. Soviet military specialists recognized that the treaty had eliminated the danger of surprise attack from US INF weapons and many also understood that the confrontational tactics of the early 1980s had only strengthened NATO. In Washington after the treaty had been signed, Akromeyev told Shultz, "My country is in trouble and I am fighting alongside Mikhail Sergeyevich to save it. That is why we made such a lop-sided deal on INF and that is why we want to get along with you."[38]

The Washington Summit

When Gorbachev arrived in Washington in December 1987 for his first ever visit to the US capital, it was slightly more than two years after the "get acquainted" session in Geneva and fourteen months after the two leaders had parted angrily at Reykjavik but the changes in the US-Soviet relationship were palpable. The Western world was in the grips of "Gorbymania," shown in Washington on the last day of the summit when Gorbachev brought his motorcade to a halt and plunged into an enthusiastic crowd, saying, "Hello, I'm glad to be in America."[39]

The Washington summit had its share of tough exchanges between the two leaders. In their first private session, Reagan hammered on human rights, leading Gorbachev to retort that the president was not a prosecutor and

Gorbachev not a defendant. Nevertheless, the meeting saw the reestablishment of the personal relationship between the two leaders. As Gorbachev said, "Both partners were becoming used to each other and stopped getting worked up at every word and every snubbing remark they disliked." In his diary, Reagan described his meeting with Gorbachev, adding, rather "I should say Michael."[40]

At the INF signing ceremony, Reagan cited the Russian proverb he had already tried out privately on Gorbachev: "I'm sure you're familiar with it, Mr. General Secretary, though my pronunciation may give you difficulty. The maxim is: Dovorey no provorey—trust, but verify." To laughter from the entire room, including the president, Gorbachev interjected, "You repeat that at every meeting!" Shultz saw the exchange as a telling sign of the "easy and friendly relationship between the two leaders."[41]

The improved relationship was evident at less exalted levels as well. The presidents and foreign ministers were accompanied by teams of lower-level officials with responsibility in every aspect of the relationship. "Dozens of aides were ushered in and out of the Oval Office as the leaders toured the superpower horizon," with White House chief of protocol Lucky Roosevelt looking "like a traffic cop" as she managed the flow of officials from both sides.[42] The prospect of jointly reporting to both leaders imposed a kind of discipline and even camaraderie among officials in both bureaucracies.

Bilateral Breakthrough on Human Rights

Early one morning, I entered the ornate prerevolutionary house on Tolstoy Street that the Soviet foreign ministry maintained for ceremonial events. Built before the revolution by millionaire merchant Sasha Morozov, its Russian "fairy-tale baroque" embellishments were cherished by generations of diplomats, Soviet and foreign alike. On this day, accompanied by a colleague from Embassy Moscow, I bypassed the ornate reception areas and entered one of the small working rooms in the back, where we met counterparts from the MFA USA desk.

By the mid-1980s, the State Department's "representation lists" had become practically public entitlement documents, a strong contrast to the early 1970s, when I had compiled them for the Nixon-Brezhnev summits and they were considered virtually top secret. Now the list was divided into four separate categories and contained hundreds of families and almost a thousand names in total.

After the November 1985 Geneva summit, when Gorbachev for the first time had acknowledged that "humanitarian matters" were a part of the US-

Soviet dialogue, the State Department began pushing actively for resolution of representation-list cases. Eventually a new tone began to creep into the responses we would hear from Soviet counterparts. Instead of "interference in internal affairs," usually accompanied by a disgusted "what, not again" roll of the eyes, Soviet diplomats began to reply in a slightly more forthcoming fashion. One of the points they made was that the information on our lists was often inaccurate. Sometimes, they would assert, when they tried to track down the people on the list, they would find that they no longer wanted to leave the USSR, had died, or perhaps had never existed at all, this accompanied with a friendly "gotcha" smile.

Finally, I suggested to my Soviet counterpart on these matters, the genial Soviet consul general Viktor Kuleshov, that it might be a good idea for us to go over the names on the list in a problem-solving manner. Given the regrettable difficulties one often experienced in trying to communicate with ordinary Soviet citizens, I acknowledged there probably were inaccuracies in our lists. Why not go through them on a name-by-name basis to exchange information and clear up any inaccuracies, which would of course make it easier for the Soviets to do the right thing by those who remained on the list. To my surprise Kuleshov, after a moment's reflection, nodded agreement.

And so, after the idea had been staffed up our respective chains of command, I found myself in Moscow. For the entire day, we slogged through every name on the lists. I would describe what we knew about the individual or family. My Soviet counterpart listened, took careful notes, and sometimes provided information in reply. It was a businesslike exchange.

At the end of the day, when we finally reached the last name, all of us heaved a sigh of relief. To save time, I had done the whole procedure in Russian. I felt mentally exhausted but at the same time elated. Standing to leave, I said we had appreciated the spirit of the exercise and added that we now hoped that everyone who remained on the lists would be allowed to leave the USSR. My Soviet counterpart replied in a positive but noncommittal fashion. Nevertheless, within eighteen months almost every person on those lists had received permission to leave the USSR. Their departures were certainly not due exclusively to our one-day exchange of information, but it was an example of the often ignored impetus that US-Soviet bilateral diplomacy had on improving the overall situation with respect to human rights in the era of perestroika.

It is often forgotten how grim the human rights situation was in the USSR when Gorbachev took office. The Moscow Helsinki group had formally disbanded in 1982, after almost everyone connected with it had been arrested, exiled, or driven into silence. The *Chronicle* had stopped appearing years ago. The few human rights activists still at liberty were isolated and silent.

Before I left for official trips to Moscow in the mid-1980s, people who were part of a human rights support network in the United States would give me supplies, generally clothing, medicines, or food. Once in the Soviet capital I would find time to peel away from official business, call a number I had been given, and arrange to meet the person at the other end of the line. Passing over my small bundle, I would offer a few words of encouragement and we would separate. Sometimes the process was more direct. Once a journalist asked me to carry in medicines for author Lydia Chukovskaya, which gave me the chance to spend a delightful afternoon with the spritely eighty-something author in her Gorky Street apartment, where books, photos, and other memorabilia constituted something of a museum to her father, children's author Kornei Chukovskiy, and to the history of the Soviet literary intelligentsia.

Behind the scenes, Gorbachev was working toward a new approach on human rights. At a Politburo session in November 1986, after Shevardnadze described the understandably skeptical reaction to his proposal to hold a human rights meeting in Moscow, Gorbachev said the USSR needed to work out its own concept of human rights. In the subsequent discussion, many on the Politburo declaimed that it was the USSR's sovereign right to decide such questions, but Gorbachev had a more nuanced view: "We need to reexamine all our practice on this issue. Look at how many applications for exit have accumulated!" It was time to end the "routine" approach to the issue that had only led to the accumulation of "dissidents." "If someone wanted to go abroad, let them," Gorbachev said.[43]

During Shultz's April 1987 visit to Moscow, he attended a seder dinner held at Ambassador Matlock's Spaso House residence with several dozen prominent refuseniks and their families. Wearing a yarmulke, Shultz had a personal message for almost every guest. I knew a number of the guests, and I can personally testify that, as Shultz writes in his memoirs, the event "moved deeply . . . all my colleagues who were present." At the time, even though Gorbachev had been in office for over two years and the pace of perestroika was accelerating, the traditional "next year in Jerusalem" still seemed like a dream. And yet, Shultz notes in his memoirs, "all of the prominent refuseniks at the seder had been allowed to emigrate by the time of Passover the following year, 1988."[44]

During Shultz's visit, the two delegations established a US-Soviet working group on human rights. On the Soviet side, the working group was headed by Anatoly Adamyshin, a soft-spoken and intelligent diplomat with long experience in Western Europe. Adamyshin later confessed that when he began his new assignment, he "was aware that our Soviet laws and particularly their implementation left much to be desired but I didn't realize how far we were below international standards."[45]

Adamyshin's counterpart was the head of the State Department's Human Rights Bureau, Richard Schifter. A Democratic politician from the Washington suburbs, Schifter made the neoconservative political migration to the right under the conviction that détente had been one-sidedly advantageous to the USSR. Schifter later acknowledged that he was slow in recognizing the true scope of the changes Gorbachev was introducing in the USSR. Yet his tenacious advocacy of tough US actions with respect to Soviet human rights abuses bore fruit in the US bureaucracy and with the Soviets.

Progress was dramatic in all three areas the working group covered: emigration, political prisoners, and the political abuse of psychiatry. By 1988 Adamyshin felt able to tell the UN Human Rights Commission that there were no longer any persons convicted for political or religious reasons in the USSR, although Schifter noted that there still remained substantial numbers in the camps who had ostensibly been convicted for criminal offenses but whose real transgressions were political.

Adamyshin and Shevardnadze used the growing prominence of human rights in the US-Soviet bilateral dialogue to push for changes within the Soviet system that many liberal-minded Soviets thought were long overdue. In 1987 Shevardnadze supported Adamyshin's proposal to collect more liberal emigration regulations in one legal framework, to bring the USSR into compliance with the UN Covenant on Civil and Political Rights. Even though Gorbachev felt compelled to oppose some of the human rights proposals Shevardnadze sent him, out of worry that they would be criticized by party conservatives, this initiative led to the adoption of the USSR's first law on emigration in 1991.

The MFA also used the US-Soviet working group to tackle the political abuse of psychiatry, one of the most loathsome of the human rights violations under the Soviet system. In the late 1970s, about 15,000 people were forcibly confined in psychiatric prisons for political reasons. In 1988, thanks in part to the ministry's efforts, new rules were adopted that reduced the grounds for coercive treatment in mental hospitals. "Political dissidents" charged with anti-Soviet activity were released from psychiatric confinement. Maximum-security psychiatric hospitals were reduced in number and those that remained were transferred from the police to the Ministry of Health.[46]

In three years, the bilateral working group had presided over an astonishing sea-change since Shultz had met Gromyko in Geneva in January 1985 and the Soviet foreign minister refused to exchange even one word on the subject of human rights. Of all the Cold War–era secretaries of state, George Shultz was possibly the most personally committed to human rights. He may have remembered this incident with Gromyko when during the Moscow summit in 1988 he said, "Progress on human rights had come further than in any other area of our four-part agenda."

Progress on human rights contributed to the extraordinary transformation of the human relationship among the top leaders on both sides which, in turn, played an important role in fostering progress across the range of issues in the US-Soviet relationship. Ambassador Matlock recounted a meeting between Shultz and Shevardnadze on the margins of the UN General Assembly in which Shultz passed over a copy of the US representation list. Instead of delivering a Gromyko-style lecture on "noninterference," Shevardnadze said he would take the list back to study, "not because you asked me but because my country needs to do it." After this, Shultz and Shevardnadze stood up and shook hands. The American replied, "I will never ask you to do anything that is not in your country's interest."[47]

Summit in the Evil Empire

Ronald Reagan landed in Moscow on May 28, 1988, a little more than five years after he had called the USSR "the focus of evil in the modern world." It was a trip rich in symbolism, the leaders of the two Cold War rivals hugging babies in Red Square, but thin on substance.

The START treaty, which both leaders had hoped to have ready for signing at the summit, was drowning in a morass of technical issues from which it would not emerge until George Bush's first Moscow summit three years later. But many of the other issues on the four-part agenda, which only two and one half years earlier at the Geneva "fireside" summit had seemed frozen into confrontation, had either been resolved or transformed into areas of cooperation. In Afghanistan Gorbachev had begun to withdraw Soviet troops. Regional issues, once the cockpit of US-Soviet global confrontation, had entered a phase where Gorbachev assured his guests that "the hand of Moscow will be a positive one."

The Moscow summit was Reagan's first opportunity to see the country he had spent most of his political career denouncing. As Air Force One approached the Soviet capital, Powell tried to brief a distracted president, who kept his eyes glued to the window. "Look," he said, "there's almost no traffic." Ordinary Soviets took advantage of the opportunity to view the man who until recently the Soviet media had routinely vilified. Everywhere Reagan went, crowds lined the street. One Muscovite told US reporters, "I'm not religious but I was delighted to hear him end his speeches by saying 'God bless you.' We never heard it said before on television."[48]

On one occasion, the enthusiasm of ordinary Soviets got out of hand and the Reagans saw the enduring hard side of Soviet reality. On the first day of the summit, the Reagans decided to walk along Moscow's Arbat Street, which under perestroika was becoming an unofficial pedestrian shopping arcade. As the presidential couple strolled along the street, they were surrounded by an enthusiastic crowd. The president's KGB escorts formed a flying wedge and without warning began to pound people aside. Surprised, Reagan was heard to mutter, "This is still a police state."[49]

At Gorbachev's alma mater, Moscow State University, Reagan delivered one of his better speeches, which his foremost biographer has described as a "Hymn to Freedom." Initially skeptical, the students warmed to the Great Communicator and at the end Reagan received a standing ovation. At the Writers Club, Reagan left the building to prolonged applause after praising the achievements of glasnost and urging the publication of still-banned works such as Solzhenitsyn's *Gulag Archipelago*.[50]

The substantive and personal progress both sides had registered in the relationship did not prevent problems from arising sometimes. At his first one-on-one meeting with Reagan, Gorbachev handed the president a short statement in English that he described coyly as merely "a question of reflecting policies as they were." As Reagan said he liked the statement, Tom Simons the note taker for the meeting, asked, "Mr. President, could I take a look at it?" and suggested tactfully that the working group chairs, Ridgeway and Bessmertnykh, should review the text.

The short statement was loaded with Brezhnev-style code words that reflected the worst of that era of bristly confrontation. It described "peaceful coexistence" as the "universal principle of international relations" and "non-interference in internal affairs" as "inalienable and mandatory," as if the two leaders were not then discussing the human rights situation in each other's country and Gorbachev himself was not introducing major changes in almost every aspect of Soviet internal and external policy.

At the last plenary session, Gorbachev turned to Shultz and Ridgeway to ask why they could not accept what the president had approved. The US team outlined its objections, but Gorbachev would not give up. At the end of the session, he turned once more to the president and said challengingly, "Tell me, Mr. President, that you will be able to accept this text after all." At this point, the US side called a recess and his advisers persuaded an uncomfortable Reagan to hold firm. After the president and Shultz walked over to Gorbachev and gave him the final "nyet," Gorbachev sighed resignedly, put his arm around Reagan and they walked together to the final ceremony.

Years later, Gorbachev told Matlock that he had pushed the statement "in order to challenge Reagan to make a decision on his own." It is also possible that Gorbachev felt a need to show party conservatives on the eve of the 19th Party Conference, when he was seeking dramatic changes on the domestic front, that in the international arena he could stand tall against the Americans. Whatever the origins of the statement, Matlock thought that if Gorbachev had explained candidly to Reagan, a fellow politician, why he needed something like it, the president might well have found some way to accommodate him, but the Soviet leader never made the effort.[51]

Gorbachev's Speech to the UN General Assembly, December 1988

On December 7, 1988, Gorbachev gave a landmark speech before the UN General Assembly (UNGA), in which he described the sweeping steps he intended to take in providing "Soviet democracy" with a legal underpinning by adopting laws on freedom of conscience, public association, and political and religious toleration. He promised to regularize emigration from the USSR and also announced an end to the jamming of all foreign radio broadcasts.

Turning at the end to what he described as "the main issue—disarmament," Gorbachev announced a reduction of 500,000 in the overall strength of Soviet armed forces. A total of 10,000 tanks, 8,500 artillery systems, and 800 combat aircraft would be eliminated in the western USSR and neighboring countries. Soviet forces "remaining for the time being in the territory of our allies" would be assigned "clearly defensive" missions.[52]

At the beginning of 1988, Gorbachev had told the Politburo, "It is now clear that without a significant reduction in military expenditures we won't solve the problem of perestroika. We must preserve parity but we also need disarmament." Over the summer, he worked to build support in the leadership for reductions in the Soviet military posture. On one occasion he invited to the Politburo a collection of the USSR's most talented scientists, who explained how far the USSR lagged behind in critical areas such as computers. Turning to the chief of the Military-Industrial Commission, in three years a member of the coup that tried to overthrow him, Gorbachev railed, "And what kind of money do you guzzle up!"

Gorbachev told the Politburo that if the real data were published, the USSR would show that it "expends 2.5 times more than the USA on military needs and that not one state in the world . . . spends more per person for these purposes than we do." With Politburo members around the table nodding in approval, Gorbachev added, "We will not resolve the tasks of perestroika if everything remains as it is with the army."[53]

Gorbachev's UNGA speech, which some have described as the real end of the Cold War, would have been a promising foundation for further dramatic changes in the Soviet internal and external order that Gorbachev intended to pursue, but in the coming year these were overtaken by events in the USSR and its East European empire.

CHAPTER 15 • 1989
Year of Miracles or Time of Troubles?

As Gorbachev was delivering his triumphal December 1988 UNGA speech a massive earthquake devastated Armenia. After meeting Reagan and president-elect George H. W. Bush on Governors Island, in New York harbor, Gorbachev canceled a planned visit to Cuba and flew with Raisa to the disaster area.

In striking contrast to Chernobyl two years earlier, the tragedy in Armenia was splashed across Soviet media from the beginning. With glasnost in full voice, criticism of Soviet relief activities was not slow in coming. For Gorbachev, after the international acclaim that accompanied his UN speech, it was a sobering plunge back into what was to become the grim reality of his domestic experience in coming years.[1]

Accounts of 1989 often treat the collapse of the Communist regimes across Eastern Europe as a "Year of Miracles," as it definitely was in many ways. In the USSR, by contrast, 1989 was the year when events began to outrun Gorbachev's ability to control them. Explanations of why Gorbachev refrained from using force to block change in Eastern Europe often overlook this domestic connection, how events in the USSR preoccupied him and also limited his ability to intervene even had he wanted to.

New Team in Washington

George Bush came to the presidency better prepared to deal with international affairs than any US president since John Quincy Adams. The Bush foreign policy team was the most capable put together by any president in the second half of the Cold War. Its senior members were experienced and skillful, the strong personalities that always rise to the top of the Washington power game. But they were used to working together and understood that if they did not the boss would show them the door. The Bush team consisted of conservative pragmatists and had no place for the ideological true-believers who populated part of the Reagan administration. It was driven by power politics and not ideology. It was capable of articulating and acting on the basis of sound principles, which served it well in dealing with watershed events such as the unification of Germany and repelling Saddam Hussein's aggression in Kuwait. It also tended to be reactive rather than proactive, which sometimes put it behind the curve in dealing with fast-moving events on a grand historical scale, such as 1989 in Eastern Europe.

Bush's secretary of state, James Baker, was the best dealmaker in Washington. He tended to see foreign policy issues in light of their impact on the president's political standing and domestic agenda. He had little interest in ideology or broad geopolitical questions but was brilliant in the role of problem-solver. Baker largely bypassed the State Department's Soviet experts and relied on a small team of talented and hardworking aides, centered around Denis Ross at the department's policy-planning office. Baker deliberately stayed away from some international hot potatoes such as the wars in Yugoslavia, but he succeeded brilliantly in the big problems he did tackle: US-Soviet relations, German unification, and the Gulf war. Baker and George Shultz, who operated very differently but equally effectively, were the two best secretaries of state in the second half of the Cold War. The United States was fortunate to have had two such capable men in charge of its diplomacy for ten critical years at the end of the Cold War.

Gorbachev and the USSR at the Beginning of 1989

When Dobrynin visited Washington in early 1989 with a message from Gorbachev seeking an early US-Soviet summit, the president asked Dobrynin bluntly, Would Gorbachev survive the tumultuous events in the USSR? At roughly the same time, the British Foreign Office asked its ambassador in Moscow, Roderic Braithwaite, whether Gorbachev was about to be sacked in a coup.[2]

Rumors of a coup were premature and yet, as Gorbachev entered his fourth year in power, the atmosphere of hope and excitement that had accompanied the flowering of reform was dissipating amid a growing cloud of problems and questions, not the least of which was what Gorbachev really wanted. The engine of change that Gorbachev had set in motion had taken on a momentum of its own and the conductor could not seem to make up his mind whether he wanted to drive the process further or hit the brakes.

People had enthusiastically embraced glasnost to the point where some were even questioning whether the 1917 October Revolution itself had been a mistake.

As Gorbachev recoiled from what he saw as the excesses of glasnost, his strongest supporters among the intellectuals began to worry about his leadership. In December 1988, *Moscow News* published a letter by six prominent intellectuals that amounted to both a declaration of support and a cry of alarm: "We will vote for you, Mikhail Sergeyevich . . . We will vote for your policies. But be careful! Too many leaders who do not want perestroika remain in their positions."[3]

On the economic front, Prime Minister Ryzhkov described to the Politburo a Soviet economy spiraling downward into crisis. In the three years since perestroika began, Soviet government spending had exceeded revenue by 133 billion rubles. Gorbachev's antialcohol campaign had cost the Soviet budget 34 billion rubles and Chernobyl an additional 8 billion. The decline in world oil prices had dealt a body blow to the Soviet economy. The value of Soviet oil exports had declined by 40 billion rubles.[4]

In the fall of 1988, Yegor Gaidar, then working as an adviser to Ryzhkov and later the architect of Yeltsin's sweeping economic reform, stumbled on a classified version of the 1989 Soviet budget, still considered a secret document even after four years of glasnost. Gaidar found the draft "absolutely suicidal," with an uncontrollable deficit to be compensated by an unsupported expansion in the money supply. The government was seemingly oblivious to, or at least powerless to address, the prospect of economic cataclysm and social tumult.[5]

But probably most dangerous, and in some ways most surprising to Gorbachev and many others in the Soviet hierarchy, was the rise of ethnic unrest. In 1972 Brezhnev had declared, "The nationalities question as we inherited it from the past, has been fully, definitively, and irreversibly resolved."[6] By 1989 it was tragically clear that Brezhnev's boast was wrong.

The first sign of trouble on the nationalities front came in December 1986, when Gorbachev's ham-handed replacement of long-serving Kazakh leader Kunayev with an ethnic Russian set off several days of bloody riots. These were halted in the old-fashioned Soviet way, through armed force, but as perestroika progressed this option became increasingly difficult to employ.

Two years later, a dispute between Armenians and Azeris over Nagorno-Karabakh, a remote, mountainous region that was predominately inhabited by Armenians but part of Azerbaijan, raised the specter of ethnic unrest in the volatile Caucasus region. In February 1988, after the local assembly in Stepanakert, the Nagorno-Karabakh capital, asked to be incorporated into Armenia, massive supporting demonstrations broke out in Yerevan. Skirmishes between Armenian and Azeri inhabitants of Nagorno-Karabakh helped trigger a bloody pogrom lasting several days against the Armenian inhabitants in Sumgait, a gritty industrial suburb of Baku.[7]

Events in the Baltic States raised a different set of challenges, less fraught with the prospect of violence but just as dangerous for the unity of the USSR. Incorporated forcibly into the USSR in 1940 as part of Stalin's deal with Hitler, the Baltic states were the only part of the USSR where Brezhnev-era dissidence became a mass movement. When I traveled around the USSR in the late 1970s, it was possible to meet people who complained about various aspects of Soviet life but it was only in the Baltics where one got the impression of being in an occupied country. Even Communist officials would sometimes let slip areas of disagreement with the official Soviet line. One did not have to spend more than a few minutes in a bar before young people would begin to speak relatively openly about their desire to be part of the West. A Catholic priest did not let the presence of Soviet officials accompanying a delegation of US visitors deter him from saying quietly that although current conditions were "not bad," someday Lithuania would be "free."

The Baltic States quickly took advantage of Gorbachev's reforms to begin pushing their own national agenda. In the summers of 1987 and 1988, large demonstrations were held to commemorate events connected with the 1940 Soviet invasion. Independent nonparty groups formed in all three republics, ostensibly to support perestroika, but their demands for economic autonomy, language and cultural rights, and the ability of young men to do their military service at home, raised questions about the place of the republics in the union. By the end of 1988, Gorbachev was plaintively asking Chernayayev, "Is it really true that the Baltic people want to secede?"[8]

The national tide was slower to appear in Ukraine, in part perhaps because of continued preoccupation with the legacy of Chernobyl and in part because of the repression that had greeted any manifestation of Ukrainian national feeling in the past. In September 1989 the Popular Movement of Ukraine for Perestroika (RUKH) had its founding meeting in Kiev. Compared with similar organizations in the Baltics or the Caucasus, RUKH's goals initially seemed moderate: economic autonomy, environmental activism, language and human rights. But the national flavor of the movement was clear from the choice of its first president, the poet Ivan Drach, who had been imprisoned in a wave of dissident nationalism in the early 1970s, and from its display of the long-banned yellow and blue Ukrainian national flag.[9]

The Tbilisi Syndrome

At 4 AM on April 9, 1989, Soviet police and airborne troops carrying sharpened entrenching tools, firing tear gas, and backed by armored vehicles dispersed a crowd that had occupied the central square in the Georgian capital of Tbilisi for several days, killing at least nineteen and wounding hundreds. In Georgia, the violence led to growing demands for independence, while in Moscow an eruption of finger-pointing among the Party hierarchy and the military leadership left the soldiers feeling bruised and abandoned.

Not until April 20 did the Politburo hold its first discussion of the Tbilisi events, eleven days after the tragedy. The blame-game was under way in full force. Shevardnadze, who had left for Tbilisi immediately after hearing about the violence, said the official version of events "was absolutely groundless." Gorbachev, who had not returned from a trip abroad until after the Politburo under Ligachev's direction had sent troops to Tbilisi, asserted that the information he received in crisis situations from Soviet intelligence agencies was often doctored. He also blamed the Georgian leadership, which had not "walked out to the people." Finally, turning to Minister of Defense Yazov, Gorbachev said, "Dmitri Timofeyevich, from now on the army cannot take part in such actions without Politburo decisions."[10]

Gorbachev disclaimed any responsibility for the use of force, an assertion that provoked bitter recrimination at the time and later. The Ministry of Defense in Moscow had issued orders to regain control of the parliament building where the crowd was gathered but left it up to local commanders to decide how the task was to be accomplished. After a menacing driveby of armored vehicles and buzzing by helicopters failed to persuade the crowd to leave, the Georgian Defense Council met in secret to consider next steps. With Yazov's deputy, General Kochetov, demanding "urgent and decisive action" and scorning Georgian civilian authorities who "fail to recognize the direness of the situation," the Defense Council approved "swift and resolute measures to restore order."[11]

Gorbachev never explained why he did not assume direct personal control as soon as he landed in Moscow the evening of April 7. As with a similarly controversial decision to use force in Vilnius in January 1991, Gorbachev cannot escape culpability. If Gorbachev failed to engage personally on the issue and allowed the military to act in a way he later claimed was inconsistent with perestroika, he was negligent on a matter of great importance to the country and himself. If, on the other hand, he was informed about what was happening, he was guilty of deceiving the Soviet public and abusing his military subordinates.

After April 1989, the Soviet military became increasingly resentful toward civilian authorities for the way, in the military's view, they allowed problems to get out of control to the point where it was necessary to send in troops to restore order and then blamed the military for casualties that occurred. It is impossible to understand the failure of the Soviet leadership to contemplate the use of force in Eastern Europe later in 1989 without taking into account what came to be called the Tbilisi syndrome.[12]

Nothing Will Ever Be the Same Again—
The Congress of People's Deputies

It is often forgotten that the first expression of democracy during the "Year of Miracles" began in the seat of the Soviet empire. Despite the imperfections of the election system for the new congress, which allocated 100 unelected seats to top party leaders and 750 others in the 2,250-member body to representatives of "public organizations" dominated by the party, people across the USSR seized on the chance to vote in an election that for the first time since 1917 offered at least some degree of choice. *New York Times* reporter David Remnick, who attended election meetings across the country, found that despite economic hardships, empty stores, and the rise of nationalism, "everywhere the talk was of freedom, of learning democracy. They had no prior experience of genuine debate or choice, and yet they seized the opportunity immediately."

The results of the March 25 elections were a stunning surprise. In almost every race where there was a choice, the official candidate lost. Of the eighty-six regional first secretaries who participated in the elections, only ten won. In order to defeat prominent officials, voters often exercised their right to cross out the name of unopposed candidates, who needed more than 50 percent of the votes cast to win. In Leningrad virtually the entire party leadership was defeated, including Politburo member Yury Solovyev. As one observer said, "It takes a special type of person to lose an election when there is no opponent," but the party leadership turned out to be heavily populated by such characters.[13]

But the election's most astonishing result and the one fraught with the most long-term significance was Boris Yeltsin's spectacular victory in Moscow, where he gained 89 percent of the votes despite intense efforts by Gorbachev to defeat him. Yeltsin was nominated in dozens of districts across the country but decided to run in Moscow, the citadel of the party apparat but also home to many members of the liberal intelligentsia and the seat of reformist media organs whose help Yeltsin would need to counterbalance the party-controlled central media. As one of his aides later wrote, "Yeltsin would not have been Yeltsin" if he had not chosen to throw down a challenge to the party at the very place where the apparat was strongest of all.[14]

Gorbachev and the Moscow party machine met Yeltsin's challenge by putting together a slate of ten candidates, which included two serious figures: Yuriy

Brakov, the head of the massive ZIL automobile factory and Gregory Grechko, a popular cosmonaut. In late February, all candidates assembled in the Hall of Columns, near Red Square, which had served as the venue for Stalin's show trials of the 1930s. Gorbachev had something similar in mind for Yeltsin. The hall was packed with apparatchiks and Gorbachev was sufficiently confident of the outcome—only the first two candidates would appear on the ballot— to allow the event to be televised live. For hours Yeltsin faced a barrage of hostile questions that he answered with characteristic vigor. Shortly before the vote Grechko withdrew his name, a stroke that had been arranged in advance with Yeltsin and that left him going head-to-head with Brakov. Realizing that the event was slipping out of control, party organizers called for a vote. As expected, Brakov came in first but Yeltsin was a solid second.

Yeltsin spent four weeks speaking to enthusiastic crowds, including a vocal rally of several hundred thousand in Manezh square, just across from the Kremlin. The official motto of his campaign was a sedate "Perestroika Will Bring Change," but the mood was better captured by a slogan that accompanied him wherever he went: "Fight on, Boris" ("Beri Boris," in the alliterative Russian). Yeltsin was virtually shut out of the broadcast media and his campaign was the victim of many dirty tricks, but none of this mattered. Yeltsin had captured the affections of the people of Moscow and his message of change was what they wanted to hear. Yeltsin received over five million votes to Brakov's 400,000. Even a majority of party members voted for Yeltsin's insurgency.[15]

On May 25, delegates assembled in the Kremlin for the congress's opening session. By the time it adjourned thirteen days later, the USSR was a different country. The proceedings were televised live and millions of transfixed viewers saw for the first time something approaching a real political process.

Before the congress could even address the first item on its agenda, the selection of its presidium, which Gorbachev, in traditional Soviet fashion, had decided in a closed party session before the congress met, an unknown delegate from Latvia strode to the podium and demanded a minute of silence in honor of the victims of the Tbilisi massacre. Next the stooped figure of Andrei Sakharov walked slowly toward the podium. Harkening back to the "Decree on Peace" that Lenin and his Bolshevik conspirators had announced after seizing power in Petrograd, Sakharov proposed a "Decree on Power" that would make the congress the supreme governing body in the land.

In coming days a former Olympic weightlifter, Yuri Vlasov, accused the KGB of running an "underground empire," while a noted Dostoyevsky scholar called for Lenin's body to be removed from its Red Square mausoleum and given a "decent burial." Delegates called attention to environmental catastrophes around the country, revealed that in parts of the USSR infant mortality exceeded African levels, and demanded that Gorbachev give an accounting for the expensive new dacha he had just finished building on the Black Sea coast. Baltic representatives questioned the right of the congress to adopt laws for their republics and asked for an honest discussion of the 1939 Molotov-Ribbentrop pact, which had paved the way for Stalin's seizure of the region. For almost two weeks, the people of the USSR watched their leaders in action, and when it was all over they found themselves distinctly unimpressed. It was "the demytholo-gizing of Kremlin power. Communist demigods were being transformed into ordinary mortals before our eyes."[16]

Despite the unruly debate, Gorbachev's ability to control the congress was never in question. Backers of radical reform constituted no more than three to four hundred liberal intellectuals supported by nationalists of various stripes. When it came to choosing the chair, 2,123 voted in favor of Gorbachev and only 87 against. Gorbachev controlled the flow of speakers to the podium and when one exceeded his tolerance he simply switched off the microphone.

But Gorbachev was also diminished by the congress. By resolutely attempt-ing to steer his own predetermined middle course, he ended up angering both proponents and opponents of change without building an independent base of his own. Watching the congress on television as Gorbachev switched off Sakha-rov's microphone, translator Tatyana Arzhanova, one of the people interviewed in Raleigh's oral history, recalled that she began to cry: "I stood in front of the television and stomped my feet. It was so intolerable." A few weeks after the Congress, *Argumenty I Fakty* polled its twenty million readers on who had been the "best deputy." Sakharov was number one with Yeltsin second—Gorbachev finished a distant seventeenth.[17]

The congress also saw the creation of what amounted to the first opposi-tion group in Soviet politics since the time of Lenin. In July approximately four hundred delegates founded the Interregional Group, arguing that "it was time to move rapidly toward a showdown with the party apparat and to make radical decisions regarding the economy and politics." To avoid the necessity of choos-ing which of the two obvious candidates, Sakharov or Yeltsin, should head the new group, both were elected to a five-person presidium.[18]

The Center Will Not Hold: Gorbachev Loses Control of Events

In the words of journalist Fyodor Burlatskiy, a congress delegate and Soviet insider since the Khrushchev era, "The First Congress of People's Deputies was the summit of the political career of Gorbachev. Earlier he had achieved a breakthrough in foreign policy. Now he had laid the basis for a democratic system." It is a tragic irony that 1989 was also the time when Gorbachev lost control of events both within the USSR and outside it. "By the second half of 1989, Gorbachev and his team were being carried along by the turbulent historical currents they themselves had created," one of his aides later acknowledged.

Gorbachev made two serious mistakes in 1989. Most damaging was failing to take advantage of the congress elections to run for office himself, perhaps for a new post of president of the USSR, as some of his advisers urged. In Burlatskiy's words, Gorbachev's failure to seize this opportunity to gain democratic legitimacy "drove the first stake in his political grave." Gorbachev's second error was in failing to break with the party. Yakovlev had long urged Gorbachev to split the party into a reform-oriented social democratic wing, which Gorbachev could use as a vehicle for real change, and leave the other half of the party to act as the home of conservative true believers.[19]

Gorbachev settled for the position of congress chair, some thought because it had the side benefit of evicting Gromyko from the sinecure to which Gorbachev had appointed him in return for his support as general secretary in 1985. According to Boldin, Gorbachev did not run for direct election to the congress because he was afraid he might lose. A more sympathetic observer, Anatoliy Chernyayev, writes that Gorbachev decided not to seek election out of "loyalty" to officials who entered the congress through one of the seats reserved for party leaders. Whatever the reason, Gorbachev's failure to gain for himself the legitimacy that went with democratic election became in the coming years an increasingly serious handicap in his competition with Yeltsin, who won resounding victories each time he put his name before the Russian people.[20]

Miners Strike

Little more than a month after the congress ended, another dramatic event unfolded that went a long way toward eviscerating the economic, and in some ways the moral, legitimacy of the system. In July, as Solidarity was ending four decades of Communist rule in Poland and setting the stage for subsequent revolutions across Eastern Europe, miners in the Siberian town of Mezhdurechensk walked off the job. Within a few days, 500,000 miners were on strike across the country and Soviet coal production fell by 60 percent.

With large segments of Soviet industry dependent on coal, the strike threatened the entire economy. But the plight of the miners and their families also struck at the heart of the country's image of itself. Stories about the suffering of miners under capitalism were a staple of every Soviet schoolchild's education. In the Soviet system, by contrast, miners were supposedly treated as something of a "labor aristocracy." Soviet miners enjoyed shorter hours than most other Soviet workers, their wages exceeded the average, and they had better benefits, such as early retirement and special sanatoria.

The reality was different and discontent among miners had been building since the 1960s when Soviet authorities began to emphasize oil and gas over coal in energy policy. Wage levels and pensions remained relatively high but the fall in investment led to a decline in working and living conditions.[21]

Reporters visiting striking villages found families living in shacks or crowded into dismal barracks. Indoor plumbing was rare and hot water nonexistent. Ration coupons were issued for food but the food itself was largely absent. Children played listlessly in the street; already their teeth were visibly rotting while those of their parents had long since gone. For Soviet viewers, the contrast between the reality of the lives of the miners that they saw for the first time on their TV screens and the regime's propaganda became one more reason to question the entire system.

In the end, the authorities had no choice but to negotiate. In August Prime Minister Ryzhkov signed a decree that granted many of the miners' demands, including increases in pay and pensions and the dispatch of food reserves to the mining regions. The miners went back to work but the relief proved only temporary.

The miners did not initially criticize Gorbachev. One of the leaders said, "People are not blaming Gorbachev." They knew they were only able to strike because of Gorbachev, but he added, "We can't wait forever." When the government's promises proved hollow, as was inevitable, given the difficulties across the Soviet economic system, the miners' mood changed. A few months after the strikes one of the leaders told a Western correspondent, "We've been destroyed by Stalinism and Brezhnev's cronies. I'm ready now for a leader other than Gorbachev. Someone like Boris Yeltsin."[22]

Ethnic Unrest

In the summer of 1989, ethnic clashes erupted in Central Asia, followed shortly by renewed violence in the Caucasus. In late May, the densely populated Fergana Valley region of Uzbekistan erupted into battles between Uzbeks and Meshkhetian Turks who had been expelled by Stalin from the Caucasus. Troops reestablished order but not before over one hundred people had been killed and 34,000 Meshketians forced to flee their homes. A feature of the riots with ominous implications for the future was the inability, or in some cases unwillingness, of local party and police authorities to stop violence perpetrated by the majority population against a group defined as outsiders.

Barely had the situation in Central Asia settled into an uneasy calm when violence returned to the Caucasus. When Armenians blockaded Nakichevan, a part of Azerbaijan separated from the rest of the republic by Armenia, Azerbaijan replied by blocking the major communication links to Armenia. By the fall of 1989, the two Soviet republics were basically at war and the authority of the Communist Party had essentially vanished.[23]

In 1989 the Baltic states began to slip out of Moscow's control as inexorably as the Caucasus, albeit more peacefully. On August 23, the fiftieth anniversary of the signing of the Nazi-Soviet Pact, three million people linked hands to create a human chain connecting the Baltic capitals. Facing a choice between irrelevance or joining the move toward independence, the communist parties in the Baltic states opted to stay with their people. In July the Lithuanian party adopted a new program that proclaimed state independence as its goal and in December it broke away from the central Soviet party, repudiating the top-down model that had governed the party since Lenin.[24]

In arguing against national separatism, Gorbachev often cited the benefit of living in a large and integrated economy as well as the threat of violence that could accompany the breakdown of the union. Gorbachev's points were valid at the time and in some ways have been vindicated by what happened after the disintegration of the USSR. Yet Gorbachev never understood how for many restive Soviet nationalities the experience of life in the USSR was the central tragedy of their twentieth-century existence. Memories of mass killings, starvation, and the deportation of entire nations had been suppressed but not forgotten. It was hardly surprising that the exhumation of this ugly history did little to encourage enthusiasm for life in a Soviet state however benign its current rulers professed themselves to be.

All Fall Down: Eastern Europe in 1989

When Gorbachev took office Eastern Europe was far down his list of priorities. The day after Chernenko's funeral, Gorbachev told East European leaders, "Where you go, how you get there—that is your business, I will not interfere." Gorbachev could promise to abandon Moscow's big-brother role because he thought the people of Eastern Europe would willingly embrace the democratic socialism he sought for the USSR. According to Andrei Grachev, Gorbachev's last press secretary, Gorbachev "believed that the driving force of perestroika in the Soviet Union would provide an inspiring example for its allies and result in a new unity of the Socialist community, this time founded on mutual interest rather than coercive pressure."[25]

By 1988 problems in Eastern Europe could not be ignored. In a long and troubled Politburo discussion in March, Ligachev admitted that "some socialist countries are facing political upheavals. In Poland everything is moving in the direction of renunciation of the party." Gorbachev told the Politburo that the situation in Eastern Europe was worsening and concluded with a prescient comment, which shows that he fully understood the stakes involved: "The stability of the socialist countries is our vital interest from the perspective of both security and our economic interests. . . . If the situation begins to crack, the very idea of socialism will be discredited."

At the beginning of 1989, Yakovlev asked the Bogomolov Institute to prepare an analysis on the situation in Eastern Europe. After he received its gloomy reply, Yakovlev commissioned reports on the same subject from the MFA, the KGB, and the Central Committee, the three key Soviet institutions responsible for policy with Eastern Europe.

The Bogomolov report called the situation potentially explosive and warned that socialism could lose its governing position in Poland. The three reports also reveal that, at least for civilian analysts, the use of force in Eastern Europe was off the radar screen, although the Central Committee and the MFA recommended some ambiguity on the subject to retain leverage in Eastern Europe.[26]

As the East European revolutions began to rise over the horizon, Moscow was well informed about the situation. No one in Moscow anticipated the scope or the speed of developments but then neither did anyone else including people in Eastern Europe itself.

Poland

On June 4, 1989, the people of Poland administered an even more crushing electoral setback to the Polish party than Soviet voters had given their own Communists three months earlier. Solidarity won 160 of the 161 seats it was able to contest in the lower house of the Polish parliament, as well as 92 out of a possible 100 seats in the senate. In an even starker indication of the revulsion that the Polish people felt for the regime that had ruled them since 1945, almost all senior party leaders failed to pass the required threshold of votes for the uncontested seats set aside for them.

The elections in Poland were the opening round in the astonishingly rapid and largely peaceful collapse of the Soviet empire in Eastern Europe. The first shots of the Second World War were fired on Polish soil and the Cold War began in a dispute over Poland's future at the end of that conflict so it was fitting that the final act of the Cold War should also begin in Poland.

By the middle of the 1980s, it had become clear that the imposition of martial law in 1981 had simply driven the regime's problems underground. In September 1987 Jaruzelski's advisers warned that the present social peace was illusory. They suggested negotiations with Walesa, through Catholic intermediaries, to avoid what they described as a humiliation similar to Gorbachev's telephone call to Sakharov a few months earlier.

On February 6, 1989, the dialogue got under way. Seated around a huge doughnut-shaped table, its size determined, according to legend, by the need to keep the parties out of spitting distance, were representatives of the regime, Solidarity, and the Church. Chaired by Walesa and his former jailer, Interior Minister Kiszcak, the Roundtable Talks resulted in an agreement on April 5 that called for legalization of Solidarity, free access to the media, and the reform of economic, administrative, and judicial systems. New political structures included an elected president and a bicameral parliament with real political power. The Soviet media welcomed the Roundtable agreement, but a certain degree of worry can be inferred from the fact that at the end of April Jaruzelski, "at Gorbachev's invitation," traveled to Moscow and for three and one half hours briefed the Soviet leader on the accord.[27]

Solidarity's sweeping electoral victory ended hopes that demands for change in Eastern Europe could be contained within the limits of perestroika. Overnight the issue changed from whether Communism could be reformed to whether the Polish authorities, and their Soviet backers, would allow a non-Communist government in Poland for the first time since the Second World War. Gorbachev seems never to have wavered. The day after the election, Jaruzelski informed the Polish Politburo that Gorbachev had told him, "A political solution will have to be found."[28]

In early August, Walesa demanded that there be no Communist ministers in a government headed by Solidarity. This was a bridge too far even for Gorbachev and his team. A foreign ministry official warned publicly that Solidarity should not push things "all the way to a destabilization of the situation in Poland." This relatively cautious warning had an immediate effect, demonstrating the strong residual fear of Soviet intervention even at this late stage of the game. Walesa said that Solidarity would leave the defense and security portfolios in the hands of the Communists and promised that "Solidarity will fulfill its Warsaw Pact commitments."

By late August, Tadeusz Mazowiecki, a former Solidarity editor, was on the verge of being named prime minister. Before that happened, Mieczyslaw Rakowski, who had taken over as head of the Polish party to allow Jaruzelski to become president, made a last-ditch effort to head it off. In a forty-minute call to Gorbachev, Rakowski pushed for an invitation to Moscow. Gorbachev refused, warning that such a meeting could be seen as Soviet interference, which is of course just what Rakowski wanted.[29]

The fact that events in Poland ended with a peaceful transition of power does not mean this outcome was inevitable. There was much enmity on both sides and a long history of violence. In August 1988, at the height of a last spasm of Solidarity strikes, the Homeland Defense Committee, the secret body chaired by Jaruzelski that had organized the imposition of martial law in December 1981, began planning a repetition. After Solidarity's electoral victory, detailed preparations for another crackdown were drawn up, including lists of people to be arrested. In the words of Mark Kramer, who has probably studied more secret files of the Soviet and Eastern European regimes than anyone on either side of the former Iron Curtain, "If the Polish authorities had received a go-ahead from Moscow in mid-1989 (as they did eight years earlier), the martial law operation of December 1981 might well have been repeated."[30]

Gorbachev did not order the tanks to roll for many reasons, including a genuine abhorrence of violence. He was also preoccupied with events in the USSR and was increasingly inclined to view Western assistance, which would have evaporated after any use of force in Poland, as necessary for his own domestic reforms. Moreover, from Moscow's point of view, the situation in Poland did not yet appear hopeless. Gorbachev's friend and ally Jaruzelski remained president and the Communists still controlled the "power ministries." The Poles had promised not to touch remaining Soviet forces in Poland and Mazowiecki declared that the "new Soviet-Polish relations, based on partnership, not domination, would only reinforce the stability of Poland's international obligations."

On September 29, the Politburo met to review a report on Poland prepared jointly by the Central Committee, the KGB, and the ministries of defense and foreign affairs, the first time the Politburo had considered the dramatic events in that country. The report took an optimistic tone by asserting that Moscow had the opportunity to "maintain friendly, good-neighborly relations with Poland." It recommended practical steps to improve relations with the new authorities, including an early invitation to Mazowiecki to visit Moscow. But the report acknowledged the potential for serious problems. Events in Poland were "increasing concerns about the fate of socialism and sometimes lead to false conclusions about the flaws of perestroika." Solidarity was already promising to reduce military expenditures and it was possible Poland would withdraw from the Warsaw Pact or restrict its participation to formalities, a development that, nevertheless, the report did not expect "in the near future."[31]

But developments in Poland were not unfolding in a vacuum. People across Eastern Europe were watching and drawing their own conclusions. Events, some as seemingly trivial as a wave of East Germans driving their slow and smelly Trabant cars along Western autobahns, quickly turned into a tectonic upheaval that swept away not just the remaining Communist governments in Eastern Europe but also Gorbachev's hopes for reforming the communist system in the USSR.

Hungary

Hungary was the first country where the Communist authorities voluntarily decided to allow creation of a multiparty system and it was the first to physically breach the Iron Curtain. In May 1988, Janos Kadar, who had led Hungary since 1956, was replaced as party chief by Karoly Grosz, a cautious conservative somewhat in the mold of Ligachev in the USSR. But in Hungary, unlike Poland or the USSR, there was a powerful faction in the party pushing for real democratic change. Miklos Nemeth told a US journalist shortly after he became prime minister in November 1988 that his "greatest ambition" was for the political clubs then springing up across Hungary to become political parties.

After Kadar's departure, the party established a committee to reassess the events of 1956, headed by Imre Pozsgay, a leading radical reformer. Pozsgay told a US journalist, "Communism does not work. It has come to the end of its days." In January 1989, Pozsgay released a 102-page report whose conclusions were as stunning as they were accurate: the 1956 revolt was not a counterrevolution but a "people's uprising." Imre Nagy was not a counterrevolutionary but a national hero and the Soviet intervention had been a tragedy for Hungary.[32]

As in Poland, the Hungarian reformers believed initially that they had to calculate their moves with regard for Moscow's potential reaction. After Pozsgay made his dramatic pronouncement about 1956 his team retired anxiously to his office to await the Soviet riposte. After two days, they nervously telephoned friends in Moscow, who assured them there would be no reaction. Its absence was not an oversight. On learning of the Hungarian move, Valentin Falin, head of the Central Committee International Department, drafted a memo to the Hungarian leadership reminding them of the counterrevolutionary character of the events of 1956. Gorbachev blocked its dispatch, citing the principle of noninterference.[33]

In March 1989, Nemeth went to Moscow, where he told Gorbachev about plans being developed in Budapest for elections, adding that the Communists might well lose. As Nemeth described the meeting, Gorbachev was "very angry" and said, "I do not agree with this Hungarian way." But when Nemeth asked specifically if the Communists were voted out would the Soviets intervene again as they had in 1956, Gorbachev replied without hesitation, "No, at least as long as I am sitting in this chair."[34]

The First Hole in the Wall

Hungary's border fence with the West was scheduled to be renovated in 1995 but Interior Minister Isvan Horvath concluded, "It was no longer in our interest to incur these costs" for a device that was activated more by rabbits and deer than human intruders. Watching televised images of Hungarian workers rolling up strings of barbed wire, East Germans vacationing in the neat pensions that lined Hungary's scenic Lake Balaton realized that a gap had opened in the prison walls their rulers had constructed for them. Small numbers of East Germans began showing up at border crossings into Austria, where Hungarian guards often just waved them through. By the end of August, over six thousand had crossed. On one well-publicized day, two hundred East German picnickers charged across an unattended border crossing into Austria.[35]

In Europe it was "the summer of the Trabi," the tiny East German auto described variously as a "sardine-can-on-wheels" or a "plastic tank," whose possession was the high point of consumer status in the East. Many of the East Germans who crossed from Hungary into Austria that summer kept chugging along until they crossed the German border. German drivers blazing past in their Mecedeses and BMWs would honk and wave a friendly greeting to the tiny Trabis, often crowded with a seemingly impossible number of people. It was probably the only time in history when Germans reacted with tolerance to anyone traveling at less than Mach speed along their autobahn system.

But removing barbed wire and watchtowers did not completely open free passage to the West. Hungary had signed an agreement that obliged it to return any East Germans caught trying to escape. Some Hungarian border guards turned a blind eye to people passing through the border without an official exit permit but as late as August 22 one East German was killed trying to flee into Austria. By August 150,000 were hovering uncertainly on the Hungarian side of the border. Thousands more were camped out on the grounds of West German embassies in Prague and Budapest.

On September 11, Budapest announced that any East Germans in Hungary could cross unimpeded into Austria. On the first day, 8,100 poured over the border and within three days 18,000 had crossed, in buses, trains, on foot, and in the ubiquitous Trabis. Over the fall of 1989, authorities in Budapest estimated that 600,000 East Germans fled across Hungary into the West.[36]

A direct line runs from the Hungarian decision to open its borders to the fall of the Berlin Wall two months later. Those whose ears were properly tuned understood that the Hungarian move was the death knell for Communist rule across Eastern Europe. In early October, the US ambassador in Hungary, Mark Palmer, one of the leading Soviet experts in the State Department, told a US journalist, "Communism is dead."[37]

President Bush Visits Eastern Europe

Even as events in Eastern Europe began to accelerate, skepticism about Gorbachev remained in the Bush administration. The Soviets had stopped sending military aid to the Sandinistas in Nicaragua, as Gorbachev had promised Reagan the year before, but in what seemed simply a shell game Cuba and East Germany had stepped up their deliveries. National Security Adviser Brent Scowcroft said later, "Soviet intransigence in the 3rd world deepened my reservations about Gorbachev."[38]

It took a previously scheduled trip by President Bush to Poland and Hungary in July to push the administration into a more activist approach. In Gdansk, the birthplace of Solidarity, Bush and Walesa jointly addressed a huge and enthusiastic crowd, alternatively chanting their two names. The president made it clear where US sympathies lay, telling "the brave workers of Gdansk" that "America stands with you." Nevertheless, Bush still believed he had to "step carefully" to avoid antagonizing the Soviets. The NSC official responsible for Eastern Europe at the time wrote later, "We wanted to facilitate democratic change without inadvertently provoking a backlash."[39]

Speaking to the Polish parliament, Bush called for Solidarity and the Communist authorities to "forge a rare alliance of courage and restraint" and made several positive references to Jaruzelski. In private, Bush encouraged the proud Jaruzelski, who feared a humiliating rejection by the parliament, to run for president. As President Bush recalled, "Jaruzelski opened his heart and asked me what role I thought he should now play. . . . I told him his refusal to run might inadvertently lead to serious instability and I urged him to reconsider. It was ironic: Here was an American president trying to persuade a senior Communist leader to run for office."[40]

According to Jaruzelski, Bush's intervention played a crucial role in his election as president on July 18, a few days after the president's departure from Poland. It was one of those quiet, behind-the-scenes moments that reflect greater historical changes. Since the Second World War the Soviet Union had called the shots in Poland. Gorbachev's backing for Jaruzelski's negotiations with Solidarity had been critical. But after Solidarity's election victory, the balance of power was shifting. Moscow's role was still important but largely negative through the residual fear of armed incursion. Now it was the American president whose intervention was decisive in determining who would be Poland's president. Gorbachev seems hardly to have noticed but Moscow's Eastern European empire was starting to slip away.

East Germany Unravels

The unexpected opportunity in the summer of 1989 to leave East Germany on vacation and end up in the West immediately exposed the paradoxes that underlay the regime since its founding and which the world had largely forgotten since the building of the Berlin Wall in 1961. East Germans lived better than people in any other Soviet Bloc country. But East Germany was also the most repressive of the Eastern European regimes, with the possible exception of Ceaușescu's Romania. The Wall was the external symbol of the regime's repressive nature, but for its citizens the day-to-day reality was the Stasi, the secret police that monitored every aspect of the population's lives through 90,000 full-time employees and 180,000 "unofficial collaborators," making it according to some calculations the largest surveillance organization in history as a percentage of population. Yet at the same time East Germans enjoyed easy access to Western television and radio just across the border. The only location in East Germany where West German television could not be received was one low area near Dresden, known as "the valley of the clueless."[41]

Before the Wall was built in 1961, approximately 3.5 million East Germans departed to the West. In the following twenty-eight years only about 5,000 managed to flee. At least 136 were killed trying to escape, the last in February 1989. Despite its seemingly solid foundations, the existence of East Germany rested in a very direct way on force. Intelligent members of the East German hierarchy, whether true-believing hard-liners such as party boss Honecker or cynical pragmatists like spymaster Markus Wolff, understood this fact. Gorbachev apparently never did.[42]

The pressure for change, swelling so visibly in Poland and Hungary, was slower to develop in East Germany. In June 1989 the Stasi estimated that there were no more than 2,500 opposition figures in the entire country, of whom only 60 were considered hardcore activists. Two events in the middle of the year deepened the sense of despair. In early May, the regime held its usual phony elections, in which 98.95 percent of the population were said to have supported the official list, a striking contrast to elections that spring in the USSR and Poland, where for the first time people had a real choice and exercised it against the Communist authorities. The vocal support that the regime gave to the Chinese suppression of the Tiananmen demonstrations was seen by East Germans as a sign of their own rulers' determination to take similar measures to crush any efforts at change.[43]

East Germany was sometimes described as the economic showcase of the Communist world. This rump portion of Germany with a population of only seventeen million had the eleventh largest economy in the world. But East Germany could not escape problems facing other Soviet-style centrally planned economies. Over the years, its industrial productivity steadily declined: in the 1950s it was 70 percent of that in West Germany but by the 1980s it had fallen to less than 50 percent.[44]

There was, moreover, the problem of reconciling the East German population to living in what amounted to a large lockup, especially when everyone could see the prosperity fellow Germans enjoyed on the other side of the wall. The Pankow regime adopted an economic strategy that was intended to "compensate for the lack of legitimacy by providing consumer goods and social security." It soon became apparent, however, that the East German economy could not support a social welfare policy aimed at placating the population. As consumption increased at the expense of investment, productive capacity declined and the infrastructure began to deteriorate.[45]

In fact, the surface prosperity of the East German economy rested on massive outside subsidies. The Soviets provided oil and other raw materials to East Germany at well below world market prices and bought in return East German manufactured goods that were often the best in the East but generally well below the quality available in the West.

West Germany provided credits on generous terms to its eastern rival, a practice pursued by both leading parties, despite the absence of any evidence that it had the slightest effect in its intended objective of encouraging moderation in East Berlin. Another form of financial subvention was less openly acknowledged since it basically involved paying ransom to the East German regime in return for allowing people to depart to the West. The practice began with the reunification of families divided by the Wall but it subsequently expanded to include the release of political prisoners. Eventually, a regular trade in human beings was established, with a schedule of fees depending on the status of the individual involved. By the time the regime collapsed, over 250,000 individuals had been reunited with family members and Bonn had additionally purchased the freedom of 33,000 political prisoners. For these "humanitarian services" West Germany paid in cash or in kind approximately 3.5 billion deutschmarks. Hard currency obtained in this way went into a special bank account personally controlled by Communist chief Honecker.[46]

As the USSR reduced subsidies to its East European satellites, Pankow relied even more heavily on Bonn, which provided billion-mark loans in 1983 and 1984 and stepped up payments for political prisoners. East Germany was being kept afloat by subsidies from its western neighbor, but the day of reckoning could not be postponed indefinitely. In May 1989, the head of the East German planning commission, Gerhard Schurer, told a small circle of leaders that Pankow's debt to the West was increasing by five hundred million hard currency marks per month and that by 1991 the country would be insolvent.[47]

The Soviets had multiple channels into the upper echelons of the East German government and Gorbachev was well informed about events there. To take only one example, in August 1989 Stasi chief Mielke asked to see privately Sergei Kondrashev, a longtime senior KGB operative then serving as personal adviser to KGB chief Kryuchkov. Mielke told Kondrashev, "I want you to tell Kryuchkov, who must then immediately tell Gorbachev, that if you persist in your present passivity in the face of what is going on in Poland, Hungary, and Czechoslovakia, then I must tell you that the DDR is doomed." Kryuchkov took Kondrashev's message to Gorbachev, who read it and said only, "Leave it with me. I'll think it over."[48]

Gorbachev Visits Berlin

There was little love lost between Gorbachev and East German party boss Erich Honecker, who told Wolff, "I will never allow here what is happening in the Soviet Union." Gorbachev, nevertheless, felt he had no choice but to attend celebrations of the fortieth anniversary of the creation of the East German regime, arriving on October 6, just as demonstrations were expanding across the country. On the ride from the airport, with Honecker sitting stolidly beside him, thousands greeted the Soviet visitor with chants of "Gorby, Gorby." Later, Gorbachev told his aides that the situation reminded him of "a boiling pot with a tightly shut lid."[49]

In his public remarks Gorbachev was guarded, saying that every country had to find its own way to renewal and frequently emphasizing the importance of East Germany as a Soviet ally. In private, perhaps with the message he had received from Kondrashev in the back of his mind, Gorbachev gave the East German Politburo a clear invitation to move against Honecker. The Soviet leader warned, "If the party pretends that nothing special is going on, if it does not react to the demands of reality, it is doomed. Now is a good moment for you to act." As the Soviet delegation left the country, it appeared the East German leadership had gotten the message. Egon Krenz, generally considered

Honecker's successor, told Falin, who accompanied Gorbachev, "You said everything that needed to be said. We understood it all."[50]

The Wall Falls

The pivotal point in the East German revolution came on October 9, when over 100,000 marched in Leipzig. Police were ordered to break up the demonstration by "any means," but after hearing an appeal for dialogue from prominent religious and cultural figures and failing to get guidance from East German leaders, the local party chief ordered police to assume defensive positions. The demonstrators chanted Gorbachev's name, called for the release of prisoners, and shouted, "We are staying here," transforming protest from an appeal to leave to insistence on internal change.[51]

On October 17 the East German Politburo, responding to pressure from the street and from Moscow, finally ousted Honecker, after first sending a secret emissary to consult with Gorbachev. Krenz, an unimaginative apparatchik who basically amounted to Honecker light, was duly chosen to take his place. In the streets, people were demanding elections, recognition of opposition groups, and freedom to travel, but Krenz, notorious for his involvement in the falsification of the May elections and for his effusive praise of the Tiananmen massacre, was incapable of stilling the popular clamor.[52]

When Krenz made the obligatory trip to Moscow, Gorbachev made it clear that as far as he was concerned unification was not in the cards. If "the tendency of rapprochement in Europe would continue for several decades," Gorbachev said, "the situation might present itself in a different light someday" but for now "one had to continue the current policy which had brought such success."[53]

Krenz, however, staggered Gorbachev when he got around to discussing the East German economic situation. He unveiled data showing that at the end of 1989 foreign exchange accounts would show an income of $5.9 billion and expenses of $18 billion. In the future, this imbalance would only get worse. East Germany had no option but to seek new foreign loans, even though Krenz admitted that interest on previous loans amounted to 62 percent of total hard currency earnings. An "astonished" Gorbachev replied that he had not imagined the country's situation "to be so precarious." He advised Krenz to find a way to promptly tell the East German population that "it had lived beyond their means in the last few years" lest he find himself blamed for the mistakes of the previous leadership.

This was classic Gorbachev: full disclosure of your predecessor's mistakes but vague on what you intend to do to correct them. It was not what Krenz wanted to hear. Uncharacteristically, he interrupted Gorbachev to say he agreed with the analysis but then asked bluntly what the Soviet leader was prepared to do to help. Krenz pointed out that, "the GDR was, in a certain sense, the child of the Soviet Union, and one had to acknowledge one's paternity." Gorbachev, however, was in no mood to take on additional parental obligations. He danced away from Krenz's plea by urging the East Germans to develop relations with West Germany but eventually admitted that the USSR "could do very little in economic terms" to support its Eastern European friends.

The street was starting to take charge of the situation. As officials of the two Germanies were discussing financial assistance to prop up the eastern regime, over a million people marched in Leipzig. On November 1, under the threat of strikes at home, the East German government reopened the border with Czechoslovakia. Approximately 25,000 East Germans quickly took advantage of the move to flee to the West. By November 9, a quarter million had left since the crisis began that summer, most of them young and well educated. The continued existence of two Germanies was being called into question by the citizens of one, no matter what statesmen might say to themselves.[54]

By November 9, when the Berlin Wall fell, the state that had erected it was dissolving. The days of the Wall were clearly numbered yet the act itself occurred through a bureaucratic snafu. Under pressure from the street—on November 4 half a million protestors had marched in East Berlin—and from Prague, which was threatening to reclose the border because the flow of escapees was stirring unrest in Czechoslovakia, the East German government adopted a new regulation allowing citizens to apply for permission to leave the country temporarily without meeting previous highly restrictive criteria. The East Germans had obtained approval for an early draft of what was intended to be a technical fix from the Soviet foreign ministry and Krenz also read the decree to the East German Politburo, which was preoccupied with political infighting and did not react. According to one recent study of the events around the Wall's fall, there was "no sign that the party leaders realized that they were essentially approving their own death warrant."[55]

Hoping to reduce the growing pressure of demonstrations, Krenz told press spokesman Schabowski to announce the new rule during a press conference already scheduled for that evening. When journalists asked when it would go into effect, Schabowski apparently decided to wing it. "Immediately, without delay," he replied. Within minutes, media across Germany and the world broadcast the sensational news that the border was open. West German television reported, "The gates in the Wall stand wide open," which was not then true but soon would be.

Thousands of people collected on both sides of the Wall, clamoring for action. Police guarding the gates, who had not been informed about Schabowski's announcement, frantically telephoned for instructions but could get none, in part because the Politburo was in an extended session discussing the country's catastrophic economic situation. The police let some of the more brazen troublemakers through to the West, thereby under existing rules depriving them of the right to return home. When they realized what had happened, some begged to be allowed back.

At 11:30 PM, after fruitless calls to superiors, the commander at the Bornholmer crossing asked his subordinates, "Should we shoot all these people or open up?" He answered his question by ordering the gates to swing open. With a roar, the crowd surged forward. "The wall is gone," people screamed, crying and laughing at the same time. Younger participants scrambled over the wall and some began to dance along the top of the once fearsome barrier. The next day, Stasi headquarters estimated that 68,000 pedestrians and 9,700 cars had entered West Berlin that evening. By the end of the month, 9 million, or over half of the country's population, had crossed the border, with 130,000 choosing to remain in the West.[56]

World Leaders Try to Catch Up

Six days before the Wall fell, after KGB chief Kryuchkov warned the Politburo that half a million people were expected to march the following day against the East German regime, Gorbachev concluded that Krenz could not be saved without support from West Germany—which led Shevadnadze to remark, "It would be better if we took down the Wall ourselves." On the day the Wall actually fell, however, it was not events in Germany but fears about the possible dissolution of the USSR itself that preoccupied the Soviet leadership. Gorbachev told the Politburo that Baltic leaders had said to him, "There is no way other than to leave the USSR." Gorbachev still seemed to believe that the Baltic drive toward independence could be blunted by granting economic autonomy. But other Politburo members were more alarmed. Prime Minister Ryzhkov warned that in the Baltics "everything is aimed at secession" and added, "What we should fear is not the Baltics, but Russia and Ukraine. I smell an overall collapse." Vorotnikov predicted that negotiations with the Baltics meant that "Russia will blow up."[57]

When Gorbachev learned about the fall of the Wall, his first public reaction, like any good politician, was to take credit for what had happened, by claiming that opening the border was a victory for the principles of perestroika. In private, Gorbachev dispatched alarmed messages to world leaders. He called

President Bush to warn against "unforeseen consequences" and to ask for "understanding" from the United States. Bush's aides found Gorbachev's reaction one of "barely disguised panic." Bush noted to himself that this call was the first time he had ever seen Gorbachev exhibit any concern about events in Eastern Europe. Heretofore, according to the president, Gorbachev had seemed "relaxed, even blasé." Now, "it was as if he had suddenly realized the serious implications of what was going on."[58]

As pictures from Berlin flooded across television screens, White House spokesman Marlin Fitzwater urged the president to hold a press conference but Bush replied, "Listen, Marlin, I'm not going to dance on the Wall." Finally, "against my better judgment," the president agreed to a short session. With the White House press corps standing around his oval office desk, Bush said, "I am very pleased with this development" and added that the United States was "handling the event in a way that would not goad the Soviets." In response to criticism from the press that he did not seem elated at this "victory for our side," Bush replied simply, "I'm not that kind of guy."[59] Gorbachev's plea for restraint was one reason for Bush's muted response. But the president was cautious by nature. The day before the Wall fell, he had written in his diary, "Changes are dramatically coming our way. . . . If we mishandle and get way out and look like [promoting dissent] is our American project, you would invite a crack-down . . . that could result in blood-shed."[60]

The day after the wall fell, German chancellor Kohl and Foreign Minister Genscher joined a rally at Berlin's city hall, where in 1963 JFK had proclaimed, "I am a Berliner." Kohl thanked Gorbachev for having recognized Germany's right to self-determination, although it was far from clear that Gorbachev had in fact done so. Warming to the moment, the chancellor asserted that Germany's road ahead led to "unity and freedom" and declared, "A free German fatherland lives! A free, united Europe lives!" Genscher also started on a cautious note, promising to avoid "unwanted advice to the East." But Genscher's personal feelings also took over: "There is neither a capitalist nor a Communist Germany but only one German nation."[61]

The prospect of one Germany was precisely what was worrying some Western European leaders. Italian prime minister Andreotti summed up the views of many by saying, "I love Germany so much that I preferred when there were two." British prime minister Thatcher publicly described the fall of the Wall as "a victory for freedom" but in private was more wary. In September she had met Gorbachev in Moscow, where she told him that despite NATO's traditional statements supporting Germany's aspirations for reunification, "in practice we were rather apprehensive."[62]

Gorbachev's panicky initial reaction and the prospect of Alliance disunity helped Washington understand that it needed to take the lead in working out a coordinated Western response. Baker's talented team produced principles to guide Western policy: self-determination, Germany must remain in NATO and the European Community, unification had to be peaceful, and Helsinki principles must be respected. This was something of a holding action, but it also captured the essence of the approach the United States would pursue over the coming year, working to persuade Gorbachev to go along with the process but also insisting that the final outcome in Germany had to reflect the fundamental principles that the West had pursued throughout the Cold War.

Mixed signals from Moscow, one day anxious and threatening and the next day calm and flexible, set a pattern the Kremlin followed for the rest of the drama around unification. "After the Berlin Wall fell, Moscow began to temporize rather than elaborate a strategy that contained a bottom line. That, in turn left it to others to set the agenda, exploiting the appearance of Soviet indecision."[63]

On November 28, Kohl presented an ambitious ten-point program for achieving German unity through "free self-determination." He called for multiparty elections in East Germany, leading eventually to a joint structure for all of Germany that would be firmly embedded in "a lasting and just European order of peace." Kohl's speech established unification as the goal of the upcoming process and overshadowed the feeble efforts of the rump East German authorities to retain a separate identity. By wrapping German unity in European rhetoric, the speech undercut efforts by some Europeans to impede unification and forced the Soviets, if they chose to oppose it, to adopt the role of spoiler through the blunt instrument of the veto they possessed as one of the four victorious powers of World War II.[64]

Kohl ensured that the full text of the speech and a lengthy explanation of its objectives landed on President Bush's desk as he was speaking. Kohl was knocking on an open door. In a phone call Bush told his German counterpart, "We are on the same wavelength. I appreciated your ten points." In public, as the Soviet media was harshly criticizing Kohl's speech, Bush said, "I feel comfortable. I think we are on the right track." With Washington and Bonn now publicly aligned on unification, the rest of the alliance had little choice but to go along. Thatcher concluded "there was nothing I could expect from the Americans as regards slowing down German reunification."

In Moscow, Gorbachev fumed. When Genscher visited Moscow a few days later, he had what he described as "my most unpleasant meeting with Gorbachev." The Soviet leader complained that he had been duped by the chancellor, who, Gorbachev asserted, "had put forward demands that resembled an ultimatum."[65]

Malta Summit

By December, when Bush and Gorbachev finally met in Malta, the world had changed. It was obvious that Gorbachev had lost control of events and that the long Cold War struggle was approaching a conclusion that was going to look a lot more like victory for the West than anyone had expected.

Within the administration, skeptics such as Scowcroft, his deputy Robert Gates, and Defense Secretary Cheney might still harbor suspicions, but policy toward the USSR was firmly in the hands of the president and his secretary of state, neither of whom any longer doubted that Gorbachev's reforms were for real. But there was little sentimentality in the administration's approach toward the USSR. The Bush team understood that the Soviet Union was a wounded giant and was fully prepared to exploit its weakness to achieve US policy goals. The president liked Gorbachev and wished him well but was also determined to lock in agreements that met US objectives lest the situation in the Kremlin change. In the words of NSC aide Hutchins, by 1989 "our task was to secure Soviet acquiescence without humiliation."[66]

Malta was the first shipboard US-Soviet summit and the experience was never repeated. What had been intended to be an informal get-together with a few close associates had mushroomed into the usual horde of advisers, assistants, guards, journalists, and other hangers-on. President Bush clung to the notion of holding the actual meetings on two warships, the USS Belknap and the Soviet cruiser Slava, largely because as a former sailor he knew that tight shipboard space would limit the number of aides who could crowd into the discussion. But as the two leaders arrived, a winter storm turned Valetta harbor into a maelstrom of wind-whipped waves that forced most of the meetings to be held on board the cruise ship Maxim Gorky, which the Soviets had thoughtfully tied up to the shore. Quarters were tight even on the Gorky. When the two delegations crowded into a stateroom for their first meeting Gorbachev quipped the room was so small that if the sides ran out of arguments they could always resort to kicking each other under the table.

Bush began the meeting by stating unequivocally that "the world will be a better place if perestroika ends as a success" and continued with a seventy-minute monologue in which he outlined a package that left the Soviet delegation visibly pleased. It included proposals to advance the pace of US-Soviet arms-control negotiations and an ambitious list of economic measures.[67] Gorbachev, who took careful notes as Bush spoke, replied that before the meeting he had considered telling Bush that the USSR expected "concrete action" to back up his previous statements of support for perestroika. Now, Gorbachev continued, he had heard both a statement and important action.

With the storm increasing, the session had to be curtailed to allow Bush to return to the *Belknap*, tossing at its anchor in Valetta harbor. The president and other senior members of his delegation got into a US Navy launch and pushed out into the heavy seas. Viewers saw the small craft bobbing and sometimes disappearing behind mounting waves. It took several approaches before the launch was able to make fast to the *Belknap* and the US party could scramble aboard. After lunch, the president bounced up, grabbed his papers and said "let's go." The *Belknap*'s captain courageously told his commander in chief that the seas were simply too rough. The president was marooned on the US warship until the following afternoon, unable to traverse the few hundred yards of wild seas that separated him from his Soviet counterpart, who remained on board the *Maxim Gorky*, choosing not to sample the *Slava*'s shipboard hospitality.

Participants were enthusiastic about Malta's results. Chernyayev described it as a "historic turning point in international developments." On the plane home, Bush told his companions, "Now I want to push, push, push on arms control, and get something done." In Washington Bush instructed the NSC that "foot-dragging" was over. He demanded active engagement from the most senior members of the administration to move forward an ambitious agenda of arms-control agreements and economic engagement.[68]

For all the genuine goodwill between the two leaders and their respective teams, the Malta summit clearly established the United States as the dominant partner in the evolving superpower relationship. President Bush had said he did not want to create difficulties for Gorbachev by "dancing on the Wall" but at the same time he was not going to be deflected from pursuing policies to US advantage. He also made clear his intention to push for the unification of Germany despite Gorbachev's wish to see the subject left for the future.

Marshal Akromeyev, a member of the Soviet delegation, wrote later that Malta showed "the correlation of forces between the USA and the USSR had shifted in favor of the USA." Akromeyev said the Americans had "won" at Malta because Bush came away with the understanding that the USSR would not strongly oppose the unification of Germany and because the Americans understood after Malta that the domestic situation in the Soviet Union would only get worse, something Akromeyev believed that Washington would take advantage of in the future.[69]

At a meeting of Warsaw Pact leaders in Moscow the day after his return from Malta, Gorbachev gave an upbeat description of the talks. But he also said it was essential that the pact continue in order to defeat the "confrontational policy" of the West in the future. When Gorbachev finished, an uncomfortable silence followed, finally broken by Romanian leader Ceaușescu, who criticized Gorbachev's optimistic picture of recent events. In a clear sign of how the earth had moved, the meeting adopted a resolution put forward by the Czechoslovak representatives that condemned the 1968 Soviet invasion as "illegal." Afterward, one Eastern European participant told the Western media, "With this declaration . . . the Warsaw Pact as we have known it is coming to an end."[70]

Sakharov Dies and Gorbachev Loses the Democrats

On November 9, the day the Wall fell in Berlin, Gorbachev told the Politburo that a second Congress of People's Deputies needed to be convened "as quickly as possible," not to deal with problems abroad but with the political and economic situation in the USSR itself. When the congress opened, Sakharov proposed modifying Gorbachev's precooked agenda to include a discussion of abolishing Article Six of the Soviet constitution, which established the Communist party as the only one in the country. Gorbachev became visibly angry and drove Sakharov off the podium in a humiliating fashion.

That evening Sakharov laid down for a rest, asking his wife to wake him in two hours. When Bonner went into his room, she found Sakharov dead. Bonner and many friends of Sakharov believed that the vehemence with which Gorbachev had criticized Sakharov contributed to his untimely death.

At Sakharov's funeral several hundred thousand paid their respects to the man who embodied the conscience of the Soviet people. Gorbachev did not attend the funeral but according to Ambassador Matlock, who did attend, Gorbachev's treatment of Sakharov "persuaded many reformers that Gorbachev was more interested in preserving his position as head of the Communist party than in carrying out the reforms he had initiated."[71]

Sakharov's death left Boris Yeltsin, who walked several miles in near zero temperatures behind Sakharov's bier, as the unchallenged leader of the democratic opposition. For the next eighteen months, politics in the USSR revolved around the deepening duel between these two men for the direction of reform and for the future of the country itself.

CHAPTER 16 · Stumbling toward Collapse
Gorbachev's Final Eighteen Months

Approaching Berlin in August 1991 on my way to assume my new duties as chief of the political section at the US embassy in Moscow, I saw to one side of the autobahn an expanse of concrete in the midst of which stood long rows of empty tollbooths. The area was cordoned off by barbed wire barricades and grass was starting to grow through the pavement. It was the former border between West Berlin and surrounding East Germany. Now, traffic raced unthinkingly past what had once been one of the major flashpoints of the Cold War.

It was a reminder of how quickly history can move on. German unification, accomplished almost completely on Western terms, seems so natural that it could appear foreordained. Other outcomes, however, were possible and even desired by some participants on both sides of the East-West divide. The result was attained through skillful negotiations led by the Bush-Baker tandem with the close cooperation of German chancellor Kohl. Gorbachev initially staked out a tough stance and Soviet national security professionals showed skill in developing positions designed to frustrate maximalist Western objectives. In the end, however, Gorbachev gave way on almost everything, in part because of Soviet weakness, in part because he hoped to use a conciliatory approach on unification to gain Western economic assistance, and in part perhaps out of sheer miscalculation.

German Unification: Early Maneuvering

Germans have a word for what happened in the year that followed the fall of the Berlin Wall: "Madness." A divided Germany, which had seemed destined to last for decades if not longer, began to dissolve in weeks. Never before in

German history had anything comparable occurred: a shift in the country's borders without a shot being fired.

Things looked different from the Soviet side of the crumbling East-West divide. In the winter of 1990, Vadim Zagladin, deputy chief of the Central Committee International Department, apologized to Condi Rice, then serving as the NSC's chief expert on the USSR, for being late to a meeting at the Kremlin. "These days are very difficult. I come to work every day to see what new disaster has befallen us."[1]

At the end of January 1990, Gorbachev convened a meeting on Germany with top national security officials. Several participants said the only way to avoid unification was to use Soviet troops to close the border between the two Germanies, an option Gorbachev categorically ruled out. Gorbachev concluded that there were simply no "realistic forces" left that could preserve East Germany. He pledged to "resolutely resist" united Germany becoming a NATO member and outlined a plan to build an international firebreak against the rush to unification. He said the USSR would only withdraw its troops if the United States would do the same, which Gorbachev admitted "would not happen for a long time." But he also ordered the Soviet military to "prepare for the withdrawal of troops from Germany," saying, "We have to put them somewhere!"[2]

While Moscow struggled to come up with a strategy to hold back the tide of history, President Bush and Secretary of State Baker outlined a US approach that included the "fastest possible achievement" of a united Germany as a full member of NATO; a separate negotiating forum, which came to be known as the "Two Plus Four," with internal aspects handled between the two Germanies and international matters by the four victorious powers in World War II; and a substantial US troop presence to remain in Europe.

When Baker met Gorbachev in early February, the Soviet leader said, "Basically, I share the course of your thinking." There was no agreement on specifics, but Gorbachev acknowledged that it was important to avoid a replay of the post–World War I Versailles treaty and added that "he could see advantages to having American troops in Germany."[3]

German chancellor Kohl arrived in Moscow on the heels of the departing American secretary of state. As Kohl was on his way, he got a letter from Bush and a detailed report from Baker about his just-completed talks in the Soviet capital. In the president's letter, which Kohl called "one of the most important documents in history of US-German relations," Bush expressed support for early German unification and pledged, "In no event will we allow the Soviet Union to use the Four Power mechanism as an instrument to try to force you to create the kind of Germany Moscow might want."

In a long meeting alone with Kohl, Gorbachev said it was up to the Germans themselves to decide whether they wanted to unify, what form of government they wanted, and the pace and conditions of the process. Gorbachev endorsed the two-plus-four negotiating framework he had just heard from Baker, saying he had been persuaded that the thirty-five-member CSCE where he had originally wished to center the negotiations, was too unwieldy. Gorbachev said he was still considering what to do about NATO and sought to ensure that subsidies for Soviet troops in East Germany, which Bonn had agreed to take over from the bankrupt Pankow regime, would be paid in deutschmarks.

The People Decide

On March 18, the people of East Germany went to the polls for the first free election in that part of Germany since 1933. The vote was a stunning triumph for Kohl, who held six massive rallies in the east during the campaign. Kohl's conservative Christian Democratic Union coalition claimed 58 percent of the seats in the new East German parliament. The Social Democratic Party won 22 percent of the votes, while the communists, running under a new name, managed 16 percent. The election demonstrated that the majority in East Germany wanted nothing more than to join their countrymen in the West and put an end to any lingering thoughts that East Germany might continue as some sort of separate entity.

In Belgrade the German embassy marked the occasion by holding a US-style election-night party. As the results were reported across TV screens, the happiness among the German diplomats was obvious. One told me jubilantly, "Now it's inevitable; Germany will be united again." A few guests were not so enthusiastic. The elderly East German political chief and his wife sat alone and watched the proceedings glumly. "We are going home soon," he said with obvious bitterness while his wife added, "And we know there will be no place for us."

Moscow Stalls

Even as its former East German satellite was gradually dissolving, Moscow began to dig in its heels. Facing growing criticism that he was giving away too much, Shevardnadze convened a meeting of the MFA collegium, which issued a statement that the USSR could never accept a united Germany as a NATO member. Gorbachev tightened up Soviet positions in other forums; progress on arms talks ground to a halt.

At the first ministerial-level two-plus-four meeting in Bonn, on May 4, Western participants were surprised by the "grim, unyielding tone of Shevardnadze's presentation." The Soviet foreign minister said a suitable international agreement would have to involve a ban on NATO membership, restraints on domestic German politics, negotiation of a new European security system, and continuation of at least some four-power occupation rights. After several hours of fruitless discussion, the ministers left the West German capital wondering what to do about a looming stalemate.

Bush took a tough line. "They're saying that Germany must not stay in NATO. To hell with that. We prevailed and they didn't. We can't let the Soviets snatch victory from the jaws of defeat." Washington and Bonn began contingency plans for unification without Soviet agreement—a concept that would have been unthinkable even a year earlier.[4]

As unification negotiations unfolded, the Western alliance was moving toward new political and military strategies, whose chief point, according to Bush, was "to make unified German membership in NATO more palatable to the Soviets." In early July, after NATO foreign ministers haggled over the text until past midnight, the alliance adopted a number of changes in its political and military strategies to reduce confrontation between two blocs. Immediately afterward, Bush wrote Gorbachev, pointing out that the NATO declaration would transform every aspect of the alliance "especially of its relationship with the Soviet Union," adding that he hoped the declaration would persuade Gorbachev "that NATO can and will serve the security interests of Europe as a whole."[5]

Breakthrough in Washington

A critical breakthrough came on the second day of the US-Soviet summit in Washington in May, when Gorbachev agreed with Bush that membership in NATO was something for the Germans themselves to decide. Bush describes himself as being "astonished" at Gorbachev's move. As the exchange between the two leaders on this point proceeded, the president said later that "the room went suddenly quiet," but the disarray on the Soviet side was obvious. Bush described it as "a virtually open rebellion against the Soviet leader." Other members of the US team recalled it as "a palpable feeling—conveyed through expression and body language—among Gorbachev's advisers of almost physically distancing themselves from their leader's words."

Gorbachev was prone to hasty and almost impulsive decisions, as his advisers were by now well aware. But by this point he and Shevardnadze were focused not on trying to block a united Germany's membership in NATO but on the conditions that would accompany the deal.

Gorbachev had, in effect, decided to go for the cash. As the two leaders were walking across the White House lawn after the summit's opening ceremony,

Gorbachev stressed to the president his interest in US economic help for perestroika. That evening, in private, a "very agitated" Gorbachev told Bush that if there was no trade agreement it would be a "disaster." Meeting US congressmen for breakfast, Gorbachev complained that the USSR was "being squeezed out of Europe," explained his economic difficulties with considerable frankness, and urged passage of a trade agreement "largely for political reasons."

During talks at Camp David, Gorbachev asked for direct financial aid from the United States, telling Bush that he had not wanted to raise the matter in front of the whole Soviet team. Bush pledged that the G-7 would consider a multilateral assistance program at its Houston meeting in July. But the US president also said that before US assistance could be considered, "he wanted to see" more progress in economic reforms, movement on Lithuania, and a reduction in subsidies to Cuba. He also pointed out that "progress on Germany would create the right political climate" to seek money from Congress.[6]

By early July, the essential elements of the Western position on German unification were on the table. Meanwhile, on the ground, Germany was rapidly becoming one country. On July 1, as economic and monetary union occurred, East Germans lined up to exchange their old money for new deutschmarks at the highly favorable rate of one to one. West German goods flooded the East and border checks disappeared. Negotiations between the two Germanies on terms of unification began in early July, but after the triumph of the CDU coalition in March the Kohl team was essentially negotiating with itself.

On the Soviet side, national security professionals continued to struggle to reassert the primacy of traditional security interests. In May former INF negotiator Yuliy Kvitsinskiy took over the Soviet team in the two-plus-four process and began, in his words, "sorting out the mess that had passed for Soviet policy." At about the same time, Adamyshin complained to British ambassador, Rodric Braithwaite, that "Soviet tolerance had its limits. It was unimaginable that East Germany should become part of NATO or that American troops should advance to the Polish border."[7]

In a second meeting of two-plus-four foreign ministers in June the Soviets presented a toughly worded draft agreement intended to slow the momentum toward unification. The Soviet draft would have established the two-plus-four agreement as a transition arrangement pending negotiations beginning in 1992 toward a final settlement on a unified Germany. It would have also allowed East Germany to maintain a separate existence for at least five years after unification, banned any changes in the scope of NATO or the Warsaw Pact, and required steep reductions in German forces but allowed troops of the four victorious powers to remain in Germany for at least five years after unification.

US officials acknowledged that the new approach was "elegant but it had come too late." The USSR, with its economy and national cohesion crumbling by the day, had only one real lever, to threaten to delay the withdrawal of Soviet troops but that would have ended any hope of Western assistance to perestroika, which by now had become Gorbachev's only remaining lifeboat. And even Soviet hard-liners, who would shed no tears if perestroika and its author disappeared, recognized that the USSR was not in a position to hold its own in the renewed Cold War struggle that would have followed a Soviet effort to thrust a spike in the diplomatic wheel of unification.

Meanwhile, Gorbachev and Shevardnadze were working out their own position on German unification, without reference to the bureaucracy. In June Shevardnadze's aide Sergei Tarasenko advised the Germans not to worry about what they were hearing from lower-level MFA officials or even from Shevardnadze at set-piece sessions of the two-plus-four. The final outcome would reflect what his boss and Gorbachev said in private sessions. Baker, for his part, warned Shevardnadze that, if necessary, the West was prepared to proceed with German unification absent Soviet agreement.[8]

Negotiations on Germany's future came to a head in July, when Chancellor Kohl paid an official visit to Moscow and then accompanied Gorbachev to Stavropol. In two days of intensive talks, which Kohl's aide Teltschik called "the most important foreign trip ever taken by the chancellor," the two leaders nailed down all of the remaining open issues, essentially completing the shape of the agreement under which Germany was united in October.

Gorbachev repeated the point he had made to the American president that "the presence of US forces in Europe is stabilizing" and disposed of any ambiguity on the NATO membership issue by saying that "a unified Germany will be a member of NATO." In the Caucasus the next day, discussions centered on the conditions under which a unified Germany would join NATO. Gorbachev accepted Kohl's proposal that German military forces be limited to no more than 370,000.[9]

At the end of August, with the treaty due to be signed in a few days, and with global diplomatic attention focused on the Iraqi seizure of Kuwait, the Soviets made a last-minute bid for more money. Gorbachev told Kohl that German unity could not be agreed without an acceptable financial package. He sought over thirty-six billion deutschmarks ($20 billion) for troop support, new housing, and compensation for Soviet property in East Germany. Eventually the

Germans bought the Soviets off with an offer of twelve billion deutschmarks and an additional interest-free loan of three billion.[10]

NATO Expansion: Did the West Renege on a Deal?

It has become an article of faith in some quarters, chiefly of course in Putin's Russia but also among some in the West, that the expansion of NATO into Eastern Europe and some former Soviet republics violated commitments made during the negotiations on German unification. The available historical record does not support these beliefs.

Early in the process leading to German unification, before anyone had settled on a final position, the notion of limiting or excluding NATO's jurisdiction in East Germany was bruited about by some as a sweetener to the Soviets. During his February visit to Moscow Baker, following advice from his German counterpart Genscher, told Shevardnadze that if united Germany were included in NATO, there would be guarantees that "NATO's jurisdiction or forces would not move eastward." But the White House was unwilling to go along with Genscher's formulation and insisted that all of German territory would be in NATO. When he learned of the new White House line Baker, skilled inside operator that he was, began to backtrack. In a press conference before he left Moscow, Baker said that with a united Germany in NATO, "you will have the GDR as part of that membership," although he added that there could be "some sort of security guarantees with respect to NATO's forces moving eastward."

Gorbachev claims that Baker's remarks in February were "the core of the formula on the basis of which was later achieved the compromise on the military-political status of Germany." But during the February meeting with Baker, Gorbachev opposed any membership in NATO for a unified Germany and did not agree to Baker's more limited formulation. Baker himself said years later, "This was a negotiating position briefly considered by the U.S. in regard to East Germany only in talks about German unification and then promptly discarded."

During the German chancellor's visit to Moscow immediately after Baker, Kohl at one point said, according to the Soviet transcript, that "NATO must not expand the sphere of its activity," but Gorbachev, still opposing any NATO membership for a united Germany, did not pick up on this vague formulation. Both Baker and Kohl, in any case, made clear that their talks were exploratory and that final agreement on unification would be worked out in the two-plus-four process.

During the Washington summit in May when Gorbachev agreed that a united Germany should be allowed to choose for itself whether to join NATO, he did not seek to add any limitations on expanding NATO's jurisdiction to the east. During Kohl's breakthrough visit in July to the USSR, Gorbachev initially sought to condition agreement on NATO membership to a commitment that no NATO troops would be deployed in the former East Germany but gave up on this point when Kohl and Genscher insisted that as a fully sovereign nation Germany should have the right to determine developments within its own borders.

The "Treaty on the Final Settlement with Respect to Germany," signed in Moscow on September 12, 1990, contains all of the formal obligations undertaken by any party with respect to German unification. It specifies that after the withdrawal of Soviet forces, German military units integrated into NATO are allowed into the east in the same fashion as elsewhere in Germany with the exception that they may not have "nuclear weapon carriers." No foreign armed forces or nuclear weapons may be deployed or based in the former East Germany, although they may be present for other purposes.

During two-plus-four negotiations, Gorbachev obtained some assurances that helped sweeten the deal—financial aid from Germany and political changes within the NATO alliance—but none of these had anything to do with the enlargement of NATO beyond Germany. Later, when NATO expansion became a controversial reality, officials involved in the process denied that it had figured in the German unification negotiations. In 1997 Philip Zelikow, a senior NSC staffer during the unification process, pointed out, "No Soviet ever said, 'NATO may extend to East Germany but no farther.'" The two sides never discussed the possibility of Poland, Hungary, or other Central European nations joining NATO. If the Soviets took Baker's remarks in February 1990 as ruling out the alliance's expansion, they failed to nail it down in writing or even to mention it in subsequent negotiations.

In 1990 all senior Soviet diplomats were graduates of the Gromyko school of nit-picking diplomatic drafting. They all also understood the Marxian (Groucho, that is) dictum that an oral agreement isn't worth the paper it is written on. In US-Soviet arms-control agreements, both sides frequently adopted the practice of making agreed or unilateral statements separate from the actual text of a treaty but including them in the public record. If the Soviets believed that limits on NATO's expansion eastward formed the basis for their concept of the unification deal, they could have made a formal statement to that effect.

Ultimately, Gorbachev settled for unification largely on Western terms because he had no real alternative. In the opinion of Andrei Grachev, a Central Committee official at the time and later Gorbachev's press secretary, Gorbachev's acknowledgment to Bush at the Washington summit that a unified

Germany could make its own choice on NATO membership was a conscious policy decision to make the best of a bad situation. By then Gorbachev understood that despite the reservations they had earlier expressed to him Western European leaders were not going to split the NATO alliance over unification. Gorbachev understood "he was left alone to face the Americans." Gorbachev was taking the statesman's long view of history. According to Chernyayev, Gorbachev took his final decision to accept full German membership in NATO after he came to the conclusion that all other options were ruled out and "if he wanted to have a friendly Germany on his side it was crucial to stop objecting."

By early 1990, the United States had adopted an ambitious strategy of using German unification to effect a fundamental realignment in the European balance of power. The architects of US policy acknowledged that the result for the USSR would resemble the consequences of a defeat in war but they sought to carry out unification in a way that the USSR could accept and not be left in a position of nurturing lasting bitterness. Hutchins wrote that "the US sought to avoid a Versailles-like result, where the Soviet Union would be deeply dissatisfied and harbor long-lasting resentment." If this objective was ultimately not achieved, it was primarily due to larger developments outside the unification negotiations themselves, most importantly the inability of Moscow after the Soviet collapse to come to grips with its necessarily diminished role in the world; the failure of Russia's post-Communist leadership to create a vibrant and prosperous new domestic system, which had the effect of undermining support for every aspect of the post-Soviet settlement; and the failure of the West to find a way to include Russia as an equal partner in the creation of the new, post–Cold War European order of which German unification was the first step.[11]

Back in the USSR: Gorbachev's Difficult Final Months

By the end of 1989, Yeltsin was blocked at the national level. Gorbachev controlled the congress and the opposition Interregional Group was unlikely ever to constitute more than a vocal minority. Yeltsin's response was to adopt a new strategy "to compel the center to change its policy because of the radicalization of Russia." If Yeltsin and his democratic insurgency could not take power at the federal level, they would seize control of Russia. Yeltsin and his team were not trying to break up the USSR but rather to use the Russian bastion to push reform to its logical next phase of multiparty democracy and market economic reform.[12]

The first battlefield was the March 1990 elections for the Russian Congress of People's Deputies. In the Russian elections there were no reserved seats for party luminaries and the process of candidate selection proceeded in a more open fashion than a year earlier for the USSR congress. A total of 6,705 candidates ran in the 1,068 electoral districts across Russia, with only 33 districts having but a single candidate.

Gorbachev maintained a posture of formal neutrality during the Russian election campaign, most likely aware of the futility of trying to stop Yeltsin in his native Sverdlovsk, where he won a thumping 85 percent of the votes in a field that included twelve other candidates. But Gorbachev pulled out all the stops in an effort to block Yeltsin's election as speaker to the new parliament.[13]

When the Russian congress opened on May 16, Gorbachev unleashed a sharp personal attack on Yeltsin, ending with what he no doubt believed was a clinching argument, that Yeltsin had no intention of sticking to the cannon of "democratic socialism." Delegates responded to Gorbachev's remarks with interruptions and ostentatious signs of disinterest. Watching the proceedings, outgoing Russian Supreme Soviet chief Vorotnikov told himself that Gorbachev simply did not understand. "His authority was greatly weakened . . . and Yeltsin's ratings had grown and therefore criticism of him was received negatively."[14]

After three votes, Yeltsin finally crossed the hurdle by a narrow margin, receiving 535 votes to 467 for Gorbachev's candidate Aleksandr Vlasov, a lackluster apparatchik. Yeltsin's victory came as a result of frantic political maneuvering by his supporters and thanks to divisions among the hard-line Communists who maintained a strong presence in the Russian Congress. It was a triumph for the man whom Gorbachev had sworn to remove from politics forever. But it also signaled trouble ahead. "Yeltsin's victory portended a most uncertain ability to steer the parliament. Most of his victories would be just as narrow and difficult, gained only under intense pressure from outside."[15]

In Moscow there were now two centers of power: one with the legitimacy of democratic election and moving to grasp the levers of authority across Russia and the other that maintained formal control over the old Soviet system but whose standing throughout the country was fading by the day. The struggle was one of power and principle. Yeltsin had a clear policy goal, a democratic Russia within a more loosely organized federal union. Gorbachev's goal seemed less clear. He continued to maneuver in various directions, seemingly hoping that something would turn up to rescue his vision of socialism with a human face. Over the next eighteen months, there were times when the two men were able to work together. In the end, however, real cooperation proved impossible because of the deep personal animosity between the two, their policy differences, and eventually because the tide of history simply passed Gorbachev by.

In his first speech Yeltsin set out a vision of Russia as a "democratic state of laws" with a multiparty system that would be fully sovereign economically. On June 12, 1990, the congress declared that "the Russian Federation is an independent, sovereign republic within the composition of the USSR." By the fall, a draft constitution had been produced based on democratic principles drawn from the United States and Europe. But it was blocked by party hard-liners, who had no wish to see the reforms they opposed at the federal level under Gorbachev introduced in Russia under Yeltsin. The critical stumbling block was the power that would be assigned to the new post of Russian president. Yeltsin was forced to settle for amendments to the existing constitution that reinforced the principles of Russian sovereignty but left unresolved the critical issue of the balance of power between the executive and legislature.

Yeltsin's move passed almost unnoticed at the time but it had fateful consequences. In the coming years the Russian leader was forced to operate on the basis of a Communist-era constitution, which was intended to function in a one-party system where all major questions were resolved behind the scenes by the party leadership. With the formal powers of the executive branch limited, Yeltsin acted in periods of crisis on the basis of emergency grants of quasidictatorial authority, which did nothing to build democratic institutions and which reinforced Yeltsin's predilection for quick, decisive, and sometimes arbitrary actions.

After the election Yeltsin visited the huge and luxuriously appointed speaker's office, on the fifth floor of the immense building that became known as the "Russian White House," located only a couple of hundred yards behind the American embassy. His aide, Lev Sukhanov told his boss in amazement, "Look, Boris Nikolayevich, what an office we've seized." Even Yeltsin, who had operated in the upper echelons of the Soviet system for many years, was "frightened" as he told himself, "After all, we haven't just seized an office. We've seized an entire Russia."[16]

Gorbachev and Yeltsin: Oil and Water

Gorbachev and Yeltsin, whose political and personal struggle shaped the final years of Soviet politics, shared many similarities in their early years. Both were born in 1931 in provinces remote from Moscow. Both were too young to fight in the Great Patriotic War, and both lived in poverty in their early years. Like almost all Soviets, both had close relatives who were arrested in the Stalin era. Both fashioned impressive provincial political careers before coming to Moscow.

Yet the differences between the two men were also profound. Gorbachev spent his entire working life within the party. He was able to enter the prestigious Moscow State University in large part because of a party award he won as a teenager. At the university he demonstrated his aptitude for a future party political career by rising to a leadership position in the Young Communists organization. When he returned to Stavropol it was to take a job at the bottom rung of the local party apparat, from which he steadily worked his way upward.

Yeltsin, by contrast, made his early career in the rough world of construction and did not join the party until he was thirty and membership had become a necessity for further advancement. Gorbachev was always a believer in Marxism-Leninism and could never bring himself to break with the party, even when it had become the chief source of resistance to his reforms. For Yeltsin the party was a means to an end that he shucked off easily once it became an obstacle on his path to the top.

Gorbachev was an intellectual. He was motivated by ideas and was a profound generator of them himself but he had difficulty putting them into practice. Yeltsin was a classic man of action, dominant, aggressive, and overbearing; he would do what it took to get the job done. Yeltsin could be harsh with subordinates but once the eruption was over he forgot the incident and tried to make amends with kindnesses or gifts. Gorbachev was a loner. He was a user of people, resented critics, and many of his closest allies seemed to end up disliking him.

The differences between the two men in style and substance were as visible to foreign observers as they were to their Soviet aides. On the first occasion I met Gorbachev, I was struck by his keenness and quick intelligence, which penetrated immediately to the heart of the issue and readily produced an insightful response, almost like a star pupil wanting to impress a professor. The first time I met Yeltsin, I was struck by the power of his physical presence and personality and by the intensity of his desire to meet his interlocutor on open terms. Yeltsin was also intelligent, of course, but his intelligence seemed more focused on finding what was necessary to get the task on the table accomplished. Gorbachev's self-confidence and even arrogance were immediately evident. Yeltsin had plenty of confidence and could easily become domineering, but behind his façade of strength and confidence there was a deep reservoir of anxiety.

Foreign travel had a profound effect on both men, as it did with most Soviets. Gorbachev's trips to Western Europe showed the individual prosperity of the capitalist system, but they also seemed to leave him with the conviction that the Soviet system performed better in social services such as health and education and, in any case, did not shake his belief in the possibility of creating some kind of democratic Marxist-Leninist socialism.

Yeltsin's first visit to the United States, in 1989, was the occasion for a critical turning point in his political evolution, one that came about during a visit to a supermarket in Houston, which he described as a "shattering experience." In his first volume of memoirs, written at the end of 1989, Yeltsin says, "When I saw those shelves crammed with hundreds, thousands of cans, cartons, and goods of every possible sort, for the first time I felt quite frankly sick with despair for the Soviet people. That a potentially super-rich country such as ours has been brought to a state of such poverty. It is terrible to think of it."[17]

Last Chance: Five Hundred Days

While Yeltsin and his team were taking power in Russia, catastrophe loomed over the Soviet economy. Decision-making at the center was increasingly paralyzed while local bosses found they had to cultivate their own power bases if they were to survive. Once local elites had absorbed the lesson that no one above them was in effective control, new possibilities presented themselves. The transfer of economic resources out of state control and into the hands of local managers, more accurately called asset stripping, got under way in this era. Over the longer term, it set the stage for the corrupt "crony capitalism" that sabotaged Yeltsin's economic reforms in the 1990s and the "kleptocracy" of the Putin regime, but in the twilight of the Gorbachev era it contributed to the growing inability of the center to manage the economy.

In a May 24 speech to the Supreme Soviet, Prime Minister Ryzhkov, in what Soviet journalists called "shock without therapy," announced that food prices were to rise 300 percent, with bread tripling by July 1. Salaries were supposed to be increased as compensation, but no one believed it. Ryzhkov's approach of increasing prices administratively before introducing structural reforms to address other accumulated problems in the economy turned out to be a disaster. Within hours, frantic shoppers had cleaned out stores across the country.[18]

As Ryzhkov and the Soviet economy were going down in flames together, radical economists created the most comprehensive program of economic reform developed over the history of the USSR, called the "Five Hundred Days" because its authors had the public relations masterstroke of establishing that period as a timetable for a phased transformation of the Soviet economy into a market system. Over the first three months the government would introduce sweeping institutional changes, including privatization of small enterprises, demonopolization of larger ones, and cuts in the military and KGB budgets. After this period, a gradual deregulation of prices would begin with approximately 80 percent of prices freed in four hundred days. Over the same period, the ruble would become internationally convertible and most large industrial, transportation, and construction enterprises would be privatized. State and collective farms would be broken up into individual plots as a first step toward the creation of private farms. Republics would be responsible for taxation and foreign trade. Functions remaining with the central government, such as defense, foreign affairs, and internal security, would be financed through voluntary contributions from the republics.[19]

The Five Hundred Days plan was as much a political as an economic document. Its strength was the explicit recognition that the Communist system had failed and needed to be replaced completely and that these changes had to be accomplished quickly and comprehensively. Its timing was probably unrealistic and some of its goals misplaced but it amounted to a last-gasp effort by liberal Soviet economists and their political supporters to transform the country into a modern, democratic, and prosperous union.[20]

Gorbachev and Yeltsin agreed to cooperate on economic reform based on the Five Hundred Days, and Gorbachev appointed a commission headed by prominent economist Stanislav Shatalin to craft the new approach. The document Shatalin produced was largely based on the Five Hundred Days. But facing strong opposition from Ryzhkov, Gorbachev sought to merge the Shatalin plan with the Ryzhkov approach. Combining the two was impossible and could only be a recipe for further dithering. In mid-October, when the new document was released, it was clear that Gorbachev had once more back-tracked. The new plan omitted the most important market elements of the Five Hundred Days and retained many administrative features of Ryzhkov's approach.

Gorbachev said that he had to support the Ryzhkov program because it was based on a strong central government and retained "the fundamentals of a socialist system." Gorbachev's economic adviser Nikolai Petrakov said simply that Gorbachev "got frightened." His popularity had dropped to new lows. Gorbachev thought he could not afford to antagonize the factory managers, bureaucrats, generals, and secret police chiefs whom he believed were his real power base and who "constituted his final line of defense against Yeltsin."[21]

Gorbachev had made a fateful choice. Yakovlev said, "When Mikhail Sergeyevich rejected the 500 Days program he was rejecting the last chance for a civilized transition to a new order. It was probably his worst, most dangerous mistake, because what followed was nothing less than war."[22]

Gorbachev Turns Right, Then Back Again

That fall Gorbachev seemed beset on all sides. During the November 7 Revolution Day parade across Red Square, a man fired two shotgun blasts at him. A few days later, Gorbachev held a disastrous meeting with over a thousand military officers who expressed furious anger over his leadership and made it clear they considered him directly responsible for the country's woes.

Facing growing pressure from party and national security conservatives and frustrated by the deepening political and economic problems across the country, Gorbachev convened an emergency meeting aimed at reorganizing the government and strengthening the office of the president. Gorbachev's reformist advisers were either not invited or kept their heads down. Hard-liners, such as Moscow party secretary Prokofiev, urged the introduction of "special measures of a police character" to ensure the supply of food to the capital, and the head of the Russian Communist party Ivan Polozkov said the answer was "to restore order by military means." At the end of the long session it was decided to "strengthen the presidential vertical . . . and be prepared for extreme measures in the country."[23]

The Presidential Council, which despite its rather ineffectual character had included respected academic and cultural figures, was replaced with a new Security Council, heavily weighted toward the "organs of force." Liberal advisers, such as Yakovlev, Medvedev, and Shatalin, were not included. On December 1 Gorbachev replaced the moderate Minister of Internal Affairs, Vadim Bakatin, with the hard-line Boris Pugo. At about this time Ryzhkov suffered a heart attack, and Gorbachev replaced him with Valentin Pavlov, the ineffectual minister of finance. For the new position of vice president, Gorbachev chose Gennadiy Yanayev, a nonentity whose only possible qualification was that he would not get in Gorbachev's way. As head of broadcast media, Gorbachev installed propaganda hack Leonid Kravchenko, who proclaimed that "state television does not have the right to engage in criticism of the country's leadership" and put deed to words by closing down or muzzling hard-hitting programs that had taken advantage of glasnost to begin reporting real news independently and accurately.[24]

On December 20, in an emotional speech that was unexpected to everyone, including Gorbachev, Shevardnadze announced his resignation and warned that the USSR was on the brink of dictatorship. His face red with emotion, Shevardnadze announced, "I cannot reconcile myself with what is happening in my country. . . . A dictatorship is approaching." Shevardnadze uttered no explicit criticism of Gorbachev, but an obviously distressed Gorbachev took to the podium and accused his longtime colleague of an "unforgivable" action.[25]

Bloodshed in the Baltics

Gorbachev was torn about how far to go in responding to the Baltic challenge. Hard-line advisers warned him that Baltic departure would cause the USSR to unravel and he had publicly drawn a line in the sand by warning that measures would be taken to block secession. The use of force was repugnant to Gorbachev by nature and tactically he was reluctant to be seen to authorize it. But the alarming public vehemence toward his policies from the traditional props of Soviet society, the party, military, and security forces, led Gorbachev to fear that if he failed to move he might well be overthrown like Khrushchev.

Sometime over the New Year, Gorbachev decided on the use of force. January 7, 1991, saw the first act in a familiar scenario. In Lithuania an anonymous National Salvation Committee appealed to Gorbachev to "restore Soviet power" in the republic. That same day the Ministry of Defense announced it was sending paratroops to Lithuania. Three days later, Gorbachev demanded that the Lithuanian leadership act "immediately to restore the USSR and Lithuanian SSR constitutions in their entirety and to rescind the unconstitutional acts adopted previously." That evening Yazov, Pugo, and KGB chief Kryuchkov were ordered by Gorbachev "to use force and to dispatch to Vilnius the KGB special forces team Alpha."[26]

On the night of January 12, a "workers militia," supported by Alpha, moved to occupy the Vilnius television center. After warning shots were ignored, Soviet attackers fired directly into the crowd surrounding the building. At least fourteen were killed and several hundred injured. By next morning, thousands had gathered around the republic's parliament, while inside several hundred volunteers, armed with hunting rifles, Molotov cocktails, and fire hoses, were busily transforming the building into a sand-bagged bunker. Lithuanian president Landsbergis tried to phone Gorbachev, who was said to be unavailable, while outside defenders displayed slogans such as "Gorbie, hell is waiting for you."[27]

Matlock and other Western ambassadors were summoned to the Foreign Ministry, where Deputy Foreign Minister Kovalev passed on a personal message from Gorbachev to Western leaders. Kovalev said the Soviet president wished to assure his foreign colleagues that "he had not been responsible for the attack on the television tower. He did not himself know who had given the order." Gorbachev "was still determined to continue the reform course he had set and to avoid bloodshed." As they were leaving, the ambassadors asked themselves which of the two possible scenarios was worse, that Gorbachev was lying and he had in fact authorized the use of force or he was telling the truth and had lost control of his own forces.[28]

On January 23, with pressure mounting in Congress, Bush sent Gorbachev a letter outlining the steps the United States would be required to take if force continued to be used in the Baltics, including freezing the US-Soviet trade deal and blocking Soviet membership in international financial organizations. On January 20, the European parliament halted a one-billion-dollar aid package to the USSR.

When Ambassador Matlock met Gorbachev to deliver Bush's letter, the Soviet leader asked for understanding that the USSR was "on the brink of civil war" and said the world should expect to see "a period of zigs and zags." Gorbachev reassured "my friend George" that despite the pressure he was under he would continue to act as he had promised in the international arena and at home would not abandon the goals he had set for himself.[29]

Battle for Moscow

Two hours after Yeltsin heard about the violence in Vilnius, he was on a plane to the region. It was a move that embodied the best of Boris Yeltsin—courageous, decisive, and demonstrating a clear view of the main chance amid fast-moving events. In the Estonian capital of Tallinn, he met the three Baltic presidents in the parliament building, surrounded by defenders armed with knives and hunting rifles. They issued a joint statement condemning the bloodshed in Vilnius, pledged to aid each other against threats to their sovereignty, and called upon international actors to take steps against the violence. Returning home, Yeltsin issued a powerful "Appeal to the Peoples of Russia" to act "to stop the slide of the Union leadership toward lawlessness and violence."[30] When I arrived in Moscow at the tag end of the August coup, during which the Baltics finally gained their independence, representatives of the three republics told me they were convinced that Yeltsin's courageous actions had prevented a full-fledged military crackdown, which could have been followed by similar moves elsewhere in the Soviet Union had it succeeded.

Over the next month, a massive outpouring of support for Yeltsin swept across Russia. In two weeks, over three million people signed a petition backing the Russian president. On February 24, over 200,000 people took to the streets of Moscow on behalf of Yeltsin and two weeks later over 300,000 demonstrated in support of him and striking coal miners, who were demanding that Gorbachev resign and be replaced by Yeltsin.[31]

Yeltsin owned the streets, but with a meeting of the Russian Congress scheduled for the end of March, Gorbachev told the Central Committee, "Things are moving toward a climax. . . . We have to seek a decision in Moscow." The apparat prepared a secret "Action Plan 28," an allusion to the March 28 opening date of the Congress, which set out specific steps to be taken by communist delegates to oust Yeltsin. Some were to speak, others were to "defend" the microphone against opponents seeking to speak on Yeltsin's behalf, and others to block Yeltsin's deputy Khasbulatov from presiding.[32]

The day the Congress opened, fifty thousand troops and riot police in full combat gear appeared in the streets of Moscow and Communist deputies called for Yeltsin to step down. But Gorbachev's heavy-handed threats backfired. The Congress demanded that troops leave Moscow and over 100,000 people, ignoring the ban on demonstrations, marched in support of Yeltsin.[33]

Facing the possibility of bloodshed, Gorbachev pulled back. The next day, troops disappeared from Moscow. Although not immediately evident, the move marked Gorbachev's shift away from the hard-line advisers who had been pushing him toward introduction of a state of emergency since 1990. And it, in turn, set off a growing belief among these advisers that they would have to take action with or without Gorbachev.

Buoyed by the withdrawal of troops, Yeltsin took the offensive in an opening speech in which he reaffirmed his opposition to virtually the entire legacy of Communist rule in the USSR. After three days of impassioned speeches, Afghan war hero Aleksandr Rutskoy led his improbably named faction, Communists for Democracy, over to Yeltsin's side and on the last day of the session Yeltsin's request for additional powers and his proposal to hold direct elections for a Russian president passed by a substantial majority.

It is difficult to come up with rational explanations for the lengths Gorbachev went in his battle with Yeltsin during this period. There were, of course, real differences between the two leaders and by the winter of 1991 the personal relationship between them had degenerated to visceral hatred. But Gorbachev must have understood that if he ousted Yeltsin the hard-liners who had become his allies would likely move next against Gorbachev's own reform program.

Observers described Gorbachev at this time as physically exhausted, isolated, and unwilling to face unpleasant realities. British ambassador Braithwaite, who saw Gorbachev in March, viewed him as "living almost entirely in cloud-cuckoo-land." Gorbachev had become profoundly weary of dealing with the unpleasant flood of domestic events and preferred to focus on his relationships with fellow global leaders. When Ambassador Matlock met

Gorbachev toward the end of January to deliver Bush's message on the Baltics, he was struck by the contrast between Gorbachev's irritable and unconvincing public demeanor and his behavior in this private meeting, where the Soviet leader seemed "collected and even judicious."[34]

In March Gorbachev did what he should have done long before, seek the opinion of the people of the country through a referendum on the future of the USSR as a united country. Approximately 76 percent voted in favor of the union. But Gorbachev had waited too long. Only four republics held the referendum exactly as Gorbachev intended. Six republics boycotted and five added qualifiers to Gorbachev's question or crafted additional questions of their own. In Russia 71 percent voted in favor of the union but approximately the same number also supported a proposal to create a popularly elected Russian president, which Yeltsin had added to the ballot with the obvious intention of running himself.[35]

A President for Russia

Yeltsin faced five opponents in the short Russian presidential election campaign. Former prime minister Ryzhkov had name recognition but was identified with the economic policies that had brought the country to the brink of ruin. Vadim Bakatin was rumored to be Gorbachev's favorite but he proved to be a lackluster campaigner. Other candidates included the reactionary general Albert Makashov, who promised if he were elected to publicly flog democrats and "cosmopolitans" in Red Square; and Aman Tuleyev, a leader in the miners' strikes, who took a strong stand against showing Western horror movies in Russia. The final candidate, Vladimir Zhirinovskiy, was a rising national fascist, generally regarded by those who met him, including myself, to be mentally unbalanced. After the collapse of the USSR, a former Central Committee official told me that he had organized the funding of Zhirinovskiy's campaign under instructions from Gorbachev.[36]

On June 12, 1991, Yeltsin became the first, and perhaps by some measures, the only democratically elected leader in Russian history. With 75 percent of the electorate participating, Yeltsin received 57 percent of the votes cast. The biggest surprise was the relatively strong showing of the two most eccentric candidates—Zhirinovskiy and Tuleyev, who received 8 and 7 percent respectively.

Nine Plus One Equals Zero

On April 23, after a marathon nine-hour session, Gorbachev and the leaders of the nine republics still willing to consider remaining within the union announced their intention "to conclude a new treaty of sovereign governments, taking account of the results of the referendum." The essence of the deal was clear: Gorbachev would agree to a decentralized structure in which virtually all internal powers were devolved to the republics, provided some external functions were left to the union and he was allowed to remain as its head.

On July 29, the three drivers of the process, Gorbachev, Yeltsin, and Kazakh leader Nursultan Nazarbayev, met privately to allocate the new government positions that would be created after the union treaty was signed on August 20. President of the new Union of Sovereign States would be Gorbachev. Nazarbayev, at Yeltsin's suggestion, agreed to take the post of prime minister. Most members of the current Soviet government would be unceremoniously fired, including "power ministers" Yazov, Kryuchkov, and Pugo. In the midst of the conversation, Yeltsin got up and strode to the balcony. "They are listening to us," he warned while the others laughed nervously.[37]

Yeltsin was right. The KGB was listening and information about what awaited the security service chiefs reached Kryuchkov almost immediately. He and his fellows had no intention of departing quietly.

G-7 Summit in London

In the summer of 1991, as Gorbachev shifted back toward the center, he made his most serious effort to attract Western economic assistance. The Soviet leader decided that if he could wangle an invitation to attend the G-7 summit scheduled for London in July 1991 his personal powers of persuasion might produce a favorable outcome. But despite the gratitude and in some cases even affection that Western leaders felt for Gorbachev, they looked at his position with considerable skepticism. The determination of republican leaders to take control over their own economies raised serious questions about Gorbachev's ability to conduct any effective economic policy, let alone sweeping reform. And Gorbachev's past economic record did not exactly inspire confidence. Reform had gone nowhere since the Five Hundred Days fiasco and by the spring of 1991 the Soviet economy was on the edge of collapse.

Nevertheless, Gorbachev made a serious effort to present a credible case for Western aid. He put Medvedev in charge of a planning group that included Five Hundred Days author Yavlinskiy, who told Matlock that he was convinced "Gorbachev was now finally committed to more radical reform measures." Gorbachev's Nobel Peace Prize acceptance speech on June 5, perhaps the finest oration he ever delivered, contributed to a groundswell of sympathy in the West for the embattled Soviet leader. Gorbachev admitted that in the beginning he had underestimated the problems facing the USSR but he presented a rosy picture of the country at that moment, claiming, "There is already a consensus in our society that we have to move towards a mixed market economy." He made a carefully couched appeal to world public opinion: "We are now approaching what might be the crucial point . . . the world needs perestroika no less than the Soviet Union needs it." Gorbachev did not put a price tag on the amount of aid he hoped to solicit but he called for "a joint program of action to be implemented over a number of years," which would include Soviet membership in the International Monetary Fund (IMF) and the World Bank.[38]

On the eve of the London meeting, Gorbachev sent G-7 leaders a long letter outlining plans for introducing a modern "mixed economy," including privatization, price liberalization, and a convertible ruble. He promised that the adoption of the union treaty would be followed within six months by a new constitution based on democratic elections. The letter also admitted that the USSR could not get out of its current difficulties without some form of external debt relief.[39]

Gorbachev's efforts were bolstered by a group of influential American scholars and retired government officials, led by Harvard professor Graham Allison, who called for a "Grand Bargain" of Western aid to the USSR to the tune of $30 billion in return for serious Soviet internal and external reforms. Yavlinskiy, whom the Western media had turned into the poster child of radical economic reform, joined forces with the Grand Bargain team to help create a global boom in favor of something like a Marshall Plan for the USSR.

Gorbachev also continued his efforts to hit up individual world leaders for aid. In March he asked the United States for $1.5 billion in agricultural credits. President Bush replied that he wanted to help but that Soviet actions in the Baltics made such assistance difficult. Behind the scenes, Bush remained skeptical. He later wrote, "I had seen no evidence that even basic economic changes were being implemented."[40]

In London, British prime minister Major opened the G-7 meeting by telling the Soviet leader: "You are among well-wishers." But he added bluntly that the assembled leaders expected explanations on a number of points including privatization, monetary policy, the budget deficit, price reform, and relationships between the center and the republics. Bush gave what a disappointed Gorbachev called a dry and businesslike statement. European leaders lectured Gorbachev on the mechanics of market reform while the Japanese continued to link assistance to the return of the four tiny northern islands the USSR had seized at the end of the Second World War.

The explanations Gorbachev provided did not impress his audience. At a late-night supper, Major found Gorbachev to be distinctly lacking in understanding modern market economies. He was well schooled in "dark satanic mills" but he was unable to grasp "even the basic essentials of the free market" which he professed to be seeking for the USSR. In the end, the G-7 agreed on a six-point program that included vague promises of a Soviet relationship with international financial institutions; technical assistance; pious calls for an expansion of East-West trade; and promises of visits to Moscow by a stream of Western economic officials, but no real financial assistance.[41]

The Last US-Soviet Summit

By the summer of 1991, the Bush administration had settled into what might be called a policy of benign toleration with respect to Gorbachev. Bush and Baker remained personally fond of the Soviet leader and wanted to encourage continued close relations with him, a policy shown by their decision to appoint fellow Texan Robert Strauss, a close personal friend of both the president and the secretary of state, despite his also being a former national chairman of the Democratic Party, to take Matlock's place as US ambassador in Moscow.

Some members of the Bush administration saw an opportunity in Gorbachev's problems. Gates said frankly that he and Secretary of Defense Cheney "wanted to see the Soviet Union broken up, thereby significantly reducing the chance it could ever threaten our security again." But for now these views were too much for the cautious Bush administration and in the summer of 1991 US policy remained as Scowcroft articulated it in a briefing for the president on May 31: "Our goal is to keep Gorbachev in power for as long as possible, while doing what we can to help him head in the right direction—and doing what is best for us in foreign policy."[42]

On July 29, President Bush arrived in Moscow for what turned out to be the last summit meeting between the leaders of the United States and the Soviet Union. Its centerpiece was the signing of the START I strategic arms-control agreement, nine long years after the two delegations first sat down together in Geneva. The treaty marked the first time the two nuclear powers had actually agreed to reduce strategic nuclear weapons and that by an amount that would have earlier seemed impossible. But in an era when most of the old Cold War flashpoints had vanished, the US-Soviet nuclear relationship no longer seemed so threatening. The mind-numbing complexity of the agreement also helped foster reserve. The document ran to over seven hundred pages and included provisions regulating the behavior of the two sides with the detailed intricacy of a puppet master gone mad.

For all its length and complexity, the treaty that the two leaders finally signed bore a striking resemblance to the basic principles the US delegation had enunciated in our first negotiating round in Geneva in the summer of 1982.

It reduced missiles and bombers to 1,600, 29 percent below the US 1990 level and 36 percent below the Soviet. For the first time, it limited the number of warheads on missiles to a maximum of 6,000 on each side, a reduction of over 40 percent in the levels of the two countries. And it led to a 46 percent cut in the throw weight of Soviet ballistic missiles, that critical component of the destructive potential of strategic ballistic missiles over which so much bureaucratic blood had been spilled in negotiations within Washington and between the two sides. The treaty contained numerous provisions sought by the United States across decades of arms-control negotiations, including a reduction by one-half in the number of SS-18 heavy ICBMs, a ban on encryption of ballistic-missile flight-test data, and twelve different types of on-site inspections.

Bush described Gorbachev as being in "marvelous" form for the summit. But there was little of substance to discuss. Most contentious Cold War issues between the two countries had vanished. In May the Supreme Soviet had finally passed a relatively liberal law on emigration, removing a roadblock in the US-Soviet relationship that dated back to the first Nixon-Brezhnev summit in 1972. Bush held separate meetings with Nazarbayev and Yeltsin, who agreed with the American president that the Baltics should be independent but added emphatically that "Ukraine must not leave the USSR."[43]

Bush's visit to Kiev attracted the most attention, although not the kind that the US president welcomed. Only a few days before the summit, Gorbachev asked Bush to cancel his already planned visit to the Ukrainian capital and spend the day with him in Stavropol instead. The White House pointed out that Gorbachev would simply be causing problems for himself if it became known that he had blocked the president from visiting the USSR's second-most populous republic. The incident reinforced Bush's already strong conviction that he should not do anything that might embarrass Gorbachev and led him to tell his speechwriters that they should use the address he was scheduled to deliver before the Ukrainian parliament to "help Gorbachev."[44]

Bush arrived in a deeply divided Kiev. The republic's opportunistic Communist leadership was cautiously embracing aspects of the Ukrainian national agenda, chiefly as a way of retaining power, while a vocal Ukrainian nationalist faction was determined to push for independence. Bush endorsed Ukraine's striving for "liberty, self-rule, and free enterprise" and also made several positive references to Gorbachev, whose policies the US president described as "pointing toward the goals of freedom, democracy, and economic liberty." But it was Bush's warning that "freedom is not the same as independence" that attracted the most attention. His remark that "Americans will not support those who seek independence in order to replace a far-off tyranny with a local despotism" proved prophetic about developments in many of the soon-to-be independent Soviet republics, if not on US policy, which in the years after the Soviet collapse tended toward bolstering the independence of the post-Soviet states despite the absence of anything approaching real democracy in much of the region.[45]

At the end of the president's speech, Ukrainian legislators gave him a prolonged standing ovation. But when columnist William Safire, relying on sources in the Ukrainian-American community who reported unhappiness with portions of Bush's remarks, called the speech "Chicken Kiev," the label stuck.

Vladimir Medvedev, the chief of Gorbachev's security detachment, knew that something unusual was destined to disturb the tranquility at Foros, the luxurious Black Sea villa where Gorbachev and his family were vacationing, when his boss, General Yury Plekhanov, chief of the KGB's Ninth Directorate, which provided security for all senior Soviet officials, appeared without any warning and told him that a high-level delegation had arrived unannounced from Moscow. Medvedev found Gorbachev and explained who was coming: Oleg Baklanov of the Military-Industrial Commission; Viktor Shenin, the Central Committee secretary in charge of ideology; General Valentin Varennikov, commander of the Ground Forces of the Soviet Army; and Valery Boldin, Gorbachev's longtime aide.

Surprised, Gorbachev told Medvedev to have the visitors wait and disappeared into the family's private living quarters. When he heard Gorbachev's reaction Plekhanov brushed past Medvedev and led the delegation to Gorbachev's office, an unpardonable breach of Kremlin protocol. Gorbachev was still nowhere to be found and when Medvedev picked up the direct phone to the general secretary, Plekhanov curtly told him, "Don't bother! The phone doesn't work." Suddenly, Medvedev understood—it was the "Khrushchev variant."[1]

As the head of Gorbachev's personal security detachment, Medvedev commanded thirty highly trained, well-armed guards who were personally loyal to the general secretary. Medvedev knew that if Gorbachev gave the order, his men would arrest the visiting delegation despite their impressive ranks. So when the meeting broke up after about two hours, Medvedev was relieved to see Gorbachev shaking hands with his visitors as they departed. For Medvedev, however, the show was over. As the delegation got into its cars, Plekhanov told him curtly, "You have three minutes to pack your things and then onto the plane and back with us to Moscow."[2]

What Happened at Foros?

According to Gorbachev, he refused to work with the plotters from the beginning. Retorting that "you will never live that long," he dismissed their demand to temporarily relinquish his powers. Gorbachev told his uninvited visitors that he would be willing to meet with a delegation from the Supreme Soviet to discuss the situation in the country. And on that basis, he said, "Let us have an emergency situation if you want" but only one that had the objective of "increasing our reforms and further cooperation with the West." Gorbachev described the meeting as a "conversation of deaf mutes" and claimed that after he had "categorically refused to have any dealings with you," the delegation departed.[3]

According to accounts provided by the coup plotters, when Gorbachev entered the room his first question was, "Is this an arrest?" On hearing that it was not, Gorbachev visibly relaxed and asked angrily why the phones had been disconnected. Baklanov took the lead in describing the catastrophic state of the country and suggested that Gorbachev step down temporarily in favor of Vice President Yanayev to allow the introduction of a state of emergency. "We will do the dirty work for you," Baklanov said at one point. When Gorbachev asked whether the state of emergency would apply to the Russian leadership, Baklanov said that Yeltsin would be arrested, news that Gorbachev appeared to take with equanimity.[4]

As the conversation dragged on, Varennikov, more used to giving commands than being lectured to, interrupted with a long harangue on the state of the country, declaiming that no one respected the actions of the president. To resolve these problems, the delegation was proposing to "shake up everything and put everyone in his proper place." At the end of the meeting, according to Boldin, Gorbachev unexpectedly changed his tone, adopting a calm and businesslike manner. He gave matter-of-fact advice on how to resolve the issues raised and explained the reasons for his policies. "Think it over and tell your comrades," Boldin records Gorbachev's concluding. According to Varennikov, Gorbachev ended by saying, "Go to hell, do what you want. But report my opinion."[5]

Backdrop to the Coup

Discussions about introducing a state of emergency had been occurring in Moscow for some time. According to Pikhoya, who had access to its records, the Security Council repeatedly discussed the matter and "Gorbachev himself often spoke about the necessity of a state of emergency."[6] KGB head

Kryuchkov said that before Gorbachev left Moscow for Foros on August 4 he instructed his security chiefs to prepare a study of the situation and draw up a list of measures that could be undertaken if it became necessary to introduce a state of emergency. A team led by Pavel Grachev, commander of Soviet airborne forces, concluded that if the Union Treaty were signed, "it would be the end of the USSR."

After the text of the Union Treaty was published by the Soviet media on August 14, Kryuchkov told his associates that Gorbachev had a psychological disorder and was incapable of dealing with the situation: "We are going to introduce a state of emergency." Two days later, Grachev's team presented Kryuchkov a list of political, economic, and military measures to strengthen state security and social order. While all this was going on, Kryuchkov was in daily contact with Gorbachev in Foros.[7]

Late in the evening of August 18, what the coup plotters called "The State Committee for a State of Emergency" held its first meeting in the Kremlin. News that Gorbachev had refused to sign the document relinquishing power brought home that participants had marched over the edge of an abyss. Without Gorbachev's agreement to step down or a Supreme Soviet decision to introduce a state of emergency, they were acting outside the law. Immediately, some began to get cold feet. Only after heavy pressure did Vice President Yanayev sign the document declaring he was assuming the duties of the president. The chairman of the USSR Supreme Soviet, Anatoliy Lukyanov, insisted that his name be removed from the list of members of the committee, arguing that as head of the country's highest legislative body he could not be seen as part of something so obviously illegal.[8]

The Coup Begins

Early in the morning, Minister of Defense Yazov ordered elements of two elite divisions stationed on the outskirts of Moscow to begin moving into the capital: 2,107 men, 127 tanks, and 144 armored personnel carriers from the Tamanskaya motorized rifle division and a detachment from the Kantemirovskaya tank division consisting of 1,702 men, 235 tanks, and 125 infantry fighting vehicles. The Tula-based 106th Guards parachute division was ordered to move to an air field near Moscow. The Ministry of Internal Affairs (MVD) deployed its special forces division, the Dzerzhinskaya, and the dreaded OMON antiriot police.[9]

At 6 AM, troops surrounded the headquarters of state broadcast media, which switched to transmitting only classical music interspersed with grim-faced announcers reading the decrees issued by the committee. When people across the USSR turned on their TV or radio that morning, they heard that Yanayev had taken over as acting chief of state in connection with Gorbachev's "inability for health reasons to carry out the responsibilities of president."

Later that morning, the committee released an "Appeal to the Soviet People," which proclaimed that Gorbachev's reforms had reached a "dead end." The Committee promised to "restore law and order, end bloodshed, and declare merciless war against the criminal world." It also included the obligation for citizens to follow "without deviation" all orders of the committee; the suspension of political parties and movements that "interfere with the normalization of the situation"; the prohibition of public demonstrations, control over the mass media, and a curfew.[10]

Yeltsin Escapes the Net

The committee initially planned to divert Yeltsin's plane on a return flight from Alma-Ata, where he was meeting with Nazarbayev, and intern him at Brezhnev's favorite hunting dacha at Zavidovo. After this option was abandoned because of the delay in the return of the delegation that met Gorbachev in Foros, it was decided to detain Yeltsin at his dacha the morning of August 19. Pavlov was supposed to meet Yeltsin there and persuade him to cooperate with the coup, a challenging task for anyone but almost certainly beyond the powers of the lackluster prime minister. In the early morning hours, a heavily armed Alpha detachment was deployed in the woods around Yeltsin's dacha. Pavlov never showed up and heavily armed Alpha troopers lurked for several hours behind trees until the Russian president, accompanied by his own security guards, left for Moscow.[11]

Yeltsin first learned about the coup when his daughter woke him crying, "Papa, get up. There's a coup!" Yeltsin and his wife Naina called his close associates and instructed them to gather at the dacha. Ruslan Khasbulatov, speaker of the Russian parliament, was among the first to arrive. The man who two years later was to become Yeltsin's chief opponent copied down by hand on the kitchen table an appeal to the citizens of Russia as it was dictated by Yeltsin and his excited associates milling around the room. Yeltsin's daughters typed the final text and it was immediately distributed via phone, fax, and through the nearest local post office.[12]

Yeltsin's appeal boldly proclaimed, "all decisions and instructions of this committee to be unlawful." It demanded that Gorbachev be given the opportunity to speak to the people of the USSR and called upon servicemen "not to take part in the reactionary coup."[13] Within hours Yeltsin's appeal was spreading through Moscow, posted on walls and metro stations, hung on lampposts, and transmitted to Soviet and foreign media.

Despite the power of Yeltsin's presence in the White House, visible support for resistance to the coup was slow in developing. Mid-morning on the first day of the coup, Roman Wasilewski, a Russian-speaking member of Embassy Moscow's economic section, walked over to the White House to observe Yeltsin's first address to the Russian parliament. After a long wait, Yeltsin appeared and called on the delegates to resist the coup until the end. Wasilewski thought that Yeltsin spoke in a "measured tone," seeming slightly uncertain at this early stage in the drama. The mood in the White House was "charged but subdued." There were few people in the corridors and outside the "living ring" of defenders had yet to materialize.[14]

Around midday on the 19th, several tanks approached the White House. Watching from his office, Yeltsin instinctively knew what he should do. "I had to be out there right away, standing with those people." With his security guards nervously accompanying him, Yeltsin marched out of the White House and approached the lead tank. He asked the commander, "Did you come to kill the President of Russia?" "Of course not," was the reply of the distraught young officer. With that, Yeltsin climbed on board and read in a loud voice his "Appeal to the People of Russia."[15]

Relatively few people were in the area at the time of the incident but CNN broadcast the event around the world live and foreign radios transmitted the news back into the USSR. The gesture immediately turned Yeltsin into the symbolic leader of all forces opposing the coup. Former foreign minister Shevardnadze, who wrote years later that he was in the crowd at the time, immediately recalled a picture that formed part of every Soviet citizen's stock of Lenin lore, when the Bolshevik leader had climbed onto an armored vehicle outside Petrograd's Finland Station after his arrival in revolutionary Russia. Lenin had issued a ringing appeal for a revolutionary offensive and Shevardnadze saw Yeltsin's dramatic move as, similarly, the transformational moment in the August coup.[16]

Divisions within the Military

The display of armed might in the streets of Moscow masked deep divisions within the Soviet military. The senior leaders who brought the armed forces into the coup had been young officers during the Great Patriotic War. From their perspective, perestroika at home had meant the overturn of the old-time Communist verities that they had imbibed since youth and, even worse, the collapse of Soviet power and prestige abroad.

But underneath these aging leaders were rising younger officers born after the war. Many had served in Afghanistan, an experience that had not filled them with enthusiasm for a system that had sent them ill-prepared into a pointless war. They were not necessarily fans of Gorbachev and perestroika but they lacked the reflexive belief of their more senior colleagues in old-style Soviet socialism.

Yeltsin had made a deliberate effort to reach out to younger commanders. Earlier in the year, he met Grachev during a visit to the paratroop division in Tula and one of the first calls Yeltsin made the morning of the coup was to him. Grachev promised to send Yeltsin a reconnaissance unit to act as a security detachment and when Yeltsin put down the phone he told his wife, "Grachev's on our side."[17] Grachev ordered General Aleksandr Lebed, commander of a paratroop division, to the White House, where he described for Yeltsin the doubts among many in the military about the coup but also made it clear that most officers felt bound by their oath of loyalty and would probably obey orders to attack the White House if it came to that.[18]

General Boris Gromov, the last commander of Soviet forces in Afghanistan and at the time of the coup serving as Deputy Minister of Internal Affairs, tried to convince Pugo not to participate. When Pugo replied that "orders must be obeyed," Gromov used "Afghan veteran" channels to get word to the White House that an attack was being planned. Gromov also contacted the commander of the MVD's elite Derzhinskiy division and told him not to enter the center of Moscow. If Pugo, nevertheless, ordered the division into the city, Gromov told them to come without ammunition.[19]

Yevgeniy Shaposhnikov, the commander of the Soviet Air Force, first learned that something was up when his duty officer called him at home at 4 AM on August 19 to say he was to attend a meeting of the collegium of the Ministry of Defense in two hours. At the meeting, Yazov informed his top commanders that a state of emergency had been declared because Gorbachev was no longer capable of leading the country. Troops were to be introduced into Moscow as a precaution. After this announcement, Yazov abruptly left the room.

By the end of the day, Shaposhnikov was convinced that the coup was not only wrong but hopeless. He contacted the White House to pass the message that the Soviet Air Force would never "go against the people." The following evening, learning about the plans for an attack on the White House, Shaposhnikov again called the White House and said that in case of an assault he would order Soviet military aircraft to fly low-level intimidation runs against the attackers.[20]

KGB chief Kryuchkov was the driving force behind the coup, but at lower levels of the spy agency there was considerable skepticism. According to

Yevgenia Albats, a courageous Russian journalist who was one of the first to write honestly about the KGB, the second echelon of the KGB leadership, "colonels and heads of departments," did not participate in the coup. Oleg Kalugin, a former senior KGB officer in Washington who had broken publicly with the KGB, reported that many of the KGB and party officials who lived in his building opposed the coup. According to an American journalist, KGB officers made available to the White House a special communications network that allowed Yeltsin's statements to go directly to six hundred key addresses across the country. Others prepared printing facilities, provided access to weapons caches, and offered to hide secret Russian governmental documents. Former KGB officers in private business reportedly delivered one million rubles in cash to the White House.[21]

The Firm Hand Wobbles

On the first day of the coup the committee took control of the streets, government offices, and traditional broadcast and print media. It was what Lenin would have done if he had been running the coup. But the conservative, middle-aged men on the committee ignored the changes in communications that had developed since the days of the Bolshevik revolutionary fathers. For some reason, they neglected to take charge of the phone system and they completely ignored the copiers, fax machines, and rudimentary computers that coup opponents used to distribute material throughout the country and into the world beyond. The committee also failed to understand that glasnost had fundamentally changed the mindset of Soviet journalists.

Sergei Medvedev, a young anchor on the main Soviet evening news program, "Vremya," was sent packing the first morning of the coup out of suspicion that he was too liberal. Medvedev took advantage of his free time to roam Moscow with a cameraman. At the end of the day, he returned with his footage to the studio and prepared a segment to be shown on that evening's "Vremya." To his surprise, the central TV leadership accepted it. That evening tens of millions across the USSR tuned in to find out what was going on. In the first half of the program, they got what might be expected, official statements of the committee and a carefully packaged commentary.

Then, as if a switch had been thrown and another planet heard from, Medvedev's material began to run. Viewers saw long lines of tanks with bewildered soldiers being berated by anxious crowds. Most astonishingly, they saw Yeltsin climbing onto the tank and calling for resistance to the "illegal" coup. With Yeltsin's voice in the background and his towering figure filling the screen, Medvedev carefully summarized the main points of Yeltsin's "Appeal to the Russian

People." For millions it was the first sign that there was an opposition to the coup and for many in Moscow it was seen as, in effect, an appeal to join Yeltsin at the White House.[22]

The most damaging wound suffered by the committee was self-inflicted, the disastrous performance of its members during a nationally televised press conference the evening of August 19. When Yanayev described the committee's actions, his trembling hands and evident confusion left many viewers with the impression that he was drunk. Foreign and Soviet journalists peppered the committee members with questions about Gorbachev's health, what new policies they intended to introduce, when suspended publications would be allowed to reappear, and whether the troops in the streets of Moscow were prepared to shoot civilians. The evasive answers they received and the uncertain manner in which the replies were delivered left the impression that the committee actually had little idea what to do with the power they professed to be seizing.

The disdain evoked by the performance of the bumbling buffoons on the podium was crystalized in a question posed by Tatyana Malkina, a twenty-four-year-old reporter from the USSR's first independent newspaper, *Nezavisimaya Gazeta*, who asked whether the committee understood that they had "carried out a coup d'etat" and "which comparison seems most apt to you—the comparison with 1917 or 1964?"[23] By the time the press conference was over, the committee had lost the respect of the country. All that was left was fear, and that would vanish the next evening.

By the end of the first day, even coup supporters were having their doubts. From Kiev, where he had been sent to bludgeon the Ukrainian leadership, Varennikov demanded that the committee take stronger action, including immediate measures to "liquidate" the group of the "adventurist Yeltsin."[24] Lukyanov said it would be impossible to gain the required two-thirds vote in the USSR Supreme Soviet to give legal cover to the actions of the committee. KGB analysts sent the committee a "merciless report," which highlighted eleven serious mistakes, including failure to establish a real emergency situation in Moscow, failure to seize leading opposition figures, failure to block communications among groups opposed to the coup, and failure to take control of antigovernment media.[25]

Assault on the White House Fizzles

By the second day, it was clear that to succeed the coup would have to crush Yeltsin. Military and police officials put together a plan that was brutally straightforward and virtually certain to succeed in purely military terms against the improvised defenses around the White House. With helicopters providing support from above, paratroopers and a special police detachment were to block approaches to the White House from the side of the US embassy. OMON would drive a hole through the defenses and secure the entrance to the White House. Once this was accomplished, Alpha would penetrate inside the building and together with a special KGB unit move directly to the Russian leadership who were to be arrested or killed, more likely the latter, judging by Alpha's behavior in seizing the presidential palace in Kabul in 1979. As Gromov left the session that planned the operation, he recalled the majority exiting in an "aggressive" mood, "almost euphoric."[26]

Around the White House, meanwhile, Yeltsin's position was growing stronger. At noon a huge meeting began that lasted for almost five hours. On the podium, together with Yeltsin and the Russian leadership, were many representatives of Gorbachev's perestroika team, including Shevardnadze and Yakovlev, who earlier had been photographed, pistol in hand, among the armed defenders of the White House. It was a combination of protest rally, intellectual happening, and celebration of Russia reborn. Some of the country's top rock bands gave impromptu concerts, knowing well that if the coup prevailed they would be giving few in the future. Yevgeniy Yevtushenko read a new poem and a comedian gave a devastating impersonation of Yanayev and his shaking hands. Mstislav Rostropovich turned up, was briefly given an AK-47 to be photographed defending the White House, and raised everyone's spirits, including Yeltsin's, with his infectious enthusiasm.[27]

Tens of thousands of people filled the square and the streets surrounding the White House and after the rally was over many stayed to join the living ring of defenders. Barricades surrounding the building were strengthened with construction materials and whatever else came to hand, including vehicles belonging to employees of the US embassy that were parked in the small street between the White House and the embassy. Defenders of the White House politely said they needed to borrow the vehicles, organized crews to move them the short distance to the barricades and, after it was all over, returned the vehicles in the same fashion, mostly without damage. The mood was resolute and almost euphoric. People understood the dangers but participants also felt uplifted about being part of a larger cause aimed at saving democratic change in the country. Many also noted how polite and good-natured the crowd was, not usually considered typical characteristics of Muscovites gathered in large numbers.

As the White House prepared its defenses, the attack plan began to collapse. The Alpha team demanded that their commander show them a written order. When he replied that the order had been oral, Alpha voted not to participate. Despite Alpha's defection, as the evening of August 20 stretched out, troops were on the move around the White House. Tensions rose among the defenders, who could hear the sound of diesel motors and an occasional gunshot. Searchlights played across the sky and loudspeakers in the White House broadcast alarming and often contradictory messages. Hearing armored vehicles moving in the streets, Shevardnadze and two close aides went on foot to join the ring.[28]

Around midnight a column of armored vehicles moving along the Ring Road near the US embassy found its exit from an underpass blocked by a barricade of parked trolleybuses. As the armored vehicles tried to break through, an angry crowd swarmed toward them. An Afghan veteran named Dmitry Komar was crushed while climbing onto the lead vehicle. A similar fate befell Vladimir Usov, who tried to rescue him. As Molotov cocktails flew and one vehicle burst into flames, the soldiers opened fire and a third victim, Ilya Krichevskiy, fell dead. As more angry people swarmed over the vehicles, an informal agreement was reached to allow the vehicles to turn around and withdraw in the direction from which they had come.

When he learned of the deaths, Yazov ordered a halt to all troop movements and abandoned the planned attack. At 3 AM, Kryuchkov called Yeltsin's aide Gennadiy Burbulis and said "It's OK now. You can go to sleep."[29] In the White House, when Yeltsin's security men heard the gunfire they bundled the Russian president into his armored limousine and tried to persuade him to take advantage of what they said was an offer of asylum from the nearby American embassy. As the vehicle was about to leave, Yeltsin suddenly came to his senses and ordered it to turn around. He was well aware that to be seen fleeing into the US embassy would completely undermine his image of courageous resistance and hand the coup plotters an undeserved victory.[30]

American Reaction to the Coup

Wayne Merry, newly arrived in Moscow as chief of the section responsible for reporting on internal political developments across the USSR, first learned about the coup when he arrived at the embassy the morning of August 19 and the Soviet guard asked, "Have you heard about the overthrow of our government?" The guard added, "I am very afraid." Jim Collins, chargé d'affaires when the coup began and US Ambassador in Moscow from 1997 to 2001, set up two teams to provide twenty-four-hour coverage of the events around the coup. For the next three days the embassy, located only two hundred yards away from the White House, was at the center of the storm, a witness and to some extent a player in the events that gripped the world's attention. The embassy's team of talented Russian-speaking Foreign Service Officers fanned out across the city to provide a detailed account of what was happening. Military personnel in the Defense Attaché's office also worked the streets and the phones to develop a picture of the military's role. Embassy officers trudged frequently across the brief space separating the compound from the White House, talking to the people in the living ring and entering the White House to meet with members of the Yeltsin team.[31]

Collins quickly decided that the embassy would have no contact with those behind the coup except as might be necessary for the security of the embassy or American citizens. "The embassy would not do anything to give a sense of legitimacy to the coup and would so advise Washington," Collins instructed.

On the first day of the coup, the Yeltsin team asked Collins to come to the White House. In a demonstrative gesture, he drove the two hundred yards in the ambassadorial limousine. Seeing the massive black Cadillac with the American flag flying on the fender, the crowd around the White House gave a cheer. Inside the White House the Yeltsin team had a message for Collins to pass to Washington: "We are trying to maintain legitimate constitutional authority." Yeltsin hoped that the United States would support the legitimate government of Russia and not be taken in by the people behind the coup. To show their determination, the Yeltsin team informed Collins that Russian foreign minister Kozyrev had been dispatched to Brussels with authorization to set up a government in exile if that became necessary.[32]

"It was heady stuff," Collins later recalled and as he returned to the embassy he had another heady moment. The embassy had set up an open phone line to the State Department operations center and just as Collins walked back into the embassy he was told that the White House was calling—this time from the United States. Collins picked up the receiver and found President Bush on the line. The president asked if everyone at the embassy was safe and sought Collins's opinion about what was going on. Collins replied that the embassy believed the coup was "an unconstitutional act" and "was not persuaded that this coup was going to work."[33]

When the coup began President Bush was at his Maine vacation home. Initially, the president, on Scowcroft's advice, adopted a public line that was condemnatory without burning bridges to the potential new authorities in the Kremlin. But as the first day wore on and taking account of information Collins had provided, Gates said, "We began to think that the coup plotters did not have their act together." Bush issued a second, stronger statement that condemned the "unconstitutional use of force" and expressly supported Yeltsin's call for Gorbachev's restoration to power. He also picked up on the embassy's line by stating, "We will avoid in every possible way actions that would lend legitimacy or support to this coup effort."[34]

On the second day of the coup, Bush telephoned Yeltsin at the Russian White House and "to our astonishment," according to Gates, the call went through. The first request Yeltsin made of the US president was to telephone Gorbachev. Bush congratulated Yeltsin on his "courage and commitment" and after hanging up issued a statement affirming his support for "Boris Yeltsin, the freely elected leader of the Russian Republic" and for "Yeltsin's goal of the restoration of Mr. Gorbachev as the constitutionally chosen leader."[35] It was a dramatic turnaround in the attitude of the Bush White House toward the Russian leader and a sign of how the coup was already altering the power situation in Moscow.

The day after the coup collapsed, newly arrived Ambassador Strauss attended a rally at Manezh Square to commemorate the three who had died. On arrival Strauss found several hundred thousand people in the square and chaos among the organizers. While his escorts scrambled to learn where diplomats were supposed to go Strauss, with a politician's instinct, headed straight for the stage. There he met Gorbachev, who asked if he wanted to speak. Strauss replied, "Yes but only after you." So the second person to speak at the rally honoring the dead heroes of the resistance to the coup was the US ambassador, whose remarks citing Patrick Henry's famous cry, "Give me liberty or give me death," received a rapturous response.[36]

Assertions that the US offered asylum to Yeltsin appear in the 1997 memoirs of Yeltsin's chief bodyguard, Aleksandr Korzhakov, who wrote that he was informed that the American embassy had telephoned to offer Yeltsin asylum. Korzhakov told Yeltsin of the offer, which Korzhakov says was seen as "strong moral support" for the Yeltsin cause. Yeltsin also mentioned the offer of asylum in his memoirs, saying that the original request came from the Russian side and the Americans "ran with it themselves."[37] Neither Yeltsin nor Korzhakov said who actually made the offer from the US and who on the Russian side received it.

There appears to be grounds for questioning the claimed US asylum offer as well as a separate claim that the US offered intelligence support to Yeltsin during the coup. The United States does not, as a matter of policy, offer asylum in its embassies abroad and such an offer to Yeltsin seems unlikely. If Yeltsin had actually sought refuge, his presence in the embassy would have been a huge complication for any US efforts to establish a working relationship with what would then have become the new leadership in Moscow. Collins said he had made no such offer of asylum and was unaware of anyone else doing so. Collins pointed out, however, that Russian foreign minister Kozyrev, in Brussels, was in touch with Baker and his team and said he could not rule out that some such discussion had occurred there, but he added that if that had happened no one had informed him. In any case, such an offer does not seem consistent with the cautious Bush administration.[38]

In 1994, respected investigative reporter Seymour Hersh wrote that US intelligence had begun to help Yeltsin months before the coup and that after the coup began President Bush ordered that essential communications intelligence be provided to Yeltsin—over the bitter protests of the National Security Agency.[39] Collins said he was unaware of any such transfer of US intelligence data to Yeltsin during the coup.[40] Passing intelligence information without the knowledge of the chief of the US mission would have been a violation of the rules of the game—not impossible, perhaps, but unlikely, given the fluid situation at the time. It is also hard to believe that the United States would formally authorize such transfer on short notice to what amounted at the time to a ragtag group of rebels in the Russian White House. There is no information in the memoirs of senior Bush administration officials to corroborate either the offer of asylum or intelligence support to Yeltsin during the coup.

The Coup Outside Moscow

One of the first things Yeltsin did after arriving in the White House the first day of the coup was to telephone leaders of the major republics. He was shocked to find their main objective was to avoid committing themselves in order to be in a position if the coup succeeded to negotiate with its leaders.[41]

The coup plotters seem to have made only half-hearted efforts to pressure republican leaders with the exception of Ukraine where after meeting Gorbachev at Foros the headstrong Varennikov flew to Kiev to meet with Kravchuk and other members of the republic's leadership. Varennikov forthrightly described the committee's actions as a "coup" and confirmed that its intention was to restore the Soviet system. He demanded that the Ukrainian leadership announce the introduction of a state of emergency.

Ukrainian leaders did not openly oppose the coup but said that "everything was in order" in their republic and there was no need for a state of emergency. Eventually, Varennikov tired of the Ukrainians' evasions and told them bluntly that the decrees of the committee were in effect in the republic whether they liked it or not. The Ukrainians bowed somewhat to Varennikov's bullying and agreed to form a joint commission to study the situation in the republic and take necessary corrective actions. That evening, Kravchuk was so equivocal in a television interview that he seemed to give indirect support to the coup.[42]

Two days later, Ukrainians greeted the news of the collapse of the coup with a rally in Kiev's October Revolution Square. Chanting "Yeltsin! Yeltsin! Down with Kravchuk!" the crowd listened to representatives of the opposition in the Ukrainian parliament and various public groups express their gratitude toward the Russian president for successfully facing down the instigators of the coup.[43]

In Central Asia, Kyrgyz president Askar Akayev issued a forthright statement opposing the coup, but other Central Asian leaders avoided saying anything in public on the first day. President Niyazov, of Turkmenistan, told Yanayev when the latter called that he would fully support the coup and there are reports that Uzbek leader Karimov sent a private message of support to the committee.[44]

As signs of disarray in the committee accumulated, republican leaders began to distance themselves. On the second day, Kazakh leader Nazarbayev criticized the "shameful" actions of the coup and declared that he was leaving the Communist party and creating a new independent party in his republic. On August 23, with the coup leaders safely under arrest, the Ukrainian leadership declared the republic independent and announced a December 1 referendum to confirm the move. Within a few days, every Soviet republic had declared independence, although exactly what this meant in practice remained to be determined.

Gorbachev Humiliated

Gorbachev returned to Moscow in the early morning hours of August 22. Soviet television showed him walking slowly down the airplane ramp, obviously tired and seemingly somewhat disoriented, not surprising, considering what he had been through. Gorbachev acknowledged that he had returned to "another country" but his actions in the coming days revealed that he had not really absorbed the lessons of the coup. Arriving in Moscow, he called the failure of the coup a "victory for perestroika," which showed how out of touch he was with popular sentiment.

Gorbachev missed a historic opportunity to go to the White House to personally thank Yeltsin and the thousands of ordinary Muscovites who had defeated the coup. The next day he returned to his Kremlin office and attempted to take up the reins of power almost as if nothing had happened. He announced that Yazov and Kryuchkov were fired, which was certainly appropriate, but to take Yazov's place as minister of defense he appointed Chief of Staff Moiseyev, who had also been an active participant in the coup. Yeltsin learned about Gorbachev's actions from the evening news and immediately telephoned Gorbachev for a "short and sharp" conversation. The next day

Yeltsin forced Gorbachev to summon Moiseyev to his office and fire him. Gorbachev had to agree to Yeltsin's choice of Shaposhnikov as new defense minister and that all future personnel changes would have Yeltsin's concurrence.[45]

At the Russian parliament, deputies asked whether Gorbachev had drawn any lessons from the fact that the leaders of the coup were men whom Gorbachev himself had appointed. Some pushed Gorbachev to acknowledge that socialism should be banned and that the Communist party was a criminal organization. Gorbachev argued, reasonably enough, against the banning of parties in a democratic system. Eventually, however, Yeltsin lost patience and insisted Gorbachev read a secretly made record of a Soviet government session on the first day of the coup, which showed that virtually all of Gorbachev's ministers had supported the coup. Gorbachev was forced to admit, "This whole government has got to resign," and they were subsequently replaced by people largely of Yeltsin's choosing.

But Yeltsin was not finished with his humiliation of the man who had once done something roughly similar to him, albeit in closed session. With television cameras rolling, Yeltsin continued, "On a lighter note; shall we now sign a document suspending the activities of the Russian Communist Party?" He signed with a flourish while a stunned Gorbachev looked on stammering, "I don't know what you're signing there."[46]

After the the coup, even as Gorbachev was struggling to come to grips with its consequences, many in Moscow questioned his role in the dramatic events of those August days. Many doubted whether Gorbachev had in reality been as resolute an opponent of the coup as he portrayed himself and some accused him of direct complicity. Typical in this regard was Shevardnadze who, when Gorbachev tried shortly after the coup to get him to join the Security Council, angrily refused saying that Gorbachev had provoked the coup, either intentionally or unintentionally. Shevardnadze added, "I have every ground for supposing that you took part in the plot."[47]

A final answer to this question may never emerge until the KGB opens its files but it is clear that in the weeks and months before the August coup Gorbachev flirted with the notion of establishing a state of emergency in the country. Only the prospect of bloodshed, and the loss of Western support for him as the leader of perestroika that would have inevitably followed, seems to have induced Gorbachev to pull back from the use of force in January in the Baltics and in March in Moscow against Yeltsin.

Before leaving Moscow for his vacation in Foros Gorbachev authorized his "power ministries" to study what might serve to trigger a state of emergency and what measures might be undertaken once one was imposed. In the days before the coup Gorbachev was frequently in contact with KGB chief Kryuch-kov but what he actually said about the plans being drawn up for a state of emergency remains unknown.

Once the coup was under way Gorbachev was apparently not as isolated at Foros as he later portrayed. Gorbachev's state communications were cut but telephones were working in the administration buildings and in official vehicles at Foros. On the first day of the coup, after the plotters had left, Gor-bachev telephoned his political associate Arkadiy Volskiy and Kazakh president Nazabayev.

There has also been speculation why Gorbachev did not order his per-sonal guards to arrest the delegation of coup plotters once he understood the nature of their mission to Foros. The chief of Gorbachev's guard detach-ment wrote in his memoirs that the men under his command would have detained the delegation had Gorbachev given the order to arrest them, a point confirmed by Raisa in 1992 during an interview with Russian prose-cutors. In his memoirs Gorbachev said he did not do so because "the main plotters were in Moscow, and they held all power in their hands." Some have found Gorbachev's assertion unconvincing but using Gorbachev's detachment of approximately thirty guards to arrest the plotters would, in fact, have been a highly risky undertaking, carrying with it the possibility of provoking a conflict among various branches of the heavily armed security services that could easily have spiraled out of control into a broader civil conflict.

Gorbachev's behavior when the coup plotters met him in Foros may well have been less than the model of forthright resistance he described immedi-ately after the coup but whatever he said to the plotters Gorbachev refused to join the coup by signing the decree they had brought along to authorize tempo-rarily handing over power to Vice President Yanayev. Gorbachev's stance forced the coup plotters to act outside the law, which weakened their own resolve and made it easier to mobilize opposition to the coup. Some have speculated that Gorbachev refused to sign in order to force coup plotters themselves to take re-sponsibility for the dirty work of "imposing order." It is probable, however, that Gorbachev refused the coup plotters' demands out of well-founded suspicion that once he signed away power the hard-line conservatives who led the coup were unlikely to ever give it back to him. This one act by Gorbachev helped lay the foundation for the coup's failure by giving Yeltsin and others solid grounds for resistance. It was a clear indication of Gorbachev's opposition to the way the inept coup plotters went about their business if not necessarily to all of their objectives.[48]

Euphoria in Moscow

The mood in the streets of Moscow in the first days after the coup was electric. On August 23, thousands demonstrated in front of the KGB building on Lubyanka Square. To cheers of the crowd, bulldozers toppled the statue of Feliks Dzerzhinsky, the founder of the secret police under Lenin.

The next day, a mob surrounded the Central Committee headquarters on Old Square. While apparatchiks inside frantically shredded documents Yeltsin's top aide, Gennadiy Burbulis, got Gorbachev to sign a decree ordering everyone to leave. They exited to the jeers of the crowd, protected from worse by a thin line of city police.[49]

I drove into Moscow shortly after the coup's collapse. Candles were still burning at the site near the embassy where the three young men had been killed. Remnants of some barricades remained around the White House and a few people were still huddled around campfires, as if reluctant to abandon the solidarity that had gripped them during the days of the living ring.

On my first visit to the Foreign Ministry, AK-47-toting police guards stood at the entrance and at each floor of the huge building. Later, a friend took me into what was by then the former Central Committee offices at Old Square. We wandered through dark and empty corridors and into the massive fifth-floor office that for decades had been the domain of the party's second secretary, where I sat in the chair once occupied by Suslov and Gorbachev. Only a few light bulbs illuminated the deserted corridors and empty offices. Some members of the Yeltsin team were visiting the building, apparently sizing up the vacant real estate, but the overall impression left by this one-time center of imperial power was to recall a seedy version of Shelly's depiction of the vanished glories of the "King of Kings," Ozymandias.

The Soviet media was exploding with the exuberant power of freedom. Journalists had been a key component of the resistance to the coup and they were determined to take advantage of the new era. On the first day after the coup's collapse, Sergei Medvedev reappeared as "Vremya" anchor. "Vzgladi," an outspoken program of news commentary that had been banned when Gorbachev shifted to the right a year earlier, reappeared with two long programs that chronicled in exhaustive detail the events of the coup.

Euphoria engulfed the citizens of Moscow. The last couple of years had been hard, politically, economically, and psychologically. Now anything seemed possible. People persuaded themselves that life would soon change for the better. Mixed up in these emotions was a strong sense of pride. The country had been through tough times but had emerged with hope from the crisis of the coup and the long nightmare of Communism. Russia would remain a superpower but it would join the other members of the world community as a "normal" country. Democracy was on everybody's lips. People assumed that with the Communist party and its institutions swept away it would be easy and relatively painless to graft the institutions of democratic governance onto the Russian body politic. Russians, after all, were a well-educated, talented, and motivated people. Soon Moscow would take its proper place with Paris, London, New York, and other world centers.

An outpouring of positive feelings toward the United States accompanied the postcoup euphoria. People believed, with good reason, that President Bush's role in rallying international opposition to the coup was one of the key reasons for its failure. It was assumed that Russia and the United States would remain the world's two leading nations but now as friends and partners, not rivals. To walk into a Russian office or meeting and be introduced as an American diplomat was to be greeted by smiles, enthusiastic handshakes, and often a warm embrace.

Looking back, this brief window of pro-American enthusiasm was probably unsustainable and even at the time there were signs of strain. Over the winter, as supplies dwindled in Moscow, the US airlifted emergency food and humanitarian aid. On one occasion, my son and I helped unload a massive C-5A cargo aircraft and accompanied a small convoy of food and medicines to a Moscow hospital, where the staff unloaded the trucks. The director was appreciative for the assistance, but as the unloading continued and a number of empty boxes turned up he flew into a rage and accused us of stealing some of the supplies and staging a show. Returning to the embassy, I asked the air attaché what had happened and he told me that empty boxes were used to distribute the load in a balanced fashion throughout the aircraft. The next day, I called the director and explained the situation. He apologized for his outburst and expressed gratitude for the US assistance, but added that he also hoped we understood just how difficult it was for a Russian to be in the position of accepting aid from the United States, however well intentioned.

After the coup, the three most important institutions that had underpinned the USSR as a unified state disappeared or were weakened to the point of incapacity. The Communist Party had vanished as a ruling institution and bearer of a mobilizing ideology. The centrally planned economy had disintegrated and economic output had plunged to the point where, as the autumn progressed, worries about survival spread across much of the country. Security forces remained large and potentially powerful but their morale had collapsed and they were looking for institutional mooring even as, under the surface, some within them were embracing the opportunities for profit and influence offered by the emerging market system.

Salvaging a New Union or Rearranging the Deck Chairs?

Within a couple of weeks, Gorbachev recovered from the confusion that had gripped him immediately after the coup. Shrugging off the personal and political humiliations Yeltsin had inflicted on him, and taking advantage of Yeltsin's absence from the scene for part of this period, Gorbachev threw himself into one last struggle to preserve some form of united entity out of the wreckage of the USSR. It seemed a hopeless task but confidence in his own abilities had always been among Gorbachev's strongest points. In the words of Andrei Grachev, who joined Gorbachev's team as press secretary in these final days, "Gorbachev had been so successful at convincing the world that he could perform miracles that he may have wound up believing it himself."[1]

Gorbachev's position was weak but he was not without cards to play. Fears that disintegration could trigger Yugoslav-style ethnic violence in the nuclear-armed USSR were on everyone's mind. Many republican leaders hesitated to cut all the ties binding them to the center. Even Yeltsin at this stage seemed to want to preserve some form of union. In early September, a confident Yeltsin "made it brutally clear that he was the master now" to Prime Minister Major, but he still insisted, "As of today we need Gorbachev to hold the Union together."[2]

On September 5 Gorbachev was forced to agree to the dissolution of the USSR Supreme Soviet, whose creation in 1989 through quasifree elections had been one of the high points of perestroika. It was replaced by a new Council of State consisting of the heads of the country's constituent republics. At the same time, Gorbachev got republican leaders to agree to resume negotiations, held at the Novo-Ogarevo dacha near Moscow, aimed at creating a new entity to be called the Union of Sovereign States.

On October 11, Gorbachev convened a meeting of the State Council to discuss a draft that he claimed pointedly, "Boris Nikolayevich and I worked out together."[3] The meeting opened under the glare of television lights, which Gorbachev had arranged at the last minute without consulting other leaders, apparently in the belief that broadcasting the meeting live would help enlist public opinion on his side. When the meeting began, Yeltsin's chair, now always next to Gorbachev's, was conspicuously empty. Not until Gorbachev had finished his remarks did a sullen-looking Yeltsin enter the room, apparently put off by the presence of TV cameras.

Once Yeltsin had taken his seat, Yavlinskiy, whom Gorbachev had once more enlisted on his team, presented an eloquent report on the virtues of a common economic zone. When Yavlinskiy finished, everyone waited for Yeltsin's reaction. In his usual peremptory style, he declaimed that Russia would go along, but demonstratively raising his index finger, he boomed out that Russia would stop financing any institution of the central government that was not included in the draft agreement.

As the brief Russian fall turned toward winter postcoup euphoria was replaced by anxiety. Soviets had experienced shortages before but goods were now scarcer than anyone could remember in peacetime. There was a sense of looming unknown as the foundations of the system that had existed for most people's lifetimes crumbled away. Yegor Gaidar, serving in this period as the head of the Russian government and the architect of Yeltsin's ambitious program of economic reform, remembered, "The autumn of 1991 was rife with expectations of catastrophe, famine, total breakdown in transport and communications systems. Primus stoves were at a premium. The most common topic of conversation was, How will we survive?"[4]

The economy was dropping off the chart. Production in 1991 fell by 15 percent and was expected to fall by an additional 25 percent in 1992. Republics had stopped financing central institutions and were issuing unsecured loans, in effect printing money, to cover expenses within their own borders. Interrepublic trade was collapsing, with customs borders appearing between republics.

When information on gold reserves, formerly considered a state secret at least as sensitive as missile data, became publicly available it hit like a bucket of cold water. From 1989 to 1991, the Soviets had sold over one thousand tons of gold and the pace was accelerating. By the end of 1991, state gold reserves had fallen to the unprecedentedly low level of 289.6 tons, insufficient to cover even the most urgent obligations. The situation with respect to hard currency was even worse. By the end of October 1991, foreign currency reserves were totally exhausted and the USSR was forced to stop all foreign payments except for debt service.[5]

Western economic assistance was now seen by all as the only hope for salvation, but Gorbachev had no plan other than to beg for handouts. When he met Bush in Madrid at the end of October he asked for $4.5 billion in credits and food aid. Despite his personal sympathy for the Soviet leader Bush felt Gorbachev "was out of touch with Soviet reality."[6] US support at this time was confined to technical assistance and humanitarian aid, including frozen chicken parts that to this day are known in Russia as "Bush legs." It was not an unreasonable position given the powerlessness of Soviet central authorities and the general chaos across the country. Yavlinskiy told Prime Minister Major that until there was a viable economic agreement among the republics and a genuine program of economic reform was in place there was no point in the West giving economic aid.[7] But the seeds for future trouble were sown as a robust public posture on the virtues of Western assistance was accompanied by modest amounts of real aid.

Soviet officials were sometimes their own worst enemies. When Baker paid his first postcoup visit to Moscow in early September, Gorbachev told him the money the Soviets had received from Germany in 1989 had simply vanished. "Things disappear around here. We got a lot of money for German unification and when I called our people I was told they didn't know where it was."[8]

The End of the Road

While Gorbachev tried desperately to preserve some kind of union, the Yeltsin team was putting together a comprehensive program of market reform for Russia, based loosely on the Five Hundred Days plan. On October 28, Yeltsin unveiled the new plan before the Russian parliament. Speaking for over an hour in a somber but resolute tone and warning of hardships to come, Yeltsin declared his intention to lift price controls, carry out sweeping privatization of state enterprises, and undertake tough financial stabilization measures, including sharp reductions in military spending. Yeltsin did not bother to inform Gorbachev in advance about the speech and he failed to mention central authorities at all, except to warn that Russia would stop financing some seventy ministries and agencies of the "former Union" as of November 1.[9]

On November 25, Yeltsin told the USSR State Council that the Russian parliament was not prepared to accept either a unified or a confederal state. Gorbachev marched out of the room, calling on the republican "boyars" to come up with some kind of solution.[10] Eventually Yeltsin and Belorussian leader Shushkevich persuaded Gorbachev to return and the impasse was relieved by a drafting fix. But none of the republican leaders signed the document and as Yeltsin wrote later, "Essentially it was the death-knell of the Novo-Ogarevo process."[11]

As the union treaty talks ground to a halt, Gorbachev seems to have made a stab at encouraging the military to intervene to hold the country together. In November 1991, Gorbachev invited Defense Minister Shaposhnikov to his Kremlin office for a late evening one-on-one conversation. After coffee and pleasantries, Gorbachev began to discuss the situation in the country, concluding that the USSR was on the verge of disintegration, that his efforts to preserve the union were not succeeding, and that "something needs to be done." Several options were conceivable, Gorbachev said, but the most acceptable would be for "you soldiers to take power in your hands, install a government you are comfortable with, stabilize the situation, and then step aside." Shaposhnikov angrily replied, "and then we could go straight to prison." Gorbachev quickly pulled back, saying, "What are you talking about? I was only discussing options, thinking aloud."[12]

On December 1 Gorbachev's string ran out when Ukraine voted overwhelmingly for independence. With 84 percent of the electorate participating, 92 percent approved the declaration of independence adopted by the Ukrainian parliament shortly after the August coup. Every region voted solidly for independence, including in the east, where Russian speakers predominated. Even Crimea, which had a strong sense of affinity to Russia, voted "yes" by 54 percent.

The day after the Ukrainian vote, Gorbachev called Yeltsin and suggested a meeting with Kravchuk and Nazarbayev but Yeltsin refused, saying nothing would come of seeking to prolong the union treaty process. He countered by suggesting a four-republic union consisting of Russia, Ukraine, Belarus, and Kazakhstan, but Gorbachev refused, complaining, "What would be my place in it?"[13] The next day Yeltsin conveyed Russia's recognition of Ukrainian independence and stressed the need for the two former republics to forge a new relationship in the future. On December 4 Kravchuk, who had not left the Communist party until after the August coup, was inaugurated with a five-hundred-year-old Ukrainian Bible on the table beside him. Afterward, he announced that the new state would no longer participate in Gorbachev's efforts to draft a new union treaty.[14]

Ukrainian Plebiscite

I was privileged to have the opportunity to witness a number of elections in former Communist countries, where people had the opportunity, often for the first time in their lives, to vote in an election with real choice. The experience always provided a moving insight into just how powerful the practice of democracy is to people who have been deprived of it. Ukraine on December 1, where I observed the independence referendum, was no exception.

Throughout the day we visited polls in Kiev and the surrounding countryside. Long lines of people waited patiently but with obvious enthusiasm to cast their ballot in the first election any of them had ever experienced where the vote would actually make a difference in their lives. Technical procedures, verifying identity, registering, counting and transmitting the votes, operated without significant glitches. In the evening, we watched the inhabitants of a village near Kiev celebrate independence by spontaneously performing Ukrainian folk dances and singing Ukrainian national songs long banned under the Communists.

It was hard to find anyone who did not support the concept of independence and there is no question that the results of the referendum accurately reflected the feelings of the people at the time. On the other hand, fair elections are about more than just what happens on polling day. In the weeks before the referendum, proindependence voices completely dominated public discussion. Voices questioning independence were absent. The December 1 ballot offered, in practice, more of a plebiscite than a choice.

There were also real questions in the minds of many about what a yes vote on independence would signify. For many, independence meant complete state sovereignty, a seat in the UN, a separate army—the works. Others offered more ambiguous views. Some saw a yes vote as primarily a repudiation of Ukraine's repressive experience under the Communists. Others saw it as opening a path to prosperity and full-fledged membership in the modern world. One ethnic Russian voter told a Western journalist, "If there is no independence, life will never get better."[15]

Shortly after the referendum, I took my son to visit the Lenin mausoleum. In the postcoup environment we assumed, incorrectly as it turned out, that the Old Bolshevik's time on Red Square was drawing to a close. After exiting the mausoleum, we found ourselves in conversation with an older Russian-speaking couple who had just come from their home in Ukraine. Both had voted in favor of independence and at that early day were still optimistic about the future. They had traveled on the train, still using their Soviet passports, and when I remarked casually at how things would change when Ukraine had its own passports and border posts, they seemed shocked at the thought. Ukraine and Russia would always remain together they said.

US Policy Adjusts

Like the rest of the world, the United States struggled in the months after the coup to come to grips with the pace of events. President Bush and Secretary Baker, watching television together when Gorbachev returned to Moscow after the coup, were "absolutely shocked" when he spoke of the need to "renew" the Communist party.[16] It seemed to the two American leaders, along with many others, that Gorbachev had failed to grasp how the world had changed during the three days he had been in Foros.

On September 5, the senior figures in the Bush foreign-policy team, known among themselves as the Gang of Eight, met to discuss how US policy toward the USSR should evolve in the wake of the coup. Only Secretary of Defense Cheney argued forthrightly that the United States should adopt a policy of encouraging the disintegration of its longtime Cold War rival. Cheney had long been skeptical of Gorbachev, whom he met at the Washington summit in December 1987 and "came away thinking he wasn't as serious a reformer as some believed." Now, Cheney argued, "it was time for a bold policy initiative that would cement the downfall of the Soviet Union."[17] Others were more cautious, although primarily as a matter of expediency. Secretary of State Baker acknowledged, "Peaceful break-up is in our interest, not another Yugoslavia." But Baker did not believe that the US should try to accelerate the process of disintegration. Rather it should be guided by what the republics themselves did and by the principle of peaceful and democratic change of borders as envisioned by the Helsinki Accords.[18]

President Bush, typically, was most cautious. He "did not consider it useful to pretend that the US could play a major role in determining what happened in the USSR." But he was still susceptible to feelings of loyalty and support for Gorbachev. As late as November, he told Chancellor Kohl, "I support the Center and I support Gorbachev even though I am criticized in the United States for doing so."[19]

Four days before the referendum, President Bush met a delegation of prominent Ukrainian-Americans who urged him to recognize Ukraine as an independent country immediately after the vote. The president, well aware that he was speaking to the leaders of a generally conservative community that tended to vote Republican, replied that after the vote "we'll salute independence and then we will take steps leading to recognition. . . . It won't take long."[20] After the meeting, "administration officials" leaked a report that Bush had authorized a major shift away from the central Soviet government toward supporting the republics.

On November 30, Bush telephoned Gorbachev to tell him, "The only question is when and how we and other countries recognize Ukrainian independence." Gorbachev reacted angrily, accusing the United States of "not only trying to influence events but to interfere." But with few options available, Gorbachev attempted to put the best face on the situation. Ignoring everything the Ukrainians were saying, Gorbachev claimed that a positive vote on independence would be just what Kiev needed to return to the union treaty process.[21]

Immediately after speaking with Gorbachev, Bush telephoned Yeltsin. The Russian president was confident that an overwhelming majority of Ukrainian voters would endorse independence and said in that event Russia would promptly recognize Ukraine as an independent country, just as it had done when the Baltics declared independence. Yeltsin dismissed any thought that Ukraine might return to the union treaty talks after a positive independence vote and added that if Ukraine withdrew from the process Russia would do so as well.[22]

The USSR Ceases to Exist

On December 8, people in the former USSR woke up to find that they were living in a new country. Overnight, Yeltsin, Kravchuk, and Shushkevich, meeting secretly at a lodge deep in the remote woods of the Beloveshka Pushcha nature preserve, announced, "The USSR has ceased to exist as a subject of international law and geopolitical reality."[23] In place of the USSR, the three leaders announced the formation of a new association called the Commonwealth of Independent States (CIS).

Participants have given varying accounts of the meeting and the genesis of the document that emerged from it. Long afterward, Kravchuk claimed that Yeltsin had begun by stating his willingness to sign Gorbachev's union treaty if Ukraine would also sign, a move that if true was likely a ploy to reinforce the point that it was the Ukrainian independence vote that had put paid to Gorbachev's efforts to preserve the union. Kravchuk, as Yeltsin knew he would, rejected the suggestion.[24]

Overnight, Yeltsin's new team of "young reformers—legal adviser Sergei Shakrai, Foreign Minister Kozyrev, and acting Prime Minister Gaidar—produced a draft agreement for the new entity. The meeting was held in such haste and secrecy that there were no copy machines present. Gaidar wrote the entire first draft by hand, finishing at 4 AM and then had to dictate the text just minutes before the signing ceremony when a flustered secretary proved unable to read his late-night handwriting.[25] In Kravchuk's telling, he tossed out the "young reformers" draft and the three republican leaders produced a new document based on the text of a "Slavic Union" he and Yeltsin had given Gorbachev earlier in 1991.

Whatever its genesis, after the document was signed, Yeltsin's first call was to Shaposhnikov to offer him the post of defense minister of the new CIS. After Shaposhnikov agreed, which ensured the support of the military, Yeltsin telephoned President Bush. To avoid using the Soviet VIP phone system, still monitored by security services subordinate to Gorbachev, the Russian team placed the call through regular international lines. The White House operator initially had some difficulty understanding why the president of the United States should take a call from a game preserve in Belarus but Kozyrev, a fluent English speaker, managed to explain what was going on and get Bush on the line. Yeltsin told the US leader, "Mr. President, the Soviet Union is no more." He emphasized that the signatories would respect all existing international obligations and promised to maintain control over Soviet nuclear weapons. Bush correctly understood that "the provisions sounded as if they had been designed specifically to gain US support." After hearing from Yeltsin that Gorbachev was as yet unaware of what was going on, Bush ended noncommittally, saying simply that he hoped for a peaceful evolution.[26]

Shushkevich was delegated to call Gorbachev, who when he heard that the agreement had already been signed asked sarcastically why the Belorussian leader had bothered to call. But when Shushkevich told Gorbachev that President Bush had already been informed, the Soviet leader exploded. "This is a disgrace. You've been speaking with the president of the United States and you failed to speak with the president of your own country."[27]

Despite the shabby way Yeltsin and the others treated Gorbachev, the Beloveshka Accord marked recognition of reality. For all practical purposes, the USSR had ceased to exist after the failure of the August coup. The Ukrainian independence vote on December 1 was merely the formal coup de grâce. Gorbachev's dogged efforts to retain some kind of union amounted to little more than trying to resuscitate a corpse.

Yeltsin described the Beloveshka Accord as a new global strategy for Russia, which was "ridding itself of its imperial mission." In the era of Vladimir Putin, Russia's imperial dreams seem to be reviving but, nevertheless, the agreement signed that snowy day, deep in one of Europe's most remote spots, has to be seen as one of Yeltsin's greatest achievements. The Beloveshka Accord provided a political framework for a "civilized divorce" among the constituent members of the USSR. Its value can be seen by comparing the process in the USSR with what happened as another multiethnic Communist state dissolved at roughly the same time in Yugoslavia. And those who wonder whether a divorce was necessary at all should ask themselves how they would feel today about a union encompassing most of the former USSR ruled by Vladimir Putin.

Golden Parachutes

Under the surface, as the USSR disintegrated, developments were occurring that were only faintly visible at the time but that ultimately played an important role in shaping the future. The Soviet party-state elite had watched as the collapse of Communist regimes in Eastern Europe was followed by the eviction of the party and its leaders from the political and economic institutions they had formerly controlled. By 1990 it was easy to see how a similar process could occur in the USSR. Around this period, as hard-liners in the party and security services fought to derail the forces of reform Gorbachev had unleashed, they also began quietly to prepare what amounted to covert escape packages that would allow them to retain control of enterprises and funds at home and abroad even if party rule collapsed.

The program of transferring state funds into banks and enterprises abroad began in August 1990, when Vladimir Ivashko, whom Gorbachev had installed as deputy general secretary, signed a decree calling for measures to protect the party's economic interests by forming new economic structures abroad. In June 1991, Gorbachev signed a secret party decree authorizing the transfer of six hundred million rubles to commercial organizations and banks established by the party. As developments heated up, the process was not always so neatly prepared bureaucratically. After the Central Committee was evicted from its Old Square quarters in the wake of the August coup, found among the papers the apparatchiks had frantically trying to destroy was one note that read, "I've taken one hundred million rubles. Hide it!"[28]

The USSR had long provided covert financial support to foreign Communist parties, revolutionary movements, and terrorist groups, a process that was run out of the Central Committee International Department with the actual transfer of funds handled by the KGB. Feliks Bobkov, formerly the head of

Andropov's campaign against the dissidents, and Nikolai Kruchina, the chief of the Central Committee Administrative Affairs department, who died in mysterious circumstances after the August coup, were placed in charge of the new program. They "created a capitalist economy within the CPSU apparatus, establishing joint ventures and bank accounts abroad both to make money and to hide money."[29] When Yeltsin banned the Communist party after the August coup, its former leadership apparently lost control of these funds to individuals and groups that controlled them, many of whom turned out to be former intelligence personnel.

On January 5, 1991, Kryuchkov signed a decree to covertly establish private commercial firms to sell military technology overseas. Taking the long view, Kryuchkov said the new institutions were to be reliable covers for KGB leaders and operatives "in case the domestic . . . situation develops along East German lines" and to provide the "financial means for underground work" if "destructive elements" came to power.[30]

Once such "destructive elements" actually did come to power in Russia, many KGB personnel moved out of the world of intelligence and into the newly emerging market structures. Bobkov reportedly took three hundred employees of his former Fifth Directorate to create the security services for the Media-Most company owned by Vladimir Gusinsky, one of the first generation of Russian oligarchs to take control of business and media enterprises. According to some accounts, as many as two-thirds of the employees of the new Russian stock exchange were former KGB personnel who, in addition presumably to building up their securities portfolios, were also using their new positions to launder KGB and party money abroad.

In the coming years, these people and the resources they controlled played an important role in the creation of the flamboyantly corrupt crony capitalism that emerged out of Yeltsin's failed reforms of the 1990s and, later, in the secretive network of friends and former intelligence personnel that constituted the backbone of the authoritarian regime established by ex-KGB Lt. Col. Vladimir Putin. These developments are beyond the scope of this book, but they are an important factor in the failure of Russia's post-Communist democratic transformation.

CHAPTER 19 · Why Did the USSR Collapse?

And so after a long march through the final quarter century of the Cold War, we come again to the question with which this book opened. What caused the once mighty Soviet Union to collapse almost overnight, less than a generation after it seemed to have achieved the pinnacle of international power, a mystery compounded by the absence of events that have usually accompanied imperial collapse, such as foreign invasion, internal revolution, natural catastrophe, or the like?[1]

The Dog That Did Not Bark

One thing that did not bring down the USSR was organized opposition or mass popular unrest. After crushing anti-Bolshevik resistance by 1920, the USSR never faced an opposition party or underground movement of a scale sufficient to threaten its existence. Outside of the Second World War and its aftermath, the last significant armed uprising against the USSR was the Basmachi movement in Central Asia in the 1920s and 1930s.

The Gorbachev era saw a significant rise in ethnic unrest but it tended to be confined to the periphery, was generally suppressed or at least contained by the authorities, and did not spread to the Slavic core of the state until Gorbachev's final years. Once it got under way, national separatism complicated the other problems facing Gorbachev and by 1991, if not before, it had reached the point of no return in several republics. But national separatism was at least as much a symptom as cause of the Soviet dissolution and in many regions it was more a phenomenon of entrenched ruling elites seeking an alternative ideology to fortify their retention of power than mass pressure from below. Had Gorbachev not relaxed the mechanism of repression and had his reforms succeeded in revitalizing the political and economic institutions of the Soviet system, there is no reason to believe that ethnic unrest would not have remained within manageable bounds.

Over the years, the Soviet regime experienced outbreaks of localized popular unrest sometimes accompanied by violence, but these were generally sporadic and were always quickly suppressed by the authorities, usually forcefully but sometimes also with modest and temporary concessions. Nevertheless, the regime never lost its feeling of insecurity toward the mass of the population, which stemmed ultimately from the contradiction between the proclaimed liberationist goals of the system and the repressive reality used to keep it in power.

In the late 1970s I attended a football game in Moscow with a Soviet friend. Emerging from the stadium after the match, the entire crowd was funneled for two blocks through a narrow corridor formed by a double line of burly policemen. Seeing me look with surprise at the heavy security presence for a peaceful if exuberant event, my nonconformist artist friend said with a laugh, "Our government gets very nervous when large numbers of Russians gather in one place."

In a groundbreaking work, *Mass Uprisings in the USSR*, historian Vladimir Kozlov drew on his years as Russia's archivist to show that the heyday of postwar unrest was actually the Khrushchev era. In the late 1950s, harsh conditions in the "Virgin Lands" of northern Kazakhstan led to eruptions of violent protest, including some in which hundreds of rioters and soldiers were killed or wounded. At roughly the same time, a wave of violent hooliganism swept across other stretches of the USSR, in part due to the release of millions of former prisoners brutalized by their experience in the Gulag. In 1957, half a million were convicted of hooliganism. On occasion, gangs of hooligans and other marginalized groups fought pitched battles against local authorities, joined in some cases by townspeople.

Spontaneous outbreaks in the 1950s and 1960s had their roots in the fact that the bulk of the Soviet population still retained a bedrock belief in the ideals of the Communist system. Most of the disorders of this era erupted in the name of return to an idealized Communism, to a mythological version of Leninism, or in some cases Stalinism. "People rebelled because they believed in the Communist mythology and were angry at it being perverted by current rulers."[2]

The apotheosis of Khrushchev-era unrest came in June 1962 in the southern Russian town of Novocherkassk. Angered by a rise in the price of meat announced shortly after production norms had been increased, workers downed their tools, and a massive crowd, marching behind a portrait of Lenin and chanting anti-Khrushchev slogans, attacked the police station and local party headquarters. After senior Moscow party officials failed to persuade the demonstrators to disperse, soldiers fired into the crowd and regained control of the city. Seven alleged ringleaders received death sentences and dozens of others got long prison sentences.[3]

The authorities imposed a blanket of secrecy on the events in Novocherkassk, but in typical Soviet fashion rumors circulated widely. Fifteen years later, toward the end of the 1970s, some of my dissident contacts gave me what turned out to be a relatively accurate picture of events there, including a report that the worst of the violence had been triggered when troops, intending to fire over the heads of the crowd, killed children the demonstrators had put on their shoulders to show their peaceful intentions.

Ironically, the most lasting consequence of the outbreak in Novocherkassk may have been the impact that the folk-memory of the incident had on the collective will of subsequent Kremlin leaders. After Novocherkassk, no Soviet leader could bring himself to raise food prices until the very end of the Gorbachev era, by which time it was too late to correct the imbalance in the economy caused by the heavily subsidized Soviet agriculture system.

Systemic Causes

IT'S THE ECONOMY, STUPID

By the end of the Brezhnev era, it was clear that the Soviet economy was in trouble, despite the boost provided by the oil bonanza of the 1970s. Even official data showed growth rates slowing, and when Soviet economists were able to look at the reality behind official data they found the picture worse than expected. In 1990, taking advantage of glasnost, the Institute of Statistics undertook a "radical revision of both levels and growth rates of the main macroeconomic indicators." Using statistics long buried in official archives, researchers found that over the period 1961–90 growth rates for gross social product had been overstated by over 1.7 times, national income by 2.1 times, and industrial production by more than 2 times. Over the period 1961–75, they concluded that national income grew at an average rate of 3.4 percent and fell to an average increase of 1.1 percent over 1976–90. Taking into account population growth, this meant that per capita income growth in the final decades of the Soviet system was under 1 percent.[4]

The Soviet economy never managed to make the transition from an extensive system, which depended for growth on ever greater inputs of human, financial, and natural resources, to an intensive system in which growth came from the more efficient use of these resources. Innovation was also a major weakness. The rigid, centrally planned system proved fatally inefficient in encouraging innovation and incorporating the fruits of scientific research, where the USSR excelled in many fields, into the production process. Stealing Western scientific secrets was no substitute for genuine internal innovation. As one KGB wag is said to have wearily, if perhaps also apocryphally, acknowledged, "As soon as we steal one industrial secret, those sneaky capitalists have put a better one in its place!"

But the most serious weakness of the Soviet economy was the very impossibility that a state-owned, centrally planned system could operate efficiently. The notion that billions, if not trillions, of decisions by producers, distributors, and consumers in a vast country like the USSR could be determined in advance by central authorities proved to be a chimera. In reality, the existence of a huge "informal economy" was essential to allow the state planning system to achieve its goals. Managers relied on "pushers" to break bottlenecks, such as finding supplies the system could not furnish, and often violated instructions in order to meet plan targets, for example, by giving workers illegal material incentives.[5] The plan, which supposedly determined the actions of all economic actors, was continually adjusted to reflect stubborn reality in the fields, factories, and mines of a vast and intractable country.

Nor could the Soviet economy be isolated from international economic trends. Underlying the Soviet economic collapse at the end of the 1980s was the fall in global oil prices over 1985–86, which essentially destroyed the Soviet hard-currency export position and deprived Soviet economic managers of the ability to use petro-dollars to import the agricultural goods and high technological products the country was unable to produce itself.

None of these systemic flaws explain why the Soviet economic system failed so quickly at the end of the 1980s. There is no reason to believe that continued tinkering could not have allowed the system to stagger along for some time. By the middle of the 1980s, Soviet economists had accumulated a stock of modest reform plans, essentially variants of the 1960s Kosygin reforms, which if they had been allowed to operate over a period of years might well have registered some gains. A return to the practice of "heroic campaigns," which had produced impressive, if temporary, growth spurts in earlier years was also theoretically possible. Nor does there seem to be any intrinsic reason why the Soviets could not have followed the Chinese strategy of dismantling the centrally planned economic system while retaining a one-party dictatorial political regime, a strategy that up to now has been wildly successful in economic terms, although its human and ecological cost has been immense and whose long-term viability remains to be seen.

The chief reason the Soviet economy unraveled so quickly at the end of the 1980s was the cumulative impact of repeated mistakes in economic management, which Gorbachev and his team committed almost from their first days in office: the antialcohol campaign, the misguided efforts to apply defense-industry techniques to the civilian economy, half-hearted and contradictory on-off efforts at reform during the middle years of perestroika, and finally the rejection of the last-gasp Five Hundred Days program of market reform in favor of a head-in-the-sand approach of begging the West for assistance.

But the final blow was political. The Soviet command economy depended for its success on a command-style political system. When Gorbachev eliminated the fear-factor, he also eliminated the grease that allowed an inherently inefficient system to function. On one level, the reduction in coercion led to a decrease in labor discipline on the shop floor. At the management level, the collapse in the party's authority undermined the ability of planners to ensure compliance with instructions. The center was no longer able to keep the informal-economy mechanisms necessary for the system to function from sliding out of control and growing into an illegal second economy aimed primarily at the enrichment of individual managers or local leaders. In the words of Vladimir Mozhin, the longtime deputy chief of the Central Committee Economic Department, "Without repression and in non-emergency (nonwar) situations, Stalin's model of the economy was not viable. This is the main reason for the collapse of the Soviet economy."[6]

The Military Burden

The high level of military expenditures that continued unchecked almost until the end did not, by itself, bring about the collapse. It did, however, constitute a crushing economic burden that made reform more necessary and at the same time more difficult. Military spending was also a component of what might be called the psychological burden of the Soviet worldview.

Until the very end, the Soviet military leadership was dominated by officers who had fought in the Great Patriotic War. Determined never to allow a repetition of the devastating Nazi surprise attack, the Soviet military saw virtually the entire world as full of potential enemies. According to Colonel General A. A. Danilovich, deputy chief of the general staff, in the 1960s and 1970s, twenty-three countries were categorized as potential Soviet enemies, with an additional forty considered neutral but with an uncertain stance in the event of hostilities. The Soviet military believed it needed to be able to fight all of these potential enemies simultaneously. In a 1987 meeting of the Defense Council in which Akromeyev discussed Soviet military doctrine, an enraged Foreign Minister Shevardnadze interjected, "You want to fight practically the entire world."[7]

Soviet military procurement was also distorted by a bizarre mechanical application of what they believed to be the lesson of US industrial mobilization in the Second World War. The Soviet military forecast that three to six months after the beginning of conflict the United States would be able to produce seventy thousand tanks a year. Since the Soviets also believed that modern war would lead to unprecedentedly high losses of men and equipment, the military argued that it needed to have tens of thousands of tanks on hand to ensure continued superiority. Soviet military intelligence accumulated vast quantities of data on the industrial potential of Western countries. This information was circulated on a very close-hold basis to a limited number of senior officials in what were called Orange Books and was used to support huge budgetary requests. According to Colonel General V. V. Shlykov, a department chief in Soviet military intelligence, "This is precisely the reason we accumulated 64,000 tanks."[8] Even though when he looked more closely he realized that the real US tank production capacity was closer to six hundred per year than sixty thousand, Shlykov found that senior Soviet military leaders "from the old guard school of tank division marshals" refused to listen.

By the time Gorbachev took office, there was quiet agreement among Soviet economists and even among many political leaders that the USSR was spending too much on the military. But efforts to reduce military spending were off the agenda. Only a handful of officials outside the military establishment knew the real figures, and officials in the military decision-making loop had a vested interest in keeping things as they were. Gorbachev understood that he would have to reduce military spending if his reforms were to succeed, one reason for his emphasis on arms deals with the United States, but the ingrained power of the military establishment and its allies among conservative political leaders led him to postpone dealing with the issue until it was too late.

In a study aimed at uncovering the size and effect of what he described as "the most militarized large economy the world has ever seen," US economist Clifford Gaddy concluded that the real reason that no one could come up with an accurate figure for the Soviet military burden "was not that those who knew the correct information continued to conceal it but rather that no one knew the truth."[9]

Moreover, the structure of the Soviet command economy made it difficult to truly measure the impact of military spending. The Soviet system established artificially low prices for inputs into the military budget, based on "a requirement that the defense establishment be allowed to 'buy' equipment more cheaply than anyone else in the Soviet economy." This had the effect of artificially lowering the apparent burden of military spending, and also, of course, of reducing incentives to economize on inputs.

In the late 1980s, a group of Soviet economists converted the output of the machine-building and metal-working (MBMW) sector of the Soviet economy to world prices for 1988, perhaps the last year in which the Soviet economy functioned more or less normally. As Gaddy noted, "The results are astounding." Official Soviet statistics showed that 30 percent of the output of the MBMW sector went for arms, with 50 percent going to investment, and 20 percent to consumer goods. But after Soviet economists recalculated for world prices, they found that 63 percent went for weapons—"direct military orders"—with 32 percent going for investment goods and no more than 6 percent for consumer goods.[10]

Militarization of the economy distorted the economic and social structure of the entire country. Throughout the final decades of the USSR's existence, a huge and growing share of its human and material resources regularly vanished into what amounted to a massive black hole, emerging on ceremonial occasions to roll menacingly across Red Square and in the fall when half-starved conscripts were herded into fields to dig potatoes across the USSR. If a portion of the capable scientists, engineers, and managers secreted in the closed network of military research and production centers had been allowed to employ their talents in the civilian sector, and if some of the bloated military budget had been available for investment in more productive resources, the impact on the civilian economy would surely have been immense.

Secrecy

The veil that enshrouded military spending underscores one of the contributing factors in the Soviet collapse that has often been overlooked: the obsession with secrecy. Secrecy was fundamentally a sign of the insecurity built into the Soviet system, whose leaders never completely rid themselves of the Bolshevik mindset of a conspiracy in power. Soviet leaders were unwilling to relax the system's absurd preoccupation with secrecy because at bottom they were never confident enough about the legitimacy of their rule to trust their own people with honest information.

Sergo Mikoyan, the son of Soviet leader Anastas Mikoyan, encapsulated the problem: "Soviet society faced a major self-contradiction: It provided large numbers of its citizens with a good education, all the way up to and through the university level. But its leaders feared any unchecked development of ideas—an unavoidable consequence of a strong, widely available education system. Eventually, this contradiction became an important factor in the Soviet system's collapse."[11]

Even Soviet leaders could find themselves on the wrong side of the wall of secrecy. Shortly after he became general secretary, Andropov tasked Gorbachev and Ryzhkov with undertaking a series of studies of the Soviet economy but when they approached him for access to the state budget, which remained a classified document almost until the end of the USSR, Andropov dismissed them by saying, "Nothing doing. You're asking too much. The budget is off limits to you."[12]

The Soviet scientific and technical personnel that I worked with in the late 1970s almost invariably returned from their first visit to the United States shaking their heads in dismay at how far their own facilities were behind those of their American counterparts in the material base of modern science, from basic laboratory equipment such as disposable test tubes; to more fundamental items such as computers and top-of-the-line instruments; to the knowledge that came from ready access to international scientific journals, which in the USSR were generally available only to specially cleared personnel. Soviet scientists were justly proud of what they accomplished on a much less impressive technical base than their American counterparts, but they also recognized—even if they could seldom say so openly—how their own isolation made it difficult to remain at the cutting edge of scientific progress.

Secrecy aimed at keeping prying foreign eyes away from the truth about Soviet domestic developments was matched by a wall of secrecy about life abroad, intended to prevent Soviet citizens from learning the truth about how their own country compared to its foreign rivals. As the opportunities for foreign travel expanded for members of the Soviet elite, the contrast between myth and reality became an important element in undermining belief in the system. All Soviet visitors to the West, even those in relatively privileged positions, report being shocked by their first impression of life and work there. In 1958 a young Roald Sagdeyev, later to become the director of the prestigious Institute for Space Research, traveled with a Soviet delegation to a scientific meeting in Geneva. Years later Sagdeyev reported how surprised the members of the Soviet delegation were to find that people seemed happy and prosperous. Where is the oppressed working class, the Soviet scientists asked themselves, and when will the Soviet Union catch up? At the time, a young and optimistic Sagdeyev thought five years; more pessimistic members of the Soviet delegation thought twenty. Only later did it become clear that it would never happen.[13]

Western radio stations, primarily the BBC, the Voice of America (VOA), and Radio Free Europe/Radio Liberty (RFE/RL), helped break through the secrecy and provide independent information to the people of the USSR and Eastern Europe. Their role has been overlooked by many commentators but it would be hard to find a better summary description of the importance of the radio stations (collectively called "voices" by Soviets), than that provided by Timothy Garton Ash, one of the most eloquent witnesses to the 1989 East European revolutions: "Anyone who traveled through central and eastern Europe under communism understood the immense importance of western shortwave radio broadcasting . . . The sheer numbers of those who listened are extraordinary: up to two-thirds of the Polish population in 1981 . . . Who could wish for a nicer compliment than the East German spymaster Markus Wolff saying in his memoirs, 'Of all the various means used to influence people against the East during the Cold War, I would count Radio Free Europe as the most effective.' "[14]

Studies conducted by the Soviet Institute of Sociology showed that "by the end of the 1970s more than half of the USSR urban population listened to foreign broadcasting more or less regularly." VOA was the most popular, in part because sometimes it was not jammed and because of the range of its programming, especially its music.[15]

During the late 1970s when I first served in Moscow, foreign radios were a regular, if generally unacknowledged, part of Soviet life. Dissidents and refuseniks were avid listeners to what amounted in some respects to their community radio service. But it was also my impression that Soviet scientists and officials regularly listened to Western radio broadcasts, although they would seldom admit it. They seemed relatively well informed about international and domestic events that were either unreported or highly distorted in the regular Soviet media. A study on popular unrest in the USSR found that a "surprising number" of those accused of anti-Soviet agitation and propaganda acknowledged listening to foreign radio broadcasts for specific information on events in the USSR and as a source of authoritative criticism of the Soviet system, even in situations where it would have been to their advantage to deny listenership.[16]

Some of the most popular programs on VOA were devoted to American music. For decades, Willis Conover's weekly broadcast of American jazz was a fixture on the Soviet cultural scene, even if it was never mentioned by the Soviet authorities. Rock music was considered more subversive but Western programs devoted to it also enjoyed a wide listenership. In the early 1970s, my graduate-school Russian-language teacher broadcast a late-night rock music program to the USSR on VOA. For several years, he told us, he never received any indication of listenership and thought with discouragement that he was talking to the empty ether. But he learned otherwise when he was a guide in one of the traveling exhibits on aspects of US life organized as part of the cultural exchange program. Once his name became known, he was mobbed by young Soviets who wanted to talk to him about the rock music they had been avidly following on his program.

Radio Liberty was heavily jammed and more dangerous to listen to than VOA or BBC. No official would ever admit to listening to RL, which in unconscious irony was usually called by Soviets simply "svoboda" meaning freedom or liberty. Outside of cities, jamming was less effective, and RL sometimes drew unexpected audiences. In the summer of 1980, I visited an artist friend at his dacha well outside of Moscow. Enjoying a shashlik in the garden, I found myself overhearing a radio program being broadcast at a high volume from a neighboring dacha. After a few minutes, I hesitantly asked our host whether it wasn't RL. He said the radio belonged to a Soviet special-forces officer who had recently returned from Afghanistan so disgusted with the system that had sent him there that he had taken to regularly broadcasting RL at high volume.

One measure of the effectiveness of foreign radio broadcasts is the extraordinary extent of the countermeasures the Soviets took to impede their activities. When jamming ended in 1988, the Soviets were employing over 1,700 jamming transmitters, approximately twenty times the total number of all transmitters broadcasting Western radio programming. Nevertheless, a Central Committee report concluded gloomily that "despite all efforts and the expenditure of billions of rubles, jamming is not achieving its aims. Hostile radio stations are listened to all over the country, with the exception of the centers of Moscow, Leningrad, Kiev, and Riga."[17] Western radio broadcasts did not, of course, bring about the end of the Soviet system. But together with other sources of outside information, such as foreign travel and access to foreign publications, they played an important and often neglected role in breaking the monopoly of information that is one of the most important props of any totalitarian regime.

The Lie Ends and the Fear Factor Fails

Coercion in service of creating a new and just socialist order was, as historian Martin Malia pointed out, the "original sin" of the Soviet system.[18] When Gorbachev took office, the apparatus of repression was functioning in good order. The human rights movement had been crushed. Ethnic discontent was present beneath the surface, but there was no reason to believe that the occasional disturbances could not be contained. By the mid-1980s, few members of the educated elite took seriously the regime's ideology but most had made their peace with the system.

Fear remained the essential glue that held the system together. The collective memory of fear was a crushing brake on the development of any large-scale opposition movement, as the KGB demonstrated in the late 1960s by the success of its campaign of intimidation against a couple of thousand individuals who became "signatories" in the intellectual protests of the era.[19]

When Gorbachev relaxed the threat of repression he inadvertently released a torrent of political, national, and social criticism that eroded the very foundations of the system. The process started gradually but by 1989 it was questioning almost everything that had been achieved over seventy years of Communist rule. In pre-glasnost years, people had accepted poverty as a consequence of war and historic backwardness, especially as long as it could be considered temporary and diminishing. It was also possible to accept repression as a temporary expedient to remove obstacles on the way to progress. Isolation could be accepted if the rest of the world was implacably hostile and driven by jealously toward presumably superior Soviet accomplishments. But after glasnost, it proved hard to accept a system that seemed to produce only poverty, repression, and isolation without any real justification or prospect of their ending.

The process probably did not have to result in disintegration. The system had achievements to its credit, even if these did not necessarily stack up well against those of other developed countries. The concept of democratic socialism probably enjoyed considerable latent support across the country. But Gorbachev ended by alienating those who should have been his strongest backers and failed to create an institutional basis for the reformed system he sought to create.

The Role of Individuals

MIKHAIL GORBACHEV

The Soviet ship of state sank on Gorbachev's watch, so he has to assume a major share of the individual responsibility. In the West, Gorbachev is seen as a hero, responsible for halting the Cold War and for initiating reforms that ended Communist rule in Eastern Europe and the USSR. In Russia, by contrast, Gorbachev is widely reviled, seen as responsible, either by ineptness or design, for policies that ended the Cold War with a Soviet defeat and the disintegration of the USSR itself.

Gorbachev deserves immense credit for recognizing that the Soviet system needed significant change if it was to survive and prosper. He also understood that an essential element of this change would have to be ending the long Soviet confrontation with the West. People on both sides of the former Iron Curtain owe a lasting debt of gratitude to Gorbachev for his unwillingness to use force to suppress the striving for liberation of the peoples of Eastern Europe.

And yet there is something odd about the way Gorbachev's Western friends ignore the impact of his actions on the country he led. On the home front, Gorbachev's six years of rule brought intoxicating political change but they also produced scarcity, impoverishment, and violence. On the international scene, Moscow lost the fruits of its hard-won victory in 1945 and its borders were rolled back to roughly where they stood at the time of Peter the Great. The process was liberating for the peoples of Eastern Europe and for at least some in the former Soviet empire, but it was deeply humiliating to the Russian people, even to many of those who welcomed the end of the repressive Soviet system. Typical of the views of many liberal intellectuals were those of Gorbachev's interpreter and adviser Pavel Palazhenko, who supported the decision not to use force to block the revolutions of 1989 but who was also "doubtful that Eastern Europe could just be allowed to go its own way" without any consideration of Soviet security or the millions of Soviet soldiers who died driving the Nazis out.[20]

Gorbachev's central insight, that reform was necessary for the USSR to survive and prosper, was clouded by a misconception that ultimately brought him down—that change could be contained within the context of what he often called the "socialist choice." To the end of his days, Gorbachev remained a man of the 1960s who believed that something like the "Socialism with a Human Face" of the 1968 Prague reformers could save the system.

In the end, Gorbachev never really got it. In Eastern Europe, he never understood that what people really wanted was not reformed Communism, however attractive that might appear in comparison with its predecessors, but out of the Soviet empire and the Communist system. At home Gorbachev never understood, or at least could never bring himself to act on that understanding, that the party and its ideology was the problem and not the solution.

BORIS YELTSIN

One Soviet leader who did get it was Boris Yeltsin. Unlike Gorbachev, Yeltsin was not a true believer. For him the party was a vehicle to achieve power, and he had no trouble breaking with the party when it humiliated him after his criticism of Gorbachev in 1987. No one who saw Yeltsin in the early years could fail to be impressed by his energy, courage, and commitment to democratic change, although even then there was an element of the manic in Yeltsin's behavior that later tragically overwhelmed him. Once Yeltsin and his team had seized control of Russia—through the ballot box—there was no way Gorbachev could continue to rule the USSR without some form of accommodation, but by then the level of political and personal animosity between the two men was so deep that compromise proved impossible.

Yeltsin was not aiming to end the USSR. He centered his political comeback on the Russian republic to sidestep Gorbachev's control over central Soviet institutions. Even after the August coup, Yeltsin sometimes seemed willing to go along with some form of union but by then the disintegrative forces unleashed by Gorbachev were too strong. Ukrainian independence in December 1991 was the occasion for Yeltsin to initiate the Beloveshka deal that formally ended the USSR but this was not so much an act of political homicide as the institutional equivalent of giving the last rites to a corpse.

RONALD REAGAN

Ronald Reagan took office with a firm belief in the power and resilience of American democracy and an intuitive sense of relative Soviet weakness. He was willing to take risks and go farther than most of his predecessors but he had no blueprint for ending the Cold War and still less for dismantling the USSR.

Reagan challenged Moscow on three broad fronts. His sharp criticism of Soviet behavior and confident affirmation of Western values crystallized a broader shift in Western political thought away from collectivism and toward freedom of choice in political and economic systems. Reagan's rhetoric put the Kremlin on the defensive internationally and even internally. In Politburo deliberations, Gorbachev was sometimes dismissive of the "dinosaur" Reagan, but it is surprising how often he justified his moderate moves as intended to dispel negative foreign images of the Soviet Union. Reagan's increase in military spending was intended to redress the relative decline in US power over the 1970s but it was also a blow to the Soviet national security establishment. The arms buildup that began after the humiliation of the Cuban missile crisis had, from the Soviet point of view, painfully and at great cost brought the USSR to a position of parity with the United States. Reagan's rearmament program threatened to unleash a new round of competition that senior Soviet officials were well aware the USSR could not win.

The final element of the Reagan offensive was a global challenge to Soviet interests that put Moscow on the defensive in ways that seemed inconceivable after Soviet successes in the 1970s. Aid to Afghan rebels was gradually stepped up to the point where, with the provision of Stinger missiles, it pushed Gorbachev toward a negotiated withdrawal. US support helped Solidarity survive the dark days of the early 1980s and laid the foundation for its astonishing victory in 1989. Washington's pleas that Saudi Arabia step up oil production in the mid-1980s may have only nudged Riyadh in a direction it already wanted to go, but the subsequent sharp drop in world oil prices had a catastrophic effect on the Soviet economy.

SDI, often cited as exhibit A in the case for Reagan as Soviet gravedigger, did not "spend the USSR into oblivion" as some have asserted, nor was that the intention of Reagan who, almost alone at senior levels in his administration, genuinely hoped that SDI might eliminate the need for offensive nuclear weapons. Some prominent civilian members of the Soviet national security elite seem to have persuaded themselves—and Gorbachev—of the reality of Soviet propaganda against SDI. Soviet military planners, by contrast, looked carefully at SDI, understood that it was unlikely to work, but took modest contingency countermeasures just in case.

Reagan's approach toward the USSR resembled a boxer's one-two punch. As he built up US strength and political will power, Reagan was also eager to begin negotiations. Reagan reached out to Soviet leaders from the beginning, but these contacts did not enjoy success until the Kremlin saw the failure of its walkout from the arms talks in 1983, and until the internal balance within the Reagan administration had shifted in favor of those, led by George Shultz, who wanted to negotiate with Moscow. Ironically, Reagan the negotiator in his second term, was probably more of a threat to the Soviet system than Reagan the anti-Communist crusader of his first. It is hard to believe that Gorbachev would have been able to go very far with glasnost and perestroika if US-Soviet relations had remained locked in the hostility and mutual suspicion of the first half of the 1980s.

By the end of Reagan's term in office, the Cold War was virtually over. The USSR was weakening, but no one, Reagan included, expected to see it disappear only three years later. Reagan played an important role in putting the USSR on the defensive but his policies were not a major factor in the disintegration of the country, which occurred through a combination of systemic weaknesses and mistakes by Gorbachev and his team.

GEORGE H. W. BUSH

It fell to Reagan's successor in the White House to preside over the final act of the Cold War. George Bush deflected almost until the end the appeals of some in his administration to encourage the breakup of the union. When the Berlin

Wall fell, Bush avoided dancing on it, but he exploited weakness and indecision on the Soviet side to advance the Western agenda on a range of Cold War disputes.

During the August coup, Bush overcame previous doubts about Yeltsin and provided important support to the Russian leader's courageous resistance. But it was not until the eve of the December 1 Ukrainian independence vote that Bush gave up on Gorbachev and what were by then his hopeless efforts to preserve some kind of union. After the USSR disappeared US diplomacy helped encourage Soviet republics to take the political steps that turned imperial collapse into a "peaceful divorce" and set the stage for another round of brilliant negotiation by James Baker to contain the dangers of nuclear proliferation. But the way the US and other Western countries rushed in to help create the trappings of independent state structures in former Soviet republics ended up looking to many in Moscow like an effort to build a wall around Russia, and helped plant the seeds of anti-Western resentment that Putin later exploited.

Bush refrained from exploiting Soviet weakness almost until the end but he also resisted providing economic assistance. Gorbachev does not conceal his bitterness over Western failure to provide aid after what he saw as major moves in the direction of the West. But Gorbachev failed to understand the rules of the game. Gorbachev successfully extracted billions of deutschmarks in assistance from German Chancellor Kohl as the price for unification. Had he really wanted to condition moves in other areas to the provision of Western aid, he should have made the link explicit and then settled down for a long, and probably ultimately unsuccessful, negotiation.

It was in many ways a tragedy that the West was unable to use its immense resources to aid the transition of the USSR into a democratic, market society. There were definitely things that could have been done more generously, for example, a more forgiving approach toward the repayment of the USSR's external debt. But the impetus for change in any country has to come from within, and Gorbachev never managed to devise, let alone actually implement, a lasting strategy for economic reform.

In retrospect, 1990 was the watershed year. At the December 1989 Malta summit Bush outlined a program of institutional measures that could have begun the process of integrating the USSR into Western political and economic institutions and provided a framework for significant economic assistance had there been a Soviet administration capable of using it. Had Gorbachev adopted and implemented the Five Hundred Days or some other viable plan for market reform and had he come up with some way to quickly defuse growing centrifugal pressures while still retaining a functional central government, even the cautious Bush administration might well have been compelled to produce significant Western financial assistance. By torpedoing the Five Hundred Days and flirting with the use of force to block change, Gorbachev made it politically impossible for the West to provide aid, even if it had wanted to. And by the time Gorbachev shifted back to the center it was too late.

THE WISE MEN

The Cold War was a struggle between two systems, two ways of life, and two views of human value. In the early years of the Cold War, it was far from a foregone conclusion that the Western democracies would triumph, or even that some of them would remain democracies. The generation of postwar Western leaders on both sides of the Atlantic who rebuilt a devastated continent; created a prosperous, democratic and united Europe; and founded a strong and enduring military alliance of democratic nations laid the foundation for the triumph of the West more than four decades later. Now, a quarter of a century after the end of the Cold War, the absence of leaders of this stature on both sides of the Atlantic only emphasizes the importance of their role at the beginning of the conflict and the need for similar qualities of leadership if the United States and other democratic nations are to find the way to overcome emerging new global challenges, some of which have their origins in the failure of US and Western leaders to deal effectively with the consequences of the end of the Cold War.

Postscript

I am a child of the Cold War and that, no doubt, helps explain the fascination with Russia and the USSR which underlies this book. I grew up in the shadow of US-Soviet rivalry and the threat of nuclear holocaust that in the 1950s and early 1960s seemed to be perilously close. My father's army reserve division was mobilized at the time of the 1961 Berlin crisis and although he did not have to go for a third time to serve his country in war or crisis, he and I built a rudimentary fall-out shelter in one corner of the basement of our Kentucky home. Interest in my country's major international rival and the residue of my unforgettable first visit to the USSR undoubtedly helped push me into undergraduate and graduate study of Russian history and society.

Despite the best efforts of the Soviet authorities to wall off foreign diplomats, while living for six years in Moscow and visiting it more times than I can remember, I developed a real affection for the people of the Soviet Union and for the Russian language and culture. Over the years and in the course of countless meetings and events—many routine and boring; some, to be honest, angering; but others electrifying and even inspiring—I also developed a sense of respect for the Soviet officials on the other side of the divide. In later years, as Cold War tensions relaxed and rivalry gradually changed into cooperation, respect evolved into mutual regard and even at times into friendship.

These memories underlie the sense of lost opportunity that prevails as I bring this book to a close. In the early 1990s Russia seemed poised to rejoin the world community from which the Bolshevik revolution had separated it. The new Russia appeared to have chosen a future path toward democracy and a liberal market-based economy. Although it soon became clear that Russia's transition away from Communism would be longer and more difficult than anyone expected it was still possible to look on the future with hope.

In the summer of 1994, as I was ending my three-year tour in Moscow and in keeping with a Foreign Service tradition, I sent to Washington a cable with my own personal thoughts about what might be expected in Russia's future. Titled "My Way" in allusion to the Sinatra song and to Gorbachev spokesman Gennadiy Gerasimov's use of the phrase to explain Gorbachev's relaxed approach toward the 1989 East European revolutions, its basic premise as I recall (I do not have the text of the classified cable) was that Russia would find its own path to future development. A return to old-style Soviet Communism was out of the question as was the wholesale and uncritical acceptance of all aspect of Western democracy. The future would probably be more restrictive than we would like but it would also preserve much of the openness in information, travel, personal choice, and other aspects of daily life that Russians were embracing with various degrees of enthusiasm and responsibility.

In the early years of this millennium when I began to research this book, before the project was sidelined for a decade by my return to my other area of foreign service specialization, the Balkans where I was one of the founders of the American University in Kosovo, it was still possible to retain some degree of hope about Russia's future. Putin seemed to be a classic Russian *gosudarstvennik* or man of the state, and rebuilding effective state institutions after the chaos and corruption of the Yeltsin era was clearly necessary. Putin tamed the corrupt oligarchs, albeit with some highly questionable methods. Buoyed by high oil prices Putin brought a certain surface stability and prosperity to at least part of Russian society. A middle class developed in Moscow and a few other cities. But Putin used the era of high energy prices to enrich himself and his corrupt associates. He failed to restructure the Russian economic system at the same time he eviscerated the institutions of the political system, leaving behind the façade of democracy but little of the reality.

As this book appears, a quarter century after the end of the Cold War, Putin enjoys broad popular support for a corrupt and authoritarian regime and polls show large numbers of Russians with nostalgia for the certainties of the Communist era. The regime's xenophobic Russian nationalism and rabid anti-Westernism offer little hope for the future of the Russian people and presents a demonstrated threat to Russia's neighbors.

Studying history is like reading a novel from back to front. We know the outcome before we begin. Living through history is different. The shape of the future is always uncertain and often turns out to be full of surprises. It is important to remember this fact in looking at post-Soviet Russia, where debate has often been dominated by finger-pointing about who is responsible for an outcome that almost no one is satisfied with, albeit often for different reasons.

It is impossible to understand Putin's Russia without also understanding the effect of the end of the Cold War on the country, its people, and their rulers. In considering this phenomenon, it is worth contemplating what might have happened if events had broken the other way and if the US had experienced roughly analogous consequences to Cold War defeat. It is hardly likely that the American people would have welcomed an outcome that saw their political system discredited and replaced by models from abroad, the country itself broken up into several weak and mutually antagonistic independent states, their standard of living drastically diminished, and former international allies eagerly embracing the victors from the East. It is quite possible that under these circumstances the American people would have come to view their now triumphant rivals with anger and resentment and looked back to the Cold War with some nostalgia.

Vladimir Putin, who in an April 2005 speech to the Russian people described the demise of the Soviet Union as the "major geopolitical catastrophe of the [twentieth] century," finds it convenient to shift the blame for Russia's current problems onto foreign enemies, especially the United States.[1] Ultimately, however, the Russians, like any other people, are responsible for their own history. In the post-Soviet era, the Yeltsin reform team obviously made mistakes. It failed to take control of the central banking system until it was too late, which allowed inflation to erode the standard of living for masses of Russians, made a mockery of the compensation people received for privatization of Soviet-era state enterprises, and undermined popular support for the new system the Yeltsin team sought to introduce.

What follows are some reflections on my own experience in the years immediately after 1991. In the summer of 1994, on my final weekend in Moscow, I strolled around the city snapping the pictures I had been too busy to take in the previous three years including new phenomena impossible to imagine under Communist rule such as the Russian capital's first Rolls-Royce dealership. But, underneath the surface glitz that was just starting to emerge for the enjoyment of a privileged few, the reality of transition for the many had turned out to be savings and pensions wiped out by inflation, jobs lost as Soviet-era institutions disappeared or lingered in irrelevancy, and daily lives blighted by crime and corruption.

One evening that spring I was jogging beside the Moscow River along an embankment where a line of seedy boats offered dubious entertainments to those with the money to pay. An obviously drunk woman lurched into me and almost knocked me down. Her heavy makeup and flashy clothes seemed to announce her profession but as I disentangled myself I saw that she was really a young girl, looking no more than twelve years old. When I offered to help she staggered off into the night behind a stream of profanity that far outpaced my Russian vocabulary in that field. As I continued on my way a policeman who had seen the entire incident and was aware that I was a foreigner remarked in a distinctly unfriendly tone, "That's our reality now."

From my perspective, the critical shift in the post-Soviet political environment came in October 1993, when Yeltsin successfully crushed a hard-line rebellion that came perilously close to seizing key institutions in the Russian capital. Yeltsin had little choice but to use force after his opponents launched an armed uprising but the tragic experience of sending tanks into the streets to shell fellow Russians left him politically weakened and personally damaged by his own demons of depression and alcohol dependency.

Two days after the October fighting, I accompanied newly arrived Ambassador Pickering to his first meeting with Yeltsin. The upper floors of the ruined Russian White House were still smoldering, but the Kremlin remained an island of tranquility. Yeltsin received us in the large ceremonial office around the corner from his private working quarters, where most of the drama of the previous two weeks had played out. He seemed tired and subdued. He walked stiffly, and although he moved briskly through the items on his agenda his speech was slow and his words slurred. His face was puffy and his eyes seemed almost swollen into slits; he looked much worse than I had ever seen him before.

When Yeltsin acknowledged that eighty people had died within the White House, he seemed to experience real physical pain. Yeltsin expressed appreciation for the public support he had received during the crisis from President Clinton. Perhaps revealing more than he intended, Yeltsin said that Clinton's support was especially valued because it came when the outcome of the crisis was still uncertain.[2]

Two months later Yeltsin, who had never before lost an election in Russia, probably allowed the results of a vote to be falsified to ensure adoption of a new constitution creating a strong presidential system that encouraged Yeltsin's growing authoritarian predilections. A year later came the crucial turning point in Russia's post-Communist history: Yeltsin's decision to launch the disastrous war in Chechnya, which broke the political back of the Russian reform movement and marked the beginning of the ascent of security forces onto the center of the political stage.

Over the period 1991–94, I ended up as an informal point of contact with the Chechen rebels, who declared independence in the fall of 1991 and for the next three years carved out a de facto separate entity. I visited Chechnya several times for meetings with self-styled president Djokar Dudayev and others. What the Chechens wanted was some form of recognition by the United States. In addition to the usual arguments based on the will of the people in favor of self-determination, the Chechens, with little previous experience in the diplomatic game, sometimes tried out unorthodox arguments. On one occasion, Dudayev leaned toward me and whispered in the late-night gloom of his cavernous two-story office at the top of what had been the headquarters of the region's Communist party organization, "We have nuclear weapons." On another occasion a burly Chechen visitor to my home in Moscow, getting impatient with diplomatic discourse, interrupted with an impassioned plea. The Russians, he said, accuse Chechens of having a Mafia-style organization. Well, he said, "It's true. We Chechens are everywhere. Just what is it you Americans want? We can deliver it. Is it Yeltsin?" He added for effect, I assume, that if what we wanted was the Russian president "with the nuclear briefcase on his wrist," that could be arranged.

None of these arguments for US engagement in the Russian dispute with Chechnya proved persuasive, although Dudayev's claim of possessing nuclear weapons provoked a secret investigation until it was proved that what the Chechens really had was some innocuous equipment left over from long-evacuated Soviet-era missile bases. US interest was in a peaceful, democratic, and united Russia. There was no way the US was going to encourage separatism in Chechnya, lest it spread and lead to further violence in nuclear-armed Russia.

In retrospect, however, looking at the enormous human and political costs associated with Russia's efforts to crush Chechen separatism through military force, it is to be regretted that we did not engage in some fashion with both sides to try to defuse the conflict before it erupted into tragic violence. There were some in Chechnya who questioned Dudayev's approach of seeking full political independence from Russia. Pointing to the strategy successfully pursued by Tatarstan, another oil-rich Muslim-majority region in Russia, some Chechens argued for focusing on securing control over their own resources. A US initiative to try to encourage the Russians and the Chechens to reach an accommodation might well have failed, but it could hardly have led to a worse outcome than what actually transpired. Without seeking to exaggerate my own modest role, I regret that I never recommended such a course.

Almost everyone involved in Russia after the Soviet collapse—Russians as well as foreigners—underestimated the extent of the political, economic, and social difficulties that needed to be overcome. To some extent, this was a consequence of the structure of the Soviet system itself, where basic information was either lacking or falsified. No one really understood, for example, how large and intractable the massive Soviet military-industrial complex was and how difficult, or in many cases impossible, it would be to find ways to restructure it into more productive uses.

Similarly, everyone underestimated the difficulty in establishing a viable democratic system in a society where it had never existed before. Institutions were created and elections were held, but a genuine democratic culture, founded on toleration, compromise, and rule of law could not be created overnight.

Both Russian reformers and their Western supporters overpromised and underperformed. Largely for domestic political reasons, US administrations exaggerated the size and significance of American assistance. Russians received a lot of advice, almost all of it well meaning and some of it good, but too much of it amounted to applying outside models to stubborn Russian reality. Russians were capable of devising democratic solutions to their own problems—for example, in Nizhniy Novgorod, under the leadership of Boris Nemtsov, one of the last of the 1990s reformers to remain true to his ideals—probably why he was tragically murdered in 2015.

Gorbachev spent the last several years of his rule pleading for financial assistance and ended up bitter about the failure of his Western friends to respond. A case could be made for massive, Marshall Plan–type Western assistance in Gorbachev's last couple of years. At the very least it would have made it more difficult to support subsequent claims of outside malevolence. But Western leaders were probably wise in not opening their checkbooks, in view of Gorbachev's failure to implement a credible program of economic reform and the way foreign resources transferred to the USSR tended to vanish, as Gorbachev himself admitted.

But Boris Yeltsin did have a plan, and he implemented it in a courageous, if ultimately flawed, fashion. Failure to support Yeltsin effectively was the key Western mistake of the immediate post-Soviet era. What the Russians primarily got was insistence that they follow an economic model whose emphasis on fiscal balance was pursued with a single-mindedness that left insufficient scope for creating new productive resources. As Europe is discovering in the second decade of the twenty-first century, there are practical and political limits to how far governments can go in cutting budgets, if insufficient attention is paid to increasing output.

In the field of national security, the United States could never decide whether its primary objective was to help create a democratic and confident Russia as a full partner in the post–Cold War world or to build up the former Soviet states as independent counters to a possibly resurgent Moscow. The US ended up trying to do both and accomplishing neither well.

The two key security challenges the West faced in the decade after the Soviet collapse were dealing with the nuclear legacy and devising security architecture to meet the challenges of the post–Cold War environment. By and large, the US and Russia engaged effectively in the nuclear arena, where they had a clear common interest, with the conspicuous exception of ballistic-missile defense. Numbers of nuclear weapons were dramatically reduced and the two countries cooperated for many years to enhance security for Russian nuclear weapons, at least until Putin canceled the Nunn-Lugar assistance program that was the foundation of this cooperative effort.

Russia and the United States had an obvious mutual interest in eliminating nuclear weapons from the former Soviet republics, and over the period 1991 to 1994 I met frequently with Russian diplomatic and military officials on these matters. On one occasion, the US defense attaché and I were called to meet with a senior officer in the Russian Strategic Rocket Force, who asked for our help in persuading Ukraine to allow Russian personnel to carry out regular maintenance on SS-18 ICBMs located on Ukrainian territory, including replacing radioactive tritium in the missile warheads, which was necessary to maintain their yield—and their stability. We passed the message back to Washington and eventually Russian technicians were allowed access. Joint resolution of this problem was an example of unprecedented cooperation between the two former nuclear rivals. But it seems unlikely that the Russian officer, who had spent most of his professional life in the Soviet military, could have welcomed the necessity of seeking American help to resolve a problem with weapons formerly at the heart of the Soviet strategic missile force.

In February 1992, I accompanied Secretary Baker in an unprecedented visit to one of the major Soviet centers of nuclear weapons design, Chelyabinsk 70. Formerly one of the most highly secret facilities in the USSR, its existence was concealed behind a post office number, and the several thousand personnel who worked there lived in virtually complete isolation from the rest of the country. To get there the secretary's party drove for over an hour out of Yekaterinburg, turned onto an unmarked road, and drove several miles into a dense forest, passing through three concentric lines of impressive security fencing. Entering the complex of yellow brick multistory buildings, we saw that almost every window was packed with people, many in white coats. Some were smiling and waving; others seemed more reserved, perhaps caught up in the incongruity of the event.

Baker met the center's senior scientists in a small auditorium. Speaking with an obvious effort to maintain his own and his country's dignity, the director acknowledged that with Russian defense spending being cut the center needed to reorient some of its efforts to civilian production. He stressed that the center was not seeking handouts but was eager to cooperate on a commercial basis with Western partners. He and his colleagues made brief presentations on projects they thought might be attractive—industrial diamonds, fiber optics, and nuclear medical equipment—somewhat in the manner of a bazaar merchant laying out wares before prospective buyers. Later, US and Russian nuclear specialists found ways to cooperate through a joint science center in Moscow, but the psychological cost of this performance to Soviet defense scientists must have been significant.

On security architecture, the Western response was to extend the existing Cold War system of military and economic alliances eastward, rejecting—and probably with good reason—the alternative model of creating a new system. In many ways, this approach has been a success. Incorporating former Communist countries of Eastern Europe into NATO and the EU has been good for those countries and for the broader political, economic, and security environment across Europe. Conspicuously absent from the new system, however, is Russia, which ended up being left on the outside as the boundaries of the West expanded up to—and in the case of the Baltics, into—the borders of the former USSR.

When Vice President Gore visited Moscow in 1993, we in the political section of the US embassy in Moscow briefed him on what would likely be the sharply negative reaction in Russia to the expansion of NATO into the former Eastern European satellites of the USSR, a move that was already gaining political momentum in the United States. After the briefing, one of Gore's aides asked us to send the information to the State Department, saying "we need that in Washington." We duly sent it in and, although our missive was surely not the only reason, the Clinton administration decided initially against NATO expansion, choosing instead to invite Eastern European countries into a kind of halfway house partnership with the alliance.

Later the administration reversed itself and encouraged Poland, Hungary, and the Czech Republic to become NATO members in 1999. In 1997, by then serving as the head of the State Department's analytical office for the former Soviet Union, I spent a week in Moscow at a seminar devoted to NATO expansion. In tones that ranged from pleading to anger, Russian diplomats, politicians, and journalists, many of whom I had known during my earlier tours in Moscow, warned that the expansion of NATO into countries that only a few years earlier had been part of the Soviet security zone would strengthen the already strong resentment against the West that was boosting the rise of xenophobia and authoritarianism across the Russian political spectrum.

Opposition in Moscow does not, of course, necessarily mean that NATO expansion was wrong. Membership in NATO and the European Union has been critical in integrating former Eastern European Communist regions into a united and democratic Europe. But the failure to work out some mutually acceptable form of cooperation between NATO and Russia, whether membership or something else, was a major setback. Russia itself bears much of the blame for this failure. Its threatening posture to its neighbors, aggressive intelligence activities, and the questionable caliber of some Russian officials sent to NATO headquarters in Brussels left the impression that Moscow had little interest in ending East-West confrontation. Nevertheless, anyone seeking to understand why Putin has enjoyed such success in Russia should start with the sense of humiliation many Russians feel at the image of NATO forces perched along borders that once formed part of the internal boundaries of the Soviet Union.

Moscow's sudden fall from superpower status, although inevitable in some ways since the USSR was, in reality, only a superpower in the military sense, was unsettling to Russians who more than most people tend to identify their own personal status and well-being with the power of the state. In the early 1990s, many democratically inclined Russians were willing to accept the loss of empire, and some even understood that ending a repressive dominion over other peoples was necessary for rebuilding Russia as a truly democratic state. But all Russians expected that their country would be treated as an equal partner in the international arena and resented it when this did not happen.

A relatively trivial example of this phenomenon, which I happened to witness, occurred during a meeting in Geneva in September 1995 of the international "contact group" dealing with the war in Bosnia. A talented US team led by Richard Holbrooke had just completed an intense round of shuttle diplomacy that produced a short statement of principles that became the basis for the later Dayton Agreement ending the war. When one member of the contact group began to suggest alterations, Holbrooke warned that any changes to the text, which had been painfully agreed to by the warring parties, could cause the deal to come unglued. Holbrooke's remark prompted the Russian member of the contact group, Deputy Foreign Minister Igor Ivanov, later foreign minister, to ask whether the US objected to the group reading the text before they approved it. Holbrooke's posture reflected the realities of the negotiating process and Ivanov's remark was intended more as a sarcastic aside than substantive objection but the accumulation of similar instances over the years eventually took its toll.

In a widely remarked speech at the inaugural summit of the Organization for Security and Cooperation in Europe (OSCE) in Budapest in December 1994, Yeltsin stunned the assembled heads of state, including President Clinton, by delivering a tough and emotional speech in which he warned that "Europe, not having yet freed itself from the heritage of the Cold War, is in danger of plunging into a cold peace." Listeners including myself heard the bitterness in Yeltsin's voice as he declaimed, "It is a dangerous delusion to suppose that the destinies of continents and the world community in general can somehow be managed from one single capital." Yeltsin's warning was dismissed at the time, but had it been given a more sympathetic hearing many future problems might well have been avoided.[3]

I will end this book as I began it, with the signing in January 1993 of the START II Treaty, which mandated the most sweeping reductions in nuclear weapons ever achieved up to that time. When high-level teams were not meeting, I served as the contact with the chief Russian negotiator, who often lamented to me that the absence of the Soviet-era "Big Five" backstopping group made it difficult to engage the Russian military in the talks. The men in uniform seemed primarily to criticize from the side and, learning to play aspects of the democracy game quickly, to get friends in the Russian parliament to join in the criticism. For a time, it seemed that internal opposition to the deal was so strong that the Yeltsin administration might prove unwilling to sign. The logjam was broken when the US "reminded" Moscow that if there was no START II agreement the United States would maintain its nuclear forces at the higher levels allowed by START I, which the Russians could not afford to do.

To Soviet-era military personnel who remembered the painful sacrifices associated with building the Soviet strategic arsenal, the optics of START II looked bad. Russia would be required to give up all MIRVed ICBMs including the SS-18 heavies, a central US objective since the inception of arms-control negotiations. But Russian critics of START II often ignored the fact that missiles eliminated by the treaty would reach the end of their service life over the term of the agreement. Russian experts calculated that START II would save the equivalent of approximately seven billion dollars over its lifetime.

START II was a good deal for both sides, but it also reflected the realities of the time. The United States took advantage of the strong position it occupied and this perception is one reason why the treaty never entered into force. After it was signed, Ambassador Strauss told his good friend the secretary of state, "Baker, you didn't leave those folks enough on the table." It was a shrewd remark that might serve as a good summation of US policy toward Russia in the years immediately after the collapse of the Soviet Union.

Twenty-five years after the end of the Cold War, it is time to move on. Understanding the missed opportunities on both sides that accompanied the aftermath of that global struggle does not mean ignoring the domestic repression and external aggression that characterize the Putin regime. Still less does it suggest walling off Russia into an isolated international ghetto. The West needs to show Putin that aggression in Ukraine and adventure in Syria and elsewhere cannot succeed and will have costs. At the same time, it is important to leave open a path for integrating Moscow into the Western community of nations. This will be difficult and require compromises on both sides, but it is not impossible. The Western statesmen who forged victory in the Cold War a quarter century ago made a start; their successors should be able to continue it.

Chapter 1: First Visit to the USSR

1. I should add that never again, in six years of living in the USSR and dozens of visits, did I bring in illicit rubles so, perhaps, the border guard's lecture did some good.

2. For a description of life at MGU by an American graduate student who was much more deeply immersed in Russian life and language than I was at the time, see *Moscow Stories*, by Loren Graham (Bloomington: Indiana University Press, 2006), who went on to become one of the foremost American scholars on Soviet science. When he arrived at MGU Graham found in his room a long list of forbidden activities, including eating, drinking, singing, rowdy behavior, and keeping pets. Graham soon discovered that raucous, alcohol-suffused parties occurred almost every evening, with the Komsomol (Young Communist) activist who was supposed to enforce the rules usually locking himself in his room. Graham concluded that "this divergence between official policy and real life was my first lesson that existence under Soviet 'totalitarianism' was not quite as regimented as we in the West were led to believe."

   On the interest in JFK and the Beatles in late 1960s Russia, see Donald J. Raleigh, *Soviet Baby Boomers: An Oral History of Russia's Cold War Generation* (Oxford: Oxford University Press, 2012), a fascinating study of the lives of sixty Soviets who graduated from two elite English-language high schools specializing in Moscow and Saratov. Raleigh found that for this generation, JFK and the Beatles occupied a special place. Despite the tough US-Soviet confrontations of that era, Soviet people tended to find JFK "irresistible." As for the Beatles, one of the individuals Raleigh interviewed said simply, "The Beatles are sacred. . . . We grew up on them." For this generation of Soviet youth—the first not to experience war, revolution, or mass purges—interest in the Beatles was a way of identifying with a larger global youth culture as well as a first, cautious way of stepping away from the official ideology— with consequences that became more evident later.

Chapter 2: Leonid Brezhnev

1. Brezhnev remains one of the least studied Soviet leaders. Still the best post-Soviet biographical treatment is in Dmitri Volkogonov's *Autopsy for an Empire: The Seven Leaders Who Built the Soviet Regime*. An outstanding short introduction to the Brezhnev era is *The Soviet Union under Brezhnev*, by William Tompson. A scholarly overview of the period, *Brezhnev Reconsidered*, edited by Edwin Bacon and Mark Sandle, begins a process of reconsidering his role. Vladislav M. Zubok's *A Failed Empire: The Soviet Union in the Cold War from Stalin to Gorbachev* provides an insightful and thoroughly researched perspective on the USSR's path through the Cold War in the Brezhnev era. Jonathan Haslam's *Russia's Cold War: From the October Revolution to the Fall of the Wall* provides a solid account of Soviet foreign policy in this era and afterward, drawing on Soviet sources.

2. R. Medvedev, *Lichnost i Epokha*, 104.

3. R. Medvedev, *Lichnost i Epokha*, 108.

4. R. Medvedev, *Lichnost i Epokha*, 124.

5. Grishin, *Ot Khrushcheva do Gorbacheva*, 77.

6. Fetisov, *Premier Izvestni i Neizvestni*, 10–19, 202.

7. Pikhoya, *Sovetskii Soyuz*, 251.

8. R. Medvedev, *Lichnost i Epokha*, 120; Fetisov, *Premier Izvestni i Neizvestni*, 130–38.

9. Pikhoya, *Sovetskii Soyuz*, 248–50.

10. Tompson, *The Soviet Union under Brezhnev*, 69–72.

11. Pikhoya, *Sovetskii Soyuz*, 253.

12. Tompson, *The Soviet Union under Brezhnev*, 23–24.

13. Korniyenko, *Kholodnaya Voina*, 114.

14. Powell, *My American Life*, 354.

15. Dobrynin, *In Confidence*, 531.

16. Gelman, *The Brezhnev Politburo and the Decline of Détente*, 74–82.

17. Herspring, *The Soviet High Command*, 51–52.

18. Zaloga, *The Kremlin's Nuclear Sword*, 101.

19. Yu. D. Maslyukov and Ye. S. Glubokov, "Planirovanie i Finantsirovanie Voennoi Promyshlenosti v SSSR," in *Sovetskaya Voyennaya Moshch ot Stalina do Gorbacheva* [Soviet military might, from Stalin to Gorbachev], ed. A. V. Minayev, 105. Maslyukov asserts that his article provided the first true public data on Soviet military spending. He also says that CIA estimates on Soviet military spending were relatively accurate. Maslyukov's figures are lower than those cited by some other Soviet specialists after the Soviet collapse.

20. Interview with Col. Vitaliy Tsigichko in December 1990. This is one of a series of revealing interviews with senior Soviet military personnel, at a time when they were probably uniquely willing to speak openly, conducted by a Russian-speaking US military officer for the firm BDM on behalf of the Pentagon's Office of Net Assessment. They were declassified many years later and are available on the "Nuclear Vault" section of the website of the National Security Archive, at http://nsarchive .gwu/nukevault/ebb285/index.htm. Also see Ellman and Kontorovich, *The Destruction of the Soviet Economic System*, 121.

21. Podvig, *Russian Strategic Nuclear Forces*, 6–7.

22. Zaloga, *The Kremlin's Nuclear Sword*, 118.

23. Blacker, *Hostage to Revolutions*, 11, 30.

24. Podvig, *Russian Strategic Nuclear Forces*, 11–12.

25. Zaloga, *The Kremlin's Nuclear Sword*, 135–36.

26. Blacker, *Hostage to Revolution*, 49.

27. Utkin and Mozhorin, "Raketnoe i Kosmicheskoe Vooruzhenie," in Minayev, *Sovetskaya Voyennaya Moshch ot Stalina do Gorbacheva*, 231–37.

28. On the missile civil war, also see Detinov and Savleyev, *The Big Five*, 18–19. BDM interviews, especially those with Mozzhorin and Col. Gen. Igor Illarionov, a longtime aide to Ustinov. Katayev, *Memoir of the Missile Age*, 152–58.

Chapter 3: Repression and Resistance

1. Mihajlov, *Moscow Summer*, 20, 168.

2. Feifer, *Moscow Farewell*, 226, 205.

3. Zubok, *Zhivago's Children*, 271.

4. R. Medvedev, *Portret Brezhneva*, 176.

5. Pikhoya, *Sovetsky Soyuz*, 254.

6. Pikhoya, *Sovetsky Soyuz*, 321.

7. English, *Russia and the Idea of the West*, 110; Sakharov, *Memoirs*, 282; Alekseyeva and Goldberg, *The Thaw Generation*, 211.

8. Pikhoya, *Sovetsky Soyuz*, 304.

9. Brutents, *Tridtsat Let na Staroi Ploshchadi*, 238–40.

10. Bukovskiy, *To Build a Castle*, 146; Rubenstein, *Soviet Dissidents*, 17–21.

11. Alekseyeva and Goldberg, *The Thaw Generation*, 108.

12. Alekseyeva and Goldberg, *The Thaw Generation*, 108.

13. R. Medvedev, *Portret Brezhneva*, 240. Alekseyeva, *Istoriya Inakomysliya v SSSR*, 240; Zubok, *Zhivago's Children*, 262.

14. Alekseyeva and Goldberg, *The Thaw Generation*, 138.

15. Van Het Reve, *Dear Comrade*, xv; Alekseyeva and Goldberg, *The Thaw Generation*, 255; Rubenstein, *Soviet Dissidents*, 71–75.

16. Shlapentokh, *A Normal Totalitarian Society*, 161.

17. Sharansky, *Fear No Evil*, xvii.

18. Sharansky, *Fear No Evil*, xviii.

19. Beckerman, *When They Come for Us, We'll Be Gone*, 104.

20. Applebaum, 2000. Komaromi, "The Material Existence of Samizdat," 606.

21. Alekseyeva and Goldberg, *The Thaw Generation*, 206; Reddaway, *Uncensored Russia*, 26.

22. Alekseyeva, *Istoriya Inakomysliya v SSSR*; Rubenstein, *Soviet Dissidents*; Reddaway, *Uncensored Russia*.

23. Lourie, *Sakharov: A Biography*, 187–89.

24. Sakharov, Memoirs, 215–17.

25. Sakharov, *My Country and the World*, 11.

26. Sakharov, *My Country and the World*, 12.

27. Sakharov, *Memoirs*, 390; Lourie, *Sakharov: A Biography*, 257.

28. Solzhenitsyn was unaware that the illness—which at the time he attributed to sunstroke—was caused by poison until after the Soviet collapse, when a KGB participant described the operation in the muckraking Russian journal *Soversheno Sekretno* (Top secret). In his memoir, *Invisible Allies*, Solzhenitsyn reprints the testimony of the KGB officer involved. Russian reporters, in that outstanding but tragically brief era of Russian journalistic courage and independence, also interviewed the doctors who treated Solzhenitsyn. Also see the *Washington Post* and the *Guardian* of April 21 and 22, 1992.

29. Alekseyeva, *Istoriya Inakomysliya v SSSR*, 293; Shlapentokh, *Soviet Intellectuals and Political Power*, 145.

30. Andrew and Mitrokhin, *The Sword and the Shield*, 311.

31. R. Medvedev, *Gensek S Lubyanki*, 50; Kozlov, Fitzpatrick, and Mironenko, *Sedition: Everyday Resistance*, 57.

32. Andrew and Mitrokhin, *The Sword and the Shield*, 311; Andrew and Gordiyevsky, *KGB: The Inside Story*, 487; R. Medvedev, *Gensek S Lubyanki*, 53, 63.

33. Bobkov, *KGB I Vlast*, 193; Andrew and Gordiyevsky, *KGB: The Inside Story*, 489.

34. Alekseyeva, *Istoriya Inakomysliya v SSSR*, 284–87; Rubenstein, *Soviet Dissidents*, 119–25, 140–45.

35. KGB Memo to the Central Committee, December 29, 1975, No. 3213A. Obtained from the Volkogonov file in the manuscript division of the Library of Congress. Also available in the Volkogonov collections of the National Security Archive.

36. Rubenstein and Gribanov, *The KGB File of Andrei Sakharov*, 210.

Chapter 4: The Nixon Years

1. Among the huge number of books on Richard Nixon, Stephen Ambrose's three-volume biography stands out for its comprehensiveness, its efforts to be objective about a man about which few can pretend to be objective, and its readability. A recent one-volume biography is Conrad Black's *Richard M. Nixon: A Life in Full*. Raymond L. Garthoff's *Détente and Confrontation: US-Soviet Relations from Nixon to Reagan* is comprehensive and erudite in covering Nixon's approach toward Moscow but is better at exposing the flaws than revealing the successes of US policy.

2. Kissinger, *White House Years*, 129.

3. *Soviet-American Relations: The Détente Years, 1969–1972*, 4–6 (hereafter *Relations*). This extraordinary volume, jointly published by the State Department and the Russian Foreign Ministry, includes US and Soviet records of all the meetings and telephone calls in the Kissinger-Dobrynin back channel and of all top-level meetings among Nixon, Kissinger, and the Soviet leadership through the May 1972 Moscow summit. Unless otherwise noted, it is the source for material dealing with these meetings.

4. Caldwell, "Going Steady: The Kissinger-Dobrynin Channel," 34.

5. Dobrynin, *In Confidence*, 205.

6. *Relations*, 20–25.

7. *Relations*, 86–100.

8. Nixon, *RN: The Memoirs of Richard Nixon*, 405–7.

9. Haslam, *Russia's Cold War*, 261.

10. Nixon, *RN: The Memoirs of Richard Nixon*, 497.

11. Dobrynin, *In Confidence*, 214.

12. Dobrynin, *In Confidence*, 214.

13. The American Presidency Project, http://www.presidency.ucsb.edu/ws/?pid=3016.

14. G. Smith, *Doubletalk*, 223–25.

15. *Relations*, 394.

16. Nixon, *RN: The Memoirs of Richard Nixon*, 544; Chen, *Mao's China and the Cold War*, 238, 245.

17. Kissinger memo to Nixon, July 14, 171, from National Security Archive Briefing Book 66, http://nsarchive.gwu.edu/NSAEBB/NSAEBB66/ch-40.pdf.

18. Kissinger memo to Nixon, July 14, 171, from National Security Archive Briefing Book 66, http://nsarchive.gwu.edu/NSAEBB/NSAEBB66/ch-40.pdf.

19. Arbatov, *The System*, 174.

20. Aleksandrov-Agentov, *Ot Kollontai do Gorbacheva*, 217.

21. Aksyutin, *L. I. Brezhnev*, 128–32.

22. Dobrynin, *In Confidence*, 233.

23. *Relations*, 422.

24. *Relations*, 441.

25. Dobrynin, *In Confidence*, 235.

26. Nixon, *RN: The Memoirs of Richard Nixon*, 586–91.

27. The US and Soviet records of Kissinger's secret meetings in Moscow in April 1972 can be found in *Relations*, 681–780. On Brezhnev and the Second World War see 684.

28. *Relations*, 615–780.

29. *Relations*, 687.

30. *Relations*, 687.

31. Nixon, *RN: The Memoirs of Richard Nixon*, 594.

32. Nixon, *RN: The Memoirs of Richard Nixon*, 594; Kissinger, *White House Years*, 1189.

33. Pape, *Bombing to Win*, 197–205, provides data on the effects of the US bombing campaign.

34. Korniyenko, *Kholodnaya Voina*, 146.

35. Aleksandrov-Agentov, *Ot Kollontai do Gorbacheva*, 223.

36. Nixon, *RN: The Memoirs of Richard Nixon*, 610; *Relations*, 831–36; "Salt II and the Growth of Mistrust" conference, 13–16.

37. *Relations*, 831–1004.

38. Barrass, *The Great Cold War*, 178.

39. ACDA 1990.

40. Collins, *US-Soviet Military Balance: Concepts and Capabilities, 1960–1980*, 459; May, Steinbrunner, and Wolfe, "History of the Strategic Arms Competition, 1945–1972," 733.

41. Barrass, *The Great Cold War*, 178, 190.

42. The official account of this meeting on Vietnam can be found in *Relations*, 886–95. An account which provides the full flavor of the rhetoric is in the memoirs of Brezhnev's assistant, Aleksandrov-Agentov, *Ot Kollontai do Gorbacheva*, 229.

43. Kissinger, *White House Years*, 1227.

44. *Relations*, 964.

45. Pikhoya, *Sovetskii Soyuz*, 343.

46. Kimball, *The Vietnam War Files*, 286.

47. BDM interviews.

48. Gaiduk, *The Soviet Union and the Vietnam War*, 250.

49. *Relations*, 912.

50. Bertsch, "US-Soviet Trade: A Sector of Mutual Benefit?"

51. FRUS 1972, 1217.

52. FRUS 1972, 1217.

53. Kissinger, *Years of Upheaval*, 249; Dobrynin, *In Confidence*, 273.

54. Aleksandrov-Agentov, *Ot Kollontai do Gorbacheva*, 230.

55. Dobrynin, *In Confidence*, 274.

56. Krasikov, "Declassified KGB Study Illuminates Early Years of Soviet Jewish Emigration."

57. On the negotiations aimed at getting around the Jackson-Vanik amendment, see Kissinger, *Years of Upheaval*, 985–98.

58. Dobrynin, *In Confidence*, 286.

59. Dobrynin, *In Confidence*, 286.

60. Sukhodrev, *Yazik Moi-Drug Moi*, 303.

61. V. Medvedev, *Chelovek za Spinoi*, 108; Dobrynin, *In Confidence*, 287.

62. Kissinger, *Years of Upheaval*, 300; Dobrynin, *In Confidence*, 290.

Chapter 5: A Tale of Two Cities

1. Dobrynin, *In Confidence*, 324.

2. Ford, *A Time to Heal*, 184.

3. Nitze, *From Hiroshima to Glasnost*, 334–36.

4. Interview with Ambassador Arthur Hartmann, who was present at Vladivostok, November 19, 2010.

5. Labrie, *SALT Handbook*.

6. Transcripts of the Vladivostok meetings are available online at the website of the Gerald Ford library, www.fordlibrarymuseum.gov/library/docur.

7. Korniyenko, *Kholodnaya Voina*, 158; Dobrynin, *In Confidence*, 335.

8. Ford, *A Time to Heal*, 218.

9. Ford, *A Time to Heal*, 218.

10. Chazov, *Zdorove I Vlast*, 128; V. Medvedev, *Chelovek za Spinoi*, 111.

11. Hyland, *Mortal Rivals*, 98.

12. Dobrynin, *In Confidence*, 355; Labrie, *SALT Handbook*; Hyland, *Mortal Rivals*, 103.

13. Labrie, *SALT Handbook*, 307; Hyland, *Mortal Rivals*, 103.

14. Labrie, *SALT Handbook*, 307; Burr, *The Kissinger Transcripts*, 426.

15. Hyland, *Mortal Rivals*, 128.

16. Ford, *A Time to Heal*, 300–303.

17. Ford, *A Time to Heal*, 300–303.

18. Ford, *A Time to Heal*, 300–303.

19. Aleksandrov-Agentov, *Ot Kollontai do Gorbacheva*, 227.

20. Hyland, *Mortal Rivals*, 114–18.

21. Burr, *The Kissinger Transcripts*, 334; Barrass, *The Great Cold War*, 199.

22. National Security Archive electronic briefing book on Helsinki.

23. Savranskaya, "Unintended Consequences," 183.

24. Adamyshin and Schifter, *Human Rights, Perestroika, and the End of the Cold War*, 153.

25. Bagley, *Spymaster*, 245.

26. Dobrynin, *In Confidence*, 351.

27. Interview with Leonov, April 21, 1999; available at the Mershon Institute for National Security Studies, Ohio State University.

28. Dobrynin, *In Confidence*, 351.

29. Alekseyeva, *Istoriya Inakomysliya v SSSR*, 310.

30. Alekseyeva, *Istoriya Inakomysliya v SSSR*, 310.

31. Sharanskiy, *Fear No Evil*, xxvii.

32. Amalrik, *Notes of a Revolutionary*, 312.

33. Orlov, *Dangerous Thoughts*, 188; Rubenstein, *Soviet Dissidents*, 216–19. Forty years later Dzhemilov was one of the leading opponents of Putin's illegal 2014 seizure of Crimea.

34. Alekseyeva, *Istoriya Inakomysliya v SSSR*, 310; interview with Ambassador Presel, Washington, DC, March 30, 2010.

35. Orlov, *Dangerous Thoughts*, 194.

36. Alekseyeva, *Istoriya Inakomysliya v SSSR*, 226, 313; Rubenstein, *Soviet Dissidents*, 231, 222–28.

37. Thomas, *The Helsinki Effect*, 131; KGB Report 2577A to the Central Committee, dated November 15, 1976; accessed through the National Security Archive Electronic briefing book on Helsinki.

38. Rubenstein, *Soviet Dissidents*, 238, 234.

39. Rubenstein, *Soviet Dissidents*, 259, 274; Alekseyeva, *Istoriya Inakomysliya v SSSR*, 342.

40. Interview with Ambassador Matlock, Princeton, NJ, September 14, 2011.

41. Rubenstein, *Soviet Dissidents*, 259, 274; Alekseyeva, *Istoriya Inakomysliya v SSSR*, 342.

42. Alekseyeva and Goldberg, *The Thaw Generation*, 207.

43. R. Medvedev, *Gensek S Lubyanki*, 77.

44. Kozlov, Fitzpatrick, and Mironenko, *Sedition*, 34, 45.

45. Pikhoya, *Sovetskii Soyuz*, 328.

46. Andropov's report, No. 3213-A, dated December 29, 1975, is in the Volkogonov File in the Library of Congress.

47. Adamyshin and Schifter, *Human Rights, Perestroika, and the End of the Cold War*, 112–14.

Chapter 6: The Unhappy Presidency of Jimmy Carter

1. Zelizer, *Jimmy Carter*, 51.

2. Bourne, *Jimmy Carter*, 383.

3. Brzezinski, *Power and Principle*, 57.

4. Conference on Global Competition, 1995, 192.

5. Dobrynin, *In Confidence*, 389.

6. The Carter-Brezhnev correspondence is widely available in reference works and online. They are available in FRUS, 1977–80, vol. 6; the Carter-Brezhnev Project, SALT II and the Growth of Mistrust. Carter's first letter to Brezhnev was sent on January 26, 1977, and Brezhnev's reply was received February 4, 1977, http://nsarchiv.gwu.edu/carterbrezhnev/docs_salt_ii.

7. Carter's February 15, 1977, letter to Brezhnev is available at http://nsarchiv.gwu.edu/carterbrezhnev/docs_salt_ii.

8. Conference on US-Soviet Relations, 1994, 12–14; Conference on Global Competition, 1995, 171.

9. Brezhnev's February 26, 1977 letter to Carter is available at http://nsarchiv.gwu.edu/carterbrezhnev/docs_salt_ii.

10. Brzezinski, *Power and Principle*, 151–56.

11. Dobrynin, *In Confidence*, 396.

12. Vance, *Hard Choices*, 52.

13. On "deep cuts" see Vance, *Hard Choices*, 52–54; Brzezinski, *Power and Principle*, 156–64; Talbott, *Endgame*, 69–75; Hyland, *Mortal Rivals*, 212–16; US Memcon of Vance-Gromyko March 28, 1977 meeting available at National Security Archive.

14. Conference on Salt II, 1994, 63. Conference on Global Competition, 1995, 172–73.

15. Memcon of the Vance-Gromyko meeting, March 28, 1977, was accessed in hard copy at the files of the National Security Archive located in the Gelman Library of the George Washington University.

16. Talbott, *Endgame*, 74.

17. Carter-Brezhnev Project, Conference on SALT II and the Growth of Mistrust, transcript, 64.

18. Arbatov, *The System*, 201.

19. Dobrynin, *In Confidence*, 399.

20. Soviet memcon of Gromyko's September 23, 1977, meeting with Carter (Zapis Osnovnogo Soderzhaniya Becedi AA Gromyko c Prezidentom Dzh. Karterom, 23 Sentyabr 1977 v Vashington) was accessed in the National Security Archive, Volkogonov file.

21. Rabbot, "The Debate over Détente."

22. Arbatov, *The System*, 188; Brutents, *Tridtsat Let na Staroi Ploshchadi*, 308.

23. On the Soviet engagement in southern Africa I drew heavily from the following: Major General V. A. Zolotarev, ed., *Rossiya (SSSR) V Lokalnikh Konfiktakh XX Veka*, an official history, drawing on Soviet military data, of Soviet engagement in Third Word conflicts across the Cold War. Shubin, *The Hot Cold War*. Shubin served for years on the Soviet Afro-Asian Solidarity Committee and from 1982–1989 headed the African section of the Central Committee International Department. Also Andrew and Mitrokhin, *The World Was Going Our Way*, 444, based on notes from KGB files Mitrokhin brought with him on his defection.

24. Westad, *The Global Cold War*, 233; Andrew and Mitrokhin, *The World Was Going Our Way*, 451.

25. Westad, *The Global Cold War*, 222, 230.

26. Zolotarev, *Rossiya (SSSR) V Lokalnikh*, 103–4; Kaplan, *Diplomacy of Power*, 587.

27. Andrew and Mitrokhin, *The World Was Going Our Way*, 453.

28. Arbatov, *The System*, 189.

29. Kaplan, *Diplomacy of Power*, 610, 613; Westad, *The Global Cold War*, 265.

30. Andrew and Mitrokhin, *The World Was Going Our Way*, 457.

31. Westad, *The Global Cold War*, 259.

32. Zolotarev, *Rossiya (SSSR) V Lokalnikh*, 109–10.

33. Kaplan, *Diplomacy of Power*, 622.

34. Westad, *The Global Cold War*, 277; Andrew and Mitrokhin, *The World Was Going Our Way*, 458.

35. Zolotarev, *Rossiya (SSSR) V Lokalnikh*, 110–15.

36. Nation, *Black Earth, Red Star*, 272.

37. Conference on Global Competition, 1995, 59.

38. Brutents, *Tridtsat Let na Staroi Ploshchadi*, 216; Andrew and Gordiyevsky, KGB: *The Inside Story*, 557.

39. Zolotarev, *Rossiya (SSSR) V Lokalnikh*, 99, 116; Conference on Middle East and Africa, 1994, 33.

40. Brzezinski, *Power and Principle*, 185.

41. Brzezinski, *Power and Principle*, 189.

42. The text of the speech is available at http://www.presidency.ucsb.edu/ws/?[id =3095].

43. Dobrynin, *In Confidence*, 417.

44. Dobrynin, *In Confidence*, 417.

45. Conference on SALT II, 1994, 130.

46. Sukhodrev, *Yazik Moi-Drug Moi*, 334.

47. Carter, *Keeping Faith*, 253.

48. Dobrynin, *In Confidence*, 429.

49. Carter, *Keeping Faith*, 260; Aleksandrov-Agentov, *Ot Kollontai do Gorbacheva*, 238; Sukhodrev, *Yazik Moi-Drug Moi*, 345.

50. Carter, *Keeping Faith*, 259.

51. Combs, *Inside the Soviet Alternative Universe*, 56.

52. National Security Archive electronic briefing book on Helsinki. Available at http://nsarchive.gwu.edu/NSAEBB/NSAEBB191/index.htm.

53. Interview with Gerber, September 16, 2011, in Washington, DC, and e-mail exchange, April 2015.

Chapter 7: Two Crises and an Olympiad

1. Pikhoya and Sokolov, *Istoriya Sovremennoi Rossii*, 95.

2. On the invasion of Afghanistan I have drawn primarily on the following: CWIHP e-Dossier No. 4, Documents on the Soviet Invasion of Afghanistan; Feifer, *The Great Gamble*, 55–84; Braithwaite, *Afgantsy*; Kuzichkin, *Inside the KGB*, 315; Lyakovskiy, *Tragediya i Doblest Afgana*, 61–136, 149–50; Andrew and Mitrokhin, *The World Was Going Our Way*, 386–402.

3. Lyakovskiy, *Tragediya i Doblest Afgana*, 110.

4. Feifer, *The Great Gamble*, 70.

5. Lyakovskiy, *Tragediya i Doblest Afgana*, 148.

6. RAN, "Sovetskaya Vneshnaya Politika," 464.

7. Braithwaite, *Afgantsy*, 237. Ambassador Braithwaite gives a devastating portrait of the shattering effect the sudden and generally unexpected arrival of these sealed coffins had on the families who received them and on the conscript soldiers whose duty it was to deliver them. In this, as in other ways, Russian president Putin seems to be following the Soviet example; families of Russian soldiers killed in the fighting in Ukraine beginning in 2014 also reportedly received little information about the fate of their loved ones.

8. Tomsen, *The Wars of Afghanistan*, 119.

9. Brutents, *Tridtsat Let na Staroi Ploshchadi*, 455.

10. Korniyenko, *Kholodnaya Voina*, 190.

11. Braithwaite, *Afgantsy*, 75; Arnold, *The Fateful Pebble*, 197.

12. The transcripts of the Politburo discussions on Afghanistan over March 17–19, 1979, and of Kosygin's telephone conversation with Taraki are available at the *CWIHP Bulletin*, no. 8–9 (winter 1996–97): 136–47. Also see the CWIHP e-Dossier No. 4, Documents on the Soviet Invasion of Afghanistan, available at the CWIHP website, https://www.wilsoncenter.org/program/cold-war-international-history -project.

13. Varennikov, *Nepovtorimoe*, 5:48.

14. Lyakovskiy, *Tragediya i Doblest Afgana*, 92–96; Feifer, *The Great Gamble*, 47; Tomsen, *The Wars of Afghanistan*, 159.

15. Conference on Afghanistan, 1995, 130.

16. Andrew and Mitrokhin, *The World Was Going Our Way*, 390; Cordovez and Harrison, *Out of Afghanistan*, 35.

17. *CWIHP Bulletin* (2003–4), 139.

18. Conference on Afghanistan, 1995, 101.

19. Lyakovskiy, *Tragediya i Doblest Afgana*, 102.

20. Chazov, *Zdorove I Vlast*, 152; Volkogonov, *Autopsy for an Empire*, 295; *CWIHP Bulletin* (winter 1996/97), 130.

21. Brutents, *Tridtsat Let na Staroi Ploshchadi*, 469.

22. Grau and Gress, *The Soviet-Afghan War*, 12; Arnold, *The Fateful Pebble*, 125.

23. Carter, *Keeping Faith*, 472.

24. Brzezinski, *Power and Principle*, 429.

25. Coll, *Ghost Wars*, 46, 58.

26. Carter, *Keeping Faith*, 476; Conference on Afghanistan, Wilson Center, 2002, CWIHP website.

27. Coll, *Ghost Wars*, 46, 58.

28. Dobrynin, *In Confidence*, 445.

29. Lyakovskiy, *Tragediya i Doblest Afgana*, 171; Conference on Afghanistan, 1995, 191, 160.

30. Cordovez and Harrison, *Out of Afghanistan*, 102.

31. Kemp-Welch, *Poland under Communism*, 230.

32. Kemp-Welch, *Poland under Communism*, 230.

33. Kramer, "In Case Military Assistance Is Provided to Poland," 102.

34. Mastny, "The Soviet Non-Invasion of Poland," 10–15.
35. Mastny, "The Soviet Non-Invasion of Poland," 20–21; Kemp-Welch, *Poland under Communism*, 308–10.
36. Mastny, "The Soviet Non-Invasion of Poland," 22; Kramer, *Soviet Deliberations during the Polish Crisis*, 92–111; Conference on Global Competition, 1995, 243.
37. Kramer, *Soviet Deliberations during the Polish Crisis*, 24; Kemp-Welch, *Poland under Communism*, 319–21.
38. Kramer, *Soviet Deliberations during the Polish Crisis*, 157–68. Mastny, "The Soviet Non-Invasion of Poland," 29; Conference on Global Competition, 1995, 248–50.
39. Volkogonov, *Autopsy for an Empire*, 301.
40. Pipes, *Vixi: Memoirs of a Non-Believer*, 73.
41. Gates, *From the Shadows*, 236–37.
42. Puddington, *Broadcasting Freedom*, 268–73; Nelson, *War of the Black Heavens*, 158–59.

Chapter 8: Interregnum: Andropov in Power

1. V. Medvedev, *Chelovek za Spinoi*, 178; Chazov, *Zdorove I Vlast*, 168.
2. R. Medvedev, *Gensek S Lubyanki*, 115.
3. Pikhoya, *Sovetskii Soyuz*, 372.
4. Raleigh, *Soviet Baby Boomers*, 309–10, 361–62.
5. Yurchak, *Everything Was Forever until It Was No More*, 84, 103.
6. Parker, *The Kremlin in Transition*, 1:85.
7. Parker, *The Kremlin in Transition*, 1:90; R. Medvedev, *Gensek S Lubyanki*, 102–5; Doder, *Shadows and Whispers*, 53–61; Chazov, *Zdorove I Vlast*, 157; Brezhneva, *The World I Left Behind*, chapter 19.
8. Interview with Byrnes, July 18, 2013.
9. Krasilnikov, *Prizraki c Ulitsa Chaikovskogo*, 107.
10. Politburo transcripts relating to Andropov's accession can be read at the Volkogonov collection in the National Security Archive, located in the Gelman Library at the George Washington University.
11. Shevchenko, *Breaking with Moscow*, 242–43; Doder, *Shadows and Whispers*, 106–7; R. Medvedev, *Gensek S Lubyanki*, 116; Parker, *The Kremlin in Transition*, 1:187–89.
12. R. Medvedev, *Gensek S Lubyanki*, 123.
13. Doder, *Shadows and Whispers*, 165.
14. R. Medvedev, *Gensek S Lubyanki*, 123.
15. Parker, *The Kremlin in Transition*, 1:197–99.
16. Volkogonov, *Autopsy for an Empire*, 345.
17. R. Medvedev, *Gensek S Lubyanki*, 138–39; Volkogonov, *Autopsy for an Empire*, 348.
18. Transcripts of the Politburo sessions of December 20, 1982, and March 10, 1983, are available at the Volkogonov collection at the National Security Archive, located at the Gelman Library at George Washington University.
19. Parker, *The Kremlin in Transition*, 1:202.
20. R. Medvedev, *Gensek S Lubyanki*, 143.
21. Pikhoya, *Sovetskii Soyuz*, 382.

22. Volkogonov collection at the National Security Archive located in the Gelman Library at George Washington University.
23. Parker, *The Kremlin in Transition*, 1:208; Doder, *Shadows and Whispers*, 169.
24. Zdanovich, *Komanda Andropova*, 127–28.
25. Hanson, *The Rise and Fall of the Soviet Economy*, 174, 149.
26. Gorbachev, *Naedine S Soboi*, 318.
27. Gorbachev, *Naedine S Soboi*, 312.
28. A summary of the Politburo discussion on this issue can be found at Pikhoya, *Sovetskii Soyuz*, 387–88.
29. Chazov, *Zdorove I Vlast*, 181, 188.
30. Volkogonov, *Autopsy for an Empire*, 378.
31. R. Medvedev, *Gensek S Lubyanki*, 168.
32. Chazov, *Zdorove I Vlast*, 195–97.

Chapter 9: Ronald Reagan's First Administration

1. Jules Tygiel, *Ronald Reagan and the Triumph of American Conservatism*, 132. Ronald Reagan is the subject of an immense literature, most of which pursues one agenda or another. Still the best biography is one of the earliest, Lou Cannon's *President Reagan: The Role of a Lifetime*, by a *Washington Post* journalist who started out skeptical but ended up admiring many aspects of the president. Raymond L. Garthoff's *The Great Transition: American-Soviet Relations and the End of the Cold War* is an indispensable starting point for relations with Moscow under the Reagan and Bush administrations but much new material has emerged since its publication. An insightful insider perspective is provided by Jack Matlock's *Reagan and Gorbachev: How the Cold War Ended*. More recent treatments are James Mann's *The Rebellion of Ronald Reagan: A History of the End of the Cold War*, and H. W. Brands, *Reagan: The Life*. Reagan repeated his quip about Soviet leaders "dying on me" many times; see the Ronald Reagan Foundation website, http://www.reaganfoundation.org.
2. Text is available at the Reagan Library website at http://www.ff.org/library/reagan-legacy/speech-reagan-1980-11-03/.
3. Tygiel, *Ronald Reagan and the Triumph of American Conservatism*, 142.
4. Powell, *My American Life*, 371.
5. Anderson, Anderson, and Skinner, *Reagan, in His Own Hand*, 25.
6. Brinkley, *The Reagan Diaries*, 166.
7. Brinkley, *The Reagan Diaries*, 153.
8. Gates, *From the Shadows*, 198–218; Andrew, *For the President's Eyes Only*, 459.
9. Daalder and Destler, *In the Shadow of the Oval Office*, 127–54.
10. The text of Reagan's speech is available at American Presidency Project, http://www.presidency.ucsb.edu/ws/index.
11. American Presidency Project, http://www.presidency.ucsb.edu/ws/index.php?pid=42614&st=&st1=.
12. American Presidency Project, http://www.presidency.ucsb.edu/ws/?pid=41023.
13. Dobrynin, In Confidence, 533.
14. Pipes, *Vixi: Memoirs of a Non-Believer*, 194.

15. Ronald Reagan Library: http://www.reagan.utexas.edu/archives/research.html.
16. Weiss, "The Farewell Dossier"; Reed, *At the Abyss*, 266; Service, *The End of the Cold War*, 49.
17. Schweizer, *Victory*, 220.
18. Schweizer, *Victory*, 220.
19. Griffin and Neilson, "The 1985–86 Oil Price Collapse and Afterwards"; Yergin, *The Prize*, 747.
20. Brinkley, *The Reagan Diaries*, 131; Shultz, *Turmoil and Triumph*, 162–64.
21. Reagan, *An American Life*, 558.
22. Dobrynin, *In Confidence*, 523–26; Shultz, *Turmoil and Triumph*, 167–71.
23. Dobrynin, *In Confidence*, 527.
24. Shultz, *Turmoil and Triumph*, 275.
25. Matlock, *Reagan and Gorbachev*, xi.
26. On the mini-thaw of 1983, see Simons, *The End of the Cold War?*, 52.
27. On the KAL shoot-down and subsequent events, see ICAO report "Destruction of Korean Air Lines Flight 007 on August 31, 1983," July 16, 1993, based on previously hidden Soviet archival material provided by Yeltsin in 1992; Murray Sayle, "Closing the File on Flight 007," *New Yorker*, December 13, 1993; James Oberg, "KAL 007: The Real Story," *American Spectator*, October 1993.
28. ICAO Report, 51.
29. ICAO Report, 53.
30. Gorden, "Ex-Soviet Pilot Still Insists KAL Was Spying."
31. Korniyenko, *Kholodnaya Voina*, 220.
32. The transcript of the September 2, 1983, Politburo session is available in the Volkogonov archive located at the National Security Archive in the Gelman Library of the George Washington University.
33. The transcript of the September 2, 1983, Politburo session is available in the Volkogonov archive located at the National Security Archive in the Gelman Library of the George Washington University.
34. John Burns, "Moscow Concedes a Soviet Fighter Downed Airliner," *New York Times*, September 7, 1983.
35. Shultz, *Turmoil and Triumph*, 362.
36. Reagan, *An American Life*, 582.
37. Korniyenko, *Kholodnaya Voina*, 224.
38. Interview with Ambassador Thomas W. Simons, then serving as head of the Soviet desk in the State Department.
39. Dobrynin, *In Confidence*, 543.
40. *Izvestiya*, October 16, 1992, accessed in FBIS SOV-92 201.
41. *Izvestiya*, October 16, 1992, accessed in FBIS SOV-92 201.
42. *New York Times* and *Moscow Times*, October 15, 1992.
43. Andrew and Gordiyevsky, KGB: *The Inside Story*, 583. In Russian, RYAN stands for Raketno Yadernoye Napadenie or Nuclear Missile Attack.
44. Andrew and Gordiyevsky, *Comrade Kryuchkov's Instructions*, 71.
45. Dobrynin, *In Confidence*, 529; Wolf, *Man without a Face*, 247.
46. Andrew and Gordiyevsky, KGB: *The Inside Story*, 585.

47. Andrew and Mitrokhin, *The Sword and the Shield*, 38.

48. BDM interviews, available on National Security Archive website; Andrew and Gordi-yevsky, *KGB: The Inside Story*, 600.

49. Barrass, *The Great Cold War*, 300–301.

50. "Implications of Recent Soviet Military-Political Activities," SNIE 11–10–84/JX, May 18, 1984.

51. Fischer, *A Cold War Conundrum*, 6–10.

52. Early, "Interview with the Spymaster."

53. Palazhenko, *My Years with Gorbachev and Shevardnadze*, 20.

54. Mastny and Byrne, *A Cardboard Castle*, 466–68.

55. BDM interviews with Bateinin and Katayev.

56. BDM interviews with Akromeyev and Danilovich.

57. Wohlforth, *Witnesses to the End of the Cold War*, 72.

58. Cherkashin, *Spy Handler*, 144.

59. Matlock, *Reagan and Gorbachev*, 50.

Chapter 10: Eagle vs. Bear

1. Noonan, *When Character Was King*, 226.

2. American Presidency Project, http://www.presidency.ucsb.edu.

3. Reagan, *An American Life*, 547.

4. MacFarlane, *Special Trust*, 230.

5. Shultz, *Turmoil and Triumph*, 247.

6. Hoffman, *The Dead Hand*, 222.

7. Utkin and Mozzhorin in Minayev, *Sovetskaya Voyennaya Moshch*, 196–99.

8. Podvig, *Russian Strategic Nuclear Forces*.

9. Podvig, *Russian Strategic Nuclear Forces*.

10. Akromeyev and Korniyenko, *Glazami Marshala i Diplomata*, 19–20.

11. Kelly, "Thinking the Unthinkable."

12. Kokoshin, *Soviet Strategic Thought*, 135.

13. BDM interviews.

14. "Remarks to Members of the National Press Club on Arms Reduction and Nuclear Weapons," November 18, 1981. The American Presidency Project, http://www.presidency.ucsb.edu/ws/?pid=43264.

15. Glitman, *The Last Battle of the Cold War*, 56.

16. Kvitsinskiy, *Vremya i Sluchai*, 343–55, provides a Soviet view of the walk in the woods episode.

17. Kvitsinskiy, *Vremya i Sluchai*, 343–55.

18. Nitze, *From Hiroshima to Glasnost*, 376–89; Kvitsinskiy, *Vremya i Sluchai*, 358–61; Parker, *The Kremlin in Transition*, 135–40.

19. Cannon, *President Reagan*, 268; Shultz, *Turmoil and Triumph*, 120; Weinberger, *Fighting for Peace*, 344.

20. Kvitsinskiy, *Vremya i Sluchai*, 361–71.

21. Kvitsinskiy, *Vremya i Sluchai*, 361–71.

22. American Presidency Project, http://www.presidency.ucsb.edu/.

23. Vogele, *Stepping Back*, 107–10; Goodby, *At the Borderline of Armageddon*, 138.

24. Palazhenko, *My Years with Gorbachev and Shevardnadze*, 19; Detinov and Savelyev, *The Big Five*, 68.

25. Korniyenko, "Kholodnaya Voina Kak Osnovoi Generator Gonki Vooruzhenie," in Minayev, *Sovetskaya Voyennaya Moshch*.

26. Conference on SALT II, 1994, 158–59.

27. G. Smith, *Doubletalk*, 56.

28. Conference on SALT II, 1994, 158–59, for Dobrynin's remarks.

29. Chervov, *Yadernii Krugovorot*, 174; Starodubov, *Superderzhavy XX Veka*, 334; Detinov and Savelyev, *The Big Five*, 84.

30. Conference on US-Soviet Relations, 1994, 15.

31. Conference on SALT II, 1994, 7, 18, for Dobrynin's remarks.

32. Conference on SALT II, 1994, 6.

33. Detinov and Savelyev, *The Big Five*, 35; Shevchenko, *Breaking with Moscow*, 269.

34. Detinov and Savelyev, *The Big Five*, 17.

35. Detinov and Savelyev, *The Big Five*, 34.

36. SALT II conference, 1994, 108. BDM interviews with Danilovich.

37. Zubok and Harrison, "The Nuclear Education of Nikita Khrushchev," 145.

38. The discussion in this paragraph is drawn from the BDM interview with Col. Vitaliy Tsygichko.

39. BDM interview with Gen. Andrian Danilevich.

40. Starodubov, "SSSR I SShA: Strategicheskoe Protivoborstvo," in Minayev, *Sovetskaya Voyennaya Moshch*, 567; Kokoshin, *Soviet Strategic Thought*, 53.

41. BDM interviews with Tsygichko and Danilevich.

42. The most extensive Western discussion of "Dead Hand" is found in Hoffmann, *The Dead Hand*, 149–53. For an authoritative Soviet discussion, see Yarynich, *C3: Nuclear Command, Control, Cooperation*, 156–59; Katayev, *A Memoir of the Missile Age*, 176; and the BDM interviews with Katayev, Surikov, Danilovich, and Korobushin.

Chapter 11: Mikhail Gorbachev

1. Yakovlev, *Omut Pamyati*, 511. For Gorbachev's final days in office also see O'Clery, *Moscow, December 25, 1991*, and Grachev, *Final Days*, and the memoirs of Gorbachev and Yeltsin. On Gorbachev's life and works, Archie Brown's *The Gorbachev Factor* and the subsequent *Seven Years that Changed the World: Perestroika in Perspective* will remain indispensable. George W. Breslauer's *Gorbachev and Yeltsin as Leaders* is a good discussion of the policies and the rivalry of both men. Jerry F. Hough's *Democratization and Revolution in the USSR: 1985–1991* is a comprehensive treatment of Gorbachev's rule by one of the best-known Sovietologists writing at the end of the USSR. Vladislav Zubok's *A Failed Empire* is a corrective to the still prevailing Western tendency to treat Gorbachev as an unreserved hero. In *Gorbachev's Gamble*, Andrei Grachev, Gorbachev's final press secretary, gives an inside account of Gorbachev's foreign policy as does his closest adviser Anatoliy Chernyayev in *Shest Let S Gorbachevim* [Six Years with Gorbachev].

2. For the text of Gorbachev's speech, see the *New York Times*, December 26, 1991.

3. For Red Square that night, see *New York Times,* December 26, 1991.

4. Yeltsin, *Against the Grain,* 57.

5. For the incident, see Gorbachev, *Naedine c Coboi,* 200.

6. Gorbachev, *Memoirs,* 115.

7. Gorbachev, *Memoirs,* 115.

8. Gorbachev, *Naedine c Coboi,* 380; Yakovlev, *Omut Pamyati.*

9. Gorbachev, *Memoirs,* 164. For more on the final maneuvering around Gorbachev's accession, also see Grishin, *Ot Khrushchea do Gorbacheva;* Boldin, *Ten Years that Shook the World;* Vorotnikov, *A Bylo Eto Tak;* and Chazov, *Zdorove i Vlast.*

10. Ligachev, *Inside Gorbachev's Kremlin,* 70.

11. On the deal between Gorbachev and Gromyko, see Anatoliy Gromyko, *Andrey Gromyko V Labirintakh Kremlya,* 94–95; Yakovlev, *Omut Pamyati,* 442–43; and Gorbachev, *Naedine c Coboi,* 382.

12. V Politburo, "TSK KPSS," 16.

13. Doder, *Shadows and Whispers,* 272.

14. Akromeyev and Korniyenko, *Glazami Marshala i Diplomata,* 35.

15. Onikov, *KPSS: Anatomiya Raspada,* 56.

16. Lourie, *Sakharov,* 339.

17. Parker, *Kremlin in Transition,* 2:11–18.

18. Vadim Medvedev, *V Komande Gorbacheva,* 30.

19. Shakhnazarov, *Tsena Svobody,* 13.

20. Pikoya, *Sovetski Soyuz,* 409.

21. Parker, *Kremlin in Transition,* 2:75, 82.

22. Text of the April 4, 1985, Politburo session can be found in the Volkogonov collection at the National Security Archive in the Gelman Library at the George Washington University.

23. Gaidar, *Collapse of an Empire,* 134–37; Bhattacharya, Gathmann, and Miller, "The Gorbachev Anti-Alcohol Campaign and Russia's Mortality Crisis."

24. Yakovlev, *Omut Pamyati,* 470.

25. Gorbachev, *Memoirs,* 185.

26. On Gorbachev's speech, see Serge Schmemann, "Gorbachev on the Soviet Economy: A Flock of Innovative Ideas," *New York Times,* February 27, 1986.

27. Parker, *The Kremlin in Transition,* 2:81–82; Pikoya, *Sovetski Soyuz,* 424.

28. Gorbachev, *Naedine c Coboi,* 281.

29. Gill, *The Collapse of the Single Party System,* 16–24; Parker, *The Kremlin in Transition,* 2:79.

30. On Yakovlev's remarks, see *Omut Pamyati,* 459.

31. On the Chernobyl accident, see *The Truth about Chernobyl,* by Grigoriy Medvedev, a Soviet nuclear power engineer who worked on the incident, and two reports prepared by the IAEA INSAG 1 and INSAG 7, published in 1986 and 1992 respectively. INSAG 1 was based largely on information provided by Soviet authorities at a special meeting in 1986, much of which was later found to be false or incomplete. After the Soviet collapse the IAEA commissioned a second report, INSAG 7, which retracted some earlier findings of operator error and stressed design problems in the RBMK

reactors and a serious lack of safety consciousness at Chernobyl and across the entire Soviet nuclear power industry. Texts of both INSAG reports are available on the IAEA website, http://www-pub.iaea.org/MTCD/publications/PDF/Pub913e_web.pdf.

32. Medvedev, *Truth about Chernobyl*, 114.

33. Volkogonov collection at the National Security Archive, Folder R9014.

34. Ryzhkov, *Perestroika Istoriya Predatelstv*, 135; Akromeyev and Korniyenko, *Glazami Marshala i Diplomata*, 99; Daniloff, "Chernobyl and Its Political Fall-Out: A Reassessment."

35. G. Medvedev, *The Truth about Chernobyl*.

36. Yakovlev, *Sumerki*, 389.

37. Palazhenko, *My Years with Gorbachev and Shevardnadze*, 49.

38. Pikhoya, *Sovetski Soyuz*, 430–33.

39. *New York Times*, May 6, 1986.

40. The text of Gorbachev's speech was published in the *New York Times*, May 15, 1986.

41. Varennikov, *Nepovtorimoye*, 5:263.

42. G. Medvedev, *The Truth about Chernobyl*, 214.

43. Interview with Ambassador Courtney, November 19, 2010.

44. Pikhoya, *Sovetski Soyuz*, 433.

45. Yaroshinskaya, *Chernobyl: The Forbidden Truth*, 125–32.

46. Marples, *The Collapse of the Soviet Union*, 23; Yaroshinskaya, *Chernobyl: The Forbidden Truth*, 129.

47. Graham, *The Ghost of the Executed Engineer*, 90.

48. Pikoya, *Sovetski Soyuz*, 431–37.

49. Pikhoya, *Sovetski Soyuz*, 431–37.

50. Pikhoya, *Sovetski Soyuz*, 431–37.

51. Dobbs, *Down with Big Brother*, 159.

52. Gorbachev, *Naedine c Coboi*, 442.

53. Gorbachev, *Memoirs*, 193.

54. Ryzhkov, *Perestroika*, 140.

55. Gorbachev, *Memoirs*, 192; Palazhenko, *My Years with Gorbachev and Shevardnadze*, 49.

Chapter 12: Gorbachev Ascendant

1. Bonner told me this story in the spring of 1987; she repeated it widely and it has since appeared in a number of places.

2. Parker, *The Kremlin in Transition*, 2:161–62.

3. Pikhoya, *Sovetskii Soyuz*, 445; Gill, *The Collapse of the Single-Party System*, 36, 39.

4. Gorbachev, *Memoirs*, 207; Yakovlev, *Omut Pamyati*.

5. Parker, *The Kremlin in Transition*, 2:122–24; V Politburo, "TSK KPSS," 345.

6. Matlock, *Autopsy on an Empire*, 59.

7. On Suslov's remarks to Vasily Grossman, see the Translator's Introduction to *Life and Fate*.

8. Aron, *Roads to the Temple*, 39.

9. Cohen and vanden Heuvel, *Voices of Glasnost*, 101.

10. Aron, *Roads to the Temple*, 74.

11. Aron, *Roads to the Temple*, 79.

12. Aron, *Roads to the Temple*, 114.

13. Aron, *Roads to the Temple*, 136–37.

14. Raleigh, *Soviet Baby Boomers*, 273–83.

15. Ellman and Kontorovich, *The Destruction of the Soviet Economic System*, 112.

16. Ellman and Kontorovich, *The Destruction of the Soviet Economic System*, 121.

17. For a comprehensive discussion of the debate by participants, see Ellman and Kontorovich, *Destruction of the Soviet Economic System*, 118–44.

18. Vadim Medvedev, *V Komande Gorbacheva*, 48–50; Ellman and Kontorovich, *The Destruction of the Soviet Economic System*, 137–44.

19. Gorbachev, *Memoirs*, 231.

20. Parker, *The Kremlin in Transition*, 2:204; Ellman and Kontorovich, *The Destruction of the Soviet Economic System*, 137.

21. Vorotnikov, *A Bylo Eto Tak*, 147.

22. Shultz, *Turmoil and Triumph*, 1001.

23. For an account of the session based on notes of participants, see V Politburo, "TSK KPSS," 258–65.

24. Boldin, *Ten Years that Shook the World*, 234–36; Pikhoya and Sokolov, *Istoriya Sovremennoi Rossii*, 204.

25. Matlock, *Autopsy on an Empire*, 111.

26. For an account of the repulsive episode, see Colton, *Yeltsin*, 146–48, and Gorbachev, *Memoirs*, 247.

27. Matlock, *Autopsy on an Empire*, 119; Chernyayev, *Shest Let S Gorbachevim*, 177.

28. Andreyeva's letter "I Cannot Waive Principles," appeared in *Sovetskaya Rossiia*, March 13, 1988. For an English language translation, see *Los Angeles Times*, April 13, 1988, http://articles.latimes.com/1988–04–13/news/mn-1026.

29. Medvedev and Chiesa, *Time of Change*, 192–93.

30. For an account of the Politburo discussions of the Andreyeva letter, see V Politburo, "TSK KPSS," 301–9; for a description of the first informal discussion during a break, 307; also see Chernyayev, *Shest Let S Gorbachevim*, 204 (the incident was described to Chernyayev by Yakovlev, who was present).

31. V Politburo, "TSK KPSS," 301–9; Chernyayev, *Shest Let S Gorbachevim*, 204.

32. Pikhoya, *Sovetski Soyuz*, 449. For other perspectives on this important episode, see Gorbachev, *Naedine S Soboi*, 516; Yakovlev, *Omut Pamyati*, 277; Vorotnikov, *A Bylo Eto Tak*, 187–88; Ligachev, *Inside Gorbachev's Kremlin*, 301–11; Boldin, *Ten Years that Shook the World*, 168; Matlock, *Autopsy on an Empire*, 119–20; and Parker, *The Kremlin in Transition*, 2:302.

33. Remnick, *Lenin's Tomb*, 117–18.

34. Remnick, *Lenin's Tomb*, 116; Medvedev and Chiesa, *Time of Change*, 218.

35. Matlock, *Autopsy on an Empire*, 122.

36. Onikov, *KPSS: Anatomiya Raspada*, 92, 112. Onikov served for over thirty years in the Central Committee apparat.

37. V Politburo "TSK KPSS," 314–31.

38. Gorbachev, *Memoirs*, 255.

39. Gorbachev, *Memoirs*, 259.

40. Remnick, *Lenin's Tomb*, 119.

Chapter 13: New Kid on the Block

1. Interview with Ambassador Courtney, November 19, 2010, Washington, DC.

2. Thatcher, *Downing Street Years*, 463.

3. Shultz, *Turmoil and Triumph*, 519.

4. Shultz, *Turmoil and Triumph*, 532.

5. Dobrynin, *In Confidence*, 577.

6. English, *Russia and the Idea of the West*, 185.

7. Yakovlev, *Omut Pamyati*, 226; Parker, *The Kremlin in Transition*, 2:41.

8. Shevardnadze, *Moi Vybor v Zashchitu Demokratii*, 58, 81.

9. Shevardnadze, *Kogda Rukhnul Zhelezni Zanaves*, 73.

10. Matlock, *Reagan and Gorbachev*, 129.

11. Shultz, *Turmoil and Triumph*, 572.

12. Israelyan, *On the Battlefields of the Cold War*, 353.

13. Kvitsinskiy, *Vremya i Sluchai*, 431.

14. Reagan, *An American Life*, 628–34.

15. Transcripts of the discussions between the two leaders at the Geneva summit are available at the National Security Archive electronic briefing book 172, "To the Geneva Summit: Perestroika and the Transformation of US-Soviet Relations," nsarchive.gwu.edu/NSAEBB/NSAEBB172/index.htm.

16. Reagan, *An American Life*, 636.

17. Shevardnadze, *Kogda Rukhnul Zhelezni Zanaves*, 88.

18. Shultz, *Turmoil and Triumph*, 605.

19. Gorbachev, *Memoirs*, 411.

20. The text of Reagan's statement is available at The American Presidency Project, http://www.presidency.ucsb.edu/ws/?pid=38087.

21. The text of the joint US-Soviet statement is available at The American Presidency Project, http://www.presidency.ucsb.edu/ws/?pid=38086.

22. Gorbachev, *Memoirs*, 408.

23. Vorotnikov, *A Bylo Eto Tak*, 79.

24. Speakes, *Speaking Out*, 138.

25. Simons, *The End of the Cold War*, 84.

26. Simons, *The End of the Cold War*, 95.

27. Nitze, *From Hiroshima to Glasnost*, 421.

28. Service, *The End of the Cold War*, 163–66.

29. Detinov and Savelyev, *The Big Five*, 92.

30. Starodubov, *Superderzhavy XX Veka*, 396; Chervov, *Yaderniy Krugovorot*, 99.

31. Nitze, *From Hiroshima to Glasnost*, 422.

32. Detinov and Savelyev, *The Big Five*, 93.

33. Roy, "The Lessons of the Soviet Afghan War," 18–21; Tomsen, *The Wars of Afghanistan*, 215.

34. Grau and Gress, *The Soviet-Afghan War*, 29; Roy, "The Lessons of the Soviet Afghan War," 20.

35. Bearden and Risen, *The Main Enemy*, 219; Coll, *Ghost Wars*, 88; Gates, *From the Shadows*, 348.

36. Interview with Ambassador Abramowitz, March 30, 2010.

37. Interview with Ambassador Abramowitz, March 30, 2010.

38. For a detailed discussion of the bureaucratic politics around the decision to supply Stingers, see Lundberg, "The Politics of a Covert Action."

39. Bearden and Risen, *The Main Enemy*, 252.

40. Crile, *Charlie Wilson's War*, 437; Gates, *From the Shadows*, 430.

41. Crile, *Charlie Wilson's War*, 437.

42. Grau and Gress, *The Soviet-Afghan War*, 23.

43. Odom, *The Collapse of the Soviet Military*, 103; Lyakovskiy, *Tragediya i Doblest Afgana*, 293.

44. Lyakovskiy, *Tragediya i Doblest*, 292; Andrew and Mitrokhin, *The World Was Going Our Way*, 450; Gates, *From the Shadows*, 251, 428; Kryuchkov, *Lichnoe Delo*, 1:223.

45. Lyakovskiy, *Tragediya i Doblest*, 293.

46. Shevardnadze, *Kogda Rukhnul Zhelezni Zanaves*, 80–91.

47. For an excerpted transcript of the November 13 Politburo meeting, see CWIHP *Bulletin* (winter 2003–spring 2004), 143–44.

48. CWIHP *Bulletin* (winter 2003–spring 2004), 145.

49. CWIHP *Bulletin* (winter 2003–spring 2004), 146.

50. CWIHP *Bulletin* (winter 2003–spring 2004), 148.

51. Shultz, *Turmoil and Triumph*, 1090.

52. Grau and Gress, *The Soviet-Afghan War*, xix, 1.

53. Arnold, *The Fateful Pebble*, 189.

54. Grau and Gress, *The Soviet-Afghan War*, 29.

55. Discussions with Ambassador Tomsen, March 2015; Coll, *Ghost Wars*, chapters 9–11.

Chapter 14: "I Guess I Should Say Michael"

1. Interview with Gerber in Washington, DC, September 16, 2011.

2. In "Intelligence in the Cold War," Christopher Andrew describes intelligence as the least understood aspect of the Cold War—often sensationalized and ignored. Many US and Soviet intelligence professionals have produced valuable accounts of their experiences but a comprehensive and balanced history of the role and importance of the US-Soviet intelligence relationship across the Cold War remains to be written. In *The Great Cold War: A Journey through the Hall of Mirrors*, Gordon S. Barrass describes the Cold War from the perspective of a senior British participant. Christopher Andrew produced a valuable contribution on the US perspective in *For the President's Eyes Only: Secret Intelligence and the American Presidency from Washington to Bush*. Andrew and Oleg Gordiyevsky in *KGB: The Inside Story* and Amy Knight in *KGB: Police and Politics in the Soviet Union* provided insightful accounts but much new information has appeared in the intervening years. Yevgeniya Albats in *The State within a State: The KGB and Its Hold on Russia—Past, Present, and Future* produced

the best account on the subject we are likely to see by a Russian until the Putin regime disappears. Most Western writing on Soviet intelligence focuses on the KGB; in *Near and Distant Neighbors: A New History of Soviet Intelligence,* Jonathan Haslam provides a comprehensive account of Soviet military intelligence, the GRU, drawing heavily on Russian sources.

3. Cherkashin, *Spy Handler,* 19–30, 143. In *Circle of Treason,* Grimes and Vertefeuille provide an account of the Ames case by members of the CIA team that uncovered him. See also David Hoffman's review of the Vertefeuille and Grimes book in the November 30, 2012, *Washington Post.* In *The Billion Dollar Spy,* Hoffmann provides a gripping account of Adolf Tolkachev, one of the most valuable spies ever obtained by the CIA, who was betrayed by Ames.

4. SSCI, "An Assessment of the Aldrich Ames Espionage Case."

5. The story of Stalin and the flags is part of the Moscow diplomatic legend but cannot be verified. It is more likely that the pressure to move the embassies came from Soviet security specialists concerned more about imperialist eavesdropping than flags.

6. Gerber interview.

7. Interview with Ambassador Hartman, November 19, 2010.

8. Matlock, *Reagan and Gorbachev,* 255; Combs, *Inside the Soviet Alternative Universe.*

9. Bearden and Risen, *The Main Enemy,* 199; Grimes and Vertefeuille, *Circle of Treason,* 108–11.

10. Interviews with Ambassador Hartman and Burton Gerber.

11. The following are my primary sources for the Daniloff incident: Daniloff, *Two Lives, One Russia,* 3–25, 214–26; Bearden and Risen, *The Main Enemy,* 50–60; Combs, *Inside the Soviet Alternative Universe,* 94–96; e-mail exchanges with Burton Gerber, April 2015, and with Daniloff, May 2015.

12. Shultz, *Turmoil and Triumph,* 728–34; Reagan, *An American Life,* 667.

13. Bearden and Risen, *The Main Enemy,* 189–91; e-mail exchange with Gerber, April 2015.

14. V Politburo, "TSK KPSS," 78; Chernyayev, *Shest Let S Gorbachevim,* 108.

15. Matlock, "The Legacy of Reykjavik," 107.

16. The discussion of Reykjavik is drawn from the US and Soviet memcons, which are available at the National Security Archive. See also Chernyayev, *Shest Let S Gorbachevim,* 110; Reagan, *An American Life,* 675; Shultz, *Turmoil and Triumph,* 760.

17. Nitze, *From Hiroshima to Glasnost,* 432; Akromeyev and Korniyenko, *Glazami Marshala i Diplomata,* 114–16.

18. Rozanne L. Ridgeway, "Legacy of Reykjavik."

19. Nitze, *From Hiroshima to Glasnost,* 433.

20. Starodubov, *Superderzhavy XX Veka,* 402; Nitze, *From Hiroshima to Glasnost,* 434.

21. Reagan, *An American Life,* 677.

22. Interview with Ambassador Simons, November 10, 2010.

23. Speakes, *Speaking Out,* 143; Reagan, *An American Life,* 679.

24. Matlock, *Reagan and Gorbachev,* 238.

25. Thatcher, *The Downing Street Years,* 471–73; Adelman, *The Great Universal Embrace,* 86.

26. Reagan, *An American Life,* 683; Shultz, *Turmoil and Triumph,* 775.

27. Chernyayev, *Shest Let S Gorbachevim*, 114.

28. Volkogonov archive.

29. An indispensable starting point for the role of the Soviet military in security policy in the second half of the Cold War remains Dale Herspring's *The Soviet High Command*. Barylski, *The Soldier in Russian Politics*, uses Russian sources to provide a detailed picture of the military's relationship with political leaders in a critical period. In *The Collapse of the Soviet Military* Odom, one of the best-informed American students of the Soviet military, gives a comprehensive picture of its final years. Andrei Kokoshin, a leading Soviet national security specialist and deputy minister of defense under Boris Yeltsin, gives an informed picture of Soviet military-security affairs in *Soviet Strategic Thought*.

30. Yazov interview at Mershon Center for International Security Studies, Ohio State University; Shakhnazarov, *Tsena Svobody*, 88.

31. V Politburo, "TSK KPSS," 194; Boldin, *Ten Years that Shook the World*, 166; Chernyayev, *Shest Let S Gorbachevim*, 159.

32. Shakhnazarov, *Tsena Svobody*, 90.

33. Barylski, *The Soldier in Russian Politics*, 48; Odom, *The Collapse of the Soviet Military*, 110.

34. Odom, *The Collapse of the Soviet Military*, 111.

35. Detinov and Savelyev, *The Big Five*, 114–20; Odom, *The Collapse of the Soviet Military*, 126; Katayev, *A Memoir of the Missile Age*, 158–63.

36. Mershon Center interviews; Kokoshin, *Soviet Strategic Thought*, 189; Odom, *The Collapse of the Soviet Military*, 114–21; Shakhnazarov, *Tsena Svobody*, 89.

37. Gorbachev, *Naedine S Soboi*, 472; Yakovlev, *Perestroika*, 85; V Politburo, "TSK KPSS," 151–52.

38. Detinov and Savelyev, *The Big Five*, 136–38; Starodubov, *Superderzhavy XX Veka*, 421–23; Shultz, *Turmoil and Triumph*, 1012.

39. *Newsweek*, December 21, 1987.

40. Gorbachev, *Memoirs*, 447; Brinkley, *The Reagan Diaries*, 554.

41. Shultz, *Turmoil and Triumph*.

42. *Newsweek*, December 21, 1987.

43. V Politburo, "TSK KPSS," 111–12.

44. Shultz, *Turmoil and Triumph*, 887.

45. Adamyshin and Schifter, *Human Rights, Perestroika, and the End of the Cold War*, 83.

46. Adamyshin and Schifter, *Human Rights, Perestroika, and the End of the Cold War*, 112–17, 84–89.

47. Interview with Ambassador Matlock, September 14, 2011. As he told me this story my friend and former boss Jack Matlock's eyes teared. The reality of this kind of sentiment on both sides, which I experienced at lower levels, is a commentary on the depth of the change in the relationship in the final years of the Cold War as well as the lost opportunities for US-Russian friendship that have transpired in the quarter century since the Cold War ended.

48. Powell, *My American Life*, 378; Cannon, *President Reagan*, 704.

49. Brinkley, *The Reagan Diaries*, 615; Cannon, *President Reagan*, 704.

50. Cannon, *President Reagan*, 705; American Presidency Project, http://www
.presidency.ucsb.edu/ws/?pid=35897.

51. Simons interview; Shultz, *Turmoil and Triumph*, 1105; Matlock, *Reagan and Gorbachev*, 300.

52. *New York Times*, December 8, 1988.

53. National Security Archive.

Chapter 15: 1989

1. In 1978, while serving in the science section of the US Embassy in Moscow, I accompanied a delegation of US seismic experts to Armenia, who told me they were
shocked by the contrast between the impressive briefings they received in offices
and the reality they observed on the ground. Although the Soviets had spoken
proudly about construction techniques, such as a system of interlocking reinforcing
rods used in buildings in seismic zones, on the site itself US experts found that the
rods were often either completely absent or not connected. US experts told me they
hoped not to be present if there ever was an earthquake in the regions we visited.

2. Dobrynin, *In Confidence*, 640; Braithwaite, *Afgantsy*, 86.

3. Medvedev and Chiesa, *Time of Change*, 237.

4. Savranskaya, Blanton, and Zubok, *Masterpieces of History*, 26.

5. Gaidar, *Days of Defeat and Victory*, 44.

6. Tuminez, "Nationalism, Ethnic Pressures, and the Breakup of the Soviet Union," 88.

7. Carrere d'Encausse, *The End of the Soviet Empire*, 53.

8. Savranskaya, Blanton, and Zubok, *Masterpieces of History*, Document 34.

9. Kramer, "The Collapse of East European Communism," 1:218; Carrere d'Encausse,
The End of the Soviet Empire, 128.

10. Savranskaya, Blanton, and Zubok, *Masterpieces of History*, 448; V Politburo, "TSK
KPSS," 472; Chernyayev, *Shest Let S Gorbachevim*, 285.

11. Kramer, "The Collapse of East European Communism," part 2, provides a detailed
account of the tragedy in Tbilisi. Mark Kramer, who reviewed secret Soviet and
Georgian records, concludes that the decision to use force was taken in Tbilisi by
the Georgian Defense Council and not in Moscow and tends to believe Gorbachev's
version of events. See also an independent report on the incident prepared by
Antoliy Sobchak for the Congress of Peoples Deputies, available in the Volkogonov
archive.

12. Barylski, *The Soldier in Russian Politics*, 63.

13. Matlock, *Reagan and Gorbachev*, 215; Remnick, *Lenin's Tomb*, 217.

14. Baturin et al., *Epokha Yeltsina*, 64.

15. Yeltsin, *Against the Grain*, 187; Baturin et al., *Epokha Yeltsina*, 63.

16. Dobbs, *Down with Big Brother*, 255; Remnick, *Lenin's Tomb*, 220–22.

17. Dobbs, *Down with Big Brother*, 261; Raleigh, *Soviet Baby Boomers*, 285.

18. Medvedev and Chiesa, *Time of Change*, 304; Pikhoya, *Sovetskii Soyuz*, 504.

19. Burlatskiy, *Mikhail Gorbachev-Boris Yeltsin Skhvatka*, 54–57; Grachev, *Gorbachev's
Gamble*, 130.

20. Boldin, *Ten Years that Shook the World*, 215; Chernyayev, *Shest Let S Gorbachevim*, 276.

21. Kramer, "The Collapse of East European Communism," 1:229, 226.

22. Remnick, *Lenin's Tomb*, 223–24.

23. Carrere d'Encausse, *The End of the Soviet Empire*, 98, 65; *New York Times*, June 12, 1989.

24. Carrere d'Encausse, *The End of the Soviet Empire*, 134, 154.

25. Savranskaya, Blanton, and Zubok, *Masterpieces of History*, 70; Grachev, *Gorbachev's Gamble*, 122.

26. Lévesque, *The Enigma of 1989*; texts in CWIHP *Bulletin* 12/13.

27. Lévesque, *The Enigma of 1989*, 115; CWIHP *Bulletin* 12/13, 112.

28. CWIHP *Bulletin* 12/13, 12, 23.

29. Lévesque, *The Enigma of 1989*, 125.

30. Kramer, "The Collapse of East European Communism," 1:196.

31. Savranskaya, Blanton, and Zubok, *Masterpieces of History*, 533.

32. Lévesque, *The Enigma of 1989*, 131; CWIHP *Bulletin* 12/13, 75; Meyer, *The Year that Changed the World*, 34.

33. Lévesque, *The Enigma of 1989*, 129.

34. Meyer, *The Year that Changed the World*, 56.

35. Pleshakov, *There Is No Freedom without Bread*, 181; Stokes, *The Walls Came Tumbling Down*, 131.

36. Maier, *Dissolution*, 126; Sarotte, *The Collapse*, 26.

37. Meyer, *The Year that Changed the World*, 56.

38. Bush and Scowcroft, *A World Transformed*, 135.

39. Hutchins, *American Diplomacy and the End of the Cold War*, 55.

40. Bush and Scowcroft, *A World Transformed*, 117; Savranskaya, Blanton, and Zubok, *Masterpieces of History*, 503.

41. Maier, *Dissolution*, 47; Sarotte, *The Collapse*, 9; Stokes, *The Walls Came Tumbling Down*, 138.

42. Pleshakov, *There Is No Freedom without Bread*, 188; Ahonen, *Death at the Berlin Wall*.

43. Maier, *Dissolution*, 49; Stokes, *The Walls Came Tumbling Down*, 138.

44. Maier, *Dissolution*, 77.

45. Hertle, "The Fall of the Wall," 132.

46. Maier, *Dissolution*, 60; Ash, *In Europe's Name*, 142–46; Sarotte, *The Collapse*, 17.

47. Hertle, "The Fall of the Wall," 133.

48. Bagley, *Spymaster*, 250.

49. Wolf, *Man without a Face*, 360; Grachev, *Gorbachev's Gamble*, 138; Falin, *Bez Skidok na Obstoyatelstva*, 440; Gorbachev, *Zhizn i Reformy*, 2:412.

50. Savranskaya, Blanton, and Zubok, *Masterpieces of History*, 544; Falin, *Bez Skidok na Obstoyatelstva*, 443.

51. Sarotte, *The Collapse*, 74–76.

52. Sarotte, *The Collapse*, 88; Hertle, "The Fall of the Wall," 131; Lévesque, *The Enigma of 1989*, 158; Service, *The End of the Cold War*, 408.

53. CWIHP *Bulletin* 12/13, 140 has the conversation.

54. Myer, *The Year that Changed the World*, 159.

55. Sarotte, *The Collapse*, 113.
56. Sarotte, *The Collapse*, 138–45; Sarotte, *1989*, 36–43; Hertle, "The Fall of the Wall," 136.
57. Savranskaya, Blanton, and Zubok, *Masterpieces of History*, 577; V Politburo, "TSK KPSS," 524; Service, *The End of the Cold War*, 411.
58. Zelikow and Rice, *Germany Unified and Europe Transformed*; CWIHP *Bulletin* 12/13, 158.
59. Fitzwater, *Call the Briefing*, 261.
60. Bush and Scowcroft, *A World Transformed*, 148–51.
61. Genscher, *Rebuilding a House Divided*, 292.
62. Hertle, "The Fall of the Wall," 138; Thatcher, *The Downing Street Years*, 792; Wiegrefe, "Germany's Unlikely Diplomatic Triumph."
63. Zelikow and Rice, *Germany Unified and Europe Transformed*.
64. See http://germanhistorydocs.ghi-dc.org/pdf/eng/Chapter1_Doc10English.pdf.
65. Thatcher, *The Downing Street Years*, 795; Maier, *Dissolution*, 252; Sarotte, *1989*, 72–76; Zelikow and Rice, *Germany Unified and Europe Transformed*; Genscher, *Rebuilding a House Divided*, 313.
66. Hutchins, *American Diplomacy and the End of the Cold War*, 54.
67. Excerpts from the Soviet transcript of the Malta summit are in Savranskaya, Blanton, and Zubok, *Masterpieces of History*, 619–47.
68. Chernyayev, *Shest Let S Gorbachevim*, 302; Meacham, *Destiny and Power*, 386.
69. Akromeyev and Korniyenko, *Glazami Marshala i Diplomata*, 254.
70. Oberdorfer, *From the Cold War to a New Era*, 385.
71. Matlock, *Autopsy on an Empire*, 275.

Chapter 16: Stumbling toward Collapse

1. Wiegrefe, "Germany's Unlikely Diplomatic Triumph"; Zelikow and Rice, *Germany Unified and Europe Transformed*.
2. V Politburo, "TSK KPSS," 542–55; Falin, *Bez Skidok na Obstoyatelstva*, 444; Grachev, *Gorbachev's Gamble*, 152; Chernyayev, *Shest Let S Gorbachevim*, 346.
3. In discussing the negotiations on German unification, I drew heavily from accounts by participants and documentary sources: Gorbachev, "Otvechaya na Vyzov Vremeni"; Savranskaya, Blanton, and Zubok, *Masterpieces of History*; and electronic briefing books at the NS Archive. See Baker, *The Politics of Diplomacy*, 205; Zelikow and Rice, *Germany Unified and Europe Transformed*; Gorbachev, *Zhizn*, vol. 2; Hutchins, *American Diplomacy and the End of the Cold War*, 115; Bush and Scowcroft, *A World Transformed*, 244.
4. Baker, *The Politics of Diplomacy*, 230; Zelikow and Rice, *Germany Unified and Europe Transformed*; Stent, *Russia and Germany Reborn*, 106; Genscher, *Rebuilding a House Divided*, 343.
5. Hutchins, *American Diplomacy and the End of the Cold War*, 135; Bush and Scowcroft, *A World Transformed*, 297. Text at American Presidency Project, http://www.presidency.ucsb.edu.
6. On German unification at the Washington summit see Bush and Scowcroft, *A World Transformed*, 282–83; Falin, *Bez Skidok na Obstoyatelstva*, 448; Zelikow and Rice,

Germany Unified and Europe Transformed; Adomeit, "Gorbachev, German Unification, and the Collapse of Empire," 197; Sarotte, *1989*, 160–67; Meacham, *Destiny and Power*, 403.

7. Braithwaite, *Across the Moscow River*, 131.

8. Zelikow and Rice, *Germany Unified and Europe Transformed*; Genscher, *Rebuilding a House Divided*, 415.

9. Sarotte, *1989*, 177–86; Genscher, *Rebuilding a House Divided*, 428–29; Zelikow and Rice, *Germany Unified and Europe Transformed*.

10. Zelikow and Rice, *Germany Unified and Europe Transformed*; Sarotte, *1989*, 186–92.

11. On the issue of whether limits on NATO's eastward expansion were part of the unification deal, I have drawn on the following: Genscher, *Rebuilding a House Divided*, 337, 429; Gorbachev, *Zhizn*, 2:167; Kim, "Baker Says Gorbachev Got No Promises"; Zelikow and Rice, *Germany Unified and Europe Transformed*; *New York Times*, May 25, 1997; Kramer, "The Myth of a No-NATO Enlargement Pledge to Russia"; Grachev, *Gorbachev's Gamble*, 159; Hutchins, *American Diplomacy and the End of the Cold War*, 113.

12. Yeltsin has been the subject of two outstanding English-language biographies: Timothy Colton, *Yeltsin: A Life*, and Aron, *Yeltsin: A Revolutionary Life*. Yeltsin's first two autobiographical volumes, *Against the Grain* and *The Struggle for Russia*, provide an unusually revealing portrait of the man as he really was in the midst of his political battles.

13. Pikhoya and Sokolov, *Istoriya Sovremennoi Rossii*, 247, 259.

14. Vorotnikov, *A Bylo Eto Tak*, 384.

15. Aron, *Yeltsin: A Revolutionary Life*, 384; Pikhoya and Sokolov, *Istoriya Sovremennoi Rossii*, 270.

16. Yeltsin, *The Struggle for Russia*, 19. Over 1991–94, I often found myself in the office Yeltsin "seized"—in meetings with him, his aides, or later his opponents when they took over the parliament and in October 1993 when it was a smoking ruin after the siege that ultimately forced Yeltsin into shelling the building where his hard-line parliamentary opponents had taken over. The suite was impressive in size, but its atmosphere was cold and it lacked the patina of history that enveloped the Kremlin offices Yeltsin later "seized."

17. Yeltsin, *Against the Grain*, 198; Sukanov, *Tri Goda c Yeltsinom*, 153. Moscow residents of all sorts could be affected by American supermarkets. In 1978, after almost two years in Moscow, our family returned for a visit to our parents' homes near Louisville Kentucky. On our first day back, I was sent to a supermarket for milk—returning hours later with half a carful of purchases. After two years in Moscow, where rusty cans of Bulgarian tomatoes constituted the height of a successful shopping experience, I found myself wandering up and down the aisles of the store, powerless to stop piling our cart with delicacies. My three-year-old son had his own form of entry into the world of capitalist abundance. I had picked up a bunch of bananas and at the check-out counter I saw the clerk staring at my son in surprise. Turning, I saw that Andrew—never having seen a banana before—was attempting to eat it without removing the peel.

18. Ellman and Kontorovich, *The Destruction of the Soviet Economic System*, 234; Aron, *Yeltsin: A Revolutionary Life*, 401.

19. Ellman and Kontorovich, *The Destruction of the Soviet Economic System*, 228–35; Hanson, *The Rise and Fall of the Soviet Economy*, 226–34.

20. Gaidar, *Days of Defeat and Victory*, 51; Aron, *Yeltsin: A Revolutionary Life*, 403.

21. Gorbachev, *Memoirs*, 377–86; Dobbs, *Down with Big Brother*, 324.

22. Yakovlev, *Omut Pamyati*, 519.

23. Pikhoya, *Sovetskii Soyuz*, 536–39.

24. Matlock, *Autopsy on an Empire*, 424–26; Pikhoya, *Sovetskii Soyuz*, 540; Remnick, *Lenin's Tomb*, 392.

25. Pikhoya, *Sovetskii Soyuz*, 539; Shevardnadze, *Moi Vybor v Zashchitu Demokratii*, 327; Bill Keller, "Crisis in the Kremlin," *New York Times*, December 21, 1990.

26. Kryuchkov, *Lichnoe Delo*, 31.

27. Dobbs, *Down with Big Brother*, 338–43.

28. Matlock, *Autopsy on an Empire*, 455.

29. Matlock, *Autopsy on an Empire*, 472.

30. Aron, *Yeltsin: A Revolutionary Life*, 410–18.

31. Baturin et al., *Epokha Yeltsina*, 109.

32. Pikhoya, *Sovetskii Soyuz*, 555–57.

33. Remnick, *Lenin's Tomb*, 422.

34. Braithwaite, *Across the Moscow River*, 180; Matlock, *Autopsy on an Empire*, 472.

35. *New York Times*, March 17, 1991; Pikhoya and Sokolov, *Istoriya Sovremennoi Rossii*, 342.

36. Baturin et al., *Epokha Yeltsina*, 113–14.

37. Pikhoya, *Sovetskii Soyuz*, 564–77.

38. Vadim Medvedev, *V Komande Gorbacheva*, 187. Speech available at the Nobel Committee website.

39. V Politburo, "TSK KPSS," 680–92.

40. Bush and Scowcroft, *A World Transformed*, 503.

41. R. W. Apple, "Summit in London, Pact Is Reached," *New York Times*, July 18, 1991; Gorbachev, *Zhizn*, 2:295; Major, *Autobiography*, 499.

42. Gates, *From the Shadows*, 502.

43. Bush and Scowcroft, *A World Transformed*, 511–12.

44. Matlock, *Autopsy on an Empire*, 565.

45. American Presidency Project, http://www.presidency.ucsb.edu; Plokhy, *The Last Empire*, 58.

Chapter 17: The August Coup

1. Vladimir Medvedev, *Chelovek za Spinoi*, 276–79.

2. Vladimir Medvedev, *Chelovek za Spinoi*, 279.

3. Gorbachev has given many accounts over the years of the meeting in Foros with the coup plotters. The first and most immediate, from which I have drawn, was in his first press conference on returning to Moscow, which is available in the *New York Times*, August 23, 1991. See also Gorbachev's *The August Coup*, 18–23. For Gorbachev's account twenty years later, see Mikhail Gorbachev, "Lessons from the USSR Coup Attempt," *Washington Post*, August 19, 2011.

4. In this short account of the hours-long meeting at Foros I have drawn on the following sources: Stepankov and Lisov, *Kremlevski Zagovor*, 7–15; written by the men in charge of the investigation of the coup, this reports the interrogations of the coup plotters and other investigatory material. In *Sovetskii Soyuz*, 583–85, Pikhoya drew on Russian archives for his account of the meeting. Also see the following accounts by two of the coup plotters who participated in the meeting: Varennikov, *Nepovtorimoe*, 6:204–12; and Boldin, *Ten Years that Shook the World*, 28.

5. Pikhoya, *Sovetskii Soyuz*, 578.

6. Kryuchkov, *Lichnoe Delo*, 146–49; Stepankov and Lisov, *Kremlevski Zagovor*, 84.

7. Kryuchkov, *Lichnoe Delo*, 148.

8. Stepankov and Lisov, *Kremlevski Zagovor*, 90.

9. Stepankov and Lisov, *Kremlevski Zagovor*, 108.

10. Bonnell, Cooper, and Freidin, *Russia at the Barricades*, 341.

11. Stepankov and Lisov, *Kremlevski Zagovor*, 119–21.

12. Yeltsin, *The Struggle for Russia*, 56–57.

13. Bonnell, Cooper, and Freidin, *Russia at the Barricades*, 170–80.

14. Interview with Wasilewski, August 17, 2010, in Whitefield, Maine.

15. Satter, *Age of Delirium*, 16.

16. Shevardnadze, *Kogda Rukhnul Zhelezni Zanaves*.

17. Yeltsin, *The Struggle for Russia*, 58.

18. Lebed, *My Life and My Country*, 300–11; Barylski, *The Soldier in Russian Politics*, 98.

19. Stepankov and Lisov, *Kremlevski Zagovor*, 174.

20. Shaposhnikov, *Vybor*, 18–44.

21. Albats, *The State within a State*; Kalugin, *The First Directorate*, 348–56; Shane, *Dismantling Utopia*, 270.

22. Bonnell and Freidin, "Televorot," 810–38.

23. A transcript of the press conference is available in Bonnell, Cooper, and Freidan, *Russia at the Barricades*, 42.

24. Stepankov and Lisov, *Kremlevski Zagovor*, 149.

25. Stepankov and Lisov, *Kremlevski Zagovor*, 150.

26. Stepankov and Lisov, *Kremlevski Zagovor*, 161–62.

27. Yeltsin, *The Struggle for Russia*, 85; Aron, *Yeltsin: A Revolutionary Life*, 450.

28. Pikhoya, *Sovetskii Soyuz*, 598; Stepankov and Lisov, *Kremlevski Zagovor*, 171; Shane, *Dismantling Utopia*, 270; Satter, *Age of Delirium*, 18; Shevardnadze, *Kogda Rukhnul Zhelezni Zanaves*, 205.

29. Remnick, *Lenin's Tomb*, 484; Stepankov and Lisov, *Kremlevski Zagovor*, 180.

30. Yeltsin, *The Struggle for Russia*, 93; Korzhakov, *Boris Yeltsin*, 93.

31. Interview with Wayne Merry, November 19, 2010, Washington, DC.

32. Interview with Ambassador Collins, November 19, 2010.

33. Interview with Ambassador Collins, November 19, 2010.

34. Gates, *From the Shadows*, 521. Gates was with the president in Kennebunkport. Text of Bush's statement is available at The American Presidency Project, http://www.presidency.ucsb.edu/ws/?pid=19913.

35. Text of the statement is available at The American Presidency Project, http://www.presidency.ucsb.edu/ws/?pid=19914. Transcript of Bush's conversation with Yeltsin

can be accessed through the George H. W. Bush Library at http://bush41library
.tamu.edu/files.

36. Braithwaite, *Across the Moscow River*, 232; Collins interview, November 19, 2010.

37. Yeltsin, *The Struggle for Russia*, 93; Korzhakov, *Boris Yeltsin*, 93.

38. Interview with Ambassador Collins, November 19, 2010.

39. Seymour Hersh, "The Wild East," *Atlantic Monthly*, June 1994.

40. Interview with Ambassador Collins, November 19, 2010.

41. Yeltsin, *The Struggle for Russia*, 66.

42. Stepankov and Lisov, *Kremlevski Zagovor*, 113–16; Varennikov, *Nepovtorimoe*,
6:248–49; Plokhy, *The Last Empire*, 156–58.

43. *Ukrainian Weekly*, August 18, 1996; Plokhy, *The Last Empire*, 158–62.

44. Najibullah, "Watching the Coup from Central Asia."

45. Yeltsin, *The Struggle for Russia*, 106; Dobbs, *Down with Big Brother*, 411; Baturin,
Epokha Yeltsina, 149.

46. I watched the broadcast live in Moscow. It was reported around the world and
is widely available in media archives. The source I used for the quotes is George
Gerbner, "Instant History: The Case of the Moscow Coup," *Political Communication*,
10:193–203, http://web.asc.upenn.edu/gerbner/Asset.aspx?assetID=883.

47. Shevardnadze, *Kogda Rukhnul Zhelezni Zanaves*, 211–12.

48. On the question of Gorbachev's role in the coup, see the following: Gorbachev,
Memoirs, 2:555–61; Shevardnadze, *Kogda Rukhnul Zhelezni Zanaves*, 211–12; Dunlop,
"The August 1991 Coup," 101–4; Knight, "The KGB, Perestroika, and the Collapse of
the Soviet Union," 67–93.

49. Dobbs, *Down with Big Brother*, 411–17.

Chapter 18: Red Star Falling

1. Grachev, *Final Days*, xvi.

2. Braithwaite, *Across the Moscow River*, 249.

3. Grachev, *Final Days*, 39.

4. Gaidar, *Days of Defeat and Victory*, 66.

5. Gaidar, *Days of Defeat and Victory*, 112.

6. Bush and Scowcroft, *A World Transformed*, 548.

7. Braithwaite, *Across the Moscow River*, 250.

8. Baker, *The Politics of Diplomacy*, 529.

9. *New York Times*, October 29, 1991.

10. Grachev, *Final Days*, 119–26.

11. Yeltsin, *The Struggle for Russia*, 111.

12. Shaposhnikov, *Vybor*, 138.

13. Plokhy, *The Last Empire*, 294.

14. *Ukrainian Weekly*, December 8, 1991.

15. *New York Times*, December 1, 1991.

16. Baker, *The Politics of Diplomacy*, 525.

17. Cheney, *In My Time*, 167, 231.

18. Bush and Scowcroft, *A World Transformed*, 540–44; Gates, *From the Shadows*, 529–31.

19. Goldgeier and McFaul, *Power and Purpose,* 34.

20. The George H. W. Bush Library has available online a large collection of the president's memcons and telcons with foreign and domestic figures. The memcon of the meeting with the Ukrainian Americans is available at https://bush41library.tamu .edu/files/memcons-telcons/1991-11-27-Ukranian%20Americans.pdf.

21. Bush's conversation with Gorbachev is available at https://bush41library.tamu.edu /files/memcons-telcons/1991-12-13--Gorbachev.pdf.

22. Bush's conversation with Yeltsin is available at https://bush41library.tamu.edu/files /memcons-telcons/1991-12-13--Yeltsin.pdf.

23. Pikhoya, *Sovetskii Soyuz,* 623.

24. Plokhy, *The Last Empire,* 302–12. Interview with Kravchuk available at http://oralhistory .org.ua/interview-ua/510.

25. Gaidar, *Days of Defeat and Victory,* 124–26.

26. Yeltsin, *Struggle for Russia,* 111–15; Bush and Scowcroft, *A World Transformed,* 544; transcript of Bush's conversation with Yeltsin is available at https://bush41library .tamu.edu/files/memcons-telcons/1991-12-08--Yeltsin.pdf.

27. Dobbs, *Down with Big Brother,* 442–45.

28. Handleman, *Comrade Criminal,* 93.

29. Dawisha, *Putin's Kleptocracy,* 24.

30. Dawisha, *Putin's Kleptocracy,* 26.

Chapter 19: Why Did the USSR Collapse?

1. The literature on the collapse of the USSR is immense. A good place to start remains Kotkin, *Armageddon Averted. The Collapse of the Soviet Union 1985–1991,* by David Marples is a short introduction to the subject with many suggestions for further reading. Strayer, *Why Did the Soviet Union Collapse?,* provides a survey of the issues from an academic perspective. In its winter 2003 issue, the *Journal of Cold War Studies* published a series of articles by outstanding specialists on many aspects of the issue. Lundestad, *The Fall of the Great Powers,* provides theoretical and comparative perspectives on the Soviet collapse. In *A Normal Totalitarian Society,* Shlapentokh provides practical and well-documented answers to the question of what caused the collapse as well as the equally important question of what did not cause the USSR to fall.

2. Kozlov, *Mass Uprisings in the USSR,* 39, 136–47, 314.

3. Kozlov, *Mass Uprisings in the USSR,* 221–79.

4. Eydelman, "Monopolized Statistics under a Totalitarian Regime," 75–76.

5. Shlapentokh, *A Normal Totalitarian Society,* 116.

6. Ellman and Kontorovich, *The Destruction of the Soviet Economic System,* 12; Shlapentokh, *A Normal Totalitarian Society,* 116, 206.

7. Ellman and Kontorovich, *The Destruction of the Soviet Economic System,* 41.

8. Ellman and Kontorovich, *The Destruction of the Soviet Economic System,* 43.

9. Gaddy, *The Price of the Past,* 10.

10. Gaddy, *The Price of the Past,* 13–14.

11. Mikoyan, "Eroding the Soviet 'Culture of Secrecy.'"

12. Gorbachev, *Memoirs*, 147.
13. Sagdeyev, *The Making of a Soviet Scientist*, 70.
14. Johnson and Parta, *Cold War Broadcasting*.
15. Bashkirova, "The Foreign Radio Audience in the USSR."
16. Kozlov, Fitzpatrick, and Mironenko, *Sedition*, 21.
17. Woodward, "Cold War Radio Jamming."
18. Malia, *The Soviet Tragedy*, 495.
19. Shlapentokh, *A Normal Totalitarian Society*, 99.
20. Palazhenko, *My Years with Gorbachev and Shevardnadze*, 144.

Postscript

1. Putin made these remarks in an April 25, 2005, address to the Russian Federal assembly. They can be accessed (in Russian) at the following Kremlin site: http://archive .kremlin.ru/appears/2005/04/25/1223_type63372type63374type82634_87049.shtml. What he said in Russian was this: "Прежде всего следует признать, что крушение Советского Союза было крупнейшей геополитической катастрофой века." Since the Russian language lacks indefinite articles, this has allowed arguments to develop about whether what the president really meant to say was "Above all, we should acknowledge that the collapse of the Soviet Union was *the* major geopolitical disaster of the century" or merely *a* major disaster. I find it a distinction without much difference. I am indebted to observer of Russia Patrick Armstrong for bringing this to public attention. See http://www.russiaotherpointsofview.com/2010/11/the -third-turn.html.
2. For a discussion of the conflict between Yeltsin and his parliamentary rivals in 1993, from which this material is drawn, see Sell, "Embassy under Siege," 43–64.
3. For a report of Yeltsin's speech, see Norman Kempster and Dean E. Murphy, "Broader NATO May Bring 'Cold Peace' Yeltsin Warns," *Los Angeles Times*, December 6, 1994. Accessed at http://articles.latimes.com/1994–12–06/news/mn-5629_1_cold-war.

BIBLIOGRAPHY

Archives and Online Sources

The American Presidency Project
Cold War International History Project (CWIHP)
Mershon Center for International Security Studies, Ohio State University, interviews
    with former senior Soviet national security officials
National Security Archive (NS Archive)
Parallel History Project
US Department of State, Foreign Relations of the United States (FRUS)

Conferences

Cold War Endgame, Princeton University, Woodrow Wilson School, March 29–30, 1996.
"Global Competition and the Deterioration of US-Soviet Relations, 1977–1980," Carter-
    Brezhnev project, Fort Lauderdale, Florida, March 23–26, 1995.
The Intervention in Afghanistan and the Fall of Détente, Norwegian Nobel Institute,
    Lysebu, September 17–20, 1995. CWIHP Bulletin, winter 1996/97.
"SALT II and the Growth of Mistrust," Carter-Brezhnev project, May 6–9, 1994, Musgrove
    Plantation, St. Simons Island, Georgia.
US-Soviet Relations and Soviet Foreign Policy toward the Middle East and Africa in the
    1970s, Norwegian Nobel Institute, Lysebu, Norway, October 1–3, 1994.

Collections of Documents

Burr, William. The Kissinger Transcripts: The Top Secret Talks with Beijing and Moscow.
    New York: New Press, 1999.
Gorbachev, Mikhail. "Otvechaya na Vyzov Vremeni, Vneshnyaya Politika Perestroiki:
    Dokumentalnye Svidetelstva" [Answering the challenge of time, the foreign policy of
    Perestroika: Documentary testimony]. Moscow: Ves Mir, 2010.

Labrie, Roger P. *SALT Handbook: Key Documents and Issues 1972–1979*. Washington, DC: American Enterprise Institute for Public Policy Research, 1979.

Rossiskaya Akadmiya Nauk (RAN). "Sovetskaya Vneshnaya Politika v Godi Kholodnoi Voini 1945–1985" [Soviet foreign policy in the years of the Cold War, 1945–1985]. Moscow: 1995.

Savranskaya, Svetlana, Thomas Blanton, Vladislav Zubok, eds. *Masterpieces of History: The Peaceful End of the Cold War in Europe*. Budapest: Central European University Press, 2010.

Soviet-American Relations: The Détente Years, 1969–1972. Washington, DC: US Government Printing Office, 2007.

US Arms Control and Disarmament Agency. *Arms Control and Disarmament Agreements: Texts and Histories of the Negotiations*. Washington, DC: 1990.

V Politburo. "TSK KPSS: Po Zapisam Anatoliya Chernyayeva, Vadima Medvedeva, i Georgiya Shakhnazarova (1985–1991)" [In the Politburo: From the notes of Anatoliy Chernyayev, Vadim Medvedev, and Georgiy Shakhnazarov]. Moscow: Fond Gorbacheva, 2006.

Yakovlev, Aleksandr. *Perestroika: 1985–1991 Neizdannoe, Maloizvestnoe, Zabytoe* [Perestroika: 1985–1991, unpublished, little known, forgotten]. Moscow: Demoktratiya, 2008.

Memoirs and Firsthand Accounts

Adamyshin, Anatoly, and Richard Schifter. *Human Rights, Perestroika, and the End of the Cold War*. Washington, DC: USIP Press, 2009.

Adelman, Kenneth L. *The Great Universal Embrace: Arms Summitry—A Skeptic's Account*. New York: Simon and Schuster, 1989.

Akromeyev, S. F., and G. M. Korniyenko. *Glazami Marshala i Diplomata: Kriticheski Vzglad na Vneshnyuyu Politiku SSSR do i pocle 1985 Goda* [Through the eyes of a marshal and a diplomat: A critical look at the foreign policy of the USSR before and after 1985]. Moscow: Mezhdunarodnoe Otnoshenie, 1992.

Aleksandrov-Agentov, A. M. *Ot Kollontai do Gorbacheva: Vospominaniya Diplomata* [From Kollontai to Gorbachev: Memoirs of a diplomat]. Moscow: Mezhdunarodnye Otnosheniya, 1994.

Alekseyeva, Lyudmila. *Istoriya Inakomysliya v SSSR* [The history of dissidence in the USSR]. Benson, VT: Khronika, 1984.

Alexeyeva, Lyudmila, and Paul Goldberg. *The Thaw Generation: Coming of Age in the Post-Stalin Era*. Boston: Little, Brown, 1990.

Amalrik, Andrei. *Notes of a Revolutionary*. New York: Knopf, 1982.

Anderson, Martin. *Revolution: The Reagan Legacy*. Stanford, CA: Hoover Institution Press, 1990.

Andrew, Christopher, and Vasili Mitrokhin. *The Sword and the Shield: The Mitrokhin Archive and the Secret History of the KGB*. New York: Basic Books, 1999.

Andrew, Christopher, and Vasili Mitrokhin. *The World Was Going Our Way: The KGB and the Battle for the Third World*. New York: Basic Books, 2005.

Arbatov, Georgi. *The System: An Insider's Life in Soviet Politics*. New York: Random House, 1993.

Baker, James A. *The Politics of Diplomacy: Revolution, War, and Peace, 1989–1992.* New York: Putnam, 1995.

Baturin, Yu M., et al. *Epokha Yeltsina* [The Yeltsin epoch]. Moscow: Vagrius, 2001.

Bearden, Milt, and James Risen. *The Main Enemy: The Inside Story of the CIA's Final Showdown with the KGB.* New York: Random House, 2003.

Bobkov, Filip. *KGB I Vlast* [The KGB and power]. Moscow: Veteran MP, 1995.

Boldin, Valery. *Ten Years that Shook the World: The Gorbachev Era as Witnessed by His Chief of Staff.* New York: Basic Books, 1994.

Borovik, Artem. *The Hidden War: A Russian Journalist's Account of the Soviet War in Afghanistan.* New York: Atlantic Monthly, 1990.

Braithwaite, Rodric. *Across the Moscow River: The World Turned Upside Down.* New Haven, CT: Yale University Press, 2002.

Brezhneva, Luba. *The World I Left Behind: Pieces of a Past.* New York: Random House, 1995.

Brinkley, Douglas, ed. *The Reagan Diaries.* New York: HarperCollins, 2007.

Brutents, K. N. *Tridtsat Let na Staroi Ploshchadi* [Thirty years at Old Square]. Moscow: Mezhdunarodnye Otnosheniya, 1998.

Brzezinski, Zbigniew. *Power and Principle: Memoirs of the National Security Adviser, 1977–1981.* New York: Farrar, Straus, Giroux, 1985.

Bukovsky, Vladimir. *To Build a Castle—My Life as a Dissenter.* New York: Viking, 1978.

Burlatskiy, Fedor. *Mikhail Gorbachev-Boris Yeltsin Skhvatka* [Mikhail Gorbachev-Boris Yeltsin Fight]. Moscow: Sobranie, 2008.

Bush, George, and Brent Scowcroft. *A World Transformed.* New York: Vintage, 1999.

Carter, Jimmy. *Keeping Faith: Memoirs of a President.* New York: Bantam, 1982.

Chazov, Yevgeniy. *Zdorove I Vlast: Vospominaniya "Kremlevskovo Vracha"* [Health and power: Memoirs of the "Kremlin doctor"]. Moscow: Novosti, 1992.

Cheney, Dick. *In My Time: A Personal and Political Memoir.* New York: Threshold Editions, 2011.

Cherkashin, Victor, with Gregory Feifer. *Spy Handler: Memoir of a KGB Officer.* New York: Basic Books, 2005.

Chernyayev, A. S. *Shest Let S Gorbachevim* [Six years with Gorbachev]. Moscow: Progress, 1993.

Chervov, Nikolai. *Yadernii Krugovorot: Chto Bylo, Chto Budet* [The nuclear cycle: What was, what will be]. Moscow: OLMA-Press, 2001.

Combs, Dick. *Inside the Soviet Alternative Universe: The Cold War's End and the Soviet Union's Fall Reappraised.* University Park: Pennsylvania State University Press, 2008.

Cordovez, Diego, and Selig S. Harrison. *Out of Afghanistan: The Inside Story of the Soviet Withdrawal.* New York: Oxford University Press, 1995.

Critchlow, James. *Radio Hole-in-the-Head/Radio Liberty: An Insider's Story of Cold War Broadcasting.* Washington, DC: American University Press, 2006.

Daniloff, Nicholas. *Two Lives, One Russia.* Boston: Houghton Mifflin, 1988.

Detinov, Nikolay N., and Aleksandr G. Savelyev. *The Big Five: Arms Control Decision-Making in the Soviet Union.* Westport, CT: Praeger, 1995.

Dobrynin, Anatoly. *In Confidence: Moscow's Ambassador to Six Cold War Presidents.* New York: Times Books, 1995.

Ellman, Michael, and Vladimir Kontorovich, eds. *The Destruction of the Soviet Economic System: An Insider's History*. Armonk, NY: M. E. Sharpe, 1998.

Falin, Valentin. *Bez Skidok na Obstoyatelstva* [Without allowances for the circumstances]. Moscow: Republika, 1999.

Falin, Valentin. *Konflikty V Kremle: Sumerki Bogov Po-Russki* [Conflicts in the Kremlin: The twilight of the Russian gods]. Moscow: Tsentrpoligraf, 1999.

Feifer, George. *Moscow Farewell*. New York: Viking, 1976.

Fetisov, T. I. *Premier Izvestni i Neizvestni: Vospominanita o A. N. Kosygina* [The premier known and unknown: Recollections about A. N. Kosygin]. Moscow: Respublika, 1997.

Fischer, Benjamin B. *A Cold War Conundrum: The 1983 Soviet War Scare*. Washington, DC: CSI Publications, 1997.

Fitzwater, Marlin. *Call the Briefing*. New York: Times Books, 1995.

Ford, Gerald. *A Time to Heal: The Autobiography of Gerald Ford*. New York: Harper and Row, 1979.

Gaidar, Yegor. *Collapse of an Empire: Lessons for Modern Russia*. Washington, DC: Brookings Institute, 2007.

Gaidar, Yegor. *Days of Defeat and Victory*. Seattle: University of Washington Press, 1999.

Gates, Robert. *From the Shadows: The Ultimate Insider's Story of Five Presidents and How They Won the Cold War*. New York: Simon and Shuster, 1996.

Genscher, Hans-Dietrich. *Rebuilding a House Divided: A Memoir by the Architect of Germany's Reunification*. New York: Broadway Books, 1998.

Glitman, Maynard. *The Last Battle of the Cold War*. New York: Palgrave, 2006.

Goodby, James E. *At the Borderline of Armageddon: How American Presidents Managed the Atom Bomb*. Lanham, MD: Rowman and Littlefield, 2006.

Gorbachev, Mikhail. *Memoirs*. New York: Doubleday, 1995.

Gorbachev, Mikhail. *Naedine S Soboi* [Alone with myself]. Moscow: Novaya Gazeta, 2012.

Gorbachev, Mikhail. *Zhizn i Reformy* [Life and reforms]. Moscow: Novosti, 1995.

Grachev, Andrei. *Final Days: The Inside Story of the Collapse of the Soviet Union*. Boulder, CO: Westview, 1995.

Grachev, Andrei. *Gorbachev's Gamble: Soviet Foreign Policy and the End of the Cold War*. Malden, MA: Polity, 2008.

Grinyevskii, Oleg. *Tainy Sovetskoi Diplomatii* [Secrets of a Soviet diplomat]. Moscow: Vagrius, 2000.

Grishin, V. V. *Ot Khrushcheva do Gorbacheva: Memyary i Politicheskie Portreti Pyati Gensekov* [From Khrushchev to Gorbachev: Memories and political portraits of five general secretaries and of A. N. Kosygin]. Moscow: ASPOL, 1996.

Gromyko, Anatoliy. *Andrey Gromyko V Labirintakh Kremlya: Vospominaniya i Rasmyshleniya Syna* [Andrei Gromyko in the labyrinths of the Kremlin: Recollections and thoughts of his son]. Moscow: Avtor, 1997.

Hutchins, Robert L. *American Diplomacy and the End of the Cold War: An Insider's Account of US Policy in Europe, 1989–1992*. Baltimore: Johns Hopkins University Press, 1997.

Hyland, William. *Mortal Rivals*. New York: Random House, 1987.

Israelyan, Victor. *On the Battlefields of the Cold War: A Soviet Ambassador's Confession.* University Park: Pennsylvania State University Press, 2003.

Johnson, A. Ross. RFE *and* RL: *The* CIA *Years and Beyond.* Washington, DC: Woodrow Wilson Center Press, 2010.

Kalugin, Oleg. *The First Directorate: My 32 Years in Intelligence and Espionage against the West.* New York: St. Martin's, 1994.

Katayev, Vitaly. *A Memoir of the Missile Age: One Man's Journey.* Stanford, CA: Hoover Institute, 2015.

Kissinger, Henry. *White House Years.* Boston: Little, Brown, 1979.

Kissinger, Henry. *Years of Upheaval.* Boston: Little, Brown, 1982.

Korniyenko, G. M. *Kholodnaya Voina: Svidetelstvo ee Uchastnika* [The Cold War: Testimony of a participant]. Moscow: Mezhdunarodnye Otnosheniya, 1994.

Korzhakov, Aleksandr. *Boris Yeltsin: ot Rassveta do Zakata* [Boris Yeltsin: From dawn to sunset]. Moscow: Interbuk, 1997.

Krasilnikov, Rem. *Prizraki c Ulitsa Chaikovskogo: Shpionskie Aktsii TsRU CShA v Sovetskim Soyuzum Soyuze I Rossiskoi Federatsii v 1979–1992 godakh* [Specters from Chaikovski Street: Espionage activities of the USA CIA in the Soviet Union and the Russian federation from 1979 to 1992]. Moscow: Geya Interegnum, 1999.

Kryuchkov, Vladimir. *Lichnoe Delo, Chast Pervaya i Vtoraya* [Personal affair]. Moscow: Olimp/ACT, 1996.

Kuzichkin, Vladimir. *Inside the* KGB: *My Life in Soviet Espionage.* New York: Pantheon, 1990.

Kvitsinskiy, Yuli. *Vremya i Sluchai: Zametnika Professonala* [Seasons and circumstances: Notes of a professional]. Moscow: OLMA-Press, 1999.

Lebed, Alexander. *My Life and My Country.* New York: Regnery, 1997.

Ligachev, Yegor. *Inside Gorbachev's Kremlin.* New York: Random House, 1993.

Lyakovskiy, Aleksandr. *Tragediya i Doblest Afgana.* [Tragedy and valor of an "Afghan"]. Moscow: Iskona, 1995.

Major, John. *The Autobiography.* New York: HarperCollins, 2000.

Matlock, Jack F. *Autopsy on an Empire: The American Ambassador's Account of the Collapse of the Soviet Union.* New York: Random House, 1995.

Matlock, Jack F. *Reagan and Gorbachev: How the Cold War Ended.* New York: Random House, 2005.

McFarlane, Robert C. *Special Trust.* London: Cadell and Davies, 1994.

Medvedev, Grigory. *The Truth about Chernobyl.* New York: Basic Books, 1991.

Medvedev, Vadim A. *V Komande Gorbacheva, Vzglad Iznutri* [On the Gorbachev team: The view from inside]. Moscow: Bylina, 1994.

Medvedev, Vladimir. *Chelovek za Spinoi* [Man behind the back]. Moscow: Russlit, 1994.

Mihajlov, Mihajlo. *Moscow Summer.* New York: Farrar, Straus, and Giroux, 1965.

Nelson, Michael. *War of the Black Heavens: The Battles of Western Broadcasting in the Cold War.* Syracuse, NY: Syracuse University Press, 1997.

Nitze, Paul H. *From Hiroshima to Glasnost: At the Center of Decision—A Memoir.* New York: Weidenfeld, 1989.

Nixon, Richard. *RN: The Memoirs of Richard Nixon.* New York: Grosset and Dunlap, 1978.

Noonan, Peggy. *When Character Was King*. New York: Viking, 2001.

Observer. *Message from Moscow*. New York: Knopf, 1969.

Onikov, Leon. KPSS: *Anatomiya Raspada: Vzglad Iznutri Apparatura TsK* [Anatomy of disintegration: A view from inside the CC apparatus]. Moscow: Respublika, 1996.

Orlov, Yuri. *Dangerous Thoughts: Memoirs of a Russian Life*. New York: William Morrow, 1991.

Palazhenko, Pavel. *My Years with Gorbachev and Shevardnadze: The Memoir of a Soviet Interpreter*. University Park: Pennsylvania State University Press, 2009.

Pipes, Richard. *Vixi: Memoirs of a Non-Believer*. New Haven, CT: Yale University Press, 2003.

Powell, Colin L. *My American Life*. New York: Random House, 1995.

Puddington, Arch. *Broadcasting Freedom: The Cold War Triumph of Radio Free Europe and Radio Liberty*. Lexington: University of Kentucky Press, 2000.

Raleigh, Donald J. *Soviet Baby Boomers: An Oral History of Russia's Cold War Generation*. New York: Oxford University Press, 2012.

Reagan, Ronald. *An American Life*. New York: Simon and Schuster, 1990.

Reddaway, Peter, ed. *Uncensored Russia: Protest and Dissent in the Soviet Union*. New York: McGraw-Hill, 1972.

Reed, Thomas C. *At the Abyss: An Insider's History of the Cold War*. New York: Random House, 2004.

Richmond, Yale. *Cultural Exchange and the Cold War: Raising the Iron Curtain*. University Park: Pennsylvania State University Press, 2003.

Ryzhkov, Nikolai. *Perestroika: Istoriya Predatelstv* [Perestroika: History of betrayal]. Moscow: Novosti, 1992.

Sagdeyev, Roald. *The Making of a Soviet Scientist: My Adventures in Nuclear Fusion and Space from Stalin to Star Wars*. New York: John Wiley, 1994.

Sakharov, Andrei. *Memoirs*. New York: Knopf, 1990.

Sakharov, Andrei. *My Country and the World*. New York: Vintage, 1975.

Sakharov, Andrei. *Progress, Coexistence, and Intellectual Freedom*. New York: W. W. Norton, 1968.

Shakhnazarov, Georgii. *Tsena Svobody: Reformatsiya Gorbacheva Glazami ego Pomoshchnika* [The price of freedom: The reformations of Gorbachev through the eyes of his assistant]. Moscow: Rossika/Zevs, 1993.

Shaposhnikov, Yevgeny. *Vybor* [Choice]. Moscow: PIK, 1995.

Sharansky, Natan. *Fear No Evil*. New York: Vintage, 1989.

Shelest, P. Ye. *Da ne Sydimy Budete: Dnevnikovye Zapisi, Vospominaniya Chlena Politburo* [To not be condemned: Diary notes, recollections of a Politburo member]. Moscow: Edition q, 1995.

Shevardnadze, Eduard. *Kogda Rukhnul Zhelezni Zanaves, Vstrechi i Vospominaniya*. [When the Iron Curtain collapsed, meetings and recollections]. Moscow: Evropa, 2009.

Shevardnadze, Eduard. *Moi Vybor v Zashchitu Demokratii i Svobody* [My choice in defense of democracy and freedom]. Moscow: Novosti, 1991.

Shevchenko, Arkady N. *Breaking with Moscow*. New York: Ballantine, 1985.

Shubin, Vladimir. *The Hot Cold War: The USSR in Southern Africa*. New York: Pluto, 2008.

Shultz, George. *Turmoil and Triumph: My Years as Secretary of State*. New York: Scribner, 1993.

Simons, Thomas W. *The End of the Cold War?* New York: St. Martin's, 1990.

Smith, Gerard. *Doubletalk: The Story of SALT I*. Lanham, MD: University Press of America, 1985.

Smith, Ray. *The Craft of Political Analysis for Diplomats*. Washington, DC: Potomac Books, 2011.

Solzhenitsyn, Aleksandr. *Invisible Allies*. London: Harvill, 1997.

Speakes, Larry. *Speaking Out: The Reagan Presidency from Inside the White House*. New York: Scribner's, 1998.

Starodubov, Viktor. *Superderzhavy XX Veka: Strategicheskoe Protivoborstvo* [The twentieth-century superpowers: Strategic confrontation]. Moscow: OLMA-Press, 2001.

Stepankov, V. i Ye. Lisov. *Kremlevskii Zagovor* [Kremlin plot]. Moscow: Ogonek, 1992.

Sukanov, Lev. *Tri Goda c Yeltsinom: Zapiski Pervogo Pomoshchika* [Three years with Yeltsin: Notes of a first assistant]. Riga: Vaga, 1992.

Sukhodrev, V. M. *Yazik Moi-Drug Moi: Ot Khrushcheva do Gorbacheva*. [My words, my friend: From Khrushchev to Gorbachev]. Moscow: Act, 1999.

Thatcher, Margaret. *The Downing Street Years, 1979–1990*. New York: Harper Perennial, 1993.

Tomsen, Peter. *The Wars of Afghanistan: Messianic Terrorism, Tribal Conflicts, and the Failures of the Great Powers*. New York: Public Affairs, 2013.

Vance, Cyrus. *Hard Choices: Critical Years in America's Foreign Policy*. New York: Simon and Schuster, 1983.

Varennikov, Valentin I. *Nepovtorimoe, Chasti 4, 5, i 6* [Unrepeatable]. Moscow: Sovetskii Pisatel, 2001.

Vorotnikov, V. I. *A Bylo Eto Tak: Iz Dnevnika Chlena Politburo TsK KPSS* [And it was thus: From the diary of a Politburo member]. Moscow: Sovet Veteranov Knigoizdaniya, 1995.

Walesa, Lech. *The Struggle and the Triumph: An Autobiography*. New York: Arcade, 1992.

Weinberger, Caspar. *Fighting for Peace: Seven Critical Years in the Pentagon*. New York: Warner, 1990.

Wolf, Marcus. *Man without a Face: The Autobiography of Communism's Greatest Spymaster*. New York: Public Affairs, 1997.

Yakovlev, Aleksandr. *Omut Pamyati* [The shadow of memory]. Moscow: VAGIRUS, 2000.

Yakovlev, Aleksandr. *Sumerki* [Twilight]. Moscow: Maternik, 2003.

Yaroshinskaya, Alla. *Chernobyl: The Forbidden Truth*. Lincoln: University of Nebraska Press, 1995.

Yarynich, Valery. *C3: Nuclear Command, Control, Cooperation*. Washington, DC: Center for Defense Information, 2003.

Yeltsin, Boris. *Against the Grain: An Autobiography*. London: Pan, 1990.

Yeltsin, Boris. *The Struggle for Russia*. New York: Belka/Random House, 1994.

Zaslavskaya, Tatyana. *The Second Socialist Revolution*. Bloomington: Indiana University Press, 1990.

Zelikow, Philip, and Condoleeza Rice. *Germany Unified and Europe Transformed: A Study in Statecraft*. Cambridge, MA: Harvard University Press, 1995.

Zolotarev, General-Maior V. A., ed. *Rossiya (SSSR) V Lokalnikh Voinakh i Voennikh Konflikti XX Veka* [Russia (USSR) in local wars and military conflicts in the twentieth century]. Moscow: Politgrafresursi, 2000.

Secondary Sources

Ahonen, Pertti. *Death at the Berlin Wall*. New York: Oxford University Press, 2011.

Aksyutin, Yuri V., ed. *L. I. Brezhnev, Materiali k Biografii* [L. I. Brezhnev, material toward a biography]. Moscow: Izdatelstvo Politicheskoi Literatury, 1991.

Ambrose, Stephen. *Nixon: The Triumph of a Politician*. Vol. 2. New York: Simon and Schuster, 1989.

Anderson, Annelise, Martin Anderson, and Kiron K. Skinner, eds. *Reagan, in His Own Hand: The Writings of Ronald Reagan that Reveal His Revolutionary Vision for America*. New York: Simon and Schuster 2001.

Andrew, Christopher. *For the President's Eyes Only: Secret Intelligence and the American Presidency from Washington to Bush*. New York: HarperCollins, 1996.

Andrew, Christopher, and Oleg Gordiyevsky. *Comrade Kryuchkov's Instructions: Top Secret Files on KGB Foreign Operations, 1975–1985*. Stanford, CA: Stanford University Press, 1993.

Andrew, Christopher, and Oleg Gordiyevsky. *KGB: The Inside Story*. New York: Harper-Collins, 1990.

Arnold, Anthony. *The Fateful Pebble: Afghanistan's Role in the Fall of the Soviet Empire*. Novato, CA: Presidio, 1993.

Aron, Leon. *Roads to the Temple: Truth, Memory, Ideas and Ideals in the Making of the Russian Revolution, 1987–1991*. New Haven, CT: Yale University Press, 2012.

Aron, Leon. *Yeltsin: A Revolutionary Life*. New York: St. Martin's, 2000.

Ash, Timothy Garton. *In Europe's Name: Germany and the Divided Continent*. New York: Vintage, 1994.

Bacon, Edward, and Mark Sandle, eds. *Brezhnev Reconsidered*. London: Palgrave, 2002.

Bagley, Tennent H. *Spymaster: Startling Cold War Revelations of a Soviet KGB Chief*. New York: Skyhorse, 2013.

Barrass, Gordon S. *The Great Cold War: A Journey through the Hall of Mirrors*. Stanford, CA: Stanford University Press, 2009.

Barylski, Robert V. *The Soldier in Russian Politics: Duty, Dictatorship, and Democracy under Gorbachev and Yeltsin*. New Brunswick, NJ: Transaction, 1998.

Beckerman, Gal. *When They Come for Us, We'll Be Gone: The Epic Struggle to Save Soviet Jewry*. New York: Mariner Books, 2010.

Beissinger, Mark R. *Nationalist Mobilization and the Collapse of the Soviet State*. Cambridge: Cambridge University Press, 2002.

Bertsch, Gary. "US-Soviet Trade: A Sector of Mutual Benefit?" In *Sectors of Mutual Benefit in US-Soviet Relations*, ed. Nish Jamgotch. Durham, NC: Duke University Press, 1985.

Blacker, Coit. *Hostage to Revolution: Gorbachev and Soviet Security Policy, 1985–1991*. New York: Council on Foreign Relations, 1993.

Bonnell, Victoria E., Ann Cooper, and Gregory Freidin, eds. *Russia at the Barricades: Eyewitness Accounts of the August 1991 Coup*. Armonk, NY: M. E. Sharpe, 1994.

Bourne, Peter. *Jimmy Carter: A Comprehensive Biography from Plains to Post-Presidency*. New York: Scribner's, 1997.

Braithwaite, Roderic. *Afgantsy: The Russians in Afghanistan, 1979–1989*. London: Profile Books, 2011.

Brands, H. W. *Reagan: The Life*. New York: Doubleday, 2015.

Brinkley, Douglas, ed. *The Reagan Diaries*. New York: HarperCollins, 2007.

Brown, Archie. *The Gorbachev Factor*. New York: Oxford University Press, 1997.

Cannon, Lou. *President Reagan: The Role of a Lifetime*. New York: Public Affairs, 2000.

Carrere d'Encausse, Helene. *The End of the Soviet Empire: The Triumph of the Nations*. New York: Basic Books, 1993.

Chen, Jian. *Mao's China and the Cold War*. Chapel Hill: University of North Carolina Press, 2001.

Cohen, Stephen F., and Katrina vanden Heuvel. *Voices of Glasnost: Interviews with Gorbachev's Reformers*. New York: W. W. Norton, 1989.

Coll, Steve. *Ghost Wars: The Secret History of the CIA, Afghanistan, and Bin Laden, from the Soviet Invasion to September 10, 2001*. New York: Penguin, 2004.

Collins, John M. *US-Soviet Military Balance: Concepts and Capabilities, 1960–1980*. New York: McGraw-Hill, 1980.

Colton, Timothy J. *Yeltsin: A Life*. New York: Basic Books, 2008.

Crile, George. *Charlie Wilson's War*. New York: Atlantic Monthly, 2003.

Daalder, Ivo H., and I. M. Destler. *In the Shadow of the Oval Office: Profiles of the National Security Advisers and the Presidents They Served*. New York: Simon and Schuster, 2009.

Dawisha, Karen. *Putin's Kleptocracy: Who Owns Russia?* New York: Simon and Schuster, 2014.

Dobbs, Michael. *Down with Big Brother: The Fall of the Soviet Empire*. New York: Vintage, 1996.

Doder, Dusko. *Shadows and Whispers: Power Politics inside the Kremlin from Brezhnev to Gorbachev*. New York: Penguin, 1988.

Drell, Sidney D., and George P. Shultz, eds. *Implications of the Reykjavik Summit on Its Twentieth Anniversary*. Stanford, CA: Hoover Institution Press, 2007.

English, Robert D. *Russia and the Idea of the West: Gorbachev, Intellectuals, and the End of the Cold War*. New York: Columbia University Press, 2000.

Feifer, Gregory. *The Great Gamble: The Soviet War in Afghanistan*. New York: HarperCollins, 2009.

Gaddis, John Lewis, et al., eds. *Cold War Statesmen Confront the Bomb: Nuclear Diplomacy since 1945*. New York: Oxford University Press, 1999.

Gaddy, Clifford G. *The Price of the Past: Russia's Struggle with the Legacy of a Militarized Economy*. Washington, DC: Brookings Institute, 1996.

Gaiduk, Ilya V. *The Soviet Union and the Vietnam War*. Chicago: Ivan R. Dee, 1996.

Garthoff, Raymond L. *The Great Transition: American-Soviet Relations and the End of the Cold War*. Washington, DC: Brookings Institute, 1994.

Gelman, Harry. *The Brezhnev Politburo and the Decline of Détente*. Ithaca, NY: Cornell University Press, 1984.

Gill, Graham. *The Collapse of the Single-Party System: The Disintegration of the Communist Party of the Soviet Union*. London: Cambridge University Press, 1994.

Goldgeier, James M., and Michael McFaul. *Power and Purpose: US Policy toward Russia after the Cold War*. Washington, DC: Brookings Institution Press, 2003.

Graham, Loren. *The Ghost of the Executed Engineer: Technology and the Fall of the Soviet Union*. Cambridge, MA: Harvard University Press, 1993.

Grau, Lester W., and Michael A. Guess, eds. *The Soviet-Afghan War: How a Superpower Fought and Lost*. Lawrence: University Press of Kansas, 2002.

Grimes, Sandra, and Jeanne Vertefeuille. *Circle of Treason*. Annapolis, MD: Naval Institute Press, 2013.

Handelman, Stephen. *Comrade Criminal: Russia's New Mafiya*. New Haven, CT: Yale University Press, 1995.

Hanson, Philip. *The Rise and Fall of the Soviet Economy: An Economic History of the USSR from 1945*. New York: Longman, 2003.

Haslam, Jonathan. *Russia's Cold War: From the October Revolution to the Fall of the Wall*. New Haven, CT: Yale University Press, 2011.

Herspring, Dale R. *The Soviet High Command, 1967–1989: Personalities and Politics*. Princeton, NJ: Princeton University Press, 1990.

Hoffman, David. *The Dead Hand: The Untold Story of the Cold War Arms Race and Its Dangerous Legacy*. New York: Doubleday, 2009.

Hough, Jerry F. *Democratization and Revolution in the USSR, 1985–1991*. Washington, DC: Brookings Institution Press, 1997.

International Atomic Energy Agency (IAEA). *INSAG 7 The Chernobyl Accident: Updating INSAG 1*. Vienna: IAEA, 1992.

International Civil Aviation Organization (ICAO). *Report on the Destruction of Korean Air Lines Flight 007 on August 31, 1983*. Montreal: ICAO, 1993.

Johnson, A. Ross, and R. Eugene Parta. *Cold War Broadcasting: Impact on the Soviet Union and Eastern Europe*. New York: Central European University Press, 2010.

Kaplan, Stephen S. *Diplomacy of Power: Soviet Armed Forces as a Political Instrument*. Washington, DC: Brookings Institution Press, 1981.

Kemp-Welch, A. *Poland under Communism: A Cold War History*. Cambridge: Cambridge University Press, 2008.

Kimball, Jeffrey. *Nixon's Vietnam War*. Lawrence: University Press of Kansas, 1998.

Kimball, Jeffrey. *The Vietnam War Files: Uncovering the Secret History of Nixon-Era Strategy*. Lawrence: University Press of Kansas, 2004.

Kokoshin, Andrei A. *Soviet Strategic Thought, 1917–1991*. Cambridge, MA: MIT Press, 1998.

Korniyenko, G. M. "Kholodnaya Voina Kak Osnovoi Generator Gonki Vooruzhenie." In *Sovetskaya Voyennaya Moshch. Sovetskaya Voyennaya Moshch ot Stalina do Gorbacheva*, ed. A. V. Minayev. Moscow: Voennii Parad, 1999.

Kozlov, Vladimir A. *Mass Uprisings in the USSR: Protest and Rebellion in the Post-Stalin Years*. Armonk, NY: M. E. Sharpe, 2002.

Kozlov, Vladimir A., Sheila Fitzpatrick, and Sergei V. Mironenko, eds. *Sedition: Everyday Resistance in the Soviet Union under Khrushchev and Brezhnev*. New Haven, CT: Yale University Press, 2011.

Lee, William T., and Richard F. Staar. *Soviet Military Policy since World War II*. Stanford, CA: Hoover Institute Press, 1996.

Lévesque, Jacques. *The Enigma of 1989: The USSR and the Liberation of Eastern Europe*. Berkeley: University of California Press, 1997.

Lourie, Richard. *Sakharov: A Biography*. Hanover, NH: Brandeis University Press, 2002.

Lundberg, Kristen. "The Politics of a Covert Action: The US, the Mujahedin, and the Stinger Missile," JFK Case Study C15–99–1546. Cambridge, MA: JFK Library, Harvard University.

Maier, Charles. *Dissolution: The Crisis of Communism and the End of East Germany*. Princeton, NJ: Princeton University Press, 1999.

Malia, Martin. *The Soviet Tragedy: A History of Socialism in Russia, 1917–1991*. New York: Free Press, 1994.

Mann, James. *The Rebellion of Ronald Reagan: A History of the End of the Cold War*. New York: Viking, 2009.

Marples, David R. *The Collapse of the Soviet Union, 1985–1991*. London: Pearson, 2004.

Mastny, Vojtech, and Malcolm Byrne, eds. *A Cardboard Castle: An Inside History of the Warsaw Pact*. Budapest: Central European University Press, 2005.

May, Ernest R., John D. Steinbrunner, and Thomas W. Wolfe. "History of the Strategic Arms Competition, 1945–1972." Part II. Washington, DC: OSD Historical Office, 1981.

Meacham, John. *Destiny and Power: The American Odyssey of George Herbert Walker Bush*. New York: Random House, 2015.

Medvedev, Roy. *Gensek S Lubyanki: Politicheskaya Biografiya Yu. V. Andropova* [Gensek from Lubyanka: A political biography of Yu. V. Andropov]. Leta Novgorod: Nizhnii, 1993.

Medvedev, Roy. *Lichnost i Epokha: Politicheski Portret L. I. Brezhneva* [Personality and epoch: A political portrait of L. I. Brezhnev]. Moscow: Novosti, 1991.

Medvedev, Roy, and Giulietto Chiesa. *Time of Change: An Insider's View of Russia's Transformation*. New York: Pantheon, 1989.

Meyer, Michael. *The Year that Changed the World: The Untold Story of the Fall of the Berlin Wall*. New York: Scribner's, 2009.

Minayev, A. V., ed. *Sovetskaya Voyennaya Moshch ot Stalina do Gorbacheva* [Soviet military might, from Stalin to Gorbachev]. Moscow: Voennii Parad, 1999.

Mlechin, Leonid. *Boris Yeltsin: Posleslovie* [Boris Yeltsin: An afterward]. Moscow: Tsentrpoligraf, 2007.

Mlechin, Leonid. *Yurii Andropov: Poslednyaya Nadezhda, Rezhima* [Yurii Andropov: Last hope of the regime]. Moscow: Tsentrpoligraf, 2008.

Nation, R. Craig. *Black Earth, Red Star: A History of Soviet Security Policy, 1917–1991*. Ithaca, NY: Cornell University Press, 1992.

Oberdorfer, Don. *From the Cold War to a New Era: The United States and the Soviet Union, 1983–1991*. Baltimore: Johns Hopkins University Press, 1998.

O'Clery, Conner. *Moscow, December 25, 1991: The Last Day of the Soviet Union.* New York: Public Affairs, 2012.

Odom, William E. *The Collapse of the Soviet Military.* New Haven, CT: Yale University Press, 1998.

Pape, Robert. *Bombing to Win.* Ithaca, NY: Cornell University Press, 1996.

Parker, John W. *The Kremlin in Transition: From Brezhnev to Chernenko, 1978–1985.* Vol. 1. Boston: Unwin Hyman, 1991.

Parker, John W. *The Kremlin in Transition: Gorbachev, 1985 to 1989.* Vol. 2. Boston: Unwin Hyman, 1991.

Pechenev, Vadim A. *Vslet i Padenie Gorbacheva* [The rise and fall of Gorbachev]. Moscow: Respublika, 1996.

Pikhoya, Rudolf G. *Sovetskii Soyuz: Istoriya Vlasti, 1945–1991* [The Soviet Union: History of power]. Novosibirsk, Sibirski Khronograf, 1996.

Pikhoya, Rudolf G., and A. K. Sokolov. *Istoriya Sovremennoi Rossii: Krizis Kommunisticheskoi Vlasti v SSSR i Rozhdenie Novoi Rossii, Konets 1970-x -1991 gg* [History of contemporary Russia: The crisis of Communist rule in the USSR and the birth of the new Russia]. Moscow: Rosspen, 2008.

Pleshakov, Constantine. *There Is No Freedom without Bread: 1989 and the Civil War That Brought Down Communism.* New York: Picador, 2009.

Plokhy, Serhii. *The Last Empire: The Final Days of the Soviet Union.* New York: Basic Books, 2014.

Podvig, Pavel, ed. *Russian Strategic Nuclear Forces.* Cambridge, MA: MIT Press, 2001.

Reisch, Alfred A. *Hot Books in the Cold War: The CIA-Funded Secret Western Book Distribution Program behind the Iron Curtain.* Budapest: Central European University Press, 2013.

Remnick, David. *Lenin's Tomb: The Last Days of the Soviet Empire.* New York: Vintage, 1994.

Rochat, Philippe. *Destruction of Korean Airlines Flight 007 on August 31, 1983.* Montreal: ICAO, July 16, 1993.

Rubenstein, Joshua. *Soviet Dissidents: Their Struggle for Human Rights.* Boston: Beacon, 1985.

Rubenstein, Joshua, and Alexandar Gribanov, eds. *The KGB File of Andrei Sakharov.* New Haven, CT: Yale University Press, 2005.

Sarotte, Mary Elise. *The Collapse: The Accidental Opening of the Berlin Wall.* New York: Basic Books, 2014.

Sarotte, Mary Elise. *1989: The Struggle to Create a Post–Cold War Europe.* Princeton, NJ: Princeton University Press, 2009.

Satter, David. *Age of Delirium: The Decline and Fall of the Soviet Union.* New York: Borzoi, 1996.

Savranskaya, Svetlana. "Unintended Consequences: Soviet Interests, Expectations, and Reactions to the Helsinki Final Act." In *Helsinki 1975 and the Transformation of Europe,* ed. Oliver Bunge and Gottfried Niedhart, 175–90. New York: Berghahn Books, 2008.

Schweizer, Peter. *Victory: The Reagan Administration's Secret Strategy that Hastened the Collapse of the Soviet Union.* New York: Atlantic Monthly, 1994.

Senate Select Committee on Intelligence (SSCI). "An Assessment of the Aldrich Ames Espionage Case and Its Implications for US Intelligence." November, 1994.

Service, Robert. *The End of the Cold War 1985–1991*. New York: Public Affairs, 2015.

Shane, Scott. *Dismantling Utopia: How Information Ended the Soviet Union*. Chicago: Ivan R. Dee, 1994.

Shlapentokh, Vladimir. *A Normal Totalitarian Society: How the Soviet Union Functioned and How It Collapsed*. Armonk, NY: M. E. Sharpe, 1997.

Shlapentokh, Vladimir. *Soviet Intellectuals and Political Power*. Princeton, NJ: Princeton University Press, 1990.

Stent, Angela. *Russia and Germany Reborn: Unification, the Soviet Collapse, and the New Europe*. Princeton, NJ: Princeton University Press, 1999.

Stokes, Gail. *The Walls Came Tumbling Down: The Collapse of Communism in Eastern Europe*. New York: Oxford University Press, 1993.

Talbott, Strobe. *Endgame: The Inside Story of SALT II*. New York: Harper and Row, 1979.

Thomas, Daniel C. *The Helsinki Effect: International Norms, Human Rights, and the Demise of Communism*. Princeton, NJ: Princeton University Press, 2001.

Tompson, William. *The Soviet Union under Brezhnev*. London: Pearson, 2003.

Tygiel, Jules. *Ronald Reagan and the Triumph of American Conservatism*. London: Pearson, 2006.

Van Het Reve, Karel. *Dear Comrade: Pavel Litvinov and the Voices of Soviet Citizens in Dissent*. New York: Pitman, 1969.

Vogele, William. *Stepping Back: Nuclear Arms Control and the End of the Cold War*. Westport, CT: Praeger, 1994.

Volkogonov, Dmitry. *Autopsy for an Empire: The Seven Leaders Who Built the Soviet Regime*. New York: Free Press, 1998.

Westad, Odd Arne. *The Global Cold War: Third World Interventions and the Making of Our Times*. Cambridge: Cambridge University Press, 2007.

Wohlforth, William C., ed. *Witnesses to the End of the Cold War*. Baltimore: Johns Hopkins University Press, 1996.

Yergin, Daniel. *The Prize: The Epic Quest for Oil, Money, and Power*. New York: Free Press, 2008.

Yurchak, Alexi. *Everything Was Forever until It Was No More: The Last Soviet Generation*. Princeton, NJ: Princeton University Press, 2006.

Zaloga, Steven J. *The Kremlin's Nuclear Sword: The Rise and Fall of Russia's Strategic Nuclear Forces, 1945–2000*. Washington, DC: Smithsonian Institution Press, 2002.

Zdanovich, A. A. *Komanda Andropova* [The Andropov team]. Moscow: Rus, 2005.

Zelizer, Julien E. *Jimmy Carter*. New York: Times Books, 2010.

Zubok, Vladislav M. *A Failed Empire: The Soviet Union in the Cold War from Stalin to Gorbachev*. Chapel Hill: University of North Carolina Press, 2009.

Zubok, Vladislav. *Zhivago's Children: The Last Russian Intelligentsia*. Cambridge, MA: Harvard University Press, 2009.

Zubov, A. V. *Istoriya Rossii XX Veka, 1939–2007, chast 2* [History of twentieth-century Russia, 1939–2007, vol. 2]. Moscow: AST, 2004.

Articles

Adomeit, Hannes. "Gorbachev, German Unification, and the Collapse of Empire." *Post-Soviet Affairs*, August–September 1994, 197.

Andrew, Christopher. "Intelligence in the Cold War." In *Cambridge History of the Cold War*, edited by Melvyn Leffler and Odd Arne Westad. Cambridge: Cambridge University Press, 2012.

Bhattacharya, Jay, Christina Gathmann, and Grant Miller. "The Gorbachev Anti-Alcohol Campaign and Russia's Mortality Crisis." National Bureau of Economic Research, Working Paper No. 18589, December 2012.

Bonnell, Victoria, and Gregory Freidin. "Televorot: The Role of Television Coverage in Russia's August 1991 Coup." *Slavic Review* 52, no. 4 (1993): 810–38.

Caldwell, Dan. "Going Steady: The Kissinger-Dobrynin Channel." *Diplomatic History* (2010).

Daniloff, Nicholas. "Chernobyl and Its Political Fall-Out: A Reassessment." *Demoktatizatsiya*, winter (2000).

Dunlop, John B. "The August 1991 Coup and Its Impact on Soviet Politics." *Journal of Cold War Studies* 5, no. 1 (winter 2003): 94–127.

Early, Pete. "Interview with the Spymaster." *Washington Post Magazine*, April 23, 1995.

Fischer, Ben B. "A Cold War Conundrum: The 1983 War Scare." *Studies in Intelligence*, September 1997.

Gorden, Michael. "Ex-Soviet Pilot Still Insists KAL Was Spying." *New York Times*, December 9, 1996.

Griffen, James M., and William S. Neilson. "The 1985–86 Oil Price Collapse and Afterwards." *Economic Inquiry*, October 1, 1994.

Hertle, Hans-Herman. "The Fall of the Wall: The Unintended Self-Dissolution of East Germany's Ruling Regime." *CWIHP Bulletin*, December 13, 2001.

Kelly, Jon Timothy. "Thinking the Unthinkable: The Civil Defense Debate in the 1980s." *Society for Historians of American Foreign Relations* (June 23, 2000).

Kim, Lucian. "Baker Says Gorbachev Got No Promises on NATO Expansion to East." *Bloomberg*, March 19, 2009.

Knight, Amy. "The KGB, Perestroika, and the Collapse of the Soviet Union." *Journal of Cold War Studies* 5, no. 1 (winter 2003): 67–93.

Komaromi, Ann. "The Material Existence of Samizdat." *Slavic Review* (fall 2004).

Kramer, Mark. "The Collapse of East European Communism and the Repercussions within the Soviet Union (Parts 1, 2, and 3)." *Journal of Cold War Studies* (fall 2003, fall 2004, winter 2005).

Kramer, Mark. "In Case Military Assistance Is Provided to Poland: Soviet Preparations for Military Contingencies." *CWIHP Bulletin* (winter 1998).

Kramer, Mark. "The Myth of a No-NATO Enlargement Pledge to Russia." *Washington Quarterly* (April 2009).

Kramer, Mark. Soviet Deliberations during the Polish Crisis, 1980–1981. CWIHP working paper no. 1, April 1999.

Krasikov, Sara. "Declassified KGB Study Illuminates Early Years of Soviet Jewish Emigration." *Forward*, December 14, 2007.

Lepingwell, John. "New Soviet Revelations about KAL-007." *History*, April 26, 1991.

Mastny, Vojtech. "The Soviet Non-Invasion of Poland in 1980/1981 and the End of the Cold War." CWIHP, working paper no. 23, September 1998.

Mikoyan, Sergo A. "Eroding the Soviet 'Culture of Secrecy': Western Winds behind Kremlin Walls." CIA *Studies in Intelligence* (fall/winter 2001).

Najibullah, Farangis. "Watching the Coup from Central Asia." RFE *Bulletin*, August 19, 2011.

Oberg, James. "KAL 007: The Real Story." *American Spectator*, October 1993.

Podvig, Pavel. "Did Star Wars Help End the Cold War?: Soviet Response to the SDI Program." Russian Nuclear Forces Project, Working paper, March 2013.

Rabbot, Boris. "The Debate over Détente: An Ex-Insider's Revelations." *Washington Post*, July 10, 1977.

Reuveny, Rafael, and Aseem Prakash. "The Afghanistan War and the Breakdown of the Soviet Union." *Review of International Studies* (1999): 704.

Roy, Olivier. "The Lessons of the Soviet Afghan War." Adelphi Papers 259, summer 1991.

Sayle, Murray. "Closing the File on Flight 007." *New Yorker*, December 13, 1993.

Sell, Louis D. "Embassy Under Siege: An Eyewitness Account of the 1993 Attack on Parliament." *Problems of Post-Communism* (July–August 2003): 43–64.

Tuminez, Astrid. "Nationalism, Ethnic Pressures, and the Breakup of the Soviet Union." *Journal of Cold War Studies* 5, no. 4 (fall 2003): 81–136.

Weiss, Gus W. "The Farewell Dossier: Duping the Soviets." *Studies in Intelligence*. https://www.cia.gov/csi-studies/studies/96unclass/farewell.htm.

Wiegrefe, Klaus. "Germany's Unlikely Diplomatic Triumph: An Inside Look at the Reunification Negotiations." *Der Spiegel*, September 29, 2010.

INDEX

Able Archer, 142–43

ABM (Anti-Ballistic Missile) Treaty, 53, 59, 226, 228

Abrahamson, James, 147

Abramowitz, Mort, 206–7

acceleration (Gorbachev early strategy), 172–73

Adamyshin, Anatoliy, 68, 75–76, 236, 237

Afanasyev, Yuriy, 186

Afghanistan: April Revolution, 99; consequences for the USSR, 211; and Gorbachev, 208–10; Herat uprising, 100; Soviet attacks on civilian population, 206; Soviet casualties hidden, 98; number of Soviet casualties, 210; Soviet decision-making, 102; Soviet invasion, 96–97; Soviets withdrawal, 209; after Soviet withdrawal, 211–12; US-Soviet dispute on aid to clients, 210
—United States: impact of US Stinger anti-aircraft missiles, 207; reaction, 103

Aganbegyan, Abel, 173

Akromeyev, Sergei: debunks 1983 "war scare," 143; devises 1986 Soviet nuclear arms control proposal, 205; Gorbachev adviser on arms control, 232; INF Treaty, 153, 233; informed about Chernobyl nuclear accident, 177; informs Politburo that Soviets have lost in Afghanistan, 209; Malta sum-

mit, 268; positive after first meeting with Gorbachev as general secretary, 171; rejects deployment of automatic nuclear launch system, 162; Reykjavik meeting (1986), 226; Soviet military doctrine, 327; WW II experiences, 16

Albats, Yevgenia, 300

Aleksandrov-Agentov, Andrei M., 48, 51, 52, 88, 121

Alekseyeva, Lyudmila, 26, 70, 72

Allen, Richard, 131

Amalrik, Andrei, 70

Ames, Aldrich, 213–14

Amin, Hafizullah, 96, 97, 98, 99, 100

Amstutz, J. Bruce, 101

Andreyeva, Nina (letter attacking Gorbachev), 191–92, 194

Andropov, Yuri: Afghanistan, 96, 102, 104; aids Gorbachev, 125; Brezhnev's death, 114; Diamond Affair, 118; discipline campaign, 122–23; on economy, 124–25; enigmatic character, 119–20; as general secretary, 120–21; Helsinki Final Act, 69; illness, 126–27; KAL shootdown, 138, 139; memo on US-Soviet relations (1971), 45; moves against dissidents, 39–40; national security troika, 115; operation RYAN, 140–41, 158, 329; opposes removal of "diploma tax," 60; Polish crisis (1980–81), 109, 110, 111

Angola: CIA in, 82; consequences for USSR, 83; Cuban role, 82; South African engagement, 82; Soviet engagement, 81–83; Soviet military aid, 83

Arbatov, Grigory, 48, 83

Ash, Timothy Garton, 330

Avrora article on Brezhnev, 117

back channel, 42–43

Baker, James, 243, 270, 271, 276, 291, 314, 317, 336, 345, 349

Bakhmin, Vyacheslav, 40, 71, 90

Baklanov, Oleg, 294, 295

Baltic republics, 245, 252, 285, 286

Bateinin, Gelii, 142, 143, 150

Beardon, Milt, 207

Beloveshka Pushcha meeting, 318–19

Berlin Wall: bureaucratic snafu causes fall, 263; Bush restrained public stance, 265; Gorbachev's reaction to wall's fall, 264, 265; numbers killed trying to cross, 259; police open the gates, 264; reaction of European leaders, 265; symbol and reality, 259

Bessmertnykh, Aleksandr, 199, 204, 226

Big Five, 158–59, 231

Blood, Archer K., 101

Bobkov, Feliks, 39, 320, 321

Bogomolov Institute, 103, 253

Boldin, Valery, 250, 294, 295

Bonner, Yelena, 72, 90, 184

Boris the Gypsy, 117–18

Borovik, Artyom, 211

Braithwaite, Roderic, 243, 287

Brezhneva, Galina, 117

Brezhnev, Leonid Ilich: Afghanistan, 96, 102; agricultural reform, 12–13; consolidates power, 10–11; correspondence with President Carter, 77–78; criticizes Carter policy, 87; death, 114; early years of rule, 9; foreign policy, 48; Helsinki Final Act, 68; international posture, 9; illness, 65; and the military, 16; at missile civil war, 20–21; Moscow summit (1972), 52–58; and Nixon, 59; opposition to détente, 51; Polish crisis (1980), 108; sexual amenities, 61; Shelepin challenge, 82; stability of cadres, 14–15; USSR at end his rule, 115, 140, 157, 161, 167, 168, 244; US visit (1973), 61–62; Vienna summit (1979), 88–89; Vladivostok meeting with Ford (1974), 64–65

Brezhnev Doctrine, 107, 110

Brutents, Karen, 26, 86, 102

Bryukhanov, Viktor, 177

Brzezinski, Zbigniew, 76, 77, 78

Bukovsky, Vladimir, 27

Burlatskiy, Fyodor, 249, 250

Bush, George H. W., 165, 197, 242; aid to Gorbachev, 290; August coup, 304–5, 311; Berlin Wall, 265; East Europe visit (1989), 258–59; German unification, 272; Kiev visit, 292; Kohl's 10 points, 266; Madrid (1991), 314; Malta summit (1989), 267–68; Moscow summit (1991), 291–92; Soviet collapse, 335–37; US policy after August coup, 317–18; Yeltsin, 319

Byrnes, Shaun, 119

Carlucci, Frank, 131

Carter, Jimmy: administration, 77; Brezhnev kiss, 89; correspondence with Brezhnev, 77–78; election, 76–77; human rights, 76, 78; letter to Sakharov, 78; Naval Academy speech (1978), 87; nuclear weapons, 76, 78; SALT negotiator, 81; SALT proposal, "deep cuts," 78–80; Soviet invasion of Afghanistan, 102; Soviet relations, 86; Vienna summit (1989), 88–89

Castro, Fidel, 82

Chazov, Yevgeniy, 114, 127, 169

Chebrikov, Viktor, 123, 126, 138, 139, 140, 169

Chechnya conflict, 343

Chelomei, Vladimir, 20

Cheney, Dick, 267, 291, 317

Cherkashin, Viktor, 144, 213

Chernenko, Konstantin, 115, 120, 125, 127, 168, 169, 197

Chernobyl nuclear accident, 176–83; causes, 176–77; consequences, 244; effects in Kiev, 180–81; initial responses, 177–78 —and Gorbachev: speech, 180; effect on Gorbachev, 183

German unification (*continued*)
Kohl coalition, 272; German economic unity, 274; Gorbachev meeting on Germany with senior Soviet officials, 271; Gorbachev motivated by need for aid, 273; Gorbachev and Shevardnadze work out their own position, 275; Gorbachev tells Bush Germans can decide NATO membership, 273; Kohl follows Baker to Moscow, 271; Kohl 10-point speech sets the stage, 266; Kohl visit to USSR nails down terms of agreement; Kvitsinskiy toughens Soviet positions, 274; Moscow seeks to stall process, 272–73; NATO changes to encourage Soviets, 273; NATO expansion did not violate German unification agreement, 276–78; Two Plus Four negotiating framework, 271

Ginsburg, Aleksandr, 29, 72

glasnost, 185–87, 243, 244

Glazunov, Ilya, 94–95

gold reserves, Soviet, 314

Gorbachev, Mikhail Sergeyevich: Afghanistan withdrawal, 208–10; and Nina Andreyeva letter, 192; and Andropov, 125, 127; Andropov denies access to state budget, 329; anti-alcohol campaign, 173–74; and arms reductions, 204; and August coup, 295, 307–9, 312; Baltic crackdown, 285; Beloveshka Pushcha agreement, 319; meets Bush in Madrid (1991), 314; Chernobyl speech, 180; Congress of People's Deputies (1989), 247–49; conservative shift (1990–91), 284; and Daniloff affair, 225; early years, 167; early days as Soviet leader, 170–71; and Eastern Europe, 252–53; visits East Germany 1989, 261–62; economic reform stumbles, 188–89; and ethnic unrest, 252; final days in power, 165–66; G-7 summit (London, 1991), 289; becomes general secretary, 168–70; Geneva summit (1985), 200–203; on German unification, 270, 271–72; glasnost, 185–87; and human rights, 236; INF agreement, 232–33; Kohl visit to USSR (July 1989) closes German unification deal, 275; meets Egon Krenz, 262–63; loses control of events, 250; Malta summit (1989), 267–68; miners strike 1989, 251; military rule, 315; on military spending, 327; Moscow summits: 1988, 238–40; 1991, 292; concedes German membership in NATO with Bush, 273–74; Nobel Peace Prize, 289; Party Congresses: 19th, 193–94; 27th, 175–76; and Polish crisis (1980–81), 111; purges Soviet military, 231; quarrels with Kosygin, 168; reaction to Berlin Wall fall, 265–66; reaction to Polish elections (1989), 254; referendum on USSR 1991, 288; Reykjavik summit, 225–29; role in Soviet collapse, 332–33; Sakharov death, 269; Sakharov return, 184; Tbilisi demonstration, 246; threatens force in Moscow, 287; UNGA speech, 1988, 240–41; Washington summit, 1987, 233–34; lack of Western economic aid, 344; Yeltsin criticizes, 189–90; attacks Yeltsin in Russian Congress, 279; contrasts with Yeltsin, 280–82

Gorbacheva, Raisa, 125, 202, 230

Gorbanyevskaya, Natalya, 32

Gordiyevskiy, Oleg, 141, 143

Grachev, Andrei, 252, 277, 312

Grachev, Pavel, 269, 299

Grechko, Andrei: Nixon visit to Moscow (1972), 51; on SALT I, 53; overruled by Brezhnev at Vladivostok meeting (1974), 65, 158, 159

Grinyevskiy, Oleg, 54, 205

Grishin, Viktor, 169

Gromov, Boris, 210, 299

Gromyko, Anatoliy, 170

Gromyko, Andrei: Afghanistan invasion, 96; Andropov selection as general secretary, 121; Brezhnev, 80; and Carter "deep cuts" arms control proposal, 79–81; meets Carter in 1977, 81; General Secretary deal with Gorbachev, 158, 197, 199; on Helsinki Final Act, 69; and INF, 152; and KAL shoot-down, 138; Madrid meeting with Secretary Shultz, 139; national security troika,

Pikhoya, Rudolf, 74, 96, 115, 192, 295
Pipes, Richard, 112, 133
Podgorny, Nikolai, 17, 23, 48, 51, 52, 55
Podrabinek, Aleksandr, 71
Poindexter, John, 131
Polish crisis (1980–81): Andropov and Ustinov keep up pressure, 109; Brezhnev calls off invasion, 108; economic difficulties, 107; Jaruzelski seeks Soviet intervention, 109; martial law imposed, 110; papal visit, 107; Polish position in Soviet empire, 107; Solidarity national congress, 109; Solidarity strikes, 107–8; Soviet alarmed reaction, 108; Soviet leadership declines to send troops, 110; US response, 112–13
Polish crisis (1989): Bush encourages Jaruzelski to run for president, 258; Bush visit to Poland, 258; contingency planning for crackdown, 255; Gorbachev rejects Rakowski appeal for interference, 255; Gorbachev urges political solution, 254; Politburo report on Poland, 255; reasons why Gorbachev did not intervene, 255; Roundtable Talks, 254; Solidarity election victory, 253
Ponomarev, Boris, 99
popular unrest in USSR, 323
Powell, Colin, 16, 131, 238
Pozsgay, Imre, 256
Presel, Joe, 70, 91
Primakov, Yevgeniy, 85, 170, 222
Pripyat, 178
Prokhanov, Aleksandr, 207
Pugo, Boris, 285, 299
Putin, Vladimir, 320, 321, 340, 341

Radio Free Europe/Radio Liberty (RFE/RL), 112–13, 330–31
Raleigh, Donald J. (oral history), 115, 187, 249
Reagan, Ronald: air traffic controllers' strike, 145; character, 129–30; and Daniloff arrest, 223–24; diary, 130; Dobrynin meeting, 1983, 135; economic warfare, 134–35; election, 128–29; Geneva summit (1985), 200–203; and KAL shoot-down, 139; military build-

up, 145; and mini-thaw (1983), 136; Moscow summit (1988), 238–40; and negotiations, 145–46; reaction to 1986 Soviet arms control proposal, 205; response to Polish martial law, 112–13; Reykjavik meeting with Gorbachev (1986), 225–29; rhetoric, 132–33; and SDI, 146–47; Soviet collapse, 334–35; Stinger missiles to Afghan rebels, 207; "trust but verify," 234; and "walk in the woods," 153; Washington summit (1987), 233–34
refuseniks, 92, 93
Remnick, David, 193, 247
Repentance (1987 film), 185
representation list, 58, 234, 235, 238
repression in USSR, 74–75
Reykjavik summit (1986), 225–29
Rice, Condileezza, 271
Ridgeway, Roz, 202, 215, 226, 239
Rogers, William, 58
Romanov, Grigoriy, 125, 171
Roundtable Talks, 254
Rowny, Edward, 136, 156
RUKH (Popular Movement of Ukraine for Perestroika), 245
Rust, Mattias, 230
Rutskoy, Aleksandr, 208, 287
RYAN (Raketnoe Yadernoye Napadenie), 140–41
Rybakov, Anatoly, 186
Ryzhkov, Nikolai, 171, 172; and Chernobyl, 177, 188, 189, 244, 264, 282, 283, 288, 329

Sagdeyev, Roald, 329
Sakharov, Andrei Dmitriyevich: and Czechoslovak invasion (1968), 25; Carter letter to, 78; and Congress of People's Deputies, 248; constitution day demonstrations, 27, 34; death, 269; Gorbachev accession, 171, 182; Inter-Regional Group, 249; Khrushchev criticizes, 33; memoirs, 36; *My Country and the World*, 35; Nobel Peace Prize, 36; *Progress, Coexistence, and Intellectual Freedom*, 34; returns from exile, 184, 193; US National Academy of Sciences defends, 35

161; Brezhnev and Kosygin "visibly terrified" by one study, 161; focus only on military aspects, 160; Soviet military unwilling to acknowledge victory was impossible, 161; studies on effects of nuclear war suppressed, 161

Speakes, Larry, 203

"spy dust," 215–16

Stalin, Josef: controversy over legacy, 23–25, 216, 245

Starodubov, Viktor, 205

START I (Strategic Arms Reduction Talks): Geneva summit (1985), 238; negotiations, 155; Reagan proposal (1982), 154; significance, 292; signing (1991), 291; Soviet proposal, 154; Soviet 1983 walkout, 157

START II, 1, 348–49

Stinger (anti-aircraft missiles), 206–7

Strategic Defense Initiative. See SDI

Strauss, Robert, 291, 305, 349

Sukhodrev, Viktor, 80, 88

Surikov, Viktor, 162

Suslov, Mikhail, 51, 98, 108, 110, 118, 186

Taraki, Nur Muhammad, 96, 99, 100

Tarasenko, Sergei, 103, 159, 275

Tbilisi demonstrations (1989), 245–46

"Tbilisi syndrome," 246

Teller, Edward, 146

Thatcher, Margaret, 142, 197, 229, 265

Tikhonov, Nikolai, 115, 126, 172

Tolkachev, Adolph, 214

Tomsen, Peter, 99, 212

trade, US-Soviet, 57–58

Trapeznikov, S. P., 23, 125

Tsvigun, Semyon, 117–18

Tumanov, Aleksandr, 94

Turner, Stansfield, 101

Two Plus Four (German unification negotiating framework), 271, 272, 274, 276, 277

Ukrainian independence referendum (1991), 315, 316–17, 319, 336

Ulyanovskiy, R. A., 99

USA Institute, 103

US embassy in Moscow, "bugged," 216–19

Ustinov, Dmitri: aids Chernenko selection as General Secretary, 127; chairs "Big Five," 158; directs Soviet national security, 115; and KAL shoot-down, 138, 140; at "missile civil war," 21; role in Andropov selection as General Secretary, 121, 126; role in Soviet invasion of Afghanistan, 96; and SDI, 147

Vance, Cyrus: on Brezhnev letter to Carter, 78; in Carter administration, 76; trip to Moscow (1977), 79

Varennikov, Valentin, 180, 208, 210, 294, 295, 301, 306

Vienna summit (1979), 88–90

Vietnam War: Gromyko and Kissinger discuss at Moscow summit, 55; Kissinger talks with Brezhnev (1972), 50; Moscow summit (1972), 54–56; and Nixon linkage policy, 42, 44; North Vietnamese offensive (1972), 49; Soviet lessons from, 56; Soviets unwilling to help Nixon escape, 44; Soviets urge flexibility to Hanoi, 55; US mines waters around, 51

Vladivostok US-Soviet meeting (1974), 64–65

VOA (Voice of America), 330–31

Voinovich, Vladimir, 31

Volkogonov, Dmitri, 96, 111

Volskiy, Arkadiy, 126

Wade, Bob, 219

Walesa, Lech, 107, 113, 254, 258

Walker, John, 143, 213

"walk in the woods" (INF proposal), 152–54

"war scare" (1983), 140–44

Wasilewski, Roman, 298

Weinberger, Caspar, 131, 134

Wilson, Charlie, 206

Wolff, Markus, 141, 259, 330

Yakovlev, Aleksandr: anti-alcohol campaign a mistake, 174; criticizes Gorbachev for rejecting the "500 Days" economic reform proposal, 283; discusses Chernobyl response with Minister of Defense Yazov, 179; enthusiastic after